Applied Research Methods in Criminal Justice

Nelson-Hall Series in Law, Crime, and Justice
Howard Abadinsky, Consulting Editor
Saint Xavier University, Chicago

Applied Research Methods in Criminal Justice

Jeffrey D. Senese
University of Baltimore

Nelson-Hall Publishers
Chicago

Library of Congress Cataloging-in-Publication Data

Senese, Jeffrey D.
Applied research methods in criminal justice /
Jeffrey D. Senese.
p. cm.
Includes bibliographical references and index.
ISBN 0-8304-1388-X
1. Criminal justice, Administration of—Research—Methodology.
2. Criminology—Research—Methodology. I. Title.
HV7419.5.S46 1996
364'.072—dc20 96-11326
CIP

Project Editor: Dorothy Anderson
Typesetter: Fine Print, Ltd.
Printer: Capital City Press
Illustrator: Corasue Nicholas
Cover Painting: Grace Cole, "Fragments in the Creation of Self"

Reprinted 1998

Manufactured in the United States of America

10 9 8 7 6 5 4 3 2

The paper used in this book meets the minimum requirements of American National Standard for Information Sciences—Permanence of Paper for Printed Library Materials, ANSI Z39.48-1984.

Dedicated to Fred Senese, my mentor . . .
dormire in la pace.

Contents

Preface ix

Chapter 1
Introduction to Research Methodology 1

Chapter 2
Research Terminology 23

Chapter 3
Research Design: Purposes, Types and Selection 43

Chapter 4
Data Measurement and Collection 75

Chapter 5
Sample Selection Techniques 103

Chapter 6
Experimental Designs 125

Chapter 7
Survey Research 143

Chapter 8
Observational Designs 173

Chapter 9
Secondary Analysis of Data 199

Chapter 10
Basic Descriptive Analyses 217

Chapter 11
Basic Inferential Analyses 243

Chapter 12
Basic Qualitative Analyses 295

Chapter 13
Research Ethics 325

Chapter 14
Library Research in Criminal Justice and Criminology 347

Notes 361

Glossary 369

References 389

Index 397

Preface

This book was written because I believe there is a specific need for a book on criminal justice research methods for criminal justice and criminology students. The study of criminal justice and criminological issues and subjects has developed a sense of specificity that has not existed in the past as is evidenced in the dozen or so academic and professional journals that are devoted solely to the study of criminal justice and criminological subjects. On the other hand, we, as faculty, do our students a great disservice by attempting to retrofit sociological, political science, or other social science methodologies or methods instruction to our classes and students. In addition, we are obliged to provide our students, and especially in their initial exposure to methods, with the most understandable and practical and direct approach as we can. I hope that you will find text to be a straightforward, understandable, and clear approach to the study of research methods in criminal justice and criminology.

The general structure of this book is in a logical order similar to the traditional process of research itself. The first chapter provides a detailed explanation of the process of research in criminal justice and criminology as well as a detailed "research-ese" lesson. The subsequent chapters are arranged in order from discussions of basic research designs in chapter 2 to basic descriptive analyses in chapter 10, inferential analysis in chapter 11, and research ethics in chapter 13. This text should be read in the order in which it has been prepared because methods is a process based learning procedure.

I would certainly be remiss if I did not provide a special thanks to several people who have assisted my work on this project. First, I would like to thank Libby Rubenstein and the editorial staff at Nelson-Hall for their superb and thorough assistance on this project. They should be credited and commended for making this book not only more readable but more understandable. I would also like to thank Dr. Dave Kalinich of Northern Michigan University for turning me on to the possibilities of criminal justice research in the applied context. His ability to formulate conceptual frameworks in a practical and understandable and ultimately useable form is something I continually strive to achieve. I also owe Dave a large debt for his contributions to my intellectual development and foundations. I also thank Dr. Jim LeBeau of the University of Southern Illinois for his contributions to my academic development. Jim LeBeau encouraged and fed my intellectual curiosity at a time when I was moving on to another career.

Thanks also are extended to Mary Senese for her confidence in my ability and her assurances during this project as well as her love and understanding. I would also like to thank Alice Frederico for her encouragement and faith in my capability to complete this project. A special thanks to Gianna and Francesca Girone and Mia Senese for their assistance on many of the examples used throughout this text as well as to the staff of the Radiation and Oncology Department of the University of Pennsylvania Hospital, especially Pat Miller-Wilson and Robert Wilson, Frank Villari, Max Bennett, and Dr. William and Roberta Powlis. Thanks to Bruno for his editorial assistance.

Finally, I would like to thank my wife, Alicia, whose continuous and unconditional love and encouragement throughout my writing of this book has made its completion not only possible but assured.

1 INTRODUCTION TO RESEARCH METHODOLOGY

Learning Objectives

1. To provide an orientation to the basic concepts of scientific research methodology
2. To emphasize the importance of developing an understanding and appreciation of the significance of research in criminal justice and criminology
3. To supply illustrations of the contributions that research can make to police, courts, and corrections

Chapter Outline

Introduction
The Traditional Method
- *The Aims of the Traditional Method*
  - Theory
  - Objectivity
  - Logical Structure
  - Empirical Data
  - Cyclical Process
- *The Concerns of the Traditional Method*

The Importance of Research
- *Research Constraints*
- *Police*
- *Courts*
- *Corrections*

Summary
Main Concepts
Discussion Questions
Exercise
Notes

CHAPTER ONE

Introduction

The study of research methods has been a somewhat recent addition to the list of required courses for students who endeavor to study criminal justice or criminology. Although not all criminal justice and criminology degree programs require the study of research methods, most of the better known and designed academic programs require a basic competency in research methods. Moreover, students that are interested in completing graduate studies in criminal justice almost certainly will be required to take a research course or two. The bottom line is that many of the students that read this text are required to take a research methods course. While you may perceive research methods as irrelevant to your career goals, unnecessary and overly academic, or perhaps even intimidating, you probably must successfully finish this course in order to graduate. The goal of this text is to make your first encounter with research methods practically based and successful.

Hence, this text is written from the perspective that students will not have had any previous experience with learning research methods. Moreover, this text assumes that practical knowledge of the appropriateness of research methods is more useful than theoretical knowledge of how research methods were developed. In sum, this text will provide students with practical and applied examples of the most commonly used research methods in criminal justice and criminological research.

While the explanations and examples in this book require no preexisting knowledge about methodology, they do require some basic understanding of the criminal justice system and its components and processes. The general aim of this text is to promote student understanding of social science research methodology as it is currently used in criminal justice and criminology in as painless and as sensible a fashion as is possible. Like other courses, however, you will be required to work at understanding ideas and an occasional abstraction.

The study of research methods should be taken as serious because, unlike the knowledge you may gain in other courses, knowledge of research methodology is much less likely to become obsolete in your lifetime. Hence, other than the ability to communicate or perhaps some very basic knowledge of the law, the only true technical skill that a criminal justice or criminology student leaves an undergraduate program with is the ability to understand and perhaps apply research methods to conduct studies or make decisions.

It is also important to understand that the faculty who design criminal justice study programs believe that an understanding of research methods is important for both practitioners and future researchers in the field. Hence, requiring criminal justice undergraduates to take a course in research methods is not done *to* students but rather it is done *for* students with the hope that it will enrich their qualifications for practical work or for further studies in the field of criminal justice.

From the practitioner viewpoint, instruction in criminal justice research methods focuses on students who have career goals of being in the operational criminal justice system (i.e., police officers, correctional officers, probation agents, victim counselors, and so on). The basic objective of this text is to make these students better informed and more capable consumers of the results of research. This objective is based on the assumption that an understanding of research methods will allow practitioners to be better able to make use of the results of research as it is associated with their work-related duties. For example, in many cases the difference between someone who is a career police officer but who aspires to command and a chief of police is the ability of the latter to use information effectively. The ability to understand research gives practitioners command over the most current information that can assist in work duties and intraorganizational relations and can separate the merely ambitious from the successful.

On the other hand, for students who intend to go to graduate school, a basic understanding of research methods is mandatory. Once students move beyond the realm of undergraduate studies into the more in-depth approach in graduate school, a competency in research methodology becomes crucial. Along with the ability to communicate in both written and oral forms, a competency in research methods often makes the difference between a difficult graduate experience and one that benefits the student. One of the keys to success in graduate school is perseverance. However, it is equally important that those who aspire to the graduate level of studies in criminal justice or criminology understand how the knowledge they are required to acquire has been created as well as how to create additional knowledge that helps to improve theory and practice.

Perhaps the largest problem many students have with learning research methods is overcoming the assumption that research methodology is either irrelevant to the practice of criminal justice functions or is useful only to academics in "ivory towers." Nothing could be farther from the truth, especially with respect to much of the current criminal justice research. Later in this chapter, the importance of knowledge of research methods for each of the main components of the criminal justice system is discussed. Suffice it to say that most of the innovations and solutions that are currently in vogue in the field of criminal justice were developed by researchers and not by practitioner innovations. In criminological studies it is easy to see the relevance of understanding traditional research methods and methodologies as the general focus is typically on building and testing theories about the cause of crime or criminality. Criminal justice studies, on the other hand, tend to be oriented to the study of criminal justice organizations and operational decisions. Research methods are as important in criminal justice studies as they are in criminological investigations, because they allow one to create more accurate and objective information.

In addition, the study of research methodology is consistent with many of the work activities of practitioners in the field of criminal justice because they are researchlike in nature. For instance, police officers, while not aware of it, conduct case studies and field research on a regular basis in the course of investigating crimes. In addition, court administrators conduct correlational studies when they analyze the rates of judicial case processing and case outcomes in order to better allocate cases to judges in their courts. The whole system of prisons in the United States was begun as a quasi-experiment. That is, prisons were originally designed to provide a treatment (i.e., "reform"). Hence, returns to the prison would indicate treatment failure. In sum, criminal justice practitioners in the operational components (and subcomponents) of the criminal justice system often conduct "research like" analyses and activities. However, because most practitioners do not rely on objective rules for conducting these "pseudostudies," the results cannot be trusted to be unbiased or consistent. Through application of accepted research methods, one can overcome many biases and inconsistencies in studies and in creating information for decision making.

The study of applied research methods is the study of the basic rules, appropriate techniques, and relevant procedures for conducting objective research. The preferred outcomes of applied research are results that are accurate and consistent. Although the general orientation of the applied focus in this text is to provide the most readily understandable and directly usable descriptions of the various aspects of research methods, the reduction in precision of some descriptions is not without cost in that some explanations may lead to less detailed versions of the relevant topics.[1] However, an applied focus is more relevant to the criminal justice field and for consuming scholarly research because it attempts to provide a more clear and unambiguous description that concentrates on how one should conduct research rather than on theoretical justifications for research (why research should be conducted).

The basic rules in conducting research have been established through the development of the scientific method in the fields of psychology, economics, political science, and sociology. The rules that have been developed involve such concepts as levels of measurement (how precise your data or observations are) and variables (counted or categorized observations that have two or more categories or values). This chapter focuses on providing a straightforward understanding of these rules so that you will be able to apply them. Moreover, a multitude of appropriate research techniques are presented throughout this text. This text also discusses the procedures for applying the presented research techniques in appropriate criminal justice settings and for answering criminal justice research questions.

The Traditional Method

The traditional method (the scientific method) has been developed over the past century or so and consists of a collection of guidelines by which most research can be compared in order to determine its quality and value. Although based on research methods in the physical or natural sciences (physics, chemistry, and biology), the so-called scientific method has been used since the beginning of the social and behavioral sciences (psychology, sociology, political science, criminology, and so on).

The *scientific method* has been defined as "the whole process of getting knowledge, including the theoretical and the empirical steps" (Northrop, 1965). Hence, the scientific method consists of a set of theoretical and technical guidelines and rather loose rules of conduct that are generally agreed upon by most researchers and that allow for a clear and unambiguous statement of findings. The scientific method, "as far as it is a method, is nothing more than doing one's damnedest with one's mind, no holds barred" (Bridgman, 1945, p. 450). The application of the scientific method to criminal justice has not, however, been clearly determined. Instead, criminal justice and criminological researchers "beg, borrow, and steal" methodologies from psychology, sociology, economics, and political science.

The use of the scientific method in criminal justice or criminologically oriented research has come into being "in the middle of the movie."[2] That is, the scientific method existed long before criminal justice or criminological studies. Criminal justice and criminological researchers have not played a significant role in developing the research methodology. Nor have criminal justice and criminology been well accepted by the other social sciences as truly academic disciplines in which research is appropriate.

Although many students and practitioners have little problem with these realities, the effects of a lack of understanding of the scientific methodology may be devastating. For example, Lipton, Martinson, and Wilks' "murdered" rehabilitation as the basic framework for criminal justice in the mid 1970s (Lipton, Martinson, and Wilks, 1975). Their murder weapon was a research report in which they concluded that the research on rehabilitation programs was generally poor, and that the research results that remained showed that rehabilitative programs have no appreciable effect on reducing recidivism. This report resulted in abandonment of a rehabilitation orientation in correctional systems throughout the country. The criminal justice professionals who worked in rehabilitation programs at that time surely understood the importance of research when their programs were reduced or eliminated. In addition, state legislatures also knew the value of research when they accepted the findings of Lipton, Martinson, and Wilks as "proof" that rehabilitation doesn't work and proceeded to develop a prison capacity in the United States that is unparalleled anywhere on our planet. In sum, while the scientific method is certainly not a cure-all for understanding complex criminological ideas or criminal justice practice, it is the most appropriate means for comprehension at this time.

The world will not stop spinning tomorrow if one does not understand the scientific method or research methodology. But such an understanding allows one to more appropriately evaluate research that assists in practical criminal justice work role tasks and in developing answers to questions that confront the operational criminal justice system. In an information-based society, those who know how to create, assimilate, and control information are more likely to be successful no matter what it is they choose to do with their lives. The control of information is what research methodology is all about.

The Aims of the Traditional Method

The basic missions of the scientific method as they relate to criminal justice research are the tangible targets of the research process. For example, your objectives for taking this course are to pass and to achieve an understanding of the approaches and applications involved in criminal justice research methods. The basic mission is based on five notions about the research enterprise. Each of these five concepts—*theory, objectivity, logical structure, empirical data,* and the *research process*—is described in the following sections.

Theory. One objective in scientific research is to base the endeavor on theory. Current statements that define theory are based on the scientific method in the context of academic research. For example, Babbie defines a theory as "a general and more or less comprehensive set of statements relating different aspects of some phenomenon" (Babbie, 1989, p. 102). Hagan defines a theory as "an attempt to develop plausible explanations of reality" (Hagan, 1989, p. 9). Binder and Geis define a theory as "a set of assumptions; concepts regarding events, situations, individuals and groups; and propositions that describe the interrelationships among the various assumptions and concepts" (Binder and Geis, 1983, p. 3).

In an applied context one can look at theories as an interrelated set of ideas about processes, relationships, or events. In a scientific context one is concerned with whether one's ideas, or those of others, make sense. Theories are usually both logical in origin and based on past research. Logical origin is established on the basis of an understanding of the topic being studied that is thoroughly developed and is supportable.

However, theories in most academic research are based on ideas that have been tested in past research. That is, current theories are constructed from descriptions of the topic in the literature. However, many applied researchers also logically create theories from experience, interviews, or participant observations. For example, assume that you believe incarceration will deter people from driving while drunk. You begin constructing your theory by searching the literature so you don't waste your time repeating what is already known about the relationship. You interview drunk drivers to find out what their perceptions are about the effects of incarceration. In addition, you observe sentencing of drunk drivers to further understand the relationship between incarceration and recidivism because you assume that judges will announce the rationale for the sentence. Although most basic research (academic and theoretical) requires that one begin the study with a thorough review of the literature, evaluative and applied studies can often be logically constructed and based on personal theory construction. However, in either case, a review of the literature is usually the best place to begin formulating theories because it prevents reinvention of the wheel and can reduce useless analysis.

Objectivity. Scientific research is objectivity oriented. The scientific method aims, whether the ideas are logically derived or research based, to achieve objectivity and to avoid subjectivity. Objectivity is presumed to reduce partiality (bias). Partiality is typically reduced through studying a representative smaller group (a sample) of a larger group (population). Objectivity entails reducing inaccuracies due to the prejudices, biases, or personal opinions of the researchers.

A concrete example of the concept of objectivity can be illustrated by multiple choice versus essay examinations. When an instructor gives students an objective (i.e., multiple choice) examination there is generally no question about whether answers are correct or incorrect. Only one answer is correct, though students often criticize the wording of the multiple choice questions. Multiple choice examinations attempt to "objectively" assess students' comprehension of the material without partiality. Hence, all students answer each question, and their grades are assumed to be comparable and indicative of their level of comprehension of the material. The instructor in this case merely counts the number of correct answers and does not influence the students' scores. On the other hand in subjective examination (i.e., essay format) instructors may or may not have guidelines to grade student responses. Essay tests are good at measuring students' ability to express themselves in writing and their ability to select and organize and evaluate facts and ideas, but they are not impartial. That is, student scores on essays may be influenced by the instructor's mood or impression of the student, or by factors extraneous to the content being measured (handwriting, spelling, and so on). Scientific research methodology provides techniques and guidelines for establishing a more objective investigation.

Logical Structure. The scientific method is based on the presumption that there is a logical structure that should be followed when conducting research. The theory is specified, hypotheses or research questions are stated, the data are collected, analyses are conducted, hypotheses are reevaluated, and conclusions are drawn.

Many researchers in criminal justice and criminological studies violate the logical structure of the scientific method. For example, while I was conducting a study of inmate rule violations in a jail, I collected daily population data. Although I had read the literature and formulated several research questions about inmate rule violations prior to collecting this data, I had no such preconceptions regarding the population data. However, later I went to the literature to determine whether anything had been written about inmate populations over time and found the "Stability of Punishment Hypothesis" (SPH). The SPH holds that a prison population should be stable around some average level. From this theory I hypothesized that jail populations should fluctuate around some average level, but also that this fluctuation should be cyclical based on the idea that jail populations are higher on the weekends, due to arrests, and lower during the week, due to bail and release on recognizance. Hence, I collected population data, formulated the hypotheses, and then investigated the theory. While the logical structure of the scientific method should not be abandoned, its violation can provide ideas that may not otherwise be forthcoming if one rigidly follows its structure. However, even where the logical structure is not followed in the prescribed and traditional order it should be used to structure research whenever possible.

Empirical Data. The scientific method is based on the presumption that research is grounded in empirical data. Empirical data are values or categories that are assigned to observations or experiences. Empirical data are either *quantitative* or *qualitative* in nature.

Quantitative empirical data are typically shown as numbers or statistics. An example of quantitative empirical data that can be collected about an individual offender is the number of prior arrests. The number of prior arrests does not measure the quality of those arrests. An example of a qualitative measure is whether the arrests are violent or not or are felonies or misdemeanors.

The most common quantitative empirical measures in criminal justice and criminological research are the crime rates as measured by the Uniform Crime Reports (UCR) collected by the Federal Bureau of Investigation. The UCR measures crime as the quantity of crimes reported to police per 100,000 people in a given area. Quantitative empirical data measure the amount of a certain characteristic, property, or experience of the individuals or groups one is studying.

Qualitative empirical data attempt to categorize observations or experiences. For example, in questionnaire research it is common for criminal justice researchers to collect data on respondents' gender. Gender is a typical qualitative empirical variable in that one can categorize whether a respondent is male or female. In sum, qualitative empirical data measures the characteristics of the individuals or groups one is studying.

While criminal justice and criminological research currently emphasize quantitative data and analyses, such data are not preferred to qualitative data. Neither are qualitative empirical data superior to quantitative data. The use of either quantitative or qualitative data should be driven by the theory that is relied on as well as on the research design to be utilized in examining the theory. Although quantitative data tend to be more reliable but not completely accurate (e.g., UCR arrest rates are consistent measures of crime over time, but they don't include crimes that are unsolved or those that aren't reported to the police), this is not always the case. Conversely, although qualitative empirical data tend to have relatively more accuracy, they may be less consistent over time (e.g., a case study in the beginning of the year may reveal that juvenile offenders report serious criminal involvement, but when they are restudied at the end of the year they report only minor offenses).

Cyclical Process. The scientific method assumes that the research process is a *cyclical process,* that is, it is never ending. Ideally, the end of the research process results in a reconsideration of the theory, which in turn results in additional hypotheses about the new theory, and the research process begins anew. Figure 1.1 demonstrates the structure of this process. The beginning stage involves the consideration of current theory or, in an applied or evaluative context, the need to make a decision that requires evaluative or applied analyses. The second stage in the process involves setting the focus of the research on the research purpose generally and the research questions or hypotheses specifically. The next step involves the execution of the research design (plan) by collecting and analyzing the data. Finally, the results of the research study are assessed in relation to the research questions asked in the present research as well as to their impacts on the need for further research.

For example, Reeves found that the color of the walls of an institution affects inmates' behavior (Reeves, 1992, p. 128). Essentially, this research shows that certain colors affect the behavior of inmates in several ways (see table 1.1).

In order to demonstrate the cyclical nature of the scientific approach, we could pose several additional hypotheses regarding the effects of color on inmate behavior. For example, while the color blue has a calming effect on inmates, what is the effect of the amount of light that is available? That is, does brighter light work against the calming effects of the blue color? Thus, we can hypothesize that the more light that is available, the lower

Figure 1.1

CYCLICAL PROCESS OF TRADITIONAL RESEARCH

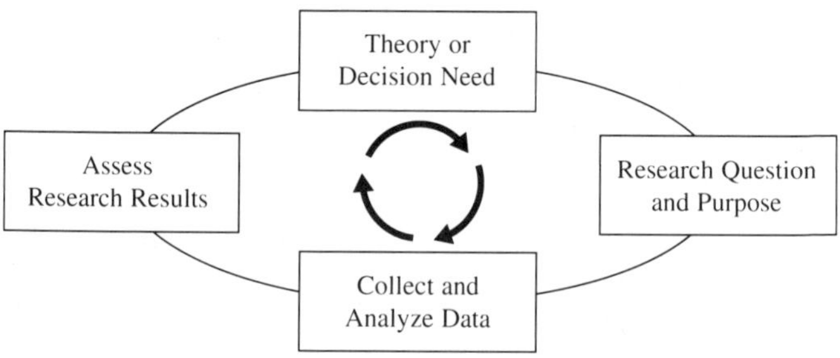

Table 1.1

THE EFFECTS OF COLORS ON BEHAVIOR IN INSTITUTIONS

Color	Effects
Blue	Has a calming effect and has been shown to reduce blood pressure. Preferred in inmate day rooms where a restful, peaceful environment is desired.
Red	Causes time to be overestimated. Appropriate for spaces where you desire people to feel as if a greater amount of time has been spent than actually has.
Green	Is the most restful color to the eye and is associated with pleasant odors and tastes. Appropriate for food preparation and dining areas.

Source: Reeves, 1992.

the calming effects of the color blue. In order to collect data about the effects of the color blue under different amounts of light, we could paint two cell blocks the same shade of blue. The first blue cell block would have the same lighting as the remainder of the prison. The second blue cell block would have all halogen lighting as well as addition natural light from skylights cut in the roof of the cell block. A third cell block painted a color other than blue could be used as a comparison, or control. This nonblue cell block allows us to make sure that the effects we find in the blue areas are due to the color or to the lighting and not to the attention the inmates receive. Data about the number and types of disciplinary infractions in each of the three cell blocks, as well as about the types of inmates involved, would be collected. Data analysis would consist of comparing the differences in the types and quantity of inmate infractions in the three cell blocks. If our results indicate that the blue cell block with the halogen and natural light has the highest rate of infractions, followed by the nonblue cell block and the blue cell block with regular lighting, we would have support for our hypothesis that light is involved in the effects of color on inmate behavior. At this point we may revise the theory and retest it. For instance, we may want to know whether the color and light interaction is affected by other physical variables such as temperature or crowding. We may want to understand why people in the nonblue cell block did worse than those in the blue cell block with regular light. Hence, the process of applying the scientific methodology continues.

The Concerns of the Traditional Method

The scientific method was developed for studying the physical world. Joseph Priestley used the scientific method to examine his belief that light particles exerted pressure on solid bodies (Preistley, 1772). The use of the scientific method in the social sciences appears to have begun in the field of psychology. The application of research methodology in criminal justice and criminology began in the 1800s with the emergence of the Positivistic School, which "symbolized that the era of faith was over and the scientific age had begun" (Schafer, 1969, p. 123). From this point on, the general adherence to the scientific method has been maintained in the study of criminal justice organizations and the causes of crime. In particular, the scientific approach has been used to study behaviors, phenomenon, and processes.

When one studies behavior in criminal justice and criminological studies one is concerned with the conduct of either criminal justice workers or inmates. In corrections studies, the majority of the current research is focused on the offender. However, there is a considerable amount of research on the behavior of the police and correctional officers, and a number of studies of community correctional programs and program participants.

Research on behavior in criminal justice and criminological studies tends to focus on *behavior* and behavioral outcomes. While criminal justice and criminological approaches to the study of behaviors rely on theories from the full range of social sciences (psychology, sociology, economics, political science, and geography), their focus is typically on behavior as an outcome. For instance, psychologists tend to focus on the underlying thought processes that lead to behaviors. Hence, they are concerned with how personality or the mind influences why criminals choose to behave the way they do. Conversely, political scientists focus on the organizational and governmental context of behavior. These scholars are interested in understanding how individual behavior influences the organization or the interactions between organizations. In an applied research focus criminal justice and criminological studies are often oriented toward assessing program outcomes in terms behavior. That is, an assessment of inmates' behavior upon release is fairly typical in criminal justice and criminological studies.

In addition to behaviors, the scientific method has been used to study *phenomena.* Phenomena are occurrences of events or actions that can be the focus of research. For instance, a researcher may be interested in studying the way police handle arrests of the mentally ill (Teplin, 1986; Kalinich and Senese, 1988). While phenomena may be comprised of several behaviors they are usually more complex. Examples of criminal justice studies of phenomena are: (1) studies of police pursuits, (2) studies of bail decisions, and (3) studies of inmate-on-inmate assaults.

The most complex level of study within the context of the scientific method is the study of *processes.* Processes are collections of behaviors and phenomena that are interrelated in some fashion. The overall functioning of the criminal justice "system" has been studied. For example, scholars have studied the criminal justice system as a process by means of an interactive computer program that enables criminal justice practitioners to assess the consequences of various system changes (Belkin, Blumstein, and Glass, 1971). This computer model (JUSSIM) was believed to allow administrators to predict case flow based on a simple diagram (see figure 1.2).

Currently, the focus on processes has been oriented toward the creation of centralized systems of data base management (Archambeault and Archambeault, 1989). This information can be integrated with a management information system and can then be used for decision making.

In summary, the scientific method is theory based, attempts to be objective, is based on a logical structure of events, relies on empirical data, and is a cyclical process. While the scientific method is difficult to use in its ideal form in policy-oriented and applied studies in criminal justice and criminology, it is the methodological basis for initiating and conducting studies. Much of the current research in criminal justice and criminology is engaged in "mopping-up" aspects of theories that remain untested (Kuhn, 1962) and in developing further understandings of specific notions within preexisting theories.

Figure 1.2
JUSSIM MODEL: DEMO SYSTEM

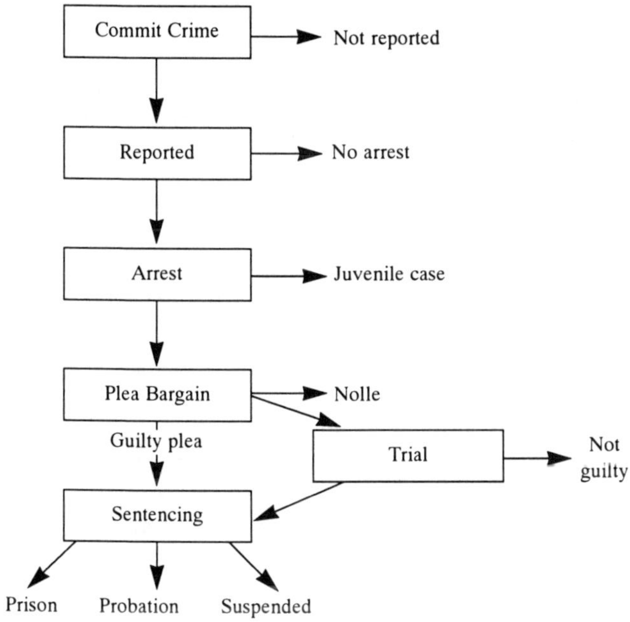

Source: Belkin, Blumstein, and Glass, 1971.

The Importance of Research

Research is important to the practice of criminal justice because it creates information upon which innovations are based. A clear understanding of research methods is a crucial requirement for criminologists because these individuals are usually concerned with the causes of crime, whereas criminal justice researchers emphasize organizational issues (Holmes and Taggart, 1989). However, the application of research to the practical world of criminal justice and other social sciences has not always been clear, as many of the "suppliers and users of social research are dissatisfied, the former because they are not listened to, the latter because they do not hear much they want to listen to" (Lindblom and Cohen, 1979, p. 1). The focus of this text is to make research more relevant to the practical criminal justice system while still maintaining scientific standards.

While those who work in the operational criminal justice system may not perceive a direct application for the results of academic research, there have been numerous effects on the "real-world" criminal justice system of both criminological and criminal justice policy-oriented research. This indicates that research has had meaningful and positive effects on the criminal justice system. Petersilia (1991), director of RAND Corporation's Criminal Justice Program, reports that research has actually affected policy and practice.[3]

- Research has helped shape the way police are deployed in our nation's cities and how they handle calls for service from the public.
- Research has also identified the existence of career criminals, provided information about the patterns of their criminality, and demonstrated the effectiveness of career criminal programs in prosecutors' offices and repeat offenders and projects in police departments.
- Research has improved the ability to classify offenders and to predict recidivism. Prediction models and the classification systems they are based on are now routinely used in bail, prosecution, sentencing, and parole decision making.
- Research has provided information about the relationship between drug abuse and crime: We now know that drug-abusing criminals commit twice as much crime as other offenders—up to six times more when they are abusing heavily. Testing has found empirical evidence that participation in rehabilitation programs necessarily reduces recidivism. (Petersilia, 1991, p. 5)

Research Constraints

Ideally, research can provide decision makers, whether they be the chief of police or prison warden, with objective and presumably the best possible information that is appropriate and relevant to the actions they intend to take. While scholars have been talking about making the information created by research relevant for decision makers for over two hundred years (Shadish, Cook, and Leviton, 1991), they have not been successful in implementing this ideal in many areas of social science. Criminal justice and criminology are not exceptions to this state of affairs.

Although research based on theoretical ideals, appropriate research methods, and quantitative or qualitative analyses is often presumed to contribute important information to the field, findings may not always be useful to decision makers. This may be because decision makers may not know how to use the information, or they may be reluctant to ask for help because it means that they are "acknowledging uncertainty, and worse, giving up some power and discretion" (Chelimsky, 1991, p. 226).

In addition, there may be *political constraints* on the use of the information generated by research. For example, in a large city on the East Coast, the State Department of Corrections recently took control over the City Detention Center. The City Detention Center was under several federal court orders to reduce its population, and the state presumed that it could run the facility more efficiently. While a research evaluation of the transition from a "city" facility to a "state" facility could have contributed to further policy development and could have helped create initial standards, the actors involved in the transition (the governor's office, the secretary of corrections, and so on) were more concerned about getting the transition achieved than understanding what was effective or ineffective about the facility or its staff or setting up objective standards to improve its functioning.

Another set of factors that reduce the utility of research in criminal justice settings are *resource constraints.* Resource constraints can be anything from lack of cooperation from the staff to lack of a unified data collection system. These constraints directly influence the type and quality of research that can be completed. For instance, if one is interested in studying judicial attitudes about sentencing drug offenders one may not be able to collect relevant information. The judges may be reluctant or too busy to cooperate. There may be little in terms of "hard data" about judicial attitudes. Moreover, access to sentenced inmates may not be possible because they are located in distant prisons or are unwilling to cooperate. Although many of the techniques of research methods attempt to bypass the problems of lack of data (e.g., surveys, questionnaires, participant observations, and so on), these problems cannot always be overcome. In addition, research that is scientifically rigorous is usually expensive, and without research grants, some research will simply not be conducted.

There are also *research constraints* that limit the influence of research. That is, there are limits to the types of research methods that can provide direct information for decision making. Social scientific research is most effective where the variables and processes one is attempting to understand are distinct enough to study (Chelimsky, 1991). In the field of criminal justice, decision making is often dynamic (e.g., the decision to grant or deny bail influences the trial or plea bargaining outcomes), unrestricted by time (e.g., bail may be more readily granted during the summer than in the winter due to population pressures), and cyclical. For example, the amount of pretrial releases may be cyclical and based on the economic cycle of recession and recovery. Therefore, exceedingly sophisticated research approaches are required that may not be available to practitioners and policymakers.

In addition, many issues in the study of criminal justice and criminology may not be distinct (i.e., they have many meanings) or may not be amenable to study. For example, Pratt states that many police departments claim they are effective by "pointing to numbers of calls handled in relation to the number of personnel handling them; number of citations written in a given period of time; increasing numbers of arrests per officer" (Pratt, 1992, p. 290). Hence, "effectiveness" may mean many things to police departments.

While research in the criminal justice system is affected by political, resource, and research constraints, it has had significant impacts. This is true even though spending for criminal justice research lags significantly behind research in other areas of study.

It is important to understand the relative importance of criminal justice research in society. One way to demonstrate the importance is to assess how much "effect" it has on criminal justice organizations or offenders. Another way to assess the importance of criminal justice research is in terms of spending priorities. Criminal justice research has done remarkably well given the level of funding it has received relative to research on health, space, energy, and other areas (Petersilia, 1991). In fact, the federal government spends most of our research dollars on health (47.8%), space exploration (28.8%), energy (16.7%), and the environment (6.5%), and spends only a paltry .2 percent on justice research.

The following sections briefly outline some of the contributions criminal justice and criminological research has made on each of the three main components of the criminal justice system: the police, the courts, and corrections. While these discussions illustrate the types of contributions that research can make to the "real-world" criminal justice system, they do not include all of the possible benefits of research. The purpose of this section is to demonstrate that research methods have helped the positive development of the criminal justice system.

Police

Research is important in policing because it can help define appropriate approaches and values. The research focus on policing has been wider than on any other criminal justice system component. The disproportionate focus of research attention toward the police is a result of the problems that resulted from the police response to the civil rights movement, protests opposing the Vietnam conflict, as well as urban riots in the 1960s and 1970s. The end result of these problems was the development of perhaps the largest federal government assistance program for criminal justice in history, Law Enforcement Assistance Administration (LEAA). While the LEAA was designed to provide direct assistance to police departments, it also supported research on police work.

The research on policing has shown that police spend the majority of their time on service activities (e.g., mediating a domestic disturbance instead of arresting someone) rather than law enforcement (Reiss, 1971). The ideas that police do not arrest every law violator and that they spend relatively little of their time on actual law enforcement have also been subjects of study. For example, Wilson found that police do not spend all their time enforcing the law, and that enforcement of the law is selective and based on the officers' abilities to "handle the situation" (Wilson, 1968). In addition, further research indicates that there may be a distinct police personality and that police are ambivalent, or cynical (Lorr and Strack, 1994).

Another area where criminal justice and criminological research has contributed to the operation of law enforcement is in the area of patrol. The incorporation of motorized patrol was undertaken because it was presumed that a fast response time was necessary for apprehension. However, in the now famous Kansas City Study, Kelling and associates found that patrol had little effect on citizens' attitudes toward the police or fear of crime (Kelling et al., 1974). Hence, police began to rethink their methods of patrol and have adopted innovations such as team policing (Sherman, Milton and Kelly, 1973) or community policing (Trojanowicz and Harden, 1985).

Other areas that have been the subject of both criminal justice and criminological research are police personality, police styles, and police discretion. Lundman (1980) found that the police personality includes aspects of authoritarianism, suspicion, racism, hostility, insecurity, conservatism, and cynicism. In addition, Niederhoffer found that police officers become cynical as a result of their day-to-day duties (Niederhoffer, 1967). Although many researchers have not found a typical police personality (Lorr and Strack, 1994; Evans, Coman, and Stanley, 1992), this issue is being further studied. The importance of this research, whether it establishes a distinct police personality or not, is in its implications for training and management. If police are cynical or racist, sensitivity programs may be designed to reduce these problems and thereby improve police service. Managers lacking information about the personality or problems of their officers may or may not commit funds to training. Either way decisions about spending or policies that have been made without objectively developed research seem unwise and may be quite costly. For instance, evidence of the potentially astronomical costs of ignoring racist attitudes of officers were demonstrated by the riots in South Central Los Angeles in 1992.

The research on police styles has shown that officers may become socialized into a particular approach to their work role. Perhaps the most well-known police style has been defined as the "Dirty Harry" style (Klockars, 1980) where officers use any means to apprehend offenders, from intimidation (e.g., "Do you feel lucky punk? Well, do you?") to outright threats of violence (e.g., "Go ahead, make my day"). While the Dirty Harry type movies may be entertaining, most citizens would rather have a police force that follows the basic rules of law. This research is important because it provides administrators with information about the potential for problem officers and styles.

Research on police discretion has also resulted in knowledge about the work role of police in our society. Skolnick claimed that because police officer decision making is "low-visibility," it is not subjected to police scrutiny or judicial review (Skolnick, 1966). This information has implications for how police supervisors and managers conduct their review of line officers. For instance, Powell (1981) found that police officers in black neighborhoods used the most amount of discretion and were more likely to be punitive toward whites than they were with blacks. When discriminatory treatment is directed at blacks or whites, it is costly in that it reduces police effectiveness and positive police community relations. An administrator can respond to this research through improving cultural diversity training or improving the guidelines for discretion. Finally, the research on police use of discretion has also pointed out that its use is complex and is dependent upon the situation and the characteristics of the officer and the offender.

In summary, the efforts of criminal justice researchers in the area of law enforcement have been important. They have produced a wide variety of knowledge ranging from the nature of police organizations to individual officers' personalities. While the research has not always directly improved police operations, it has created the initial and critical information necessary for the further development of effective and productive law enforcement.

Courts

There has been a fair amount of important research on the courts and various functions within the courts that has had a meaningful impact on the way courts function. For example, there have been several studies of the pretrial processes within the criminal courts. Toborg (1982) studied Baltimore, Washington, D.C., Miami, Tucson, Louisville, and San Jose and found that most defendants receive bail before trial (about 85%). Of those who receive bail, about 30 percent are either arrested for an additional crimes or do not show up for trial. The result of research such as this has been tightening release criteria and further analysis of safety and appearance considerations. Information about more effective case management, such as this, is crucial to the operational criminal justice system because of the extremely large case load now and in the foreseeable future.

Another area of important research at the pretrial stage has been bail. One of the most influential studies in this area was done by the Vera Institute of Justice (1972) in the Manhattan Bail Project. In the Vera project certain factors were identified as indicators of appearance. These indicators are currently widely used as measures of whether an individual offender should be released on their own recognizance or detained at the pretrial stage. In addition, this research resulted in the Federal Bail Reform Acts of 1966 and 1984. While the results of bail reform have not been uniform, they have been one of the more important successes for criminal justice research.

Plea bargaining has also been a consistent focus of criminal justice research attention. After several years of study the National Advisory Commission on Criminal Justice Standards and Goals recommended several responses to the problems involved in plea bargaining on which the federal government would spend $1 billion per year (Rosett and Cressey, 1976). The practical result of the work of the commission was to recommend that plea bargaining be prohibited (National Advisory Commission, 1973). However, while this recommendation was never implemented, addition research suggests that sentences for defendants who take advantage of the plea bargain are less severe than those given to defendants who chose to go to trial (McDonald, 1985).

Significant research studies have described the nature of the plea bargaining process and the relative amounts of plea bargaining. For instance, Boland and Forst (1984) studied the prevalence of plea bargaining and found that for each trial that is held there are eleven plea-bargained cases. In addition, they found that not all areas had a high proportion of plea bargains were high crime rate areas. This information is important for case-load management in the courts in that it allows for a more rapid processing of court dockets.

Another response to the National Advisory Commission studies by a few areas was to eliminate plea bargaining. However, research indicates that this is a difficult undertaking that may not produce the desired results. For instance, a study was conducted of the effects of this policy in Alaska. It was found that the elimination of plea bargains increased sentence severity for minor cases, but the ban had no effect on serious cases (Rubenstein, Clarke, and White, 1980). Similar results were found in New York (Department of Justice, 1978). Thus, research has shown that there are several inherent problems with the plea bargaining process, and it has also shown that plea bargaining is very difficult to eliminate. It is clear that additional research that demonstrates how the problems inherent in plea bargaining may be reduced is needed.

Research on the criminal courts has revealed that the people who work in the courts (i.e., the judge, attorneys, and so on) form courtroom work groups. That is, instead of the assumed adversarial system of justice, the courtroom process seems to be a system of exchange relationships.

Another area of research on courts is court case loads. Studies have determined that state court systems handle tens of millions of cases per year (Bureau of Justice Statistics, 1983). The Bureau of Justice Statistics has also determined that the popular view that criminal appeals "clog the nation's court system because so many convicted criminals try to 'beat the rap' on a technicality" is not supported by research (Bureau of Justice Statistics, 1983). There is also current research literature concerning the development of computer applications and records systems. Research on the court component of the criminal justice system, while far from complete, has produced direct effects on the operational criminal justice system.

Corrections

The effects of correctional research have been substantial. Evaluations of probation classification (Kratcoski, 1985) have shown that although such classification is not helpful in reduing recidivism it is an effective means to manage cases and provide treatment. Other researchers have determined that probation case-load classification facilitates community protection, because it increases the supervision for more dangerous or risky offenders (Clear and O'Leary, 1983).

Extensive research on intensive supervision probation and parole programs indicates that these are effective alternatives to incarceration (Erwin and Bennett, 1987; Pearson and Bibel, 1986). Because of the initial successes of probation, indicated by research evaluating its effectiveness, legislatures are trying to sponsor supervision alternatives to incarceration (Clear and Hardyman, 1990).

In their review of the effectiveness of probation, Allen, Carlson, and Parks (1979) found the following:

- Probation is most effective with first-time offenders.
- Probation is less expensive than incarceration.
- Probationers that are employed are more successful.
- For misdemeanants, there is no difference in success between supervised and unsupervised probation.
- Professional probation officers aren't necessarily more effective than nonprofessional probation officers.
- Sentencing decisions are typically based on probation officers' recommendations.
- Reduction of caseloads doesn't necessarily increase effectiveness.

Overall studies of the effectiveness of probation reveal that about 80 percent of the offenders who were released from probation case loads were released because they were successful (Greenfeld, 1986).

A substantial amount of research by criminal justice, criminological, and sociological researchers has been conducted of prisons as organizations. Several scholars have identified the problems (e.g., loss of liberty, autonomy, and so on) involved in housing inmates in total institutions (Sykes, 1958; Johnson, 1987). Others have studied the inmate subculture to determine the informal coping techniques utilized by inmates (Gleason, 1978; Kalinich, 1980). Research has also shown that inmates may develop their own "niche" in prison, which reduces the "pains of imprisonment" to some extent (Toch, 1977).

Recently there has been more research on correctional officers, which has had important implications for the development of more effective training and management support of these primary inmate managers. In the literature on correctional officers are studies of the influences of officer characteristics on inmate management, stress, cynicism, and job roles (Walters, 1992; Van Voorhis et al., 1991; Whitehead and Lindquist, 1989;

Hepburn, 1985; Gardner, 1981; Cullen et al., 1985; Hepburn and Albonetti, 1980; Poole and Regoli, 1980), inmate communications and management (Senese, 1991), and studies of officer characteristics (Zupan, 1986; Klofas and Toch, 1982).

In summary, although the research in corrections is far from complete, it has contributed greatly to the development of innovative programs and the professional development of correctional workers. The contributions of academic and policy-oriented research can be seen across the whole range of correctional functions from pretrial services through probation and parole. Criminal justice and criminological research is important because: (1) it can provide better and more objective information, (2) it can promote better decision making, (3) it allows for objective assessment of programs, (4) it has often been the source of innovation, and (5) it has been shown to be both directly and indirectly relevant to criminal justice practice. The study of research methods will allow you to more appropriately consider and consume information that is important to your career as a criminal justice practitioner or researcher.

Summary

This chapter has described the basic concepts of research methods in criminal justice and criminology. While the traditional research method is the ideal method, it is rarely completely adhered to in practice. However, the traditional methodology is a logical starting point for understanding research methods. You need to understand past research in order to understand where it is going and how it is used. Research in criminal justice and criminology has made substantial contributions to the operational criminal justice system. These contributions are across all major components of the system.

Main Concepts

applied research methods
theory
logical structure
qualitative versus quantitative
behavior
processes
resource constraints
scientific method
objectivity
empirical data
cyclical process
phenomena
political constraints
research constraints
research process

Discussion Questions

1. Discuss the importance of research to each of the criminal justice system components.

2. Can the traditional scientific method be applied in most criminal justice settings? Why or why not?
3. What are the potential contributions that research can make to the future of community policing?
4. Discuss and speculate about the effects of constraints on research utilization in criminal justice settings or agencies.

Exercise

Debate the value of criminal justice and criminological research. First, form into two groups (randomly or purposively). One group must argue that criminal justice research has value. The other group must argue that criminal justice research has no value. Each group should then list the points in its argument. Count the number of valid points each group makes. Each group should then offer counterarguments or critique the other group. At the end of this exercise make a general summary of the arguments.

2

RESEARCH TERMINOLOGY

Learning Objectives

1. To provide an explanation of the basic dichotomies in research methodology
2. To discuss and provide examples of the key concepts in research methods
3. To discuss and provide examples of the four key levels of measurement
4. To discuss and provide an understanding of the issue of time and its relationship to research studies

Chapter Outline

Introduction
The Basic Dichotomies
  Pure versus Applied Research
  Qualitative versus Quantitative Data
  Descriptive versus Inferential Analysis
  Discrete versus Continuous Data
Individual Concepts
  Units of Analysis
  Levels of Measurement
  Variables
  Concepts
  Theories and Models
  Research and Time
  Summary
Main Concepts
Discussion Questions
Exercise

CHAPTER
TWO

Introduction

Many students in criminal justice and criminology have difficulty understanding obtuse "researchese" language that is relied on to describe techniques and approaches to problem analysis. This chapter describes terminology and shows how it is applied. These terms cannot be avoided, because they are endemic to reported research in criminal justice and criminology. However, students should not be intimidated by these terms. Learning these terms is similar to learning legal terms. Like legal terms, research terms represent summary concepts that allow language in explanations to be streamlined. This section discusses the basic dichotomies that define the appropriateness of specific methodologies as well as the concepts that define the focus of research efforts.

The Basic Dichotomies

The basic dichotomies in research methods represent the ideal, mutually exclusive ends of four conceptual ranges. For instance, a conceptual range of income could be described as the dichotomy of rich versus poor, which has on the one extreme the "filthy rich" and on the other extreme the "filthy poor." The four dichotomies in research methods occur in (1) the application of research, (2) the kinds of data, (3) the level of analysis, and (4) the level of precision in the data.

Pure versus Applied Research

The first dichotomy in research that will be discussed is related to the purpose of the research. Certain research is basic or pure, whereas other research focuses on practical applications.

Pure research, at one extreme, generates knowledge for knowledge's sake (Babbie, 1989). For example, a criminologist may determine that work is a form of social control in that it keeps people so busy that they have little time to commit crime. Such knowledge may fit into one of the more generally accepted criminological theories and therefore will contribute to the general knowledge available about the causes of crime. Although pure research is oriented toward creating knowledge, one can often forecast its potential effects in application. For example, David Greenberg attempted to model criminal careers through the use of formal mathematical procedures (Greenberg, 1991). His focus was to create knowledge, and his analysis "addressed primarily scientific questions, not public policy." However, he suggests that his research may have implications for developing improved penal policies. Pure research tends to focus on the "big picture" questions such as what causes crime or criminality (see figure 2.1).

On the other extreme of the application continuum is *applied research.* In essence, applied research is oriented toward creating facts or information that have direct relevance to policy or immediate decision making. In figure 2.1, the focus of the applied research question is not so much on the global aspects of what causes crime as it is on how a particular criminal or group of criminals can be better dealt with by the criminal justice system.

Another example of an applied focus was a project I conducted for the Baltimore City Pretrial Services Division. The director of the division was interested in determining whether a newly designed risk assessment instrument would allow his department to make more accurate and consistent decisions about releasing defendants on recognizance than would their current Vera-type instrument (i.e., he wanted facts about the new assessment instrument). The director of Pretrial Services did not want to create basic

Figure 2.1

PURE VERSUS APPLIED RESEARCH QUESTIONS

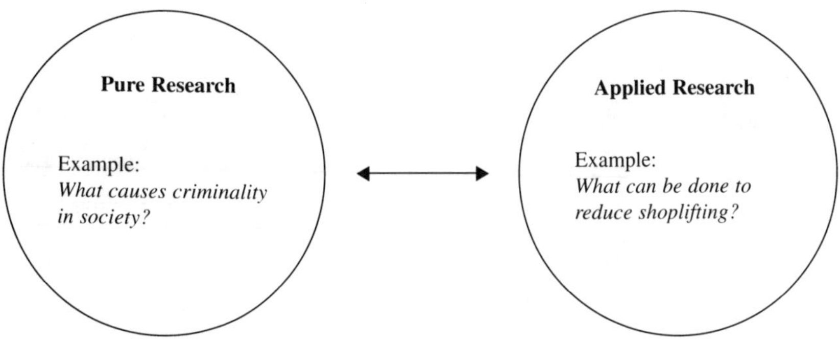

theoretical knowledge about the causes of crime or even the predictors of appearance (although it's likely he would have found the latter interesting).

While not all applied research is as limited as the pretrial services example, applied research tends to focus on the creation of specific information about particular programs or events. Although many criminological researchers presume that an applied research approach is less academic, and therefore less rigorous, this is a naive perception. As a matter of fact, some argue that the current trend in criminal justice and criminological research is to make its results more applied and practice relevant.[1]

Qualitative versus Quantitative Data

The second dichotomy focuses on the kind of data used in the research. On one extreme are qualitative data, which allow one to categorize observations for the cases in the study into distinct types (see figure 2.2). An example of a qualitative variable is gender. One can categorize gender as either male or female. Qualitative data is primarily nonnumerical in format and measures the qualities possessed by the things, groups, or people that one is studying.

Researchers often attach numbers to qualitative data, but these numbers are merely labels for the categories and have no mathematical meaning. For example, if a researcher assigns the number 1 to males and the number 2 to females, the average gender in a group of ten males and three females based on the assigned numbers is 1.2308. But this statistic has no meaning, as there is no useful interpretation of the value 1.2308. All that one can say about the distribution of gender is that there are more males than females.

Figure 2.2
QUALITATIVE VERSUS QUANTITATIVE DATA

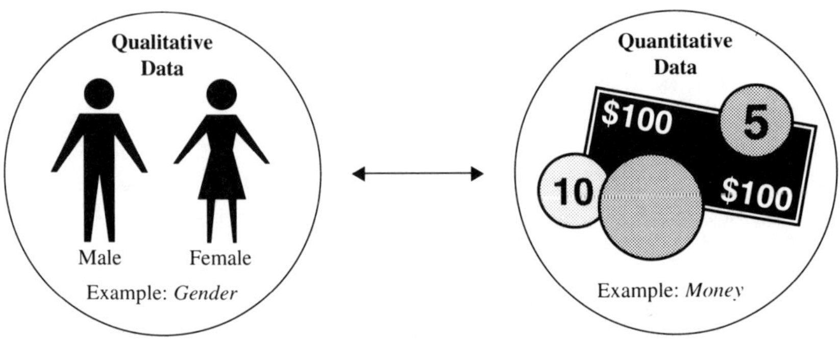

It is very important to note that when we collect qualitative data, we may rely on structured observations, interviews, or some other form of data collection that allows the categorization of observations. Qualitative data collection is similar to quantitative data collection in the sense that it is composed of collecting the number of observations of individuals or groups based on the categories we are studying. For example, we could categorize students in a class according to their opinions about the use of the death penalty in order to see whether that particular class fits with the national pattern discovered by public opinion polls.

Qualitative data are analyzed by means of logic rather than statistical techniques. In my senior seminar in criminal justice, I require students to construct a research proposal that incorporates data analysis. Many students elect to use qualitative research designs because they usually feel uncomfortable with statistics or because they believe the analysis of data will be easier. However, for many researchers qualitative data is more difficult to analyze than statistics. While there are computer based programs that allow one to analyze observational categories, they generally only organize the information and do not allow statistical testing or inference.

At the other end of the data continuum are quantitative data, which allow us to measure the amount of a characteristic the cases in the study possess. For example, a common quantitative variable in criminal justice studies is the recidivism rate (the number of rearrests). We can measure the amount of recidivism in the groups or individuals under study. Quantitative data is exclusively numerical in format. That is, the characteristics in quantitative variables can always be represented by mathematical symbols (numerical values). Although some may assume that quantitative data (hard data) are superior to qualitative data, this is not necessarily true. In fact, we should not presume that either quantitative data or qualitative data are more accurate or consistent. While there has been debate about which kind of data is better (more accurate or consistent), the issue is unresolved. Notwithstanding this debate, one should collect the kind of data that are most appropriate to the purpose of the research object. For instance, if I wanted to assess the relationship between crime rates and employment rates, then my data would likely be quantitative. On the other hand, if I wanted to study the character or patterns of criminality in poor neighborhoods, then my data are likely to be qualitative. Research may rely on both quantitative and qualitative data. For example, I may be concerned with the relationship between the amount of crime and employment as well as the quality of criminality in the areas I am studying.

Descriptive versus Inferential Analysis

The third dichotomy is concerned with the focus of the analysis and ranges from descriptive to inferential analyses. A *descriptive analysis* is a uniform and impartial explanation of certain aspects of the persons, places, or things that are the subject of study. An example of a descriptive study would be a descriptive study of AIDS in correctional institutions. Since 1985 the National Institute of Justice has funded several follow-up studies on the prevalence of AIDS in correctional institutions. The reports that result describe the incidence of AIDS in the prisons and jails across the United States. There is relatively little inference in descriptive analyses, and they are likely to be completed on topics that have not been well researched. In addition, descriptive studies provide initial information for more advanced theory development, for the creation or modification of policies and procedures, and for developing more accurately specified research (figure 2.3).

Inferential analysis uniformly and impartially explains certain aspects of the large population from a small sample of the persons, places, or things that are the subject of study. For example, in an analysis of sex differences in sentencing, a criminal justice researcher was interested in understanding whether women receive more lenient sentences than men. He collected data on 108 women and 228 men who had committed felonies. Based on his analyses he was able to infer that the relationship between gender and sentencing is more concerned with maintaining families and protecting children than with discrimination on the basis of sex (Crew, 1991).

Inferential analyses allow one to test whether the values obtained from a study group (i.e., a sample) are reasonable. For example, is it reasonable to find that the group of women we are studying receive, on average, three months more time on their prison sentences than do men? Inference allows us to evaluate whether the difference in male and female sentence lengths is due to the uniqueness of our study group or whether the difference is important, that is, statistically significant. If the statistical tests of inference show that the values found for a group are reasonable (i.e., we get the same values when we study a number of groups of women and men), then inferences from such a study group to the larger population can reasonably be made. On the other hand, if the values found are not reasonable, then we usually conclude that the values are due to inaccurate measurement or that the group we relied on is somehow different from the larger population that we are interested in.

Discrete versus Continuous Data

The fourth dichotomy involves the level of precision in the data and ranges from discrete data to continuous data. *Discrete data* fit into specific and nonoverlapping categories. For instance, assume you are interested in collecting discrete data that measure the religion of the individuals in your study. Assume further that you are interested only in knowing whether subjects are Protestant, Roman Catholic, Jewish, or some other religion. You would place each of the individuals in your study into one of these four categories.

These categories are specific in that they clearly indicate which religion belongs in which category, and they are nonoverlapping in that a Roman Catholic cannot be placed in any other category but Roman Catholic. In general, discrete data are also qualitative data.

Continuous data measure the quantity of some characteristic and do not necessarily fit into specific and nonoverlapping categories. For example, we can measure the intelligence of a group of inmates using a standard I.Q. test. Suppose we study the I.Q.s of a group of ten inmates. Because I.Q. tests result in continuous data, we could end up with ten categories (each inmate has a different I.Q.). However, continuous variables are not considered to be appropriate for categorizing observations. They allow us to

Figure 2.3
DESCRIPTIVE VERSUS INFERENTIAL ANALYSIS

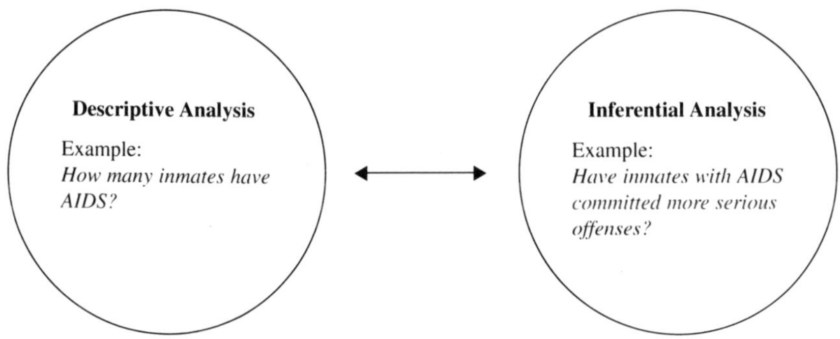

Figure 2.4
DISCRETE VERSUS CONTINUOUS DATA

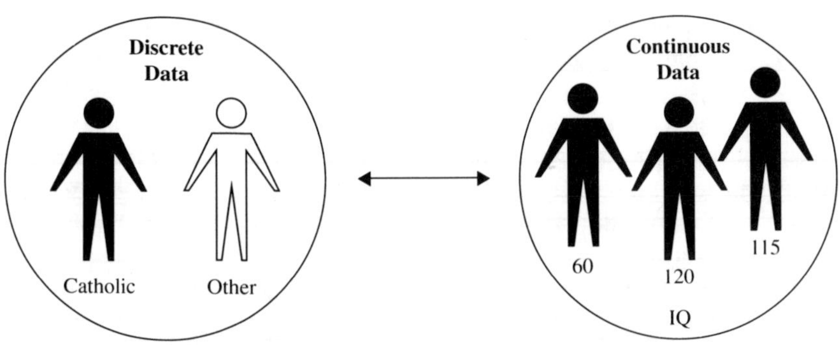

measure the relative amount of a characteristic. Let's say that we had one inmate in our group of ten that had an I.Q. of 80 and another inmate who had an I.Q. of 160. We could say, if we believe in the accuracy of I.Q. tests, that the second inmate is twice as intelligent as the first inmate. Thus, continuous data are amenable to statistical manipulation and allow us to make inferences.

Individual Concepts

Several individual concepts are important to understand before learning the details of research methodology. These individual concepts represent crucial considerations for selecting study subjects or groups as well as for determining the appropriate techniques of analysis of the collected data. The four most important individual concepts in research methods are (1) the units of analysis, (2) the levels of measurement, (3) the variables, and (4) theoretical concepts.

Units of Analysis

The typical *units of analysis* in criminal justice and criminological research are people, groups of people, organizations, and products of human activity such as records, newspapers, and so on (figure 2.5). The most often analyzed units are people—inmates, police officers, judges, victims, and so on. However, it is also common to see studies of groups such as gangs and families. Organizations are relevant units of analysis in criminal justice studies. A researcher, for example, may be interested in studying jails throughout the country in order to describe their differences or to develop inferences.

Units of analysis are often selected for both descriptive and inferential purposes. If you are interested in conducting an inferential analysis, you must be certain that the sample units of analysis are the group about which you want to generalize. It is important that the units of analysis match the description or inferences you intend to make; otherwise, generalization errors will result.

We should not attempt to generalize about an individual's behavior from group data. Suppose that our units of analysis are cell blocks and that we are interested in studying the rates of assaults on staff in each of the cell blocks in a representative group of prisons. Let's assume that our analyses indicate that the highest rates of assaults on staff were in the "segregation" and "mental health" cell blocks. We might then suppose that we had shown that segregation and mental health cell blocks are areas where staff are more likely to be assaulted.

However, it would be a mistake to make any conclusions about the inmates within the segregation and mental health cell blocks. Suppose we had data about the inmates' ages in the cell blocks we studied and found

Figure 2.5
UNITS OF ANALYSIS

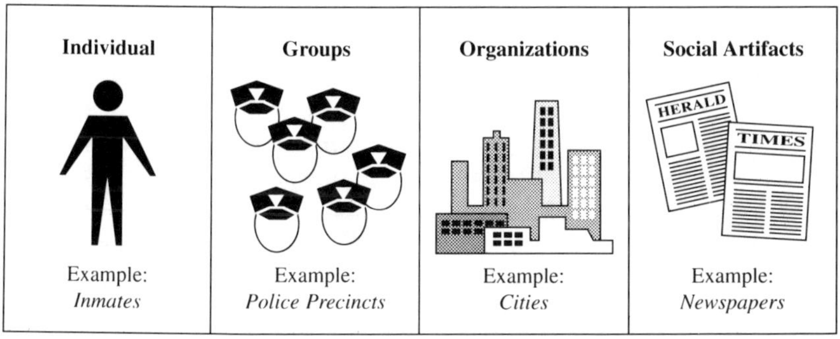

that both segregation and mental health cell blocks tended to have much younger inmates than the prison as a whole.[2] It would be a mistake to generalize that the assaults in segregation and mental health cell blocks were committed by young inmates, because the older inmates may be the ones who assaulted the staff. The fact that inmates in the segregation and mental health cell blocks are younger doesn't allow us to connect that information with the assault rate for the cell block as a whole. Of course, we could measure assaults on staff by individual inmates, which would allow such an assertion to be made.

Similarly, we should not dismiss general patterns because of individual exceptions. Suppose that we determined that assaults on staff generally occurred in cell blocks that had high staff-to-inmate ratios (for the purposes of this illustration, a high staff-to-inmate ratio is one correctional officer for every fifty inmates). Perhaps the inmates assaulted the staff because there were more opportunities to do so. Let's suppose that out of the one hundred cell blocks with high staff-to-inmate ratios ninety-eight had disproportionately high assault rates. It would be illogical to use the two exceptional cell blocks to explain the general pattern.

A basic rule of thumb about units of analysis is that they should be appropriate to the research purpose. While conclusions should be drawn only about like units of analysis, that doesn't mean that one study cannot contain several parts using different units for analysis. For example, in a study of jails, you can study both the cell blocks and individual inmates. Analyses can be done on both units. In addition, the selection of the appropriate units of analysis in criminological and criminal justice studies are often multidisciplinary in that sociological, psychological, political science, economic, and geographical variables are used to explain behaviors.

Such multidisciplinary approaches are important because they reduce the chances of a narrow interpretation of the causes and relationships in studying behavior or organizations.

Levels of Measurement

The second important individual concept is the level of measurement of the data. There are four *levels of measurement:* nominal, ordinal, interval, and ratio. The levels of measurement are related to the relative precision or accuracy of the data. The levels of measurement are also relative positions on the quantitative/qualitative continuum.

At the *nominal level of measurement* one can only separate the data by the kind of the observations. For example, if we are measuring the variable gender by relying on the categories of male and female (see figure 2.6) we can only determine whether the people in our study belong in the male female categories. The categories of "male" and "female" are both exhaustive and mutually exclusive in that we can place each individual into one or the other category. The categories, however, have no mathematical properties (i.e., one cannot add the number of males and females and divide by the total number of people in the study to produce a number that means anything). However, data analyses can be conducted on the frequencies of observations in each, or across, the categories. The nominal level of measurement is primarily at the descriptive, discrete, and qualitative ends of the respective dichotomies.

The *ordinal level of measurement* allows us to rate observations by kind as well as by order (figure 2.7). For instance, if we collect data on the

Figure 2.6

NOMINAL LEVEL OF MEASUREMENT: GENDER

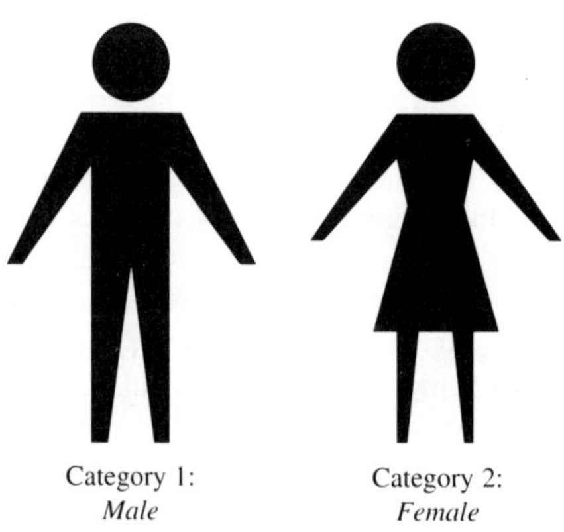

Figure 2.7
ORDINAL LEVEL OF MEASUREMENT: OFFICER RANK

rank of police officers we can determine that captain is, in fact, a different rank from sergeant or lieutenant. Additionally, the ordinal level of measurement allows us to determine the rough ordering of the categories (i.e., captain is a higher rank than lieutenant, which is in turn a higher rank than sergeant). Other examples of typical ordinal level variables in criminal justice and criminological studies are the inmate social class (high, middle, low), offense seriousness (very serious, serious, minor, not serious) and maturity (very mature, mature, immature). While the ordinal level of measurement is generally considered more precise than the nominal level, it still is not exact. That is, even though we can determine that captain is a higher rank than lieutenant, the difference is not exact (i.e., we only know captains are ranked higher), nor can we determine how much higher a rank it is.

The interval and ratio levels of measurement allow us to separate observations by kind, order, and interval and can therefore be used in inferential and quantitative studies where continuous data are required (figure 2.8). In studies of the relationship between I.Q. and delinquency, I.Q. is an *interval level of measurement.* We clearly know that an I.Q. of 70 is different in kind from an I.Q. of 80. A person with an I.Q. of 90 is more intelligent than a person with an I.Q. of 70. Interval level of measurement also allows us to differentiate the relative differences in the order of categories (i.e., the relative order can be mathematically calculated). For example, a person with I.Q. 100 is twice as intelligent as a person with an I.Q. of 50. This property is important for most statistical analyses.

The *ratio level of measurement* is the most precise level (figure 2.9). Hence, we can clearly separate the observations by kind (four prior arrests are *different from* one prior arrest), by order (four prior arrests are *more than* one prior arrest), and by interval (two prior arrests are precisely 50% more prior arrests than one prior arrest). In addition, the ratio level of measurement has a true zero point indicating the absence of the quantity that is being measured (i.e., no prior arrests). While ratio data is generally more precise than interval level data, for all practical purposes and statistical analyses either level of measurement is suitable. In addition, one may change a higher level of measurement (ordinal, interval, or ratio) into a lower level but not vice versa.

Variables

Through the process of defining variables we move from the theoretical to the measurable. Research questions and hypotheses are usually stated in terms

Figure 2.8
INTERVAL LEVEL OF MEASUREMENT: INTELLIGENCE

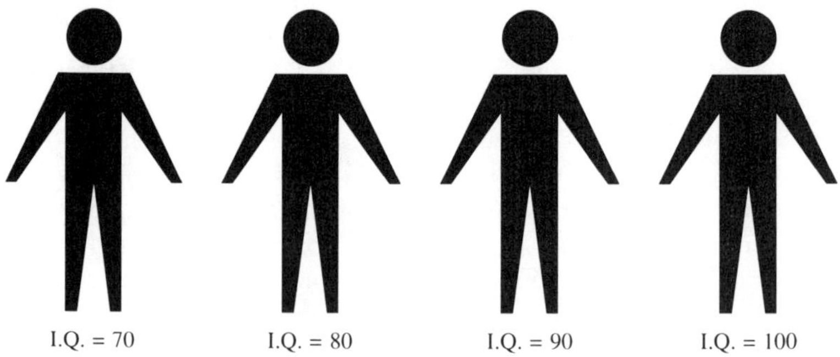

Figure 2.9
RATIO LEVEL OF MEASUREMENT: PRIOR ARRESTS

of expectations about the variables. *Variables* are empirical properties (data) that consist of two or more values. Variables may be used for descriptive or inferential purposes. They can be collected across all levels of measurement and may be qualitative or quantitative. The values that make up variables are often referred to as attributes (figure 2.10). For instance, the variable "gender" has two attributes, male and female. Data collection and analysis focuses on the collection and analysis of variables.

There are also different types of variables. The main types used in criminal justice or criminological studies are dependent variables, independent variables, and control variables. *Dependent variables* are usually the variables that we wish to explain. Typically the explanation is based on one or more independent variables. For example, we may wish to explain the dependent variable "crime rate" based on several independent variables such as employment rate or poverty rate.

Independent variables are those that influence or explain the dependent variable. While variables are intrinsically neither dependent nor independent, we create a logical basis for these labels based on the needs or focus of the research. An independent variable in one study could, therefore, be a dependent variable in another study. For example, we could assess whether the poverty rate can be explained by the relative proportion of single female headed households in a particular area.

Figure 2.10

VARIABLES AND ATTRIBUTES

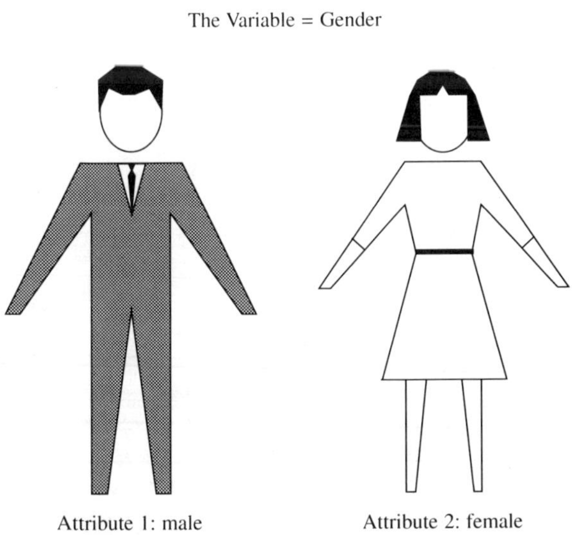

Control variables allow us to reduce the risks of falsely crediting an independent variable with explanatory power. For instance, if we attempt to explain the crime rate based on the poverty rate there may be many variables such as police arrest practices, plea bargaining, and sentencing rates that may influence or explain the crime rate. Control variables, therefore, allow us to determine whether the independent variable explanation of the dependent variable is bogus.

Concepts

Most current research is based on analyses of individual "concepts." Understanding this term will help you to understand the linkages between theory and research methodology. *Concepts* can be defined as ideal representations of objects, properties of objects, processes, or phenomena. In addition, concepts are smaller, more manageable parts of theories. For example, Einstein's theory of relativity ($E=mc^2$) consists of the concepts of "energy" and "mass." An example of concepts in criminology is demonstrated by Shaw and McKay's "Social Disorganization Theory," which maintains that crime is the product of pathological environments rather than individual abnormalities (Hagan, 1986, p. 439). The concepts of "pathology" and "environment" are abstractions that should be measured in any study that tests the veracity of Social Disorganization Theory.

Concepts can communicate ideas or introduce a point of view, or they can be the means for generalization. In terms of communicating ideas, concepts are important to research because they are the foundations of communication and thought. They allow us to let others know what we think and allow information to be shared. Thus, instead of telling you that correctional officers have less education than police, are not well trained, work in poor environments, have few positive communications with supervisors, and so on, I might rely on the concept of "unprofessionalism" to communicate my idea.

If we use concepts to introduce a point of view, we are attempting to give order to the otherwise unordered. For instance, many people report that the most appropriate way for our correctional systems to handle offenders is to "lock them up and throw away the key." We might suggest that the concepts of income, gender, race, education, and so on influence such punitive attitudes. Similarly, concepts can be used to categorize opinions (e.g., agree or disagree to the use of the death penalty), structure opinions or ideas (e.g., the inmate contraband system is based on a structure of conceptual beliefs), or establish order (e.g., in labeling theory an offender is arrested before he or she can assume the stigma of being labeled).[3]

In order to conduct research, whether it is applied or basic, we must first define the relevant concepts that we will rely upon. One of the most important reasons we read studies or books about a topic before we construct our research approach is that past research can often identify the most relevant concepts. When we use concepts they should be clear and precise, and should be generally agreed-upon. The concept of "arrest" clearly and precisely transmits the perception of apprehension by the police into the criminal justice system process, a generally agreed-upon perception.

There are basically two ways in which concepts may be defined. First, concepts may be defined through the use of other abstractions or notions that define the idea or point one is attempting to make. The use of abstractions to define concepts can be based on primary terms (those that cannot be further abstracted such as colors and sounds) or on generally shared agreements.

Table 2.1 demonstrates that primitive and shared agreements might be used to define the concept "recidivism." The primary terms "bad," "negative," and "inferior" attempt to include the most basic ideas about recidivism in terms of its use for criminal justice decision makers perhaps relative to some program or program activity. In addition, there are generally shared agreements about what the concept of recidivism measures. Both the primary terms and the shared agreements could be combined to further define the concept of recidivism. Once this has been done, the researcher will still have to convert his or her conceptual definition into something that can be empirically measured (i.e., counted or categorized).

The second way we can define concepts is operationally or through the use of empirical measures. Under this method we are able to measure a concept directly. Table 2.1 lists the operationally based definition process. We might create a composite measure of the concept of recidivism by measuring rearrests, reconvictions, and reincarcerations. This method of defining concepts tends to be less theoretically based. However, the end result of this method is a process of empirical assessment of the concept we are

Table 2.1

EXAMPLES OF DEFINING THE CONCEPT OF RECIDIVISM

Abstract Terms	Operational Definitions
Primary Terms	Number of arrests
Bad	Number of reconvictions
Negative	Percentage reincarcerated
Inferior	Composite measures
Shared Agreements	
Individual failures	
Program failure	
Inefficiency	

interested in studying. This is not to say that one method for deriving concepts is superior to the other. The method one relies on depends on the purpose of the research study.

In summary, while conceptual definitions are neither true nor false they have quality. Some are better than others, and this is based on both consistency with past research as well as completeness. Researchers should be concerned with the relationship of the concepts with the actual measures that will be used to measure them. For example, one may denote recidivism as the principal measure of correctional program failure, but this may be poorly indicated by rearrests alone, because a program can have other effects—it can reduce substance abuse or it can improve the life skills of the offender—or police may simply label known offenders more readily. Therefore, offenders may be rearrested simply because they are easily identifiable, not necessarily because they are guilty of an offense.

Theories and Models

Theories and models are general systems that are used to explain concepts. Theories can be defined as systems of well-established concepts that allow the explanation of occurrences, organizations, or processes. The basic building blocks of theories are concepts. While theories are generally substantial explanations and are usually consistent, this may not always be the case. Some theories may be shown to be poor explanations. For example, in the 1920s Burgess formulated the "Concentric Zone Theory" to explain social disorganization such as crime and poverty (Burgess, 1923). He found that social disorganization was related to the distance of a community from the central business district or downtown of a city. That is, his theory held that social problems are greatest where there is the greatest social disorganization—the Zone of Transition (figure 2.11). While Burgess's theory was perhaps appropriate in the United States of the 1930s, it was shown to be a poor explanation of social disorganization within the dynamic and rapidly expanding cities of the 1980s and early 1990s.

Another important aspect about theories is that they can range from simple explanatory classifications to complex theoretical systems. If we were to rely on a simple classification theory, for example, we would only be able to order and summarize observations. Such a theory might be used to explain whether or not inmates control the correctional environment. We would determine only whether or not the inmates control the environment and would not focus on why or why not.

On the other end of the continuum of complexity in theories are theoretical systems. Theoretical systems are combinations of categorical theories (ordering and summation) and descriptions of the interconnections between one or more categorical systems. Complex theoretical systems can both describe and infer relationships between relevant variables. For example,

Figure 2.11
BURGESS'S CONCENTRIC ZONE THEORY

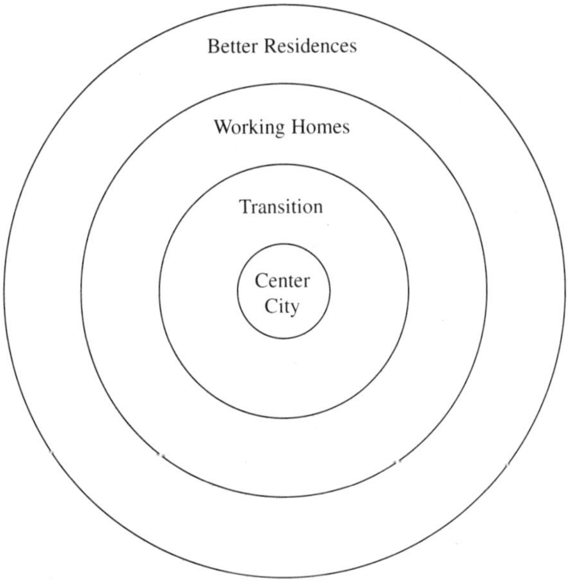

Source: Adapted from Burgess, 1929.

Reckless's "Containment Theory" can be viewed as a complex theoretical system (Hagan, 1986, p. 448). Containment theory maintains that people have various social controls (containments) that help them to resist criminality. Containment theory also describes the interactions between containments (e.g., values, personality, family) and the layers of social pressures (e.g., living conditions, minority group membership). Theories can be developed or discovered. They consist of abstract and/or operational concepts, tend to be well established, and attempt to explain something about the nature of the concepts.

Models differ from theories in that they are less developed and tested. Perhaps an area has only recently been studied, such as spouse abuse, or this lack of development may be due to the newness of the topic, such as AIDS in corrections. I am currently constructing a model for the interactions between jail officers' perceptions across a range of variables or collections of variables. From the literature on prison correctional officers (there is almost no research on jail officers), I have constructed an a priori model (from reading the literature, not through statistical analysis) that supposes relationships between several variables or sets of variables. The next step in my research will be to measure these relationships. If my model holds, then there would be support for my assumptions, but this would not elevate my ideas to a theory. That would take consistent and independent verification of the model.

Research and Time

An issue that is basic to most criminal justice and criminological research is time. In a broad sense, there are only two types of studies: those that are done at one time (*cross-sectional studies*) and those that are done at more than one time (*longitudinal studies*). One-time studies do not provide the benefits of studying a topic over some longer time period. In an applied approach, analyses tend to be cross-section, because the researcher is interested in generating policy or decision-making inputs and may not have the luxury of conducting longitudinal research (figure 2.12). However, in the field of business, which lives and dies by the bottom-line, longitudinal research is common (e.g., forecasts of profits or losses).

The main advantage of longitudinal studies is that they tend to produce a more accurate view of the research problem under study. In general, there are three approaches in longitudinal studies, series, groups, and particular. First, *series longitudinal studies* examine changes in a measurement or a population over time. Series longitudinal studies tend to focus on changes in quantitative measures. For example, a court administrator may be interested in studying the court's docket over time. She may be interested

Figure 2.12

CROSS-SECTIONAL TIME FRAME (DIFFERENT SAMPLING UNITS AT ONE POINT IN TIME)

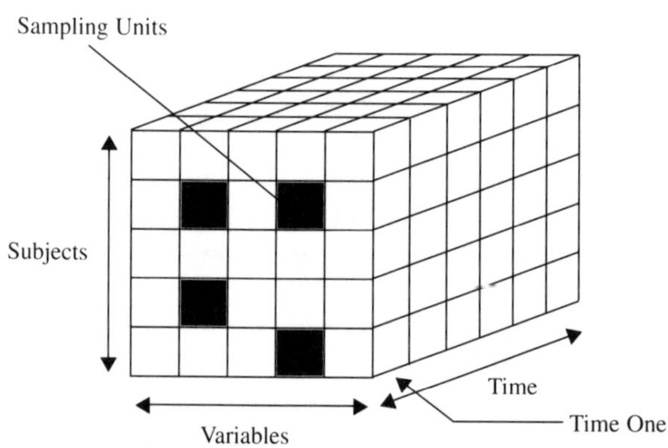

Figure 2.13
SERIES TIME FRAME (ONE VARIABLE AT MANY POINTS IN TIME)

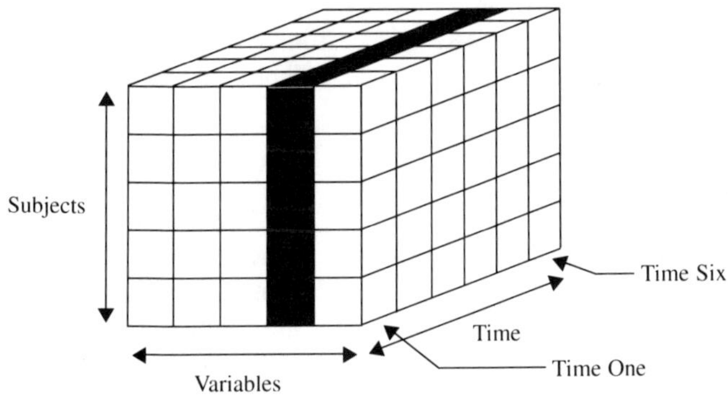

in whether the case load has a cycle and, if so, when that cycle peaks—whether the heaviest docket days are Wednesdays or Mondays—so she can manage the docket and her staff accordingly.

Second, *group longitudinal studies* can be conducted on certain groups, or any other units of analysis, in order to find out whether they change over time (figure 2.13). For example, Crowley studied the relationship between delinquency and employment. She was interested in determining "to what extent delinquent activity directly reduces labor force participation by providing substitute income and other rewards" (Crowley, 1984, p. 239).

Particular longitudinal studies focus on one group and study that group longitudinally. While it is usually difficult to maintain study participation over time, this approach is oriented toward improving the accuracy of assessment through a focus on one group of people. An example is to study a group of female offenders over a ten-year period in order to examine their criminal careers.

Summary

This chapter has defined and provided examples of the basic dichotomies and concepts involved in the study of research methods. The dichotomies are pure versus applied research, qualitative versus quantitative data, descriptive versus inferential analysis, and discrete versus continuous data. Each has a particular balance in research. The needs of a particular project dictate the nature of the research with regard to these dichotomies.

The key concepts in this chapter include the units of analysis, levels of measurement, variables, concepts, theories, and models. These important terminology labels are universally used in scientific research methods and allow us to use the accepted research language in the remainder of the text.

Finally, the issue of time in research is discussed and illustrated. There are two time frames: the one-time, here-and-now study and the study that takes place over time. Cross-sectional studies focus on the here and now, whereas group and series studies rely on variables that are measured at several different times.

Main Concepts

pure research
applied research
descriptive analysis
inferential analysis
discrete data
continuous data
units of analysis
levels of measurement
nominal level of measurement
ordinal level of measurement
interval level of measurement
ratio level of measurement
variables
dependent variables
independent variables
control variables
concepts
models
cross-sectional studies
longitudinal studies
series longitudinal studies
group longitudinal studies
particular longitudinal studies

Discussion Questions

1. Discuss the relevance of pure research to criminal justice practice.
2. Which data are better—quantitative or qualitative? Why?
3. How do units of analysis differ from levels of measurement?
4. Which research time frame is best—the one-time study or the series study? Why?

Exercise

Divide into small groups. Each group defines the concepts "deterrence," "incapacitation," and "retribution" using both the abstraction and operational methods. Make your definitions as clear and complete as possible. In addition, list a few appropriate variables that could be relied on to measure the concepts as you have defined them.

3

RESEARCH DESIGN: PURPOSES, TYPES, AND SELECTION

Learning Objectives

1. To define the concept of research design
2. To provide basic overview of quantitative research designs
3. To provide basic overview of qualitative research designs
4. To describe evaluation-based research designs

Chapter Outline

Introduction
Research Design Is a Deliberate Activity
Research Design Is a Purposive Activity
Research Design Requires Planning
Research Design Specifies the Process
Research Design Is Logical Inquiry
The Purpose of Research Designs
Simple Reporting
Clarification
Investigation
Evaluation
Constructing a Research Design
Idea Formulation
Conceptualization
Operationalization
Sample Selection
Data Collection
Data Analysis
Quantitative Designs
Description
Relationships
Experiments
Qualitative Designs
Content Analysis
Observational Designs

(Continued)

Evaluation Designs
Needs Assessment
Process Evaluation
Outcome Evaluation
Summary
Main Concepts
Discussion Questions
Exercises

CHAPTER THREE

Introduction

The idea of a *research design* usually seems overly complex or foreign to most students who have not had a research methods class. This perception is likely to be intensified when students are introduced to the broad range of specific ideas in research design. However, having a design to guide research is necessary. The research design section of a study sets the conditions under which the research is conducted. This straightforward purpose of the research design is complicated only because the considerations involved in criminological and criminal justice research are multifaceted and numerous and involve such concepts and activities as sampling, units of analysis, data collection, survey design, and statistical analyses, to name just a few. For example, if you were interested in studying a group of inmates, your research design would have to specify how the inmates in the study would be selected (sampling), the nature and manner of the data to be collected from or about the inmates, and the method of making sense of the data once it is collected (data analysis). The research design is set up to facilitate the objective and systematic process of executing a research plan.

The primary reason for constructing a research design in practice is to create a strategy upon which ones study approach is based. The research design is the basic plan to be followed when one conducts a study or a program evaluation. A definition of research design is presented in figure 3.1.

Figure 3.1

DEFINITION OF RESEARCH DESIGN

A research design is the deliberate, purposive planning of the process of scientific research and/or an evaluative study.

The following sections of this chapter describe in more detail what is meant by this general definition of research design. A clear understanding of the general definition of research design will facilitate better understanding of the research designs that are described in this chapter and throughout this book.

Research Design Is a Deliberate Activity

Constructing a research design is a deliberate activity. It is not typical for researchers to stumble upon the most appropriate research design while conducting their studies. Usually, researchers begin with determining the questions they want to ask as well as the pertinent analyses for answering these questions. While some criminal justice researchers and practitioners conduct preliminary analyses called "pilot studies" (Babbie, 1992) before they construct a full-blown research design the products of research are usually better (more objective and informative) when the research design is clearly specified prior to the beginning of a study. Ad hoc or after-the-fact research designs that attempt to fit questions of interest to analyses that have already been conducted not only are more difficult but also are much more likely to be less objective and/or less informative.

The conscious or deliberate creation of a research design prior to conducting a study is very important. For example, let's assume that a jail administrator is concerned about how the community views her facility. She is particularly interested in knowing how much support the community will provide for various programs at the jail given recent reductions in the county budget. She wants to continue the programs at the jail. If she informally questions a few of her friends, the police chief, and her neighbors, and asks some of her staff about their opinions on the issue, she would be informally trying to answer her question. These data (unstructured and informal interviews) are more likely to provide limited information and may even be biased because they were not based on a scientific research design and principles of objectivity. That is, the administrator would have no way of estimating the representativeness of the group she questioned. She would not know how representative they were of the public in general. She may have asked each person different questions, because she did not design an "interview guideline" (see chapter 8). In addition, the administrator based her investigation on her memory of conversations she had had with the various people on the subject. The data would undoubtedly be more accurate if a systematic data collection design were employed. Her experiences with the press and the public give her a logical basis for understanding public opinion but her experiences are limited and may not be representative of the experiences of other jail administrators. She is also likely to forget many of the details of the interviews unless she records them in a usable format. While, in many cases, policy decisions are made on the basis of such administrator experience or very limited analyses, the results of these types of studies are seldom sufficient to answer research or evaluative questions. Although the administrator's experience would help her to ask the right questions, it would probably not be sufficient to allow her to collect either accurate or consistent information about the subject. This casual interviewing is certainly not rigorous enough for most criminological and criminal justice research. The bottom line is that the informal approach taken by the jail administrator is much more likely to result in the collection of biased information. Without a predetermined research design, she cannot collect accurate and consistent data from a representative group of the public.

In order to select a representative group the administrator in the example would have to use a research design. She would have to specify a sample (a representative subgroup of the general public) in her research design prior to conducting her study. Without a design, the administrator is not likely to be able to analyze (make sense) of the interview information she collected other than to form an opinion about it. The procedures for analyzing data, whether these be qualitative (interviews) or quantitative (numbers), are also a necessary component of the research design and should be specified before the study is conducted. In the end, the jail administrator may be able to sell her budget request to the county council, but the effectiveness of her arguments would be due to her reputation with the council or her presentation abilities rather than the quality of the information she collected or her analysis. In this case if she were successful it would be because she was an effective politician rather than because she was an effective researcher. The big gamble here is that she may be wrong about the public supporting the programs. If the council goes along with her nonscientific appeal, she and the council might be subject to negative public opinion or even a public outcry for more punishment rather than programs in the jails.

The following example demonstrates how a deliberate research design could be constructed that would allow the jail administrator to collect accurate and consistent data about how the public feels about the programs in her jail. The administrator could construct a sound research design that uses telephone interviews with a random sample of citizens. The interview survey would be pretested and well designed, and should result in more concrete as well as less biased information. The data could be analyzed either statistically or qualitatively (these methodologies will be explained later). In addition, a research design based study allows further analyses that may explain the extent of citizen support and the characteristics of the citizens that support jail programs and those who do not.

While deliberateness is not a universal antidote for creating unbiased and concrete information, it does help researchers decrease the likelihood of incorrect or biased results. Personal experiences are rarely adequate substitutes for deliberate studies of research questions, especially if one's goal is to create accurate and consistent information.

Research Design Is a Purposive Activity

The construction of a research design is a purposive activity. A researcher usually has a specific aim in mind when he or she constructs a research design. For instance, the jail administrator in the example may believe that the public would support jail programs if they knew more about them. Her research purpose could be to examine her belief that the public would support the jail programs. A researcher would not attempt to "prove" his or her assumption or aim but would focus on thoroughly investigating the issue under study. The jail administrator would collect information from a representative sample. She would focus on collecting information that supports and refutes her presumptions to better understand how people view the topic.

The expectation or purpose of the research should be clearly stated in the research design section of the study. The general purposes that are usually stated in the research design section of a study can be theoretical, practical, or a combination of theoretical and practical.

A *theoretical purpose* is usually based on past theory or ideas as reflected in the literature (books, trade journals). In traditional scientific research designs the statement of the purpose usually entails the construction of a theoretically based research hypotheses. For example, Edwin Sutherland has suggested the following theoretical hypothesis: *Delinquents associate more with other delinquents than they do with nondelinquents.*[1] This hypothesis is based on specific aspects of Sutherland's "opportunity theory." There have been quite a few studies of opportunity theory over the years. Hence, in order to reduce the possibility of re-creating knowledge that already exists you should investigate the research literature prior to formulating a new analysis of this theory. For instance, the purpose of continued research might be to understand the differences between male and female delinquents in relation to Sutherland's theory. This is a typical example of a theoretical purpose in criminology. That is, theoretical purposes are more likely to have been explored and tested in the past than have practical purposes. Therefore, if your project is oriented toward a theoretical purpose, your research design should consider the research designs that have been used in the past to establish the details about the theory to date. In many cases the prior research designs can hint at where your study should proceed and can provide a list of the variables used in past studies that should be included in the current research efforts. These should also be considered when the purpose is practical, but you are less likely to find as much past research in the latter case, and this is especially true in the case of program evaluations.

In order to consider completed research designs you must search the research literature, for example, the *Journal of Criminal Justice, Criminology,* and *Justice Quarterly,* and determine the appropriate variables and analyses that have been used in the past. Theoretically oriented purposes are as close as criminal justice and criminological researchers come to "basic research" (see chapter 1), and such studies typically have direct value to academics and indirect value to practitioners and the operational field of criminal justice.

A more practically oriented hypothesis is one that suggests a research question. While this distinction is not one that is universally agreed upon, I use it to help students to remember the differences between theoretical and practical purposes. A research question is more limited and focused on creating information than is a theoretical hypothesis. Although the term "research question" may sound similar to the idea of "theoretical hypothesis," the basis as well as the outcome of the research from the former is more direct. The researcher who examines a research question is often motivated by an operational or a policy-level "need to know" rather than scientific "curiosity" as is the case for researchers who develop theoretical hypotheses. For example, the jail administrator may want to answer the following question: *Do "stressed" correctional officers take more sick days than "nonstressed" officers?*

There are no essential differences in the statistical or qualitative analysis techniques that one uses with theoretical purposes and with practical purposes. However, there are differences insofar as a theoretical purpose allows the researcher to refine and in some cases build upon past efforts of theory development. A *practical purpose* is more utilitarian in the sense that the researcher is more typically interested in the production of pragmatic policy-relevant information about an operational criminal justice agency, function, or program. In the practical or applied purpose a researcher is typically interested in answering operational questions or making decisions. Theoretical and practical purposes can be combined in the research design.

Research Design Requires Planning

Research design is based on conscious planning. The process of planning a research design, at its most basic level, entails anticipating the study to be conducted. The researcher anticipates a research design that best provides evidence that supports and/or refutes the research hypotheses or research questions. Anticipating the results of various statistical analyses, which are based on a deliberate choice of tests for specific purposes, is a necessary component of a well-constructed research design. Moreover, the research design is not just a plan on paper, but is an actual working outline for conducting the research project. Thus, a research design not only anticipates the results of research based on the presumed purpose of the study, but also is a guide for actually conducting the sample construction, data collection, and data analysis stages of the research.

Researchers should follow their research design, but when the situation calls for revision to improve the data collection or analysis to make it more consistent with the purpose of the research, then the design should be modified. Data collection and analysis problems are common in executing social science research, and researchers must be flexible enough to deviate from their design when necessary. This is not to say that the design should be abandoned if problems are encountered. The research design should be viewed as a design in progress, and revisions should be anticipated. An example of a research plan is presented in figure 3.2.

Research Design Specifies the Process

The research design specifies the process for conducting the research. Most research, to be objective and logical, presumes a desirable order of completion. For example, the data must be collected prior to the data analysis stage, and a representative group of people must agree to be in the study prior to any interviews that collect data about their opinions.

While it is necessary to place certain steps in the research design before others, that may not always be required. For instance, occasionally I am given access to some very interesting data before I formulate a theoretical hypothesis or a research question. While data collection is a later stage in the traditional cycle of scientific research (it comes after the theoretical considerations), there is no reason why, once the data were in hand, I could not then choose a theory or research question and proceed through the traditional steps.[2]

Many researchers follow the traditional process because it is both logical and well established. However, there are some who have not followed the traditional approach (e.g., Albert Einstein) and have nonetheless contributed greatly to scientific knowledge. The point here is that there is a generally accepted process that should be implicitly or explicitly followed in the design of a research or evaluation project *unless* there are compelling reasons to proceed otherwise. But there is more than one way to "skin a cat" and an overly rigid approach may not always fit research goals or one's "need to know." As long as a research design is oriented toward creating objective, accurate, and consistent information, there is no compelling reason to inflexibly follow the traditional research method.

Research Design Is Logical Inquiry

The research design is concerned with logical inquiry. Inquiry is the justification for the existence of the research design component of any research project or study. When we conduct an "inquiry" we want to discover objective usable

Figure 3.2
STUDENT ATTITUDES TOWARD CAPITAL PUNISHMENT

1. *Sample:* Simple random sample of all students enrolled at the college.
2. *Data Collection:* Closed-ended self-report questionnaire.
3. *Procedures:* Graphs, descriptive statistics, and inferential tests of the differences between male and female students.

information rather than collect personal stories or anecdotes. For example, when a coroner conducts an inquiry about the death of a person, he or she tries to get information about the cause of death. The coroner bases the cause of death decision on systematic, scientific, and logical inquiry. Similarly, in the research design component of studies the researcher is interested in establishing information that will help substantiate or refute the hypotheses or research questions that have been constructed. Thus, the process of executing a research design is the process of scientific inquiry.

The remainder of this chapter will further discuss the concepts and considerations involved in constructing a research design. While this chapter describes three major types of research designs—quantitative, qualitative, and evaluative—this categorization is used only to more clearly explain the concept of research design. This categorization is by no means universally accepted in criminal justice or other fields. However, this categorization helps facilitate explanations of the issues involved in specifying research designs. It is much easier to understand the idea of a research design if it is illustrated in its basic form. For example, a descriptive research design should be used with qualitative data. However, even though a distinction has been drawn between qualitative and quantitative data, neither should be given precedence. One approach is no better than the other. A four-door luxury car and a jeep are both personal automobiles that can adequately transport people from Baltimore to Philadelphia. However, a conventional car would probably be a better choice if you were to take Interstate 95 (it would get better gas mileage) whereas a jeep would be better if you traveled a dirt road. Similarly, qualitative and quantitative approaches to research are more or less appropriate in different situations. Select the data type that is most appropriate for your purpose, not because you have a fear of statistics or for other reasons outside of the needs of the study.

The evaluation designs can fit either the quantitative or qualitative approaches in terms of their analyses, but their purposes tend to be more practically oriented. While the discussions of specific research designs in this chapter should not be viewed as all encompassing (I have not included some of the more complex and advanced designs that are more appropriate for graduate-level studies), they are the most commonly utilized approaches and are more than sufficient for most research projects.

The Purpose of Research Designs

The purpose of the research design section of a research study is to explain the theoretical or practical purpose of the study and how the researcher plans to assess his or her research hypothesis or research questions. The research design typically has one or more specific purposes within either a theoretical or a practical framework. Consequently, the theoretical or practical research frameworks can further emphasize one or several more specific research purposes for the study. The most common emphases or purposes of research are: (1) reporting facts; (2) clarifying facts or relationships; (3) investigating interdependencies; (4) appraising the worth of programs or theories; and (5) understanding theories or program effects.

Simple Reporting

Simple reporting provides a description of events or subjects under study. This is the most commonly utilized purpose of research in criminal justice and criminology. Many times, however, reporting is used in conjunction with some other research purpose. Simple reporting attempts to establish basic information about the units of analysis one is studying, ideally with reference to a more general population.

An example of a simple reporting research purpose is a study that selects a representative group of jails and reports summary statistics for several relevant variables. For instance, if you could study the variable "jail population" and determine that the average daily jail population of a group of suburban jails is 320 inmates or that the average number of inmates per correctional officer is 20. Hence, the focus in simple reporting is summarizing characteristics that are relevant to the research topic you are interested in studying.

Simple reporting can be used in a theoretical framework. For example, you could use a simple reporting research design to report on the "functional-adaptive" theory of institutional adjustment (Sykes, 1967). In essence, Sykes' theory holds that inmates create a series of informal rules and behaviors in order to better cope with the institutional environment. One particularly apparent and measurable manifestation of this informal rule structure is the formation of "argot roles." That is, prisoners label each other within the informal rules with some inmates being known as "wolves" (i.e., assaultive) and others are known as "punks" (i.e., targets of homosexual assaults). If you were to study the functional-adaptive theory in a group of jails using the simple reporting research design, you would count and report the number of argot roles that exist and report the percentage of the most common type or types. While the result of the simple reporting design would not "prove" the functional-adaptation theory, they would constitute basic information supporting the theory and the proportion of inmates in each category.

The simple reporting research design could also be used in a practically oriented study. For example, you could study practical aspects of jails using the same group of jails in the study of the functional-adaptive theory. Jail administrators may or may not see the relevance of Sykes' theory; however, they would no doubt be interested in how many management problems are caused by the "wolves." A simple reporting research design in this case has information production as its goal, for example, the number of disciplinary infractions committed by assaultive inmates. The questions about how many and what types of problems are caused by inmate "wolves" could be answered, directly contributing to policy development aimed at dealing with these problem inmates.

In summary, the basic goal in simple reporting research designs, whether they are theoretical or practical, is to provide a quality description that is representative of the larger group (population) from which the study group (sample) is drawn.

Clarification

The *clarification purpose* of a research design would be exemplified by an explanation of events or a description of the subjects under study. The clarification purpose is broader than simple reporting in the sense that the researcher is interested not only in reporting characteristics but also in why certain characteristics are present in the study group or event. The researcher with a clarification purpose may also be interested in understanding the relationships between characteristics or why characteristics are related.

For example, a researcher might study the group of jails in the examples above to clarify the issue of functional-adaptation. The researcher would not only describe how many "wolves" or "punks" are in each jail but also would attempt to identify distinguishing factors (i.e., age, race, offense, criminal history) that could further explain why inmates are in one or the other category. A clarification purpose, therefore, develops the simple reporting design to more completely explain why certain factors have been found. In the example of jail inmate subcultures, clarification could help differentiate the types of inmates involved in these subcultures (see Kalinich, 1980, for a more complete description of inmate subcultures).

A practical example of clarification is a study of the effects of disciplinary sanctions against the "wolves." In general, when inmates are brought up on rule violations in jails and prisons, the staff holds formal hearings to determine the nature of these violations and the sanction that will be assigned or whether the charges are unfounded. Under a clarification purpose, you could design the research to determine what kinds of sanctions various types of inmates receive and which ones "work" the best in terms of reducing the incidence of the rule violation in the future. In this context you could also examine the effects of programs that could improve the lot of the targets of predatory inmates, for example, segregation and special housing.

Investigation

Another purpose of research is *investigation.* Investigation is done where little or relatively little is known about the people or events under study. That is, investigation is a process of inquiry that is used to establish basic information upon which further study may be based. An example is the investigation done by police at a crime scene. Investigation should be systematic and inquiry-based rather than based on personal experiences. While investigation-based research designs may be theoretical, they tend to be more practically focused as they are used to generate more general information.

An example of an investigation based research design purpose might be an investigation of the time it takes a particular court to process cases. In order to determine how long it takes a court to process a representative group of cases, you have to conduct a systematic study. This study would follow the selected cases through court disposition (i.e., sentence, dismissal, nolle prosequi, and so on). Your study could also be inquiry-based in the sense that the purpose is to create useful information for the court about how much time it takes to process its caseload. Investigative research designs tend to be inductive. That is, they begin with a broad collection of information about the situation under study and attempt to discern or understand the characteristics of that situation.

Another investigation study example is employment and criminal histories of offenders and how the two are related. There is a great deal of research literature on the employment-crime relationship (see Chiricos, 1987 for a review). Although the literature does not universally hold that crime and employment are related, much of it does suggest that an inverse relationship exists. As employment decreases, criminality increases. At present much of the literature on this topic is based on quantitative data. I would like to conduct an investigation of the individual work histories of inmates to better determine the interrelationships between a person's employment history and criminal history. My focus under the purpose of investigation would be to collect as much information as possible about both crime and employment directly from a sample of inmates to better understand the nature of the relationship.

Evaluation

A research design may have an *evaluation purpose.* The purpose of evaluation is usually more practical than theoretical. In fact, evaluations are the most typical form of program appraisals. That is, in an evaluation the researcher is interested more in program utility—was the program "good" or "bad," "successful" or "unsuccessful"—than in a theoretical explanation or clarification. Evaluation research is much more appraisal oriented than either theoretical or practical research. Where theoretical research attempts to satisfy the curiosity of the academic researcher, evaluation or appraisal research addresses specific operational or policy-oriented questions for the operational field of criminal justice. Evaluations are usually based on logic rather than academic research theories.

For instance, suppose a police training officer is interested in the effects of a high-speed pursuit training program he is planning to give to a class of new recruits. The training officer believes that the program will reduce unsuccessful police pursuits and the number that result in accidents or injuries. From an appraisal perspective he should follow a research design as well as select a representative group of officers or incidents to study. However, his goal is simply to answer a limited question about the effectiveness of the program in order to justify the training department's existence or perhaps to institutionalize the high-speed pursuit training program. Thus, the *appraisal purpose* is limited to a practical and specific issue.

Table 3.1 summarizes the basic purposes of the research design portion of research studies. In a research journal article, the research design should be clearly specified in the "Method," "Methodology," or "Procedures" section of the study. Often, researchers separate the technical aspects of research methods (i.e., sampling, statistical analysis techniques) from the specifications of theories or ideas as well as the variables or indicators that they use to measure or test their selected theories or ideas. However, these are usually apparent in any well-written research report or journal article. In fact, journal articles are usually good sources for examples of research designs and can help you in your own research efforts.

The purposes described here are not the only valid ones. Researchers may use these or combinations of these and others. The point is that these

Table 3.1
PURPOSES OF RESEARCH DESIGN

Purposes	Orientation
Simple reporting	Theoretical or practical
Clarification	Theoretical or practical
Investigation	Preliminary study
Evaluation	Answering questions or making decisions

are common purposes of research. In conducting research it is not conformance to textbook definitions that is important. What is important is a clear and understandable as well as defined purpose for the research.

Constructing a Research Design

You may have the impression from what you have read so far that the research design component of a research study is a complicated activity that consists of many considerations and that can be used for a variety of research purposes to answer different types of questions. While such an impression is certainly accurate, the procedure for constructing a research design for a specific study you wish to conduct can be framed in a more simplified logical format.

The basic considerations to be followed in the construction of a research design are shown in figure 3.3. While these considerations move from general to specific stages, one should not presume that this linear or rational model is the only way to construct a research design. It is the most readily accepted logical format and is more appropriate for a first attempt in research methods. The following sections provide a more detailed description of the construction of a research design within an example-based context.

Idea Formulation

The beginning stage in any research design should be the formulation of a researchable idea. This idea can be based on reading (e.g., newspapers, magazines, research journals, books) or on "real-world" experiences. Academic researchers typically base their ideas on theories as they are reported in research journals such as *Criminology, Justice Quarterly,* and the *Journal of Criminal Justice.* However, research ideas come from a variety of sources. In fact, ideas for applied research studies may even be derived from trade journals such as *Police Chief* and *Corrections Today* or operational agency experiences and needs rather than from academic research journals. This is due in a large part to the fact that many practitioners do not have ready access to criminal justice research journals or because practitioners are more interested in policy-level information for decision making rather than theoretical research studies (most academic journals publish the latter).

An example of an applied research problem formulation can be gleaned from a recent issue of *American Jails* (the magazine of the American Jail Association). Ken Kerle, the editor, wrote about the need to improve community relationships between jails and their communities:

> Unless a constant effort is made to gain public support through a continuing public information program designed to point out the community benefits from its programs, then the leadership must bear the

Figure 3.3
CONSTRUCTING A RESEARCH DESIGN

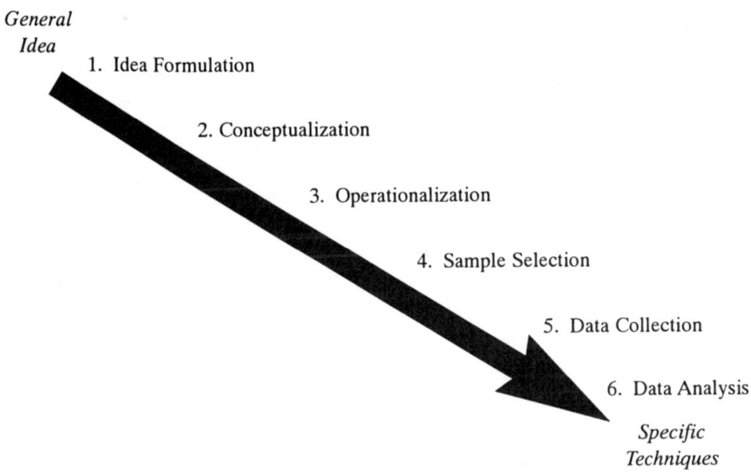

consequences of inadequate communications with the public it serves. (Kerle, 1992, p. 9)

This information might lead to a research problem that focuses on the consequences of inadequate communications or relations with the public. The focus of this study might be to describe and define the issues with a study of a group of jails (simple reporting), or the researcher may wish to investigate the linkage between efforts in community relations and the consequences of inaction (investigation). At the idea formulation stage, many options concerning the direction of the research are available and can be decided upon as the research design proceeds.

It is important to note that researchable ideas may also come from practical experiences within the criminal justice system. While this is rarely sufficient for most traditional academic or applied research projects, it can be a good beginning point. For example, in an evaluation study of correctional officer attitudes at a midwestern jail agency that I conducted a few summers ago, I interviewed a female matron who had worked in the jail for nearly thirty years. When I asked her about her "most significant impression of her job as a matron" she related how she viewed the inmates under her supervision. She explained that she had seen many of the same women from the time they were young women through their forties. That is, the same women were constantly in and out of the female section of the jail. Practical information such as this is rich in researchable ideas. For instance, is this matron's experience universal? What kinds of offenses do these women commit? How often and for what length of time do these inmates come to the jail?

While many students prefer to base their research papers and projects on practical level experience and informal sources, there are problems with an exclusive focus on these sources. That is, there is a problem with exclusive reliance on informal logic or practical experience alone. For example, while I could develop a research design based on my interview with the matron, a more complete search of the literature is necessary. Other researchers may have already studied the idea and may have answered my questions. Without consulting what has currently been done on a topic, I may be "reinventing the wheel." I may further refine the idea and contribute additional information about female jail inmates that wasn't revealed in the interview but that is very important to explaining the topic.

At the idea formation stage, the objective in constructing a research design is to focus the project on a viable and researchable problem. The statement of a researchable idea is general and is similar to the purpose of the study. It is useful to keep in mind that some problems are not researchable. For example, it is very difficult, if not impossible, to study the thoughts and beliefs of offenders who have been executed about their execution (or even those about to be executed). This would probably not be researchable (that is, unless you figure out a way to contact these offenders in the afterlife). One should simply keep in mind that there are likely to be topics that are not researchable.

For the purposes of illustration the researchable idea that will be used in demonstrating the process involved in constructing a research design is: *Are community relations important for jail operations?*

While this researchable idea is stated as a question, that need not be the case. For instance, you could make a statement: Community relations may (or may not) influence jail operations. The focus in the idea formulation stage of the research design is to state as concisely and accurately as possible the basic topical area that is to be studied.

A topic is researchable if it is amenable to objective and, in the realm of criminal justice research, empirical study. For example, one can clearly measure citizen fear of crime objectively by surveying a random sample of citizens. One can also measure citizen fear of crime empirically by using a standard survey instrument. Topics that are not amenable to research are difficult to conceptualize, as explained in the next section.

Conceptualization

The second stage of constructing a research design is *conceptualization.* Conceptualization is the process of refining the research idea into specific terms or ideas. In conceptualizing you transform the general idea into specific areas of research interest. This stage is the beginning of your own interpretation and approach in the study you are designing.

The process of conceptualization focuses the research design on the specific concepts or ideas that will be the subject of the study. For example, suppose I were interested in studying police officer on-the-job behaviors. I may choose to study the specific concepts of "stress," "corruption," "authoritarianism," "professionalism," or "brutality." These concepts are ideas within the context of the study. I will need to further define what I mean by these concepts, but they could serve as the conceptual basis for further study. A conceptual basis is a set of basic expectations about what you believe you will find. In the example of studying police on-the-job behaviors I expect to be able to observe and study "stress" and "professionalism" and the like. Hence, the conceptualization step provides an explanation of these general expectations. Both theoretical and applied studies set out expectations. They differ only in the basis of this conceptualization. In theoretical studies concepts are typically derived from literature, and in applied studies they are derived from decision making needs or practical applications.

However, concepts are often rather "slippery" notions. They may have many meanings. For instance, "stress" can be defined in several ways such as hypertension, high blood pressure, irritability, and so on. The point is that concepts may have several meanings, and it is up to the researcher to define and explicitly state in the research design the specific meaning that will be used in the study. While the definitions of concepts for a researcher's study are usually imperfect, studies should be based on a stated conceptual framework or defined concepts.

The delineation of concepts is rarely perfect. The quality or precision of measurement is always questionable as is a basic definition. One can measure the weight of a group of judges using a balance and a pile of rocks, a bathroom scale, a doctor's scale, and a water displacement tank with incremental increases in precision of the measurement of weight. However, even the best measures are not perfect, empirically or conceptually. An example of a conceptualization is shown in figure 3.4. In this conceptualization

Figure 3.4
CONCEPT EXAMPLES

Concept 1:
Community relations is the amount of knowledge the community has of the jail.

Concept 2:
Important for the daily operation of jail programs is the amount of outside support that is needed to run the jail programs.

there are two concepts or terms that I believe are important and should be dealt with in the study of this idea. First, the idea of community relations is intrinsic to the research idea that has been formulated in this example. That is, one needs to clearly define the concept of community relations as it relates to the jail. One possibility is to define the concept of community relations as citizens' perceptions about the jail. This would also require the researcher to define who are "citizens" and what is meant by the concept "perceptions." Another possible definition of community relations could be the conscious effort of the jail staff to inform the relevant communities about its functions and programs. Once again, the concepts within this example should be defined. Although I could continue to list additional definitions of the concept "community relations," the research will never get started unless I make a decision about the conceptual definition that will be used in my study.

Therefore, for this example I will use the first conceptualization, wherein community relations are measured by the perceptions of citizens toward the jail. As stated above the concepts within this definition should be further explained. Hence, for the purposes of this example, "perceptions" are defined as the reported beliefs (either positive or negative) toward specific functions and programs within the jail, and "citizens" are people over eighteen years old living within the jurisdiction (the county) of the jail. My choices, while reasonable, reduce the precision of the concepts, because they exclude some of the possible definitions.

Likewise, the concept of "importance" can be defined in several ways. One way to define "importance" is the relative influence on jail operations and management of the community perceptions. "Importance" can also be defined in terms of other community or social problems. As was true in defining community relations, the definition of "importance" is multifaceted and imperfect. However, a definition should be adopted in order to move the research design forward.

For the example I am developing, I will define importance as the influence of community perceptions on jail operations and management. "Influence" is the amount of change that the community relations cause in the jail programs. "Jail operations" are the day-to-day functions and activities that take place in the jail (inmate feeding, hygiene, programs, and so on). "Management" is the administrative functions and activities (supervision of staff, budgeting, scheduling, and planning).

In summary, for the purposes of the example research design process, I have conceptualized that reported beliefs of adult citizens toward specific functions and programs within the jail influence jail operations and management. While this conceptualization gives us a much better understanding of the research problem than the simple statement in the idea formulation stage, it does not create clear empirical (measurable) variables. The operationalization stage of the research design process focuses on that issue.

Operationalization

The next step in the process of constructing a research design is to turn the abstract concepts into measurable variables. This process further reduces the precision of the concepts because they must be measurable. It does, however, commit the project to specific defensible measures. The reason one needs to operationalize is because it is impossible to directly measure concepts like "importance," "community relations," or "police officer stress." Because these concepts are difficult to measure, it is important for researchers to clearly identify the variables that are empirically measurable and that represent the concepts in their research design. *Operationalization* is a process of developing abstract concepts into "real world" measures. While most researchers operationalize concepts in the initial stages of the project, further refinement is sometimes necessary as measurement proceeds or as variables become available.

In order to operationalize concepts we need to consider several issues. Not the least of these is the method of data collection that will be utilized. However, prior to data collection, the issue of "variation" in the operationalized concepts should be considered and defined. We should define how crude or precise the measure of the concepts will be relative to the research purpose. For example, we could construct a very crude measure of the effects of citizens' knowledge of jail programs with two simple attributes: they have knowledge or they do not. We could then collect data on this nominal variable and rely on it as our measure of the concept of "influence." Conversely, we may be interested in measuring as much of the variation in the community beliefs and their effects on the jail as exists, because we are interested in explaining the different belief profiles of different categories of people (e.g., gender, race, income level) in the community (i.e., strongly opposed, opposed, moderately in favor, in favor, strongly in favor . . . of jail programs).

The question of "variation" in the operationalization of concepts is related to the number of attributes that you include in each of the variables. The fewer the attributes of each variable, generally the less variation in the measures. This consideration should be influenced by the purpose of your study and your beliefs about the distribution of attributes across the sample. Hence, if you are studying citizens' attitudes toward management in jails, you would be more likely to be interested in greater variation if you were doing an explanatory study than if you were conducting a simple reporting study.

While there is no ideal amount of variation in the variables we operationalize from the concepts in the research idea, it is best to collect data on variables that have as much variation as possible. It is possible to reduce variation in collected variables only after they are collected. Hence, we can reduce the variable "inmate age" (internal level of measurement) to an ordinal level (e.g., very old, old, young, and very young) or nominal level (e.g., born before World War II and born after World War II). However, we cannot increase the variation in a nominal level variable. For instance, if we ask police officers to tell us whether they were stressed out (yes or no), it would be impossible to increase the variation in the data on a scale of strongly agree to strongly disagree.

Therefore, operationalization is a process for specifying the concepts such that they are measurable in terms of specific attributes of variables. In addition, the attributes of variables are typically exhaustive and mutually exclusive. Exhaustive variables are those that allow us to classify every possible observation that could be made. For example, if we were going to study the charges of inmates in prison, every inmate could be classified in terms of three attributes: violent, property, or other. There are no charges that do not fit this classification. Mutual exclusivity is the idea that observations fit one, and only one, category. That is, a violent offender in the example above could not also fit into the property crime attribute category. Of course, we would need to decide where observations fit and set specific rules for assigning attributes, but the idea here is that we will objectively apply the schema to all observations in a similar fashion.

It is also important to keep in mind while operationalizing the concepts that certain levels of measurement apply to certain statistical analyses. Hence, if we are interested in conducting tests of differences between the crime rates in a sample of suburban and urban communities, the most powerful tests require at least an interval level of measurement of the data. Although the data we collect should not drive the research design, we should not make any promises in constructing the researchable problem that the data cannot keep. Any hypotheses or research questions should be relevant to the kind and level of data we can collect. Once the variables have been clearly determined, the next consideration in the research design process is to determine from whom to collect data. In social science research it is typical to rely on samples of the population one is interested in studying because of the variability in populations, the high costs of studying an entire population, and the need to conduct timely research.

Sample Selection

Once you have clearly specified "what" variables you are going to measure, a representative group of the population must be selected. Through a structured and logical sample selection process you can select a representative group of the population in as unbiased a manner as is possible, Ideally, everyone in the study population should have an equal and independent chance to be included in the sample. For instance, if you are studying a prison that has one thousand inmates, every inmate, from those in minimum security housing to those on death row, should have the same chance of being included in a sample. In addition, the inclusion of one inmate from the minimum security unit would not exclude others from that same unit from being included in your sample.

Continuing the example from the conceptualization stage, we could take a sample of the population of the 3,318 jails in the United States to study the effects of community relations on operations (Kerle, 1992). We would begin selecting our sample with an alphabetic listing of the jails for each state. (Lists are a typical starting point for the best sampling techniques. This will be more fully discussed in chapter 5.) It is important to select a broad cross-section of jails throughout the country, because it is likely that there are regional and intrastate differences in community influences on jail operations. Moreover, we may further speculate that the influence of the community on large jails (i.e., those over one thousand inmates) is potentially different from community influence on small jail operation. Based on these considerations, we could select a sample based on the location and size of the jail for a nationally representative sample of facilities (see chapter 5 for further explanation of stratified sampling). We will consider both the location and size of the jails across the country and randomly select a sample group, making certain that each jail has an "equal" and "independent" opportunity to be included in the sample.

Once the sample is determined, the next stage is to measure the variables that we have operationalized. The data collection could be quantitative and based on numerical indicators or it could be qualitative, based on interviews or observations.

Data Collection

Following the sample selection procedures we collect the data needed for the study from the sampling units. In the operationalization section, I stated that we would like to have a greater degree of variation in our data. That is, we would be interested in the effects of the community on jail operations ranging from the community exerting a "great deal" of influence to "no influence at all." In addition, we believe that jail size, location, and age of the jail are all variables that must be considered in the community influence study. For example, we could collect data from our sample of jails by questioning the jail administrators and classifying their responses in terms of the variables in figure 3.5. The four variables in this example are either ordinal (Community Influence, Jail Size, and Jail Age) or nominal (Location) levels of measurement. The issue of the level of measurement should be considered at this point as it is important that the data one collects is amenable to helping address the research questions or hypotheses proposed in the conceptualization step. Moreover, statistical analyses are linked to the level of measurement of the data, that is, certain tests are applied to certain levels of measurement. A general rule of thumb about the level of measurement is that one should collect the highest possible level of measurement for the data. If I were to follow this rule in our example I should collect the actual daily population averages rather than categorizing population as either large or small. In addition, the number of years of operation is a ratio measure of jail age that is more precise than the example categorization. The reason I did not collect the higher levels of measurement is because I am more interested in the effects of community perceptions on jail operations than on the specific characteristics of the jails and because this example is a simple reporting purpose.

In order to complete the next stage, data analysis, the data must be placed in a logical or readable format. It does not matter whether one is using quantitative or qualitative data; both need to be placed in a logical or usable order. For the example variables proposed, that logical format could be as shown in table 3.2.

Data Analysis

The data analysis section specifies which analyses—statistical tests, descriptive statistics, or graphical displays—are the most appropriate for the selected research design and purposes of the study (see chapters 10, 11, and 12). While

Figure 3.5

EXAMPLE VARIABLES

Perceived Community Influence (PCI)
- 1 = none at all
- 2 = some
- 3 = large
- 4 = a great deal

Location
- 1 = Northeast
- 2 = Midwest
- 3 = South
- 4 = West

Jail Size
- 1 = large (over 1,000 inmates daily population)
- 2 = small (under 1,000 inmates)

Jail Age
- 1 = built before 1960
- 2 = built after 1960

Table 3.2

LOGICAL DATA FORMAT

Jail Name	PCI	Size	Location	Age
Frederico County	3	2	3	2
DeAntonio County	1	2	1	2
Girone County	3	1	3	1
Ricci County	4	1	2	1
Kalinich County	3	1	2	2

many criminal justice students are intimidated by the mere thought of conducting statistical analyses, these techniques are commonly employed in research studies. Students who plan to work in the field, as well as those who wish to attend graduate school, must have a basic understanding of which statistical tests are appropriate to the questions asked and the available data. Without this understanding, you will not have the ability to discern between the "lies, damn lies, and statistics" (Mark Twain), nor will you be able to take advantage of truly valuable information in the research literature.

The types of data analyses you plan to conduct should be predetermined and clearly stated in the research design section of the project. For instance, in our example on jail community relations and programs we could specify that we will conduct descriptive analyses that are appropriate for the nominal and ordinal variables we collect (mode and median and/or index of dispersion and range). We could also determine whether there are significant differences in the perceptions of jail administrators according to the size of the jail or the age of the facility (chi-square independence test).

Once the analysis has been set, the research design process is completed. All that remains is to execute the research design. Another issue that is important to consider is that there are several standard research designs that can be used to focus the studies. While the following sections list the most common of these accepted research designs, this listing is by no means comprehensive. However, these designs are clearly the most commonly employed designs.

Quantitative Designs

While I have divided the example design sections into quantitative and qualitative sections, these are not exclusive. Researchers could employ a quantitative design in a qualitative project and vice versa. The categorization and explanations, however, are the most commonly employed contexts for each general type of research design and are categorized to clarify their meaning.

Description

Most studies have some element of description in their design. The basic goal in the *descriptive design* is to systematically and comprehensively describe the subjects of the study in terms of the project or study being conducted. Descriptive designs can usually be portrayed through graphical or frequency table presentations. While some studies have only a descriptive approach, it is important to keep in mind that more complicated studies often begin with a basic descriptive context. For example, if we were interested in studying police patrol time in a descriptive design, we would have to collect data on several variables that describe the patrol activities of officers.

That is, we could collect data on how much time officers spend patrolling businesses versus residential areas, the potential different approaches of experienced versus inexperienced officers, and so on.

Descriptive studies are systematic in the sense that they attempt to describe the entire situation. In the example of the patrol activities of police, we would have to examine the internal rules for patrol as well as the community expectations and perhaps also the effects of case law or research on patrolling as well as officer preferences. Discretion is also a key indicator of how patrolling is actually done versus what is printed in policy manuals, so we might measure the percentage of "free time" the officers have while they are patrolling as opposed to the amount of time they are responding to calls. The purpose of simple reporting it clearly covered in a descriptive research design.

Relationships

A second common quantitative research design is that of measuring the *relationships* between variables. The focus here is to determine the coincidence or joint occurrence of the variables of interest. For example, what is the relationship between the age of the respondent and the level of fear of crime? Most research shows that older persons tend to be more fearful than younger persons. In an investigative purpose, the researcher may decide to further pursue this question through examining other relationships. For example, he or she may decide to research the relationship between residence (urban versus suburban) or gender and fear of crime. All three of the purposes described earlier (simple reporting, investigation, and exploration) could be addressed to some degree in a relationship-oriented research design. While this design is still technically descriptive, it moves beyond the mere reporting of observations to a more concrete examination of the data and the data's significance to a research question or hypotheses.

Experiments

Experimental designs attempt to discover the cause-and-effect connection between dependent and independent factors in a controlled setting. (This section provides only an introduction to this topic. See chapter 6 for a more detailed description and application examples.) Experimental designs also attempt to measure specific effects of variables within specific contexts. For example, we could attempt to measure the specific effect of providing more correctional officer training in use-of-force situations on the attitudes and perceptions of inmates toward the officers. Increased training would be expected to result in better inmate attitudes or perhaps even more cooperation. In an experimental design, the researcher is typically attempting to discover the cause-and-effect relationship between independent and dependent variables. In this example, the independent variable is the amount of use-of-force training for the officers. This variable is independent in this case because we presume that it can influence or "cause" an improvement in inmate attitudes toward correctional officers. Conversely, the attitudes of inmates are dependent upon the improved training of officers in the use of force.

Prior to conducting the experiment, a decision needs to be made about which individuals, inmates in this case, will be assigned to the control group and the experimental group. This is usually accomplished through random assignment or through matching of characteristics of the two groups. In random assignment, for example, we could number all the cell blocks in the study prisons and then assign the first cell block to the experimental group and the second to the control group and so on until we have assigned all the cell blocks on our list. When the units of analysis are essentially equivalent, the use of random assignment to the experimental and control groups contributes to the validity of the experiment. However, while this method would certainly remove any bias in the way cell blocks are assigned there are clear differences in the type of cell blocks in prisons, for example, high security, confinement, general population, and so on. This may influence the results of our experiment. Hence, matching the specific types of cell blocks in the experimental and control groups might be undertaken so that there are equal numbers of each type of cell block in each group.

In experimental designs, the dependent variable is typically measured at two points in time (see figure 3.6). In our example, inmates' attitudes toward correctional officers would be measured prior to the correctional officers receiving any use-of-force training. This is referred to as the "pretest." The pretest establishes the amount and quality of the attitudes of the inmates toward the officers before any change is made in the situation. Without this key information it would be difficult, if not impossible, to determine the magnitude of the effects of officer use-of-force training.

Another aspect of most experimental designs is the use of a control group. The control group is used to provide additional information to isolate the effects of the independent variable on the dependent variable. In the example we have been developing, we could provide the use-of-force training

Figure 3.6

EXPERIMENTAL AND CONTROL GROUP STUDY ACTIVITIES

Experimental Group	Control Group
1. Measure inmates attitudes	1. Measure inmates attitudes
2. Provide officer training	2. Do nothing
3. Measure inmates attitudes	3. Measure inmates attitudes

to officers in several cell blocks and provide no training to officers in other cell blocks (the control group). The attitudes of inmates in the control group cell blocks would also be measured prior to any officer training in the experimental cell blocks. The control cell blocks provide additional information about the influence of the independent variable in that there may be changes in inmate attitudes over time that are unrelated to our independent variable. The control group cell blocks will help us determine changes in inmates attitudes over time where officers have not had use-of-force training, thus allowing us to isolate the effects of training when all other variables are equal.

Once inmates attitudes are measured for both the control and experimental groups, the second step in the experimental design is taken—providing the training to the experimental group officers (those officers that work in the experimental cell blocks). The training should be provided only to the officers in the experimental cell block and not to those who work in the control cell blocks. This step is the attempt to instill the influence of the independent variable—officer training—on the dependent variable—inmate attitudes toward officers.

The third step in an experimental design is to remeasure the attitudes of inmates after training has taken place. We would measure the attitudes of both the experimental and control groups. It is typical in such a "real world" experiment to allow the passing of some time after the training to let the training "take effect." If the inmates' attitudes toward officers improve in the experimental group (which is what one would expect), it may then be possible to further explain the improvements in attitudes. On the other hand, if inmates' attitudes are unchanged or get worse, it may be possible to conclude that the training had negative effects on attitudes. Suffice it to say that the end result of an experiment is not "proof" of the existence of a cause-and-effect relationship, but it provides some rationale to support or refute the research questions or hypotheses one is researching.

As stated earlier, there are many other accepted quantitative approaches. In particular, criminal justice and criminology researchers have recently been strongly oriented toward multivariate quantitative designs. However, these more advanced designs are beyond the scope of this text and are not as clearly illustrative as are the most basic designs. In the remainder of this text additional research designs will be described at a greater level of detail. Suffice it to say that there are several approaches in addition to the few touched on in this section.

Qualitative Designs

Qualitative designs are not necessarily exclusive to non-numerical data. However, it is much more likely that the types of data collected in certain situations will be qualitative (interviews or observations) rather than statistics or numbers. This is not to say that qualitative designs do not also include descriptive statistics, for they often do.

Content Analysis

One type of qualitative design is content analysis. In *content analysis* the focus of the design is on systematically determining the "content" of the data. (The details of content analysis are explained in chapter 12). Typically, content analyses focus on the direct evidence of communications. For example, there has been much study of the crime and criminal justice related "content" of newspapers.

The focus in content analysis can be on the blatant aspects of communication (e.g., newspapers over-report the amount of violent crime) or the more subtle or latent aspects. An example of a content analysis that focuses on latent content would be to determine the types of descriptive adjectives used to describe offenders in newspaper articles.

Observational Designs

Observational designs are a common qualitative research approach. There have been many very well done studies of criminals and criminal behavior that have been observational in nature. However, observational studies tend not to be the norm in criminal justice and criminological research. In observational designs the data for research can be numerical or qualitative, but data are likely to be collected through some sort of participation in the situations to be observed. The data tend to be qualitative in most observational studies.

In observational studies the researcher typically takes notes. Note-taking might be done during observation or reconstructed afterward. Either way, note-taking is a key activity of observational studies and is much more flexible than in quantitative designs. The flexibility in this data creation is also problematic, however, in that it can create a situation where the data are less reliable because collection changes over time.

Another important issue in observational studies is gaining access to study populations of a sufficient size. Generalization may not be a typical observational study goal. Observational studies are more oriented toward investigation or exploration than they are toward generalization. (See chapter 8 for a more complete description of observational designs.)

Observational studies tend to be more in-depth and flexible than quantitative studies. They are also much more "real-world" oriented than are many surveys or analyses of official statistics. There is a consistent friction between qualitative researchers and quantitative researchers. Some on the qualitative side of the argument suggest that quantitative researchers are like "arm chair quarterbacks" in that they are not sensitive to the subtle nuances of the operational criminal justice system or study situations. Similarly, quantitative researchers suggest that qualitative researchers have inherently invalid and unreliable data from small, biased samples. Although there is a grain of truth in these criticisms, the research purpose and questions should be the guides for the design that is selected. Aggregate questions such as, What is the average daily inmate population? cannot be answered by qualitative designs, and a study that endeavors to understand gang membership rituals cannot be sufficiently addressed through quantitative data collection and analysis.

Evaluation Designs

Evaluation designs focus on the appraisal purpose; that is, they are oriented toward answering practical-level questions or decision making. In general, evaluation designs utilize the same techniques as more research-oriented designs. However, the results of evaluation research are utilized for different purposes. Evaluation designs are used for studies that fulfill the information needs of decision makers within the context of their agency or organization. For example, a police executive may need to make decisions about patrol allocation in his department's patrol districts. He could conduct an evaluation design to create information upon which he can base his decisions.

The following sections categorize the several contexts or purposes for evaluation designs. Although these are not mutually exclusive categorizations nor are they detailed designations, they define the range of foci that can be taken in evaluation designs.

Needs Assessment

One general type of evaluation design is a *needs assessment.* This design is similar to exploratory analysis in traditional research. However, the focus is typically on determining programmatic needs. For example, a court administrator is told by the chief judge that she is concerned with the current process for handling trial appearance dates and times of witnesses. The judge tells the administrator to design a program for improving the handling of witnesses and asks the administrators to find out what components should be included in this program, for example, what do witnesses need? In conducting a needs assessment evaluation design the court administrator could focus on the stated needs of witnesses determined through surveys or interviews. Perhaps she would also ask other courtroom workers as well. The goal would be to collect as much information about the situation as possible.

The goal in a needs assessment evaluation design is to establish, as clearly as possible, the "information" that will help a decision maker make an informed decision. In many cases, needs assessments are used prior to program designs. Objective research methods would increase the decision makers understanding of the full range of needs related to the problem at hand.

Consider the court administrator who makes her decision based on her perceptions and experience alone, without evaluation or study. She decides that witnesses should be housed in the available waiting room in the courthouse. The administrator's decision is not informed by objective information. Witnesses have had no input into the witness program, and

Table 3.3

PATTON'S EVALUATION DESIGNATIONS

Evaluation Type	Question Asked
Accreditation	Does program meet licensing standards?
Appropriateness	Are current services appropriate?
Awareness	What do people know about the program?
Cost/Benefit Analysis	What are the program costs and what effects result?
Cost-Effectiveness	What is the relationship between costs and outcomes?
Criterion-Referenced	Have the program objectives been achieved?
Decision-Focused	What decision information is needed?
Description	What happens in the program?
Effectiveness	Is program effective at attaining goals?
Efficiency	Can reduced inputs still achieve the outcomes?
Effort	What does the program require?
Extensiveness	To what extent does the program deal with the problem?
External	Evaluation conducted by non-program people.
Formative	How can the program be improved?
Goal	To what extent have the goals been achieved?
Impact	What are the impacts on the community?
Internal	Program staff conduct evaluation.
Longitudinal	What happens to program participants over time?
Meta	Was the evaluation well done? Is it worth using?
Norm-Referenced	How does program population compare with others?
Personnel	How effective are staff at carrying out program?
Product	What are the products of the program?
Quality Assurance	Are standards being met with the program clients?
Social Indicators	What social or economic data reflect program effects?
Summative	Should the program be continued?
Systems Analysis	What is the optimum way to do this program?
Utilization-Focused	What information do decision makers need?

Source: Patton, 1982.

the full range of problems and concerns have not been addressed with a more general study of their needs. In many courthouses, the available waiting room is the waiting place for witnesses from both the prosecution and defense. In addition, this decision does not address the problems witnesses have getting to the courthouse—finding transportation, finding parking, locating where in the courthouse they need to be, and so on.

Process Evaluation

A *process evaluation* is oriented toward defining the reality and utility of processes or sequences of events. The key interest in process evaluations is on systematically defining the significant events in the process. Process evaluations are often used in concert with outcome evaluation designs. However, the goal is to define the events of the process and the correspondence between what is desired and what actually happens. Process evaluation can also be used to assess the effects of programs over time (i.e., educating or providing therapy).

For example, a process evaluation can be conducted of the jail booking process. In the booking process an offender is brought into the jail and relevant information is collected, such as name, address, offense, and so on. One can define the key stages as (1) initial information gathering, (2) fingerprinting, (3) photographing, (4) health screening, and (5) holding cell confinement. Policies and procedures typically drive the booking process, and it has become routine in most jails. However, a process evaluation may reveal additional key stages that are important steps in the process. For instance, a jail that has a health screening process but has had several suicides in the past few months may determine in the course of a process evaluation that the current screening process is flawed. A process evaluation would indicate that a new suicide assessment procedure at the health screening stage should be added to the booking process.

Additionally, a process evaluation could identify key bottlenecks or snags in the booking process. For example, there may be a significant backlog at the holding cell stage—too many inmates are being housed in the holding cell area before they are transferred into the general jail population. This stage could be examined further to determine whether inmates could be moved into the general population more quickly.

Outcome Evaluation

Evaluation designs often focus on the documentation of the effects of programs or decisions. The study of outcomes can also be an attempt to determine the relative return on the dollar of the programs or treatments. Did the costs of the program result in valuable benefits? Alternatively, or concurrently, outcome evaluations can focus on measuring the achievement of program goals. For example, does the program designed to reduce recidivism actually reduce recidivism?

Outcome evaluations can use any of the traditional approaches listed earlier. However, they are often experimental or quasi-experimental. The focus in outcome evaluation is not on improving theory but on determining whether the program outcomes are consistent with the predetermined goals.

Summary

The research design provides the planning structure for the research project. The research design is the basis upon which the study is executed. A well-thought-out research design will contribute greatly to the success of a research study.

A few of the more common quantitative and qualitative research designs are described. These designs provide a context for the typical approaches of researchers in the construction of their research designs. Many of these designs will be described in much more detail in the following chapters. In this chapter they are used as illustrations of the concept of research design in general.

Several of the research design orientations in the evaluation and research design paradigm are described. While evaluation research designs rely on the same technical procedures as quantitative and qualitative designs, they are different in the sense that they are more likely to be practically oriented.

Main Concepts

research design
idea formulation
theoretical purpose
practical purpose
evaluation purpose
operationalization
data collection
descriptive design
experimental designs
observational designs
process evaluation
simple reporting
clarification purpose
investigation purpose
appraisal purpose
conceptualization
sample selection
data analysis
relationships
content analysis
needs assessment
outcome evaluation

Discussion Questions

1. Why is the development of a research design important?
2. What distinguishes a qualitative design from a quantitative one?
3. When would one use a needs assessment based evaluation design?
4. When are experimental designs appropriate?
5. What is content analysis?

Exercise

Constructing a Research Design

In an issue of *Law and Order* magazine (January 1992) Pratt writes the following:

> Nationwide, police are conducting what may well be the largest and longest search ever. Although several departments have apprehended, briefly held, then allowed the subject to slip away, few can provide an accurate description of the subject. Despite the scope of this effort, it has received little public notice. Today, as never before, the search must go on, widen, and be brought to a successful conclusion. Though money is scarce and time is short, authorities know that they must capture this elusive subject whose real name—though there are many aliases—is "police effectiveness." (Pratt, 1992, p. 290)

Form in small groups of two or three. Formulate one researchable idea within the context of this problem. For your researchable idea formulate at least one concept, and operationalize that concept. Discuss your concept in the class as a whole.

4

DATA MEASUREMENT AND COLLECTION

Learning Objectives

1. To provide an understanding of the concept of validity and methods for increasing accuracy in studies
2. To provide an understanding of the concept of reliability and methods for increasing consistency in studies
3. To describe quantitative data collection
4. To describe a qualitative data collection
5. To introduce the three main sources of criminal justice data

Chapter Outline

Introduction
- *Composite Measures*
- *Redundant Measures*
- *Quantitative and Qualitative Measures*

Data Collection and Cause and Effect
- *Time Order*
- *Relationship*
- *No Interference*

Validity
- *Face Validity*
- *Predictive Validity*
- *Content Validity*
- *Construct Validity*

Reliability
- *Test-Retest*
- *Split-Half*
- *Improving Validity and Reliability*

Quantitative Data Collection
- *The Codebook*
- *Logical Structure*

(Continued)

Qualitative Data Collection
Qualitative Framework
Qualitative Data Collection Forms
Existing Criminal Justice Data
The Uniform Crime Reports
National Crime Victims Surveys
Self-Report Data
Summary
Main Concepts
Discussion Questions
Exercises

CHAPTER FOUR

Introduction

After one decides on the basic research design, the next major consideration is usually data collection. Because data collection is fraught with potential sources of error, this chapter will include data collection problems. However, the primary focus is on the identification of problems and concrete solutions to these problems.

It is important to keep in mind that research and data collection are imperfect. For instance, the Uniform Crime Reports (UCR) are data collected by the Federal Bureau of Investigation (FBI) on crimes that are known to the police. Yet it would be naive to believe that the police are aware of all crimes that occur in society. Because we have so few police (around 90,000) relative to our national population of over 250 million people, the police cannot possibly know of every crime that is committed. In fact, police in the United States rely heavily upon citizen reports of crimes to become aware that a crime has actually occurred. While these realities bode ill for the accuracy of the UCR, this is perhaps the only quantitative data set that provides a reasonable basis for making comparisons of crime rates across the country. Hence, while the UCR is an imperfect data collection, it is the only appropriate data for certain comparative research questions.

Suppose we decide to measure the abstract concept of rehabilitation. It is not readily apparent what we could or should "count" or "observe" to measure rehabilitation. One way would be to measure the number of positive changes offenders make in their lives. Positive changes would include steady employment or going back to school. While counting the number of days employed or in school is certainly an acceptable measure of rehabilitation, it is not complete. This definition does not deal with the complexity of the term "rehabilitation." A common measure of rehabilitation is a lower post-program recidivism rate for offenders. While we could counter this line of reasoning by stating that lower recidivism, unless measured over an offender's life time, is not a measure of change that is directly attributable to rehabilitation programming alone. Also influential are the police, the courts, and the processing capabilities of the criminal justice system.

When researchers measure concepts that they have operationalized there is likely to be continued disagreement about the actual meanings of the variables in the study. The value of the data collection in a study is based on the extent to which researchers can objectively and logically justify the definitions that they employ in the study. When they have a topic with a large literature base, they can use that as support for the data measurement and conceptualizations. When there is little prior research, they should endeavor to establish the most objective measurement technique as possible. Others should be able to readily understand the meaning of the measures utilized in research studies.

Composite Measures

One of the key issues that researchers have dealt with is the creation of accurate measures of complex concepts or phenomena. For example, the measurement of *probation officer effectiveness* is necessarily complex. Effectiveness could be measured through an assessment of job duties—such as the number of contact hours with clients and the number of presentence reports written. Probation supervisors may also believe that probation officer effectiveness can be measured through the assessment of policy and procedure conformance or through annual reviews. County budget officers may speak in terms of probation officer "productivity," the number of clients per probation officer (they often assume that the more clients officers handle, the more productive they are). Judges, to whom most probation officers answer, could suggest yet another measure based on the reasonableness and timeliness of their reports. In order to understand the full range of probation officer effectiveness researchers might even ask offenders about their perspectives on the characteristics of an effective probation officer, for example, are they helpful in assisting in finding jobs, drug treatment and so on. It is clear that the concept of probation officer effectiveness is not easily measured.

How should researchers handle this complex situation? One way would be to include a variable for each of the proposed measures and to create an overall or composite measure of probation officer effectiveness. For instance, the data in table 4.1 could provide a composite measure of effectiveness.

The *composite measure* takes into account all of the different perspectives involved in the consideration of officer effectiveness. The end result (the column labeled Composite Measure) is a newly created variable that takes into account all of the perspectives involved in effectiveness. Based on this composite measure researchers can quickly state that Sue appears to be the most effective officer overall and Jack the least.

Table 4.1
COMPOSITE MEASURE OF PROBATION OFFICER EFFECTIVENESS

Name	Contact Hours	Annual Review	Productivity	Timeliness	Helpfulness	Composite Measure
Bill	51	98	250	98	65	562
Sue	52	84	300	94	64	594
Lee	58	82	125	95	63	423
Jack	51	85	68	85	75	364
Pat	62	97	55	80	90	384

Unfortunately, there are several problems with such a simplistic additive composite measure that should be apparent. For instance, the number of contact hours is a measure of the average number of hours in contact with clients per month. Hence, there are times each month when there are more or even less contacts with clients, and this average does not address these contact fluctuations. Second, in the annual review, timeliness and helpfulness measures were created through asking each group (supervisors, judges, and offenders) to rate each probation officer on a scale of 1 to 100. These summary measures could also mask extreme scores and would likely depend on the number of people evaluating the probation officers. They are also very rough measures of the concepts with the exception of the annual review variable, because it is likely to be based on a more contextual consideration of the officers. Last, if we look at the productivity measures, we can see that it influences, more than any other variable, the overall composite measure. The reason for this is because it is a raw score based on the number of clients the probation officer is supervising. Pat is supervising an intensive case load, and Sue a general or administrative case load. It is likely that they are equally productive, because intensive case loads require considerably more time per client; however, the productivity measure does not capture this reality.

Although there are problems with the composite measure, it simultaneously considers a broad range of concepts. In general, the summary measure is typically a more accurate measure than the individual variables by themselves. It is important to keep in mind, especially when using quantitative composite measures, to consider the mathematical effects of combining averages, absolute values, and percentages. The best course of action, if it is available, is to make all of the variables in the composite similar in scale (i.e., all percentages or rates). Ideally, composite measures are developed from statistical models that look at hundreds of variables and combine only those that are strongly interrelated through a technique called Factor Analysis (see Rummel, 1970) or it can be as simple and as logical as the example in table 4.1. Composite measures can greatly increase the range and quality of measures, but it is important that the composite make sense conceptually as well as mathematically. The inclusion of variables in a particular composite measure should make sense conceptually and fit the research question. In the example in table 4.1, if we were interested in testing whether male or female officers were more effective it would make conceptual sense to include as many different indicators of effectiveness as possible. The conceptual fit of the several variables is usually supported by the literature and logic of the problem statement of the research.

On the other hand, making the individual variables of a composite measure consistent may require the use of complex statistical analysis (factor analysis). When we have only a few variables as in table 4.1, it is likely that we could figure out how to make the measures consistent. In table 4.2, an attempt has been made to create consistency in the measures in the effectiveness example.

When we divide each measure (variable) by the number of cases that each officer has, we are attempting to standardize the measures based on the number of offenders each officer is assigned. This is called "controlling" for the number of offenders each officer has on his or her case load. This process of dividing by the number of offenders creates a more equitable set of measures by which officers can be compared on productivity.

In table 4.2 the new standardized composite measures show that Pat is most productive and Sue is the least productive based on the four variables that comprise the composite score. Hence, when we control for the number of offenders the probation officer is assigned we get a much more accurate picture of the productivity based on case load size.

Table 4.2

COMPOSITE MEASURE OF PROBATION OFFICER EFFECTIVENESS

Name	Contact Hours	Annual Review	Timeliness	Helpfulness	Composite Measure
Bill	20.40	39.20	78.40	26.00	164
Sue	17.33	28.00	31.33	21.33	97.99
Lee	46.40	65.6	76.00	50.40	238.4
Jack	75.00	125.00	125.00	110.29	435.29
Pat	112.72	176.36	145.45	90	524.53

These measures were divided by the total number of cases. For example, for Bill 51 contact hours was divided by 250 cases and multiplied by 100 to produce the contact hour rate of 20.40.

After having gone through this example I would be remiss if I did not mention that there are times when researchers like some variables to be worth more than others and would purposely create an imbalance in the values in the composite. For example, in the effectiveness example let's assume that the annual review score should be worth five times the other values because of the structure and strength of the annual review process. The resulting calculation of weighted composite measures are shown in table 4.3. In this case Bill and Sue are clearly more effective than Lee, Jack, and Pat. The use of weighted composite measures can be based on simple multiplication (as in this example) or on a much more complex statistical modeling. In either case, the reasons for weighting any of the variables that make up the composite measure should make sense conceptually and should be consistent with the research questions and purposes.

Redundant Measures

Another method for creating more accurate measures is to collect *redundant measures,* several variables that measure the same concept. A researcher would do this in order to assess the accuracy and consistency of the variables as a measure of the concepts of interest. For example, suppose we are interested in studying gang-related crime in a particular neighborhood, because a newly instituted police intervention program has as its main purpose the reduction of gang criminality. Because there are no UCR statistics for neighborhoods (they are reported at the city level) there are no readily available statistics to measure crime rates at the neighborhood level. Hence, we may have less confidence in the measures we rely on, and therefore we

Table 4.3

WEIGHTED COMPOSITE MEASURE

Name	Contact Hours	Annual Review	Productivity	Timeliness	Helpfulness	Composite Measure
Bill	51	490	250	98	65	954
Sue	52	420	300	94	64	930
Lee	58	410	125	95	63	751
Jack	51	425	68	85	75	704
Pat	62	485	55	80	90	772

These measures of the Annual Review Score are multiplied by 5. For example, Bill's review score of 98 is multiplied by 5 and results in a weighted score of 490.

Figure 4.1
REDUNDANT MEASURES OF GANG-RELATED CRIMINALITY

- Police calls for services that are gang related
- Citizen gang victimization surveys
- Observational study of gang graffiti
- Self-reported gang criminality

might collect several measures of the same concept in order to be certain that we are measuring the concepts relevant to our research questions. Figure 4.1 shows an example of four redundant variables of gang crime that we could use.

Redundant measures should all point in the same direction. That is, if the police calls for gang-related incidents and crimes are increasing in the neighborhood, the victimization surveys, observational study, and self-reported criminality should also show increases. Redundant measures also allow us to identify the accuracy and consistency in the measures. These issues will be explained later in this chapter.

Quantitative and Qualitative Measures

The use of quantitative and/or qualitative measures is also an important consideration in planning for the data collection phase of a research project. *Quantitative measures* are typically numerical, and *qualitative measures* are textual. Quantitative variables are aggregate indicators of the magnitude of concepts. Qualitative variables show the character or content of concepts.

It is important to keep in mind that neither quantitative nor qualitative variables are better or worse. The use of either type of data should be consistent with the research questions one is asking and not because one has a preference for statistical or qualitative analyses. That is not to say that the quantitative and qualitative measures cannot be consistent and used concurrently. In fact, in the ideal situation both types of data should be used, as a complete research focus would likely include considerations of the magnitude and quality of the concepts of interest.

For example, we could construct a study of overcrowding in a jail using consistent quantitative and qualitative measures. Clearly there are readily available quantitative measures of the magnitude of jail overcrowding, such as the number of inmates per the number of beds, the average daily jail population, or the admission rate per rated capacity. On the qualitative side, measures such as the opinions of staff or inmates on the level or nature of crowding in the facility could be relied upon. The qualitative measures would be obtained through interviews, whereas the quantitative measures could be gleaned from the official population counts or logs. The quantitative measures would provide a clear indication of the magnitude of the overcrowding relative to the amount of space that is available. The qualitative variables would provide more detail about the interaction between the space available and the resulting "feeling" of overcrowding. The qualitative measures could act as a check on the qualitative measures and vice versa. A system of checks and balances between quantitative and qualitative variables is important, because a jail could be overcrowded quantitatively, yet the inmates, because they get along, might not feel overcrowded.

Chapter 3 discussed how one would go about moving from a theory to the conceptual and operational levels of study. In this chapter the discussion focuses on the collection of operationalized variables.[1] The key issues involved in establishing cause and effect and several methods for identifying both validity and reliability are included. In addition, several methods for improving both the accuracy and consistency of data collection are explained, and a brief overview of the main criminal justice data sources is provided.

Data Collection and Cause and Effect

Another issue that is important in data collection is the notion of *cause and effect.* Researchers are often interested in establishing whether a particular cause results in a specific effect. An example is the attempt to establish that education (CAUSE) can reduce recidivism (EFFECT). Although the question of cause and effect appears to be straightforward and often should be built into the research design section of the study, there are specific considerations that must be taken into account when collecting data that are appropriate for determining the plausibility of the presumed cause and effect. Figure 4.2 shows a simple cause and effect relationship.

Figure 4.2
CAUSE AND EFFECT EXAMPLE

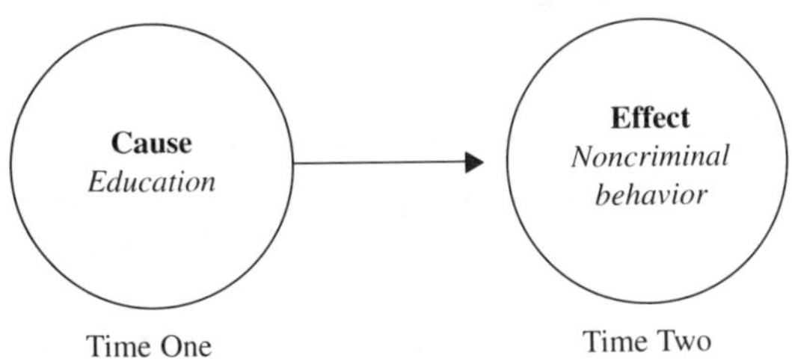

While cause and effect is primarily a research design issue, it is also a crucial data collection issue, because there are certain specific requirements for the collection of data for a cause and effect research design. These three considerations are (1) time order, (2) relationship, and (3) no interference. The following sections provide more detailed discussion of these data collection requirements for establishing cause and effect.

Time Order

One consideration in the establishment of cause and effect is time order. Essentially the cause *must* happen before the effect for one to establish cause and effect. In the example in figure 4.2 it is clear that in order for the effect (noncriminality) to be produced, the education program must occur before the noncriminality. Without a logical time order there can be no assertion of cause and effect.

Relationship

Another key component of establishing cause and effect is the establishment of a relationship between the variables. A relationship is most typically indicated by statistical measures (i.e., correlation coefficients; see chapter 10), but it can also be demonstrated through logic for qualitative variables. At its most basic level a relationship between two variables is such that there is some coincidence in the increases and decreases in magnitude of the variables. For instance, if there is a relationship between education and criminality, one would find that for every increase in the number of years of education there is a similar magnitude decrease in criminality. Similar to the time order there can be no establishment of cause and effect without some level of relationship. Unless there is this crucial evidence of coincidence between the variables it is difficult to support an argument of cause and effect.

No Interference

The third requirement for establishing cause and effect relationships is that there are no other variables that effect the relationship.[2] Not only must the cause occur before the effect and the variables must be related but there should be no other variables that are better explainors of the effect than the supposed cause. There can be other variables that improve the explanation of the effect, and in many cases researchers would look for multivariate cause and effect relationships, but the primary cause should be the best explainor. In figure 4.3 several other interfering variables are demonstrated. That is, age and prior criminality would also be likely influences on the cause and effect relationship supposed in this example.

In summary, the consideration of cause and effect is complex and should not be supposed on the basis of a relationship alone. While the establishment

Figure 4.3
CAUSE AND EFFECT: OTHER VARIABLES

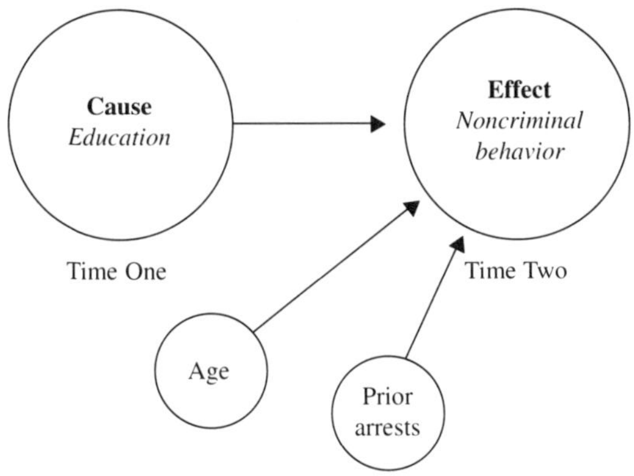

of a proper time order and relationship is usually quite apparent, it is difficult to establish that there are no other interfering variables that explain the cause and effect. The establishment of cause and effect is even more difficult, and somewhat problematic, if one is relying on qualitative data.

Validity

One of the key considerations in the collection of data about the concepts that are the focus of research is to create accurate variables. *Validity* is the extent to which the data one collects accurately reflect the concepts and operationalizations that are pertinent to the study one is conducting. There are several types of validity as well as techniques for increasing the validity of measures. The following sections provide additional detail about these considerations.

Types of validity are different insofar as they look at the accuracy of the measures researchers collect from different perspectives. Researchers often select one or two of these perspectives or types of validity to assess the accuracy of their measures. This increases their confidence in the accuracy of their measures.

Face Validity

The simplest way of looking at the accuracy of measures is to consider their "face" validity. *Face validity* is an assessment of the accuracy on the basis of what makes logical sense. For example, in a study of jail utilization the variable "average daily population" is face valid insofar as it makes sense that this variable measures the concept of jail utilization. One can argue that the average daily population, if correctly recorded by the staff, is clearly an accurate measure of how the jail is used, and is therefore face valid. Face validity is established through logical argument, and its basis is the reality of the concurrence between what one supposes one is measuring and what the collected variable actually measures.

Predictive Validity

Another type of validity is predictive validity. *Predictive validity* can be defined as the accuracy of the collected variable in terms of its ability to forecast the concept of interest. For instance, if scores earned on the Law School Admissions Test (LSAT) are valid predictive measures of success as a law student then those who earn higher scores will be more likely to graduate from law school. Predictive validity, based on this definition, is not as apparent nor as easy to establish as face validity. The establishment of predictive validity may require the use of an invalid measure only to discover that it is inaccurate. Therefore, predictive validity should be used only in situations where measures can be readily validated or assessed.

However, it is sometimes difficult to establish the predictive comparison (i.e., LSAT and law school success). For instance, police officer academy test scores could perhaps be used to measure how good police officer candidates would be in police practice on the streets. However, what should be the comparison variable to the academy test scores? Perhaps the average number of arrests or the conviction rate (convictions per arrests), but these variables are not clear or certain reflections of academy training as they are descriptive of street experience. In essence, the establishment of predictive validity is a strong basis for the accuracy of measured variables, but it is not easily established.

Content Validity

In order to establish *content validity,* you must have several measures that are accurate indicators of the complexity of the concept of interest. For example, in the redundant measures example, it was supposed that several measures of the concept of gang crime be taken. That is, police calls for service, victimization surveys, observational study of gang graffiti, and self-reported gang criminality should all be indicators of gang criminality. Insofar as these indicators are similar (e.g., increasing or decreasing) they would accurately reflect the concept of gang crime. Establishing content validity can be done through logical argument or through inter-item assessment of relationships (see table 4.4 for an example).

The logical basis for each of the four measures can be argued. That is, both crimes reported to police through calls for service and the admission of criminality by gang members can be argued to be accurate measures

Table 4.4
CONTENT VALIDITY EXAMPLES OF LOGICAL AND STATISTICAL BASIS

Measures	Logical Basis	Statistical Basis		1.	2.	3.	4.
1. Police calls for gang incidents	Direct measure		1.	1.00			
2. Victimization study	Effects measure		2.	.87	1.00		
3. Observations of graffiti	Indirect measure		3.	.85	.79	1.00	
4. Self-report gang criminality	Direct measure		4.	.91	.94	.81	1.00

of the concept of gang criminality. The victimization study of the effects of gang crimes, while indirect, also is a measure of the effects of gang crime and may reflect a component of the general impacts of such criminality on the community. The use of a statistical basis is established by assessing the inter-item correlation coefficients (assuming all four variables are measured on an interval scale). All four variables could be correlated with all other variables. The closer the correlation statistics are to +1.0 or −1.0, the more accurate the set of measures. In the example in table 4.4 all of the correlations are very high, and therefore, there appears to be a conformance between the content of the concept of gang criminality and the four created variables.

Construct Validity

Construct validity can be defined as the conformance between what one measures and what one expects the data to reflect on the basis of theory or logic. For example, Weberian Bureaucratic Theory (Archambeault, 1982, p. 68) supposes that all organizations must be structured in a hierarchy around several levels of authority. Hence, if one were measuring the flow of communications in an organization, the measures are valid if they reflect that communications flow through a hierarchy. The obvious problem with establishing construct validity is that it is based on the veracity of the theory upon which the accuracy assessment is based. Hence, there have been several more contemporary theories of how organizations are structured that may be more appropriate than Weberian theory. While the theory that one uses to validate the constructs should be relevant to the context of the study one is conducting, it is still difficult to rule out rival theories that may weaken any validity of measures arguments.

Reliability

Reliability is the consistent measure of concepts or variables over time. Consistency is not the same as accuracy (validity). In fact, the accurate measurement of a concept does not guarantee that the measure will be consistent. If, for example, we measured the opinions of the public toward the police through an open-ended interview format, such a technique would be an accurate measure of citizens' opinions about the police. However, the information may be inconsistent, because different questions may be asked each time citizens were asked, or the citizens might respond to different aspects of each question each time they were asked.

In order to show whether there is reliability in measures we can use three generally accepted techniques: test-retest, split-half, and consistency assessment. Each of these techniques can be applied in a quantitative or qualitative context. However, the use of quantitative data makes these assessments not only much easier but also more clear. There are also specific statistical indicators that have been used to assess reliability (Kuder Richardson Test and Cronbach's Alpha), but these are clearly beyond the scope of this textbook.

Test-Retest

One way to assess the reliability of measures is to measure the variables of interest over two time periods and compare the measures. If they are reliable measures, we should expect to find very little difference in the variables over the time of measurement. Typically researchers rely on statistics to establish the *test-retest* reliability of measures.

For example, let's suppose that we are interested in developing a reliable measure of public opinion toward capital punishment. We would first attempt to develop a series of questions that would measure the most important issues in regard to public opinions. In the example in figure 4.4, one question of the series we may ask is listed. If the question is a reliable measure of public opinions toward the death penalty, then the results from the test and retest should be similar. In table 4.5, results from a test-retest for seven subjects on the question in figure 4.4 are shown.

Figure 4.4

TEST-RETEST EXAMPLE

Test: Time 1		Retest: Time 2
1. Are you in favor of or opposed to the use of the death penalty. ____ In favor (1 pt.) ____ Opposed (2 pt.)	→	1. Are you in favor of or opposed to the use of the death penalty. ____ In favor (1 pt.) ____ Opposed (2 pt.)

Table 4.5
TEST-RETEST DATA EXAMPLE

	Test Score	Retest Score
Jack	1	1
Jill	1	1
Bob	2	1
Alicia	2	2
Gina	1	1
Joe	2	2
Allyssa	1	1

A summary percentage can be calculated by dividing the number of similar scores over the two tests out of the total number of cases. In this case 6 of the 7 gave the same answer over the two tests, yielding a summary percentage of 85.71%.

The results of this test show that the test and retest of the public opinion measure is fairly reliable. How high the summary percentage should be, or must be, is up to the researcher and the topic at hand. The point of attempting to show consistency with a test-retest technique is to demonstrate that respondents will say essentially the same thing over time. This can also be demonstrated by correlating the test and retest scores (see chapter 10). In essence, the higher the percentage of similarity, or correlation coefficient, the more reliable the data measures.

Split-Half

Another technique for assessing the reliability of measures is to use a *split-half technique.* In a split-half technique we would use redundant measures of t he same concept and randomly divide the measures into two groups. The assessment of consistency between the two groups can then be conducted. We would have to begin our split-half assessment with the collection of several variables that measure the same concept. This can be done in a survey or questionnaire design, because questions can be reworded to essentially measure the same concept without substantially altering their meaning. For example, in figure 4.5, several additional opinions of capital punishment questions are listed for the purpose of our split-half comparisons. We could randomly or systematically assign each of these questions to one of two groups (through reliance on a random numbers table or systematically counting through the questions listing). If we used the random numbers table, we would pick the questions one, six, and two out of the list of questions and assign them to group 1 (as shown in figure 4.5 in the Random Assignment box). Conversely, we could systematically assign every other question to group 1 (resulting in questions one, three, and five to group 1; see Systematic Assignment box). The assessment of reliability could then be done through comparing the scores for the two groups.

The split-half assessment technique relies on the comparability of the measures in each group. If the measures are reliable, they should yield similar results. For example, if people report being in favor of the death penalty on the first group then they should also report their support on the second group if the measures are in fact reliable.

Improving Validity and Reliability

There are several specific ways to improve the validity and *reliability* of measures. The balance between validity and reliability is also important to keep in mind. Just because measures are accurate (i.e., valid) does not mean they will be reliable (i.e., consistent). For instance, if we are counting the number of minor inmate infractions in a prison this year and the rules change next

Figure 4.5

SPLIT-HALF RELIABILITY ASSESSMENT EXAMPLE

1. Are you in favor of or opposed to the use of the death penalty?
   ___ In favor (1 pt.)
   ___ Opposed (2 pt.)
2. Should the death penalty be used for convicted murderers?
   ___ Yes (1 pt.)
   ___ No (2 pt.)
3. Are you in favor of or opposed to judicial sentences of death?
   ___ In favor (1 pt.)
   ___ Opposed (2 pt.)
4. Are you in favor of or opposed to jury sentences of death?
   ___ In favor (1 pt.)
   ___ Opposed (2 pt.)
5. Should the death penalty be used for convicted rapists?
   ___ Yes (1 pt.)
   ___ No (2 pt.)
6. Should those who receive death penalties actually be executed?
   ___ Yes (1 pt.)
   ___ No (2 pt.)

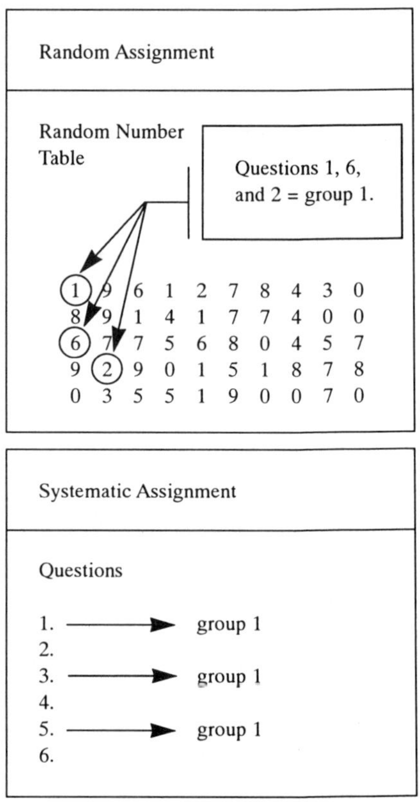

year, our measure would be valid but not reliable. On the other hand, when a measure is consistent (i.e., reliable) there is a strong tendency for it to be accurate (i.e., valid). In this latter case we could suggest that the Law School Admissions Test has resulted in very consistent scores over time and has, in fact, been shown to be a good (accurate) predictor of success in law school. There are several ways to improve validity and reliability. First, the use of redundant and/or composite measures improves the range and quality of the measurement of any concept. Although there are limitations on the number of composite and/or redundant measures that can be incorporated for each concept, the inclusion of more than one variable measuring each concept is one way to improve validity.

Second, the basic standard of "face" validity should be maintained before proceeding to data collection. That is, the variable should at the very least appear to measure the concept that one intends to measure. For example, victimization studies are poor measures of crime rates (the number of crimes per population). Hence, if one is interested in comparing the crime rates between different types of cities (e.g., manufacturing cities, university cities, capital cities, and so on), it would make little sense to use victimization data. On the other hand, the UCR appears, on its face, to be an accurate measure of crime rates in various types of cities.

Another way to improve the validity of measures is to use accepted measures for the concepts included in the study. For example, if one is interested in assessing the climate of a jail or correctional facility, the Moos Correctional Institution Environment Scale (Moos, 1968) might be selected because it is an accepted, albeit imperfect, measure of the organizational characteristics and qualities of correctional institutions. There are also many surveys and questionnaires that have been developed in criminal justice and criminology that have already been validated by their authors and are available for additional use in continued studies.

Fourth, reliability and validity can be established through pretesting the measures prior to the actual collection of study data. If they are shown to be inaccurate or inconsistent on the basis of content or construct validity, then they can be improved or developed to remove the problems. Similarly, the reliability could be assessed and problems could be corrected prior to collection of the actual study data.

Quantitative Data Collection

The quantitative data collection procedures should be based on a logical order. The data collection procedures should allow the researcher to move from the raw data forms, surveys, or interview notes to a usable analysis format. The purpose of the data collection is, therefore, to convert the data into an analyzable format. Regardless of the approach one takes to collecting data, there is usually some need to organize what has been collected for the analysis stage of the study. The following sections describe the general considerations for constructing a quantitative data base structure for the analysis stage of research projects.

While quantitative data structuring should be based on logical ordering, the requirements of computer based analysis programs should also be considered in the design of quantitative data collection. In the 1990s there are a multitude of user-friendly statistical analysis programs (BMDP/386 Dynamic, Genstat, 5.2, SAS 6.08, Minitab Release 8, NCSS Version 5.03, P-Stat 2.15, SPSS 6.0, Stata 3.0, Statgraphics 6.0, Statistica 3.1, and Systat 5.03; see Canter, 1993), and it is inconceivable that any but the most rudimentary studies would be conducted without relying on these technologies. Most spreadsheet programs allow one to create graphical displays of data, and on occasion standard deviations or means. They do not, however, allow one to conduct a full range of analyses.

The Codebook

The primary method for determining the logical structure should be based on a written and organized codebook. The *codebook* is the "road map" of the data structure. Table 4.6 shows an example of a quantitative codebook. In the codebook the exact locations of the variables and attributes of each of the variables can be exactly located.

Table 4.6

EXAMPLE OF A QUANTITATIVE CODEBOOK

Columns	Variable	Code	Abbreviation
1-3	Identification Code	V1	IDCODE
4	Gender	V2	SEX
	1 = male		
	2 = female		
5-6	Age (number of years)	V3	AGE
7	Race	V4	RACE
	1 = African American		
	2 = White		
	3 = Other		
8-9	Prior Arrests (number of)	V5	ARRESTS
10-11	Prior Convictions (number of)	V6	CONVIC
12	Security level (in last confinement)	V7	SECLEV
	1 = maximum		
	2 = medium		
	3 = low		
	4 = other		
13-14	Age at first arrest (number of years)	V8	AGEFA

The codebook typically has information about the physical locations of the scores on the variables in the data structure as well as conceptual labels. In table 4.6, the "column" category shows the physical location of the variable that is recorded in the data set. The identification code for each inmate in this study, for example, is recorded in the first, second, and third columns of the data set (see table 4.7). Conceptually, the variable labels clearly establish the conceptual categorization of the variables (in addition to the labeling of attributes of the nominal level variables). The "code" and "abbreviation" columns are used to streamline the use of the computer analysis programming (i.e., it requires much less typing to use the label "V6" than "prior convictions"). While ease of programming is certainly not the only priority in setting up a codebook, it makes little sense to make additional difficulties when these are easily avoided.

Logical Structure

Another key consideration in setting up the data for quantitative analysis is the *logical structure* of the coding scheme. Most statistical data analysis programs assume that each person in the study (research subjects) should appear on one or more logical records. These logical records are simple streams of data that hold the variables in the codebook in the same location for each research subject. For example, assume that case 001 in table 4.7 is one person; in the physical data set all the data for that person appears on the first line (or row) of the data set. In the past computer abilities have restricted this logical record length to eighty columns, but this restriction is much less relevant with more modern computing systems (this is rarely the case with state-of-the-art microcomputer-based statistical analysis programs, assuming the computer being used has enough memory). The limitations to the logical structuring of data are few and are likely to continue to decrease in the future as computer technology improves.

Therefore, in the 1990s there is little reason to set data into a logical format that is visually verifiable (i.e., one that you can read on a computer

Table 4.7

EXAMPLE OF QUANTITATIVE DATA BASED ON CODEBOOK

V1	V2	V3	V4	V5	V6	V7	V8
001	1	22	1	0	0	4	25
002	1	23	1	1	3	1	17
003	2	27	2	0	0	4	21
004	2	32	1	2	4	2	16
005	1	24	2	3	6	2	14
etc.							

screen or printout). If you need a more flexible format, you can find a program that can handle a more complex structure. For example, in a study of inmate prison activities some inmates will have participated in educational, vocational, work, and other programs whereas other inmates will have done very little. There would be incomplete information about each of the inmates in the sample, but the logical structure of the data coding should be constructed to collect as many pieces of data as possible for as many inmates as possible.

In summary, the logical structure should serve the needs of the analyses that need to be conducted based on the research questions. The purpose of the research should drive the project from construction of the research design through the analysis and conclusions.

Qualitative Data Collection

The collection of qualitative data is not quite as easy as that of quantitative data. It is important to keep in mind that just because qualitative data may be in a verbal or written form rather than numbers does not mean that it is not data. Not only is the collection of qualitative data time consuming, but the analysis of qualitative data is not as easy as analyzing quantitative data.

For one thing, qualitative data tends to be quite voluminous. For example, I once conducted over one hundred interviews of correctional officers and inmates (each interview lasting about one hour). I had a stack over two feet high of interview notes from this project. For the same project I have quantitative data on over fourteen hundred official reports, which amounts to less than half the amount of paper and data collection efforts as the interview data. In order to create the interview data I had to sit down with each interviewee and then write up my notes—a task that was tedious and time consuming, not to mention uncomfortable as the interviews were conducted in July and August in Florida. On the other hand, analyzing the official reports of inmate-officer contacts involved sitting in front of the photocopy machine and reproducing the official forms, which was accomplished in one day. My interview notes and the copies of records are raw data that must be converted into analyzable data—the subject of this chapter.

Another key consideration in the collection of qualitative data is structuring that data. Whereas the structuring process for quantitative data collection should be set up to deal with computer-based analysis, the data collection of qualitative data needs a different logical structuring. Qualitative analyses can be conducted on a computer, and there are several such programs currently available. However, there are many limitations to these programs, and by-and-large they do not complete the data analysis in the same way as do statistical or quantitative programs. Most qualitative analysis computer programs merely help in the organization and analysis. In statistical analyses, researchers make decisions on the basis of probability theory. However, in qualitative computer analyses, there is no such basis for decisions; these must be made by the researcher on the basis of his or her logic.

Suppose you were interested in studying police reports, particularly the written narrative section. You could structure your data to assess the manifest content for officers' opinions about suspects (e.g., how many times did a report state the suspect cursed at the officer). On the other hand, the data collection could focus on a more subtle level, such as grammar (e.g., the number of adjectives and adverbs used by officers) so as to reflect officers' ability to communicate on a professional level.

Qualitative Framework

One particularly helpful framework for qualitative data collection has been developed by Patton (1990). While his framework has been developed for qualitative evaluations, it is applicable to research methods in general. This framework also provides a concrete structure upon which the collection of data can be based. Figure 4.6 shows the five dimensions in the Patton framework. Each dimension may not apply in every case, but consideration of these issues is important for designing a qualitative data collection format.

The first dimension in qualitative data collection considers how much the researcher will be involved in the research scene and/or with the research subjects. This dimension ranges from full participation to observation as an outsider. A full participation data collection would involve the study of a situation as a full member. There have been professors who have, for example, joined police departments to study policing. They have become full fledged participants in the study situation with the other police officers. On the other hand, studies can be totally conducted by an outside onlooker. An example studying video tapes. In this situation the study subject or scene is not aware of the researcher, and the research does not influence behavior. The decision to do one thing or another on the first dimension should be driven by the research purpose or questions.

The second of Patton's dimensions is consistent with the first. While it is difficult and perhaps unethical to conceal one's identity if one is a full participant, it can be done. There are several very well done studies of street gangs (Hagedorn, 1988; Virgil, 1988) based on qualitative data collection from full participation. The explanation of the purpose of the research can range from a full explanation of the real purpose to a false explanation. When I studied a jail in Virginia I was required to complete a full explanation of the research I wanted to conduct prior to being granted permission to collect data. The jail administration deemed it crucial that they understand what research was to be done and that the confidentiality of the inmates and staff would be protected.

Figure 4.6

PATTON'S FIVE DIMENSIONS OF QUALITATIVE OBSERVATIONS

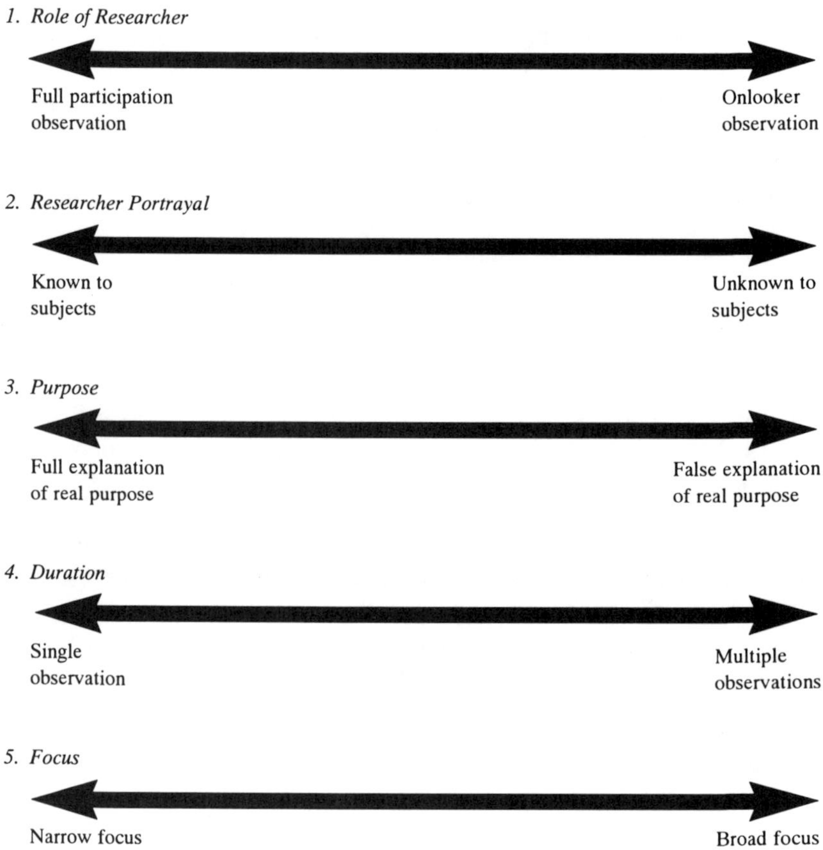

The focus of the data collection could also be narrow or broad. A narrow focus is directed at a single element, for example, a focus on the number of negative sentences about defendants by police officers in their official reports. A broad focus is looking at the entire situation, for example, studying the outcomes of particular cases based on the "picture" that was painted about the defendant.

I have also conducted a quasi-experimental study of students in one of my courses without telling them the purpose of my study. The study I conducted of my courses was based on twenty minute open-ended interviews. I did not tell students that I was using the interviews for self-evaluation purposes; rather, I told them that I wanted to discuss their term papers. The reason for not telling the students the purpose of the study ahead of time was that I felt that students might not be open about problems with the course if I told them they were required to tell me what they liked most and least about the course. I believed that by asking students about the course while talking about their term paper, I could collect more valid information about how students evaluated the course. After my study was over, however, I disclosed the purpose and findings of my interviews. Although this design seemed to work for my purposes, there are ethical problems with my approach—I did not predisclose the purpose of my study and did not give students the choice to voluntarily participate in the study (see chapter 13 for a discussion of the ethics of research).

The final two issues are the duration and focus of the data collection. The duration can range from a one-time study to multiple observational and long-term studies. Many qualitative data collections are based on one-time observations, because it takes a great deal of time and expense to study more than one time frame. However, there are qualitative studies that are conducted over a period of years. In order to understand concepts or topics such as prostitution or drug sales, it may take observations over a period of years.

Qualitative Data Collection Forms

There are several general forms of recording qualitative data. The data collected from interviews or observations should be structured in a way that allows the researcher to analyze its relevance to the research questions developed for the study (table 4.8).

Field notes are the most common form of qualitative data, and these can be based on a structured or unstructured format. Field notes are similar to notes taken during class lectures. The goal of taking notes in class

Table 4.8

SELECTED QUALITATIVE DATA FORMS

Forms	Definition
Field notes	Notes based on direct interviews taken in direct contact with the research subjects
Reconstructed notes	Notes that are written after the interviewee leaves the interview situation
Tape recordings	Dictaphone or tape-recorder based notes
Video tapes	Fixed or camcorder based multimedia notes
Photographs	Still depictions of situation or scenes

is to accurately and completely record the content of the lectures. Similarly, the collection of qualitative data through field notes is based on taking notes during an interview or observational study. In some cases the notes are constructed after the fact (i.e., they are reconstructed). For example, I was invited to tour a juvenile prison in Hong Kong when I was there for a conference. The only stipulation that they placed on me was that I could not bring anything into the prison (my camera and note pad were left at the front gate). When I returned to my hotel I reconstructed the two-hour tour of the facility as best I could from my memory of the event. While direct field notes are certainly more accurate, reconstruction is sometimes necessary and can be a perfectly valid method of data collection. Reconstruction of notes can also permit the addition of of details that could not be recorded when one was in the observed environment. Such reconstructions may include the researcher's reflections on the experience, impressions about the organization or structure, and so on—anything that helps construct a more complete picture of the observed setting can be added when the researcher reconstructs his or her field notes.

New technologies for data collection have been a boon for qualitative researchers. The development of inexpensive camcorders and other real-time recording instruments have contributed greatly to qualitative research studies. In addition, computer-based data input through the use of scanners, devices that allow pictures to be recorded on a computer, and video management systems allow basic analysis of qualitative records. With the development of computer-based multimedia management and more powerful multitasking computers, the ability of qualitative based research to consider a multitude of variables simultaneously is likely to continue to improve.

Existing Criminal Justice Data

Criminal justice data are collected by local, state, and federal agencies as well as private researchers and associations. These data are readily available and can be used for many purposes beyond the reason the data were collected. In fact, many researchers rely on these data to study crime, criminal justice, and criminological issues and theories. The focus of chapter 9 is on the use and integration of these sources. However, the following provides a brief introduction to the main sources of preexisting criminal justice data.

The Uniform Crime Reports

Perhaps the best known continuous source of crime data for the United States is the *Uniform Crime Reports (UCR)* compiled by the Federal Bureau of Investigation (FBI).[3] The UCR is a voluntary and nationwide effort to collect statistics on all crimes known to police. Over sixteen thousand city, county, and state law enforcement agencies report crimes to the UCR, representing 96 percent of the total population of the country (Uniform Crime Reports, 1991).

Data published in the UCR are collected for the purposes of law enforcement administration, operation, and management. The focus is on creating general indicators of the crime problems confronted by law enforcement. The UCR is also used by various researchers and the media as a key indicator of the relative crime rates in the United States.

The UCR has been criticized in regard to both its reliability and its validity. In terms of accuracy some argue that the different law enforcement agencies use different definitions of crimes. Over the longer term the definitions of crime have also changed, thereby reducing the consistency of the data collection.

In the early 1980s, the FBI began the long process of redesigning the data collection focus of the UCR. One of the major changes to the UCR that is being implemented in selected areas at this point is the use of incident-based reporting, called the National Incident Based Reporting System (NIBRS). This system will record each crime as a separate incident. The UCR also is focusing on hate crime statistics and the number of police officers killed and assaulted.

Data published in the UCR is collected either directly from law enforcement agencies or from forty-two mandatory state reporting systems.[4] Statistics are based on reports from victims, witnesses, police officers, and "other sources." The focus has been on reporting what the UCR labels the "Crime Index" or "Part I" crimes: murder and non-negligent manslaughter, forcible rape, robbery, aggravated assault, burglary, larceny-theft, motor vehicle theft, and arson (Uniform Crime Reports, 1991). Only the most serious offense is recorded when there are multiple offenses during one crime incident. The UCR also publishes information on "Part II" offenses, which are all offenses not included in Part I offenses except for traffic offenses.

The UCR attempts to eliminate false or unfounded crime reports, so it includes only the "actual offenses known" (Uniform Crime Reports, 1991). The UCR also includes the number of crimes known that are "cleared," or where there is an arrest. Cleared crimes are those for which an arrest has been made. They are thereby "cleared" from the police work load.

The Uniform Crime Reports provide statistics of the crimes known to police in various geographic areas and the Crime Index each year.

National Crime Victims Surveys

The *National Crime Victims Surveys (NCVS)* collect data on personal and household victimization. The goals of the NCVS are (1) to develop information about victims, (2) to create an estimate of crimes not known by police,

(3) to provide a uniform measure of crime, and (4) to permit comparisons over time.

The NCVS is based on a national sample of addresses in the United States. The U.S. Bureau of the Census interviewers conduct the interviews both in person and by telephone (National Crime Survey Codebook, 1992). Several initial screening questions determine if the interviewee has been a victim of crime. The collection of data about victimization is designed to obtain detailed information on the characteristics and circumstances of the victimization.

The sample consists of approximately fifty thousand persons in the fifty states and the District of Columbia. The sample of housing units is divided into six rotation groups with each group being interviewed every six months for a period of three years. The NCVS, like the UCR, has been under development to improve the data collection. The new data collection techniques include computer-aided telephone and personal interviewing. While the NCVS is very good for studying victims and the crimes they are involved in, it is not a crime rate measure per se, and geographic comparisons generally cannot be made on the basis of this data.

Self-Report Data

Individual researcher-created data sets, or *self-report data,* can often be utilized for current studies. These will be discussed in detail in chapter 9, but this section provides a basic introduction to the source of these data.

A great deal of data on criminal justice and other social issues in the United States can be found at the Interuniversity Consortium for Political and Social Research (ICPSR) at the University of Michigan. The ICPSR is a central archive for all independent and grant created criminal justice data sets. The basic goal of the ICPSR is to "maximize the availability and utilization of social science resources and to minimize the inconvenience and cost of teaching and studying social and historical phenomenon" (Guide to Resources, 1994).

The ICPSR houses the National Archive of Criminal Justice Data, which is funded by the Bureau of Justice Statistics. In the role as archivist for criminal justice data sets, the ICPSR is "responsible for acquiring, processing and distributing data sets concerned with crime and the criminal justice system" (Guide to Resources, 1994). Studies of crime, criminal justice, and criminological issues, as well as of general social issues, are housed at the ICPSR and can be used in further studies.

Summary

This chapter provides a description of the collection of data. The introduction discusses the issues of composite and redundant measures as well as the differences in quantitative and qualitative data. Composite and redundant measures can increase the accuracy and consistency of the data collected. However, one should take care as to how these measures are developed and utilized. Like the research design process there are distinct processes for collecting data, whether data are qualitative or quantitative in nature. It is also important to ensure that the data one collects is both valid (i.e., accurate) and reliable (i.e., consistent). Several recommendations for improving these factors are provided. Finally, a brief introduction to the readily available data sets of the UCR, NCVS, and ICPSR is given.

Main Concepts

composite measure
quantitative measures
qualitative measures
validity
predictive validity
construct validity
test-retest
codebook
Uniform Crime Reports (UCR)
National Crime Victims Surveys (NCVS)
redundant measures
cause and effect
face validity
content validity
reliability
split-half techniques
logical structure
self-report data

Discussion Questions

1. What is more important for your study, validity or reliability?
2. How could we create a composite measure of rehabilitation?
3. Could we determine the reliability of student evaluations? How?
4. How could we set up a cause-and-effect relationship between community policing and citizens' attitudes about fear of crime?

Exercise

As a class construct a short, five-question survey about a current criminal justice issue. Administer the survey to the entire class. Form into smaller groups. Perform one of the validity assessment techniques and one of the reliability assessment techniques on the survey results. As a group discuss how composite or redundant measures could be used and ways to improve the accuracy and consistency of the survey as a data collection instrument.

5

SAMPLE SELECTION TECHNIQUES

Learning Objectives

1. To explain the most common quantitative sampling techniques
2. To explain the most common qualitative sampling techniques
3. To provide an appreciation for creating non-biased and representative samples for research studies

Chapter Outline

Introduction
Probability Sampling
Simple Random Sampling
Systematic Random Sampling
Stratified Random Sampling
Nonprobability Sampling
Purposive Sampling
Quota Sampling
Accidental Sampling
Qualitative Research Sampling
Extreme Case Sampling
Focus Group Sampling
Criterion Sampling
Snowball Sampling
Sample Size Considerations
Summary
Main Concepts
Discussion Questions
Exercises

CHAPTER FIVE

Introduction

Reliance on scientific techniques of sampling is one of the most important practices in research methods. Researchers improve the power, and potentially the accuracy, of the data they collect by accurate sample selection. Most statistical analysis techniques assume that the sample is selected in as unbiased a fashion as possible.

The basic idea behind sample selection is that each member of the group to be studied could be selected for the study sample. Samples should not be selected because of the availability of subjects or because it is easy to collect data due to subjects' availability.

Sampling is required in most research projects because researchers are constrained by time and costs. For example, there is a reported grand total of 913,739 prisoners in United states jails.[1] Let's assume we want to study this population. Assume further that we want to survey these inmates using a rather short, one page survey. The potential costs involved in studying this group are listed in figure 5.1. Clearly, there are few researchers, if any, that can afford to conduct such a project out-of-pocket, and these costs are probably on the conservative side. In addition, there is not one federal or state agency that is willing to, or capable of, providing funding at such a level, and there are few if any agencies that fund criminal justice research that have budgets of this magnitude. The investment of over $1 million for a small, arguably superficial, one page survey may not be worth the cost. The large amount of time needed for mailing and processing returns and coding this data prohibits studying the entire population group.[2] Hence, researchers use samples rather than total populations as the basis of study.

Researchers have argued that a smaller group can be studied with a negligible loss in the validity and can be the basis for data collection. They believe that the sample has the same essential characteristics as the general

Figure 5.1

COSTS FOR INMATE POPULATION STUDY

Item	Cost
Paper (.02¢ per sheet)	$18,274.78
Copying of surveys (.37¢ per sheet)	$338,083.43
Mailing surveys (1,361/$15.00 each)	$292,396.48
Outgoing envelopes (.12¢ each)	$109,648.68
Return mail (50% response rate)	$173,610.41
Data coding (5 minutes/record/.83¢ each)	$379,201.68
Total	$1,311,215.46

population from which it is drawn. The idea that a sample, if selected scientifically and without bias, is representative of the population from which it is drawn is based in probability theory. The logic of sampling is based on the idea that over the long run it is more likely that our sample will represent the actual population. For instance, suppose we selected several samples of 1,000 inmates from the 913,739 inmates and compared the average age in these samples with that of the average age in the population. We would find that the average age for the several samples of 1,000 inmates that we selected would be close to the population average age. That is, more of our samples, if selected randomly, would approach the population average age than would not be close to the population average. Thus, over the long run, samples have been shown to approximate populations on both a probability and logical basis. The difference between a particular sample and the population value can also be estimated through the calculation of a standard error.[3] Knowledge of the standard error of a sample allows one to determine how much error exists in a particular sample and thus allows for an assessment of the worth or representativeness of the population.

We can also check the sample against what is known about the population. For instance, most prior correctional research shows that the prison populations in this country are male, usually 90 percent to 95 percent. If we select a representative sample of 900 inmates from the population of all inmates, the sample should have nearly the same proportion of males as the general inmate population. There are other important variables besides gender that could help us to determine how closely our sample approximates the population from which it is selected. However, we should assume that the sample rarely will be an exact replication of the characteristics and variables in the population from which it was drawn but that the amount of error should be kept to a negligible level.

In general there are two types of sampling approaches: probability and nonprobability. *Probability sampling* is based on probability theory and mathematically based subject selection. Probability sampling is considered to be superior to nonprobability sampling for this reason. The theoretical basis of probability sampling essentially boils down to the rationale that over the long run probability sampling techniques will result in more representative and less biased samples of the population.

Probability sampling is directly linked with inferential tests (discussed later in this text) in that testing hypotheses is based on an assessment of whether the sample is likely to be found or whether it is too unusual to be a probable finding. The probability basis for hypothesis tests are considered more powerful statistics than are nonprobability statistics.

We can compare probability sampling to making a salad at a salad bar. If we select the items for a salad on a probability basis, all items, even those we do not care for, have an equal chance to be included in the salad. In addition, we would use a mathematical basis for the selection of items (random numbers table, computer). The end result would be a representative sample of all the salad bar items (the population). The salad is representative of the salad bar on a probability basis and is not influenced by our person biases or preferences.

Conversely, *nonprobability sampling* is an attempt to approximate probability sampling. The basis of nonprobability sampling, however, is not probability theory but a sound and logical rationale for selecting study subjects. Nonprobability sampling relies on the ability of a researcher to select a sample without bias and through inspection or logical reasoning rather than through probability theory.

If we go back to the salad bar and select a nonprobability salad, for instance, we might take a few items from the righthand side of the salad bar because that is all that is available to us—the other side is being restocked by the salad bar worker. We might attempt to improve this by determining that we need to select a vegetable, lettuce, and dressing and then take the first type of each of these we come across. The salad would exclude many items. The nonprobability sampling method of constructing a salad may or may not result in a better tasting salad but it was selected without bias or the benefits of probability theory.

The following sections describe in more detail some of the key techniques involved in the selection of samples. Probability sampling is covered first, because it is considered to be the preferred method. There are times, however, when a probability sample cannot be used, so a discussion of nonprobability sampling follows that of probability sampling. Also included is a section on qualitative sampling, because the approach in these techniques is somewhat different than sampling techniques that use only numerical data.

Probability Sampling

Probability sampling is based on the idea that the sample selected will be a mathematically representative subgroup of the larger population. The greatest advantage of probability sampling is that the techniques are crucial for many inferential hypothesis tests and statistical analysis methods. In probability sampling we can also more directly determine the level of inaccuracy of the sample. Along with these advantages are certain disadvantages.

First, probability sampling techniques require a list of the population elements. This often makes selecting a sample a large and tedious job. For example, I once did a study in the Baltimore City Pretrial Services Division. I determined that there were nearly 60,000 cases in 1992, the year I wanted to study. In order to use a probability sampling technique I had to first create a list of all of these cases. This task alone took me over two weeks to complete. This effort was important, because I wanted to generalize to the population of 1992 cases from a sample of only 1,000. However, often a list of all the members of a population cannot be compiled. For example, there is no list of all the citizens in the United States or even of those in one state. It would be extremely difficult, if not impossible, to get complete lists of inmates or police officers for studies. These may exist in many jurisdictions, they may not be available for research purposes. Without a list, or the ability to sample from a list, probability sampling cannot be utilized.

Second, the researcher must use either a random numbers table or a computer to select the sample. This creates the possibility for errors in sample selection, because the researcher must transfer the cases selected by the table, computer, or calculator to the listing of the population. To select a sample of 1,000 takes a considerable amount of time and is quite tedious if a random numbers table is used.

All in all, however, the benefits of probability sampling outweigh the disadvantages. The better the sample, the greater the likelihood that the data collected are valid. The goal should be to select the best sample possible given the time and material constraints of the research project.

Simple Random Sampling

Simple random sampling is the most direct reflection of the concepts and techniques of probability sampling. It most closely approximately the ideals in probability theory in that each subject or case has an equal and independent chance of inclusion in the sample to be studied. It is extremely important to note that a simple random sample *is not* selecting a sample of people "at random" at a particular location. Students often mistake the word *random* with the technique of simple random sampling. Suffice it to say that it is impossible to select a "random" sample without relying on the techniques described. One cannot "randomly" select a sample without relying on a random numbers table, computer, or other form of random numbers or a list of the population.

Simple random sampling starts with a list of all subjects in the population (people, places, events, and so on). Once the list of all elements is constructed, each member of the list is consecutively numbered starting with the first item and ending with the last item on the list. The next step is to decide the sample size to be selected from the list. Once the sample size is determined, a random numbers table, computer, or calculator is used to select the sample. Figure 5.2 demonstrates selecting a simple random sample from a population of inmates.

In figure 5.2 the names of the twenty inmates (the population of inmates) in the very small jail under study are numbered from 1 through 20. Once the list has been numbered, a random start is found in a random numbers table.[4] A random starting place in the table is found by closing your eyes and placing the point of a pencil on the numbers in the table. Once the starting place is determined, a scheme for traveling through the random numbers table is adopted and followed until the desired sample size is selected. The sample size in this example is five inmates. For this example I decided to move from left to right across the rows and start at the beginning of the following row until my sample of five is selected. The numbers in the random numbers table represent the listing numbers. For example, my randomly selected starting point is 49, but there is no inmate 49, so I

Figure 5.2

SIMPLE RANDOM SAMPLING: USING A RANDOM NUMBERS TABLE

Number	Inmate List
1	**Billy**
2	Jack
3	Joe
4	David
5	**Joey**
6	Al
7	Marc
8	Fred
9	Jeff
10	Chris
11	Ben
12	**Doug**
13	Shawn
14	Fritz
15	Gina
16	Karen
17	**Alice**
18	**Crystal**
19	Patricia
20	Alicia

Random Numbers Table:

77	34	56	17	55	29	88	60	12	90
30	13	49	(12)	68	78	(17)	81	26	64
27	82	76	46	47	67	50	(01)	45	98
45	76	40	80	(05)	99	55	36	(18)	09
44	17	51	60	04	88	32	42	69	75
39	91	55	56	97	47	56	82	76	46

A random start was selected here. The random start is determined by closing one's eyes and placing a pencil point on the table. In this case, it landed on the number 49.

[shaded box] = selected for the sample

moved to the next pair of numbers to the right in the population listing—12. Hence, Doug is included in the sample because his assigned number is 12. The result of this process is a sample including inmates Billy, Joey, Doug, Alice, and Crystal. As you can imagine, if I had to select a sample of 1,000 inmates, this process would be tedious and time consuming.

A simple random sample can also be gathered using many major spreadsheet programs and statistical or scientific calculators.[5] In a spreadsheet program, select a column in the spreadsheet and calculate random numbers for each cell (see your computer manual for the formula for this operation). In Microsoft Works®, the spreadsheet program I use, the command RAND( ) is placed in each cell for the total sample size. For the example in figure 5.2 I would place the random number generator formula in twenty cells. I would then select the sample of five from the created random numbers in the twenty cells. If I were unable to select a sample of five from the first twenty cells I would create twenty more until a sample of five was selected.[6] While the numbers generated by the computer and by scientific calculators are not mathematically as good as those found in a random numbers table, they are sufficient for most research studies, and there is very little chance for major bias in the sample selection as long as the sample size is large.

Systematic Random Sampling

Systematic random sampling is more commonly used than simple random sampling because it is easier to select a sample in this manner. However, this method should be used with caution, and it requires closer scrutiny of the list from which the sample is to be selected.

The first step in systematic random sampling is to create a list of all subjects in the population (or available population) to be studied. Once the list is created it should be scrutinized for bias or patterns. This is not necessary when using the simple random sampling technique because each subject has an equal probability, based on random numbers, to be included. In systematic random sampling this may not be the case if the list is patterned.

For example, I was one of several researchers involved in a study of prison staffs in several prisons in the state of Florida. Given the time and expense of traveling to and from Florida we requested a list of all staff before we visited each prison. Upon close examination of these lists we determined that every eleventh person on the list was a supervisor in more than one of the prisons. Hence, the list was biased or patterned and could not be directly used in our systematic sampling technique. For the prison lists that showed no patterns we used the systematic random sampling technique.

Systematic random sampling begins with an unstructured listing of all possible population subjects (those who are available for study). The list can be consecutively numbered for convenience. The numbers are merely labels for each subject. The position of the subjects on the list is the basis for selection. Figure 5.3 shows an example of a systematic sample of domestic violence offenders.

The first step in selecting a systematic sample is to determine the *sampling interval* based on the total sample size one wants to collect. For example, in figure 5.3, a sampling frame[7] of sixteen domestic violence offenders is listed. In reality we would not have such a small population or sample, but it is easier to show how systematic sampling is done if we use a smaller population. To determine the sampling interval to be used on the population of sixteen offenders we should decide on the size of the sample we want. The determination of the sample size can be either quantitative or qualitative, or both.

Figure 5.3

SYSTEMATIC RANDOM SAMPLING EXAMPLE

(shaded box) = selected for the sample

Possible Subjects	Number	Selected Sample
Joe	1	
David	2	
Al	3	
Mark	4	Included in sample
Jeff	5	
Fred	6	
Glenn	7	
Chris	8	Included in sample
Ryan	9	
Brandon	10	
Shawn	11	
Michael	12	Included in sample
Jack	13	
Wayne	14	
Bruno	15	
Omar	16	Included in sample

Suppose we want to select 25 percent of the population because that is all we can afford to study. We calculate the sampling interval by multiplying the sample size by the proportion of the population we wish to collect for our sample:

Formula 5.1: Calculating a Sampling Interval

$$p \times N = \text{sampling interval}$$

Where: p = desired sample proportion
N = population size

In the example in figure 5.3, the proportion is .25 (25% ÷ 100) and the sampling interval is 4 (.25 × 16 = 4). Once the sampling interval is known, the selection of a systematic sample is a matter of selecting each subject that falls on the sampling interval (e.g., every fourth person in the example in figure 5.2), proceeding through the entire sampling frame or population. A random start is accomplished by closing your eyes and placing a pencil point somewhere on the list. The selected subjects are shown in figure 5.3 under the sample column. In this example we moved from the random start at the top of the list where the pencil icon appears.

The advantage of the systematic sampling procedure is that it is much less time consuming than matching a random numbers table or computer generated random numbers. In addition, a systematic sample can be completed on a population of subjects without creating a list by counting the total number in the population, calculating the sampling interval, and selecting the appropriate sample by systematically going through the sampling frame. For example, in a study of parolees I was involved in the Michigan Department of Corrections had twelve file boxes with four drawers in each one of these boxes. I counted all of the files in each of the forty-eight drawers to determine that there were approximately 24,000 files. I was interested in a 10 percent sample of the parolees. Therefore, I collected 2,400 files for the study. I then systematically "sampled" every tenth file in the file boxes.

Systematic sampling can create a biased sample if there is a pattern or structuring of the list or of the manner in which a list or organization was created. For example, official records (e.g., court files, DOC files) are often placed in storage alphabetically. This can introduce bias into the systematic sample you select. There are certain biases introduced by surnames (last names) that may influence the quality of the systematic sample one selects. Because the letters "M" and "S" tend to be the most common for last names one may end up with a biased sample that contains a disproportionate number of Millers or Smiths. A way to avoid this bias is to count the number of files in each letter of the alphabet and to systematically sample the appropriate sampling interval for each letter.

Stratified Random Sampling

Stratified random sampling is a compound sampling procedure in that it includes either simple random or systematic random sampling as well as a stratification schema. Stratified sampling is a way to reduce the amount of bias in either a simple random or systematic random sample. This is accomplished through the use of stratifiers, key variables that one believes could influence the nature of the sample selection or the representativeness of the sample of the population. For example, if we were going to study prison inmates, one key variable that should be taken into account is the security level of the prison in which the inmates are housed. If this were not taken into account we may end up with a sample that disproportionately represents maximum security inmates and not the full range of inmates from minimum security to death row. The stratifiers are used to create subsets of the population, which can then be used to select the sample for the research project. Figure 5.4 demonstrates a stratified and systematically drawn sample of inmates based on security level.

In order to select a systematic sample based on the security stratifiers, we need to know how much of the total sample population or sampling frame of forty-one inmates is located in each stratifier category (i.e., death row and maximum, medium, and minimum security). The box in the lower right hand corner of figure 5.4 shows these proportions as reported by the prison warden. In order to take into account the fact that the maximum security inmates in the population are the greatest proportion of the inmates, and the minimum security inmates are the smallest, each proportion should be taken into account, and each group should be sampled separately. First, we should decide how large a sample we desire. For the purposes of this example, we need a sample of ten inmates (a quarter of the inmates).

There are seven death-row inmates, representing 17 percent of the total sampling frame of forty-one inmates across all security levels. If we multiply the desired sample size (10) by 17 percent (.17), we get 1.7, which is the size of the sample we should select from the death row group. In order to determine the sampling interval for a systematic sampling of the death-row inmates, we divide 7 by 1.7 and get a sampling interval of 4.1. Hence, we should select every fourth inmate from the death-row group.

For the maximum security inmates a sampling interval of 4.05 was calculated based on the fifteen inmates in this group and the fact that they represent 37 percent of the total sampling frame or population. The calculation for the medium security group is a sampling interval of 4.19, and for the minimum security inmates the interval is 4.00.

You may or may not have noticed that the stratified sample that we ended up with in this example is two subjects short of our goal of ten inmates.

In a very small sample two inmates would make a world of difference. However, small samples of inmates are rarely used in most viable research projects. The simplest way to increase the representativeness is to increase the sample size by a few inmates in each category.

In summary, the probability sampling techniques that have been demonstrated reduce bias in selecting a study sample. They accomplish this by setting selection rules that require researchers to remove their biases from the selection process. In addition, they are based on numerical schemes and probability theory.

Figure 5.4

STRATIFIED RANDOM SAMPLE EXAMPLE

Death Row	Maximum Security	Medium Security	Minimum Security
1 Alicia	8 Glenn	23 Jackie	36 Gianna
2 Joe	9 Wayne ☑	24 Florence	37 Franco
3 David	10 Fritz	25 Alice	38 Biaggio
4 Jack	11 Shawn	26 Frank	39 Pasquale
5 Harry	12 Ryan	27 Fortunato	40 Pepino ☑
6 Billy	13 Brandon	28 Tony	41 Juan
7 Bob ☑	14 Michael	29 Mark ☑	
	15 Robert	30 Al	
	16 Willie	31 Crystal	
	17 Ben	32 Chris	
	18 Mohamed	33 Camaron	
	19 Ron	34 James	
	20 Howard	35 George	
	21 Patricia		
	22 Bruno		

[shaded box] = selected for the sample

☑ = point of random start

Total N = 41

Death Row = n = 7 (17%)
Maximum Security = n = 15 (37%)
Medium Security = n = 13 (31%)
Minimum Security = n = 6 (15%)

Nonprobability Sampling

Nonprobability sampling is based not on probability theory but on logic and structured efforts to create a quasi-random sample. Nonprobability samples are generally drawn when the researcher does not have access to a list of all the potential subjects in a population or when access to records is limited. On occasion, researchers are presented with interesting and useful data that may not have been collected from a random sample. In the field of marketing research, nonprobability samples are often the norm, and some of this research is quite good in spite of this basis. Nonetheless, in social science research, and criminal justice research in particular, the ideal sampling techniques are probability methods. Nonprobability sampling procedures are designed to approximate these ideal techniques.

Another reason for the use of nonprobability sampling is because much criminal justice research needs to take place in the "real world." That is, if you are conducting research in a fully operational prison it is sometimes difficult to select a simple random sample because some inmates are unavailable (they are in confinement) or because there simply is not enough staff to cover for the officers you select to interview. It is important to keep in mind that conducting research in criminal justice settings is rarely perfectly scientific. However, the benefits of conducting less than perfect research clearly outweigh the problems that arise when studies on criminal justice topics and in criminal justice agencies are not conducted. Perhaps one of the reasons academics and research results are presumed by many practitioners to be irrelevant to their jobs is that researchers fail to attempt to work within the rules and polices of the operational criminal justice system and agencies and are quick to criticize extremely complex functions and practices on the basis of "empirical" data alone rather than a greater understanding of the realities of practice. Nonprobability approaches should be used where it is not possible to use probability techniques.

The following sections describe three common nonprobability sampling techniques. These were selected because they are the most commonly employed techniques, not because they are the best nonprobability methods. You should select the best, most representative sample possible and in some cases that may be a nonprobability sample.

Purposive Sampling

Purposive sampling is based on the researchers' knowledge of the population from which the sample is drawn and their level of experience with the study population. A purposive sample is also based on the reason or purposes for the study. For instance, if a researcher wanted to study juvenile gang leaders in Los Angeles County, California, he or she would have to select a purposive sample based on knowledge of the gangs. Researchers such as Malcolm Klein or Cheryl Maxson, who have conducted many gang studies, would probably be able to identify those who should be included in this study.[8] Klein and Maxson would be qualified experts on the gangs in Los Angeles County, California, and would likely be able to select a representative sample of gang leaders based on both their knowledge of the gangs and their contacts in the communities where gangs exist.

Let's consider an example of purposive sampling. Suppose I am interested in studying criminal justice students at the University of Baltimore. I have taught at the university for five years and have developed a reasonable understanding of the types of students the university serves and the particular problems encountered in teaching in an urban environment such as mid-town Baltimore. Suppose further that I contact the university Office for Institutional Research and asked them to provide me with basic statistics on the criminal justice majors on campus, and they give me the information listed in figure 5.5.

Because I am busy doing research and teaching I cannot study a large sample, but I believe I can select a representative sample of University of Baltimore students. I am particularly interested in the fact that only 15 percent of the students are African American. I decide that I want to know more about this portion of the student body. The purpose of my research is to understand why African American criminal justice majors select to attend the University of Baltimore rather than the two traditionally African American schools in Baltimore (Coppin State College and Morgan University). I select a purposive sample of African American criminal justice students based on my purpose, the basic research data, and my knowledge of the criminal justice program and its students generally (see figure 5.6). If I decide to study a sample of ten African American criminal justice majors, I would try to select nine males, four or five of which are practitioners and four or five between twenty-one and thirty-one years of age. While I would not select the sample in direct proportion to the statistics in figure 5.4, I would try to approach these characteristics levels. The group of students in the second column meet my requirements, so they constitute my sample. In summary, purposive sampling is a logical sample selection technique that

Figure 5.5

SELECTED CHARACTERISTICS OF CRIMINAL JUSTICE STATISTICS

90 percent male
45 percent practitioners (police and correctional officers)
40 percent 21 to 31 years of age
20 percent 32 or more years of age
15 percent African American

Figure 5.6
PURPOSIVE SAMPLING EXAMPLE

1	Bill	11	Robert	21	George
2	Bob	12	Harry	22	Gerry
3	Jack	13	Riddick	23	Jason
4	John	14	Rich	24	James
5	William	15	Abdul	25	John
6	Sam	16	Malcolm	26	Jamie
7	Shawn	17	Jesse	27	Jackson
8	John	18	Jerry		
9	Pete	19	John		
10	Paul	20	Jack		

(shaded) = selected sample

is based on the purpose of the research and knowledge of the study population.

Quota Sampling

Quota sampling is a technique that relies on the establishment of basic characteristics of the population from which one desires to draw a sample. Most, if not all, of the national polls that are taken and reported on by the national media are based on quota samples.

In order to select a quota sample, a researcher needs to clearly establish the full range of characteristics of the population about which a generalization is to be made. Organizations that regularly conduct polls, such as the Gallup, Harris and Roper, typically use samples of 50,000 or 60,000 and attempt to generalize to the general population of the United States. Results from quota-based samples should be viewed with suspicion, because they are not clearly representative of the population but merely representative of the quota characteristics that have been identified by the pollsters.

In much of the social science literature there are general and specific references to a group of variables that I call the "correlates"—age, race, education level, family situation, housing situation, urban/suburban location, and income. These variables tend in one way or another to explain social problems like criminality. This is not to say that these variables cause criminality but only that they tend to coexist with this social problem to varying degrees. In quota sampling these correlates could be used to establish the categories of each quota stratifier in the quota sampling approach. The collection of variables used to select a quota sample is labeled the "quota sampling frame." The quota sampling frame establishes the proportions of each characteristic that must be included in the sample. The subjects in the sample quotas, however, are selected not randomly but on the basis of their availability. For example, if a researcher's quota on race in the quota frame that required inclusion of fifteen Asian Americans in a survey of public attitudes toward crime, the researcher would take the first fifteen citizens of that race regardless of how representative they were of Asian Americans. If this group was collected outside of a Mercedes Benz dealership, the researcher would get a much different sample of Asian Americans than if he or she found people outside a used car lot. Quota sampling does not generally account for such differences. Quota sampling can be used to improve purposive sampling but it is still not as good as probability sampling in terms of being able to select a representative sample of the study population.

Suppose we are going to conduct a quota sample of correctional officers. There are over 300,000 correctional employees in the United States, and a unified list of correctional staff does not exist. Hence, we are forced into a nonprobability sampling technique.[9] We decide on a quota sample because we know that 70 percent of correctional staff are male and 73 percent are white.

If we presume that that gender and race are the key characteristics we would like to include in our quota sampling frame, we could select representative correctional staff from each state. Once we collected 70 percent male and 73 percent white respondents and 30 percent female and 27 percent nonwhite respondents from each staff of each sampling site (states or individual prisons), we could stop our sampling and begin our study.

Clearly, it would be difficult to collect these quotas in any nonbiased way. Moreover, the bases of race and gender alone probably are insufficient for selecting a representative sample of correctional staffs as they may vary by many other factors, such as job experience, job functions, training, state, and so on. Although quota sampling can produce reasonable samples if an accurate enough quota sampling frame is built, there is certainly no guarantee that such samples will be representative. In general, the major polling organizations in the world (Gallup, Harris, and Roper) produce fairly unbiased samples from their quota sampling frames. However, they are required to collect very large samples to accomplish this level of accuracy.

Accidental Sampling

In *accidental sampling,* a sample is selected on the basis of availability. For example, I regularly conduct pretests of surveys using students at the University of Baltimore because they are available. Accidental samples usually are not selected on the basis of either logic or probability theory but on the basis of convenience.

When I was in graduate school I regularly ate breakfast at McDonald's because it was close to my apartment, it was inexpensive and quick, and their pancakes were excellent. McDonalds often surveys its customers while they are waiting in line to determine what they like and dislike in order to make adjustments to their preparations or menu. How representative of the population are individuals waiting in line for McDonalds food? If I were McDonalds I would want to know why my roommate rarely ate breakfast at McDonalds ("Because their coffee is too hot and they never give you enough sugar"). The accidental sample that McDonalds collected on a regular basis gave them a good idea how people who patronized that particular McDonalds viewed the service or food but it would not tell them anything about other restaurants and other McDonalds in the area.

Accidental or availability samples are appropriate when a researcher is interested in pretesting a research design or survey (albeit not always) but are not appropriate for generalization purposes. For example, in my Advanced Criminal Justice Studies course I require students to conduct a mini-research project. Students construct a researchable problem based on literature or logic, create and execute a research design, describe their findings, and make several conclusions about the results of their work. The first question I ask students is: How will you select your subjects? Without fail most students tell me they will, of course, select a "random" sample. I say, "Va bene," which means "very well" in Italian. Then I ask them how they will select the subjects. About half the time they tell me they will ask students in the student lounges "at random" to participate in their study. I explain to them that without a list of the population of all student lounge users and the use of a random numbers table or computer selection process, what they think is a random sample is in fact an accidental sample. I also ask what types of people might be included in the so-called "random" sample and they often say men, women, younger students, and older students. I then respond that that sounds more like a quota sampling technique than accidental and it is certainly not random if certain types of people have an unequal chance of being included in the study sample.

You are better off collecting a sample that is based on some logical process. Subjects are included in accidental samples because of their luck (bad or good, depending upon the research) rather than because they represent some background population.

Qualitative Research Sampling

The following sections describe four commonly used *qualitative sampling techniques*. These may or may not be the best qualitative sampling techniques, but they all have been deemed appropriate in many cases where nonnumerical data are collected or where the goal of research may not be generalization to a specific population as much as it is exploration of concepts or theories based on a reasonably representative group.

Extreme Case Sampling

In *extreme case sampling* the researcher collects only those cases that are rich in information and likely to be the most informative about a particular research question or problem. The rationale is that extreme cases should help to explain both consistency and inconsistency with the research question or purpose. For example, suppose we design a research study on police arrests of minorities in Baltimore. We decide that it is likely that the three thousand or more police officers have had numerous contacts with citizens and that there is a range of police "handling" from quick and appropriate resolution of interracial situations to race riots. If we want to use extreme case sampling to conduct interviews with the police involved in interracial situations we first define well-handled interracial arrests (read rights, discussed the situation with the offender, and so on) and poorly handled arrests (use of physical force, spraying of chemical weapon inappropriately, and so on). The contrast between the well-handled arrests and poorly handled arrests is likely to provide us with many useful insights about the differences in both the situations and the officers. We select the extreme cases to learn the most about interracial arrests in Baltimore.[10]

Focus Group Sampling

Focus group sampling is regularly used by pollsters and marketing businesses. The subjects for this type of sampling are selected because they are similar. The goal is to understand as much as possible about the opinions or perspectives of the subsamples of subjects. Typically more than one focus group is studied, and the information from all such groups is combined to form an overall view of these different groups toward the topic of interest. The focus group sampling technique uses group interviews with between five and ten people on specific issues that affect them or their functional roles.

If we are interested in studying how people view the selection of trial judges (i.e., election, appointment, merit), we might interview several focus groups. We could, for instance, construct groups of prosecutors, defense attorneys, citizens, and judges and focus on the issue of appointment. The individuals in each of these focus groups would be selected because we believe them to be representative of the group of which they are members. The idea behind focus groups is that each group will have a different perspective of the issue.

Criterion Sampling

Criterion sampling is a special case of the extreme case sampling approach. In criterion sampling, the researcher determines a specific criterion as the basis for selecting subjects to be interviewed or studied. In the industrial world criterion sampling is commonly used to assure the quality of a product. For example, if the weight of cases of beer on the bottling line in a certain brewery drops below 288 ounces, those cases are sampled to determine if there is a problem with the production process. Here criterion sampling focuses on the cases because they are indicative of system or functional problems and can suggest program or theory development.

A criminal justice example of criterion sampling is the study of recidivism (rearrests) of program participants. Suppose that we are interested in evaluating an education program that attempts to facilitate community reintegration for several groups of half-way house inmates in locations throughout the city. If we used rearrests as a measure of success we could base our criterion sample on a specific failure level in order to better understand who fails. Then we could develop programs to reduce the numbers of these failures. Our criterion in this case could be: when more than four of the twenty half-way house residents are arrested, that program would be selected for qualitative study.

Snowball Sampling

Snowball sampling is a developmental process of sampling wherein earlier subjects give insights into the selection of subsequent subjects. That is, the initial subjects are asked to refer the researcher to other subjects and the sample is incrementally built to the desired size.

The use of snowball sampling is common in qualitative research on gangs. For example, Hagedorn conducted an in-depth study of the gangs in Milwaukee, Wisconsin, in 1987. He selected his initial subject by questioning gang members he identified through his work with the criminal justice system. Then he asked the gang members he interviewed who should be interviewed next. His study is an excellent, and detailed, account of gang activities, membership, and problems in Milwaukee. It is very unlikely that he could have conducted his study without the use of snowball sampling.

Sample Size Considerations

A question my students often ask is: "How large should the sample size be?" As I see it, there are three ways to determine the *sample size.* The first way is relatively easy to state: Collect as large a sample as you can given your time and material constraints. Generally, the larger the sample you can collect, the better the data will be. This has a probability basis in that larger samples tend to be a closer approximation of the variation and characteristics of the population.

A second way to determine the size of the sample necessary for a particular study is to use logical reasoning based on the specific project at hand. Consider the size of the population, the potential amount of variation in the subjects, and the nature of the study.

Where the population is large, the sample should be relatively large. For example, if you are interested in studying the attitudes of citizens in

Philadelphia, Pennsylvania (population of over 2 million), toward the police, you should select a larger sample than if you want to study a small town such as Kingston, Pennsylvania (population 34,000). This is necessary because there tends to be many more differences in larger populations than in smaller populations. The simple fact of numbers is that a 1 percent sample of Philadelphia is 20,000 citizens, whereas a 1 percent sample of Kingston is only 340 citizens.

It is also important to have a sufficient amount of variation in the data that is largely tied to the sample size. That is, the data should have at least as much variation as there is in the population. If there is little or no variation in the data, then the variables collected will be constants and will allow you to explain very little. The control and explanation of variation and variables is perhaps one of the key activities in most criminal justice and criminological research.

In the study of citizen's attitudes toward police in Philadelphia, a small sample of a traditional Italian-American neighborhood in South Philadelphia may not have much variation because people may have very similar attitudes toward the police. This is not to say that all Italian Americans have the same viewpoint, but the selected neighborhood is more homogeneous than most other areas in the city and is not representative of the entire population of Philadelphia. To increase the representativeness of the sample it makes more sense to sample citizens from each of the neighborhoods in the city to ensure that the actual differences are reflected in the data that are collected.

The third logical basis for sample size selection is the purpose of the study. If you are interested in determining how a specific group within the population views some issue, then the sample could be smaller than if you want to study a total population. For example, if a researcher wants to study the attitudes of inmates on death row about the forms of execution, the sample would be smaller than if he or she wants to study the attitudes of all inmates toward forms of execution.

The fourth way to determine the appropriate sample size is to use accepted quantitative estimation techniques. The available quantitative estimations of the sample size focus on the issue of power. That is, they are based on the desire to not reject a research hypothesis when it is true. Most statistical tests (see chapter 12) focus on the believability of the null hypothesis (e.g., there is no difference in the average age of male and female burglars) rather than the alternative or research hypothesis (e.g., there is a difference in the average age of male and female burglars). Probability theory and inferential statistical tests allow us to determine if our null hypothesis is believable given our sample data. Thus, after testing with our statistical measure and using an appropriate probability value, we can only decide whether to believe or not believe the null hypothesis that the average ages are different.

If we reject the null hypothesis we typically believe that we have support for our alternative—in this example, that there is a difference in the average ages of male and female burglars. This decision is based only on the sample we collect and a typical value we could expect based on the sample size and characteristics (probability value). It does not take into consideration whether the sample is of sufficient size. The power of a test, which is crucial in determining the necessary sample size, is the percentage of times we will reject a false null hypothesis or keep a hypothesis that is incorrect.

Let's take an example of quantitative sample size determination. The four considerations that must be taken into account in the determination of sample size are (1) significance level, (2) the power of the test, (3) an estimate of population variance, and (4) the effect size (Hinkle, Wiersma, and Jurs, 1994). We decide to study male and female burglars and believe that a five-year difference in ages is an important difference. We then predetermine the sample size needed for our study before we go through the trouble of selecting it.[11] We could then use the Hinkle, Wiersma, and Jurs (HWJ) formula to determine the sample size (figure 5.7).

Based on the past population variation and the presumed effect size a sample of fifteen or more would be necessary to produce an 80 percent power to detect a three-year difference in ages of burglars. While the issue of power may be confusing and is beyond the scope of an introductory research methods text, the considerations of the appropriate sample size are crucial to research studies and should be addressed in as objective a manner as possible.

Figure 5.7

DETERMINING QUANTITATIVE SAMPLE SIZE

What is known about the research situation

1. Past studies have shown burglars' ages vary by 4.65 years (σ^2).
2. Significance level (α) = .05 (We will make errors about our decision about the null 5% of the time)
3. Power (1 − 4(α)) = .80 (We will be correct about the null 80% of the time (β = .20)
4. We presume that a 3-year difference is important.

$$\text{sample size} = \frac{\sigma^2(z_\beta - z_\alpha)^2}{(ES)^2}$$

where:

σ^2 = 4.65

z_β = −.842 (z value at .20)

z_α = 1.645 (z value at .05)

ES = 5 years

$$\text{sample size} = \frac{4.65^2 - (-.842 - 1.645)^2}{(3)^2}$$

sample size = 14.86 or 15

Summary

This chapter provides examples and explanations of the most common qualitative and quantitative sampling techniques in the social sciences. The techniques of sampling are crucial for the subsequent considerations of data collection and analysis. Nowhere is the saying "garbage in, garbage out" more appropriate. If a researcher does not take the time to select the best possible sample for the purposes of the research at hand, then the data collection and analysis phases are more likely to be flawed and problematic. The issue of the size of the sample is also important and should be carefully considered.

Main Concepts

probability sampling
simple random sampling
stratified random sampling
quota sampling
extreme case sampling
qualitative sampling techniques
criterion sampling
sample size

nonprobability sampling
systematic random sampling
purposive sampling
accidental sampling
quantitative sampling techniques
sampling interval
focus group sampling
snowball sampling

Discussion Questions

1. Which sampling techniques are considered to be the best? Why?
2. Why would quota sampling be inaccurate?
3. Can you think of an example of a study in criminal justice or criminology that would use snowball sampling?
4. Discuss the differences between probability and nonprobability sampling.
5. Discuss the differences between quantitative and qualitative sampling.
6. Speculate about the necessary stratifiers in a study of police officers.

Exercise

Select a population of about fifteen students and practice selecting samples of five students using simple random sampling, systematic sampling, and stratified sampling based on gender. Discuss how representative each sample is in reference to the "population." Speculate about ways to improve the representativeness of the samples.

6

EXPERIMENTAL DESIGNS

Learning Objectives

1. To define the pre-experimental designs
2. To explain the classical experiment design
3. To explain the quasi-experimental designs
4. To explain the main variations on the classical design
5. To discuss internal validity problems that are particularly relevant to experimental designs

Chapter Outline

Introduction
Single Group Experimental Designs
Single Group Design
Pretest and Posttest Design
Posttest Only Design
The Classical Experiment
Matching
Randomization
Variations on the Classical Design
Solomon Four-Group Design
Factorial Design
Quasi-Experimental Designs
Contrasted Design
Time-Series Designs
Validity Problems
External Validity
Internal Validity
History
Maturation
Experimental Mortality
Instrumentation
Testing
Summary
Main Concepts
Discussion Questions
Exercises

CHAPTER SIX

Introduction

The experimental design has been presumed to be one of the most powerful approaches one can take to research in the social sciences. This has been the case because experimental designs help establish cause-and-effect relationships between variables and phenomena. That is, experiments can establish whether a particular independent variable is related to a dependent variable and whether there are other variables that could explain the relationship between the two or more variables. Hence, we can meet the criteria for the establishment of causation: time ordering, relationship, and non-spuriousness (i.e., we can isolate causes from rival possible explainors).

The experimental design has also been presumed to be the ideal design given its ability to control irrelevant variables and to focus on specific co-variation between particular dependent and independent variables. Some researchers believe that the experimental design is the best approach for conducting accurate and consistent research. But even though the experimental design has brought great improvements in knowledge in some research areas, this has not been the case for all experimental studies, particularly criminal justice and criminological research. The execution of a classical experimental design in "real world" criminal justice agencies is difficult to complete. Yet, the experimental design is a powerful research design and just because it is difficult to achieve in a pure sense does not mean that it lacks value or should not be attempted where it is appropriate.

The basis of the experimental design can be seen in the procedures and techniques of research developed by the "hard scientists" of the last century.[1] In sciences such as chemistry and physics it is easy to isolate samples and to control variables, and therefore to conduct true experiments. This is not the case in the real world of social science and criminal justice, where true or "classical" experimental designs must be adjusted for research purposes and variables in criminological and criminal justice research settings.

The following sections in this chapter discuss the pre-experimental, classical experimental, and quasi-experimental designs. These designs are discussed in this order to clarify what has been done with these approaches as well as to keep them clearly separated. In each case, specific examples of the approaches are provided and illustrated.

Single Group Experimental Designs

Single group experimental designs are simplified versions of the true classical experimental designs. They are appropriate research designs in some situations, but they do not approach the power of classical models to control and assess research. Cook and Campbell (1979) list these designs not because they are particularly good but because they are common approaches. They are a good place to begin to learn the concepts of experimentation. These pre-experimental approaches, however, are not recommended by researchers (Babbie, 1989; Nachmias and Nachmias, 1981; Fitzgerald and Cox, 1987).

This section discusses the single group study, the pretest and posttest study, and the posttest only study approaches to pre-experimentation. The following descriptions focus on the essential elements of each of these models by providing visual examples. But you should not emulate these designs. It is important to understand these pre-experimental designs only insofar as they help you to design experimental studies and to understand the limitations of these approaches.

Single Group Design

The *single group design* is sometimes referred to as the "one-shot case study" (see Babbie, 1989; Nachmias and Nachmias, 1981; Hagan, 1993). The single group design examines the effects of an independent variable on a dependent variable over time. Figure 6.1 shows a graphic mode of the single group design.

In the single group design the effects of treatment are measured after it is applied to the study group. In experimental designs it is presumed that the treatment process (i.e., independent variable, stimulus, or criterion variable) causes the changes in the study subjects. The single group, or one-shot, pre-experimental design is the simple assessment of the effects of treatment after the fact. For example, we might assess the effects of a Narcotics Anonymous program with inmates with such a design because we would have no easily identified control group and because this program is voluntary.[2] No measures are taken of the study subjects before they participate in Narcotics Anonymous. The single group design is acceptable for exploratory or pilot studies, but it is generally a weak design.

Pretest and Posttest Design

The *pretest and posttest design* tests or measures the key variables of interest before any treatment is given to the study subjects. Once the treatment is given the study subjects are remeasured or tested to determine if there has been a change. The treatment can be viewed as the independent variable, and the change is measured in terms of the dependent variable. Figure 6.2 shows an example of a pretest and posttest design.

In the pretest and posttest design one measures the existence of the dependent condition in the subjects before a treatment is given. For example, I surmised, based on conversations with prison officials in Florida and Pennsylvania, that inmates who are in vocational educational programs are more manageable in the prison. If I were to examine this idea with a pretest

Figure 6.1
SINGLE GROUP DESIGN

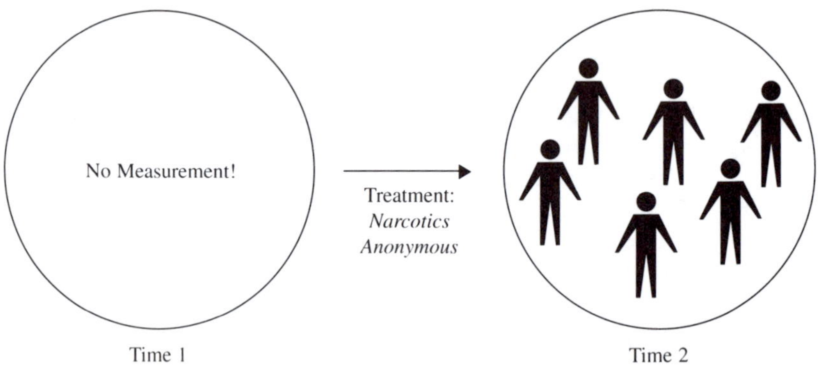

Figure 6.2
PRETEST AND POSTTEST DESIGN

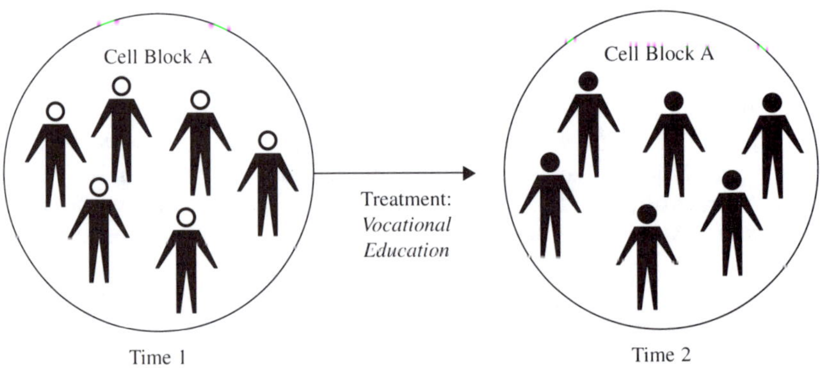

and posttest design I would assess the "manageability" of the inmates both before and after they participated in a vocational education program (figure 6.2). The concept of manageability could be measured through the number of rule violations of the inmates in the program. Hence, "manageability" is dependent upon the amount of hours in vocational education programs. This design allows you to demonstrate that the effect (manageability) is the direct result of the treatment (vocational education).

There are several problems with the pretest and posttest design. First, the changes in manageability may be related to factors other than the vocational education. That is, inmates in vocational education may be more manageable because they are older inmates who are serving long sentences, exactly the types of inmates that tend to be most easily managed. Second, the vocational educational programs indirectly teach students to cooperate and to share equipment and this indirect training may influence the inmates who participate in these programs to be more manageable outside of the programs. The content of the educational programs in this case may have little or nothing to do with the reductions in rule violations (manageability).

Posttest Only Design

The *posttest only design* is similar to the single group design in that it only measures the effects of the treatment after the fact. However, it is different from the single group design in that it includes a comparison group. It is typical for the two posttest groups not to be assigned on the basis of randomization or matching. Therefore, these groups are not necessarily equivalent but are usually pre-existing groups before the study (e.g., cell blocks). Figure 6.3 shows a posttest only design.

Perhaps the largest disadvantage with the posttest only design is that the two groups may not be equivalent. For instance, the inmates in cell block A could be short-term inmates whereas those housed in cell block B could be serving life sentences. The posttest design is clearly an improvement over the other pre-experimental designs but it still has weaknesses. This leads us to the ideal experimental model in the classical experimental model.

The Classical Experiment

The classical experimental model involves the use of an experimental group and a control group. Both groups are comparable in terms of characteristics such as age, race, offense history, gender, and so on. The experimental group is exposed to the treatment and the control group is not. Measurements are taken of the experimental group and the control group both before treatment and after treatment. The differences found in the experimental group that are not also present in the control group are generally attributed to the influence of the treatment.

Figure 6.3
POSTTEST ONLY DESIGN

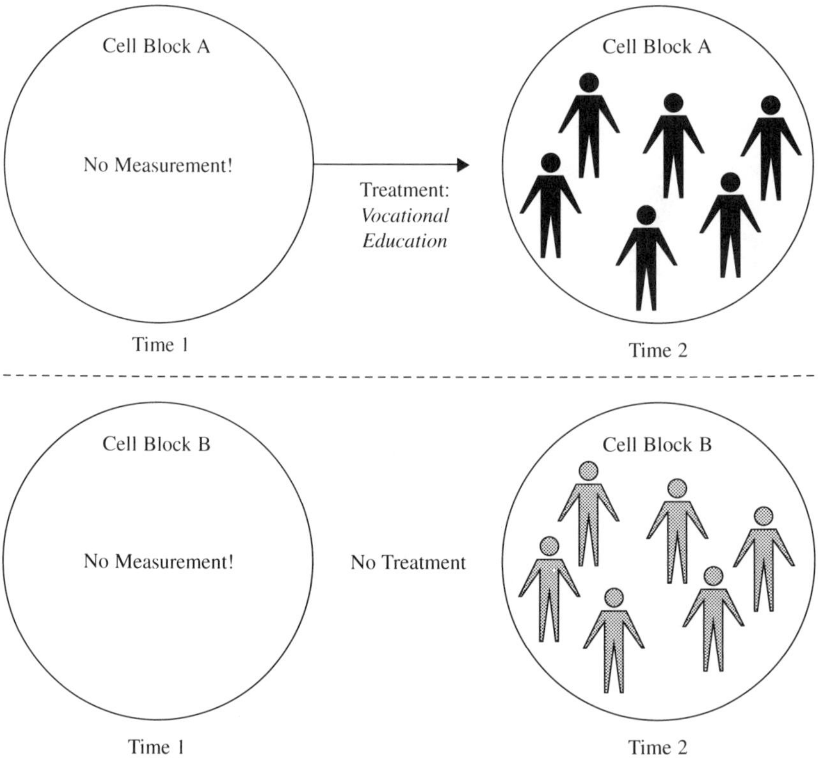

The addition of the control group in the classical experimental design is crucial to improving both the strength and power of the research results from this model. The control group allows researchers to say that "all things being equal" the treatment appears to influence, or even cause, the changes in the study subjects.

The *classical experiment* meets the three causal criterion. First, the treatment that is presumed to have an effect occurs before the measured effects. For example, we could measure the blood pressure of police officers before and after they take a course in stress reduction to determine if the training has had any effect. The control group would not take the course. We use it to determine if the officers' stress would have gone down anyway due to factors other than taking the course.

Second, and implicit in the example I have been developing, is that the course in stress reduction is related to reduced levels of stress in the police officers (i.e., those who participate in the course will have less stress). Finally, the control group allows us to rule out other causal factors, because the control group is equivalent to the experimental group. Hence, if both groups are essentially the same, other than that one group participates in the stress reduction course, then any other variables that tend to reduce stress will act on both groups. The only difference related to stress reduction can be attributed to the course the experimental group took. Figure 6.4 shows the classical experimental design. The top half of the figure shows that the experimental police officers are given a stress course (the treatment). It is presumed if the stress reduction course causes reduced stress there will be a change in these officers. The lower part of the figure (the control group) shows that no treatment is given to this group of officers. Stress is measured before and after the experimental group officers take the stress course.

Figure 6.4

THE CLASSICAL EXPERIMENTAL MODEL

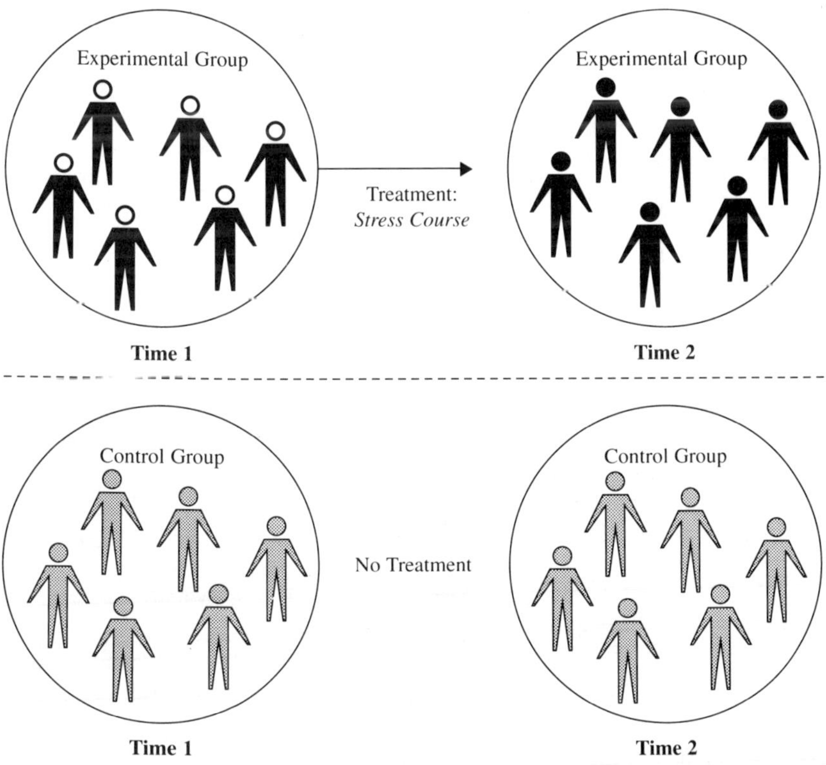

Matching

One way to insure that the experimental and control groups are similar is through a technique called *matching.* When matching or randomizing, we attempt to assign subjects to both the experimental and control groups so that the differences in the groups are minimal. Matching involves the use of knowledge about variables that are related to the research at hand. We want to make sure that the proportions of these variables are the same, or very similar, in both the experimental and control groups.

One method for matching subjects in the experimental and control groups involves assessing particular cases and assigning like cases to each group. Assume that we are doing a study of the gang activities of males. Certain variables are important in such a study—race, gender, age, and residence. We could use these variables to select the control and experimental groups. For example, if a white male, between eighteen and twenty-four years of age, from the inner city is assigned to the experimental group a similar person should be assigned to the control group. This technique is known as "pairwise matching." It is sometimes quite difficult to include all the relevant and important variables in such a selection process, and it would be a tedious job to use this approach on a large sample.

We could select subjects for the control and experimental groups based on the general characteristics of our study population. That is, if the study population is 56 percent male, then the control and experimental groups should have 56 percent males. The focus in this second approach (known as listwise matching) is on the general characteristics of the two groups.

The problem with both methods of matching is that we are never quite sure that all of the important variables are taken into account. We are not sure that the control and experimental groups are equivalent. The differences found after the treatment is applied may therefore be due to these differences and not the effects of the experiment.

Randomization

The second general approach to selecting subjects for the control and experimental groups, and one that is generally considered to be superior to matching, is *randomization.* The big benefit in using a randomization procedure is that the effects of other variables are virtually eliminated by assigning cases, and therefore characteristics, at random to the control and experimental groups. Because randomization is based on probability theory, we would expect the important characteristics to be evenly distributed across the two study groups.

Randomization can be accomplished by simply flipping a coin for each case—heads means assignment to the experimental group and tails means assignment to the control group. We can also use a random numbers table, calculator, or computer to assign cases.

Variations on the Classical Design

The classical experimental model has also been built upon to improve and focus the analyses researchers wish to conduct. Three of these extensions will be described and illustrated.

Solomon Four-Group Design

The idea behind the *Solomon four-group design* is that pretesting subjects influences how they perform after the treatment and this effect is independent of the other treatment effects. That is, simply pretesting subjects may influence how they perform on posttest measures. People tend to figure out what it is we are looking for in our research, and the more opportunities we give them to do so, the more likely it is they will tell us what we want to hear.

For example, suppose we are interested in studying prejudice of male inmates toward female correctional officers because we believe we have come up with an improved orientation to prison that reduces this form of prejudice. Pretests include questions about the female staff and inmates views about these staff. Inmates may decide that it is better to tell us what we want to hear rather than their true feelings, because what they say may affect them in some way. They may also tell us what we want to hear because the inmate culture prohibits cooperation with researchers. Either way the pretesting may affect how the subjects perform on the experiment separate from the treatment effects.

The Solomon four-group design was created to avoid or reduce the effects of the pretesting in an experiment. This design includes the same elements as the classical experimental design. However, the addition of a second set of control and experimental groups is intended to improve the design. Figure 6.5 illustrates this design. In essence, the Solomon design can show whether the independent variable, or treatment, had an effect even without the pretest. This creates the added benefit that the results of this design can be generalized to populations that were not measured prior to exposure to the treatment. The replication of treatments also strengthens the power of the conclusions from this model. Hence, Campbell and Stanley suggest that the instabilities of experimentation are such that if these comparisons are in agreement, the strength of the inferences is greatly increased (1963, p. 25).

Factorial Design

Another extention of the classical experimental design is the *factorial design.* Researchers are usually interested in the effects of several treatments on dependent variable simultaneously rather than the simple effect of one independent variable. In addition, the advent of modern mainframe and

Figure 6.5
SOLOMON FOUR-GROUP DESIGN

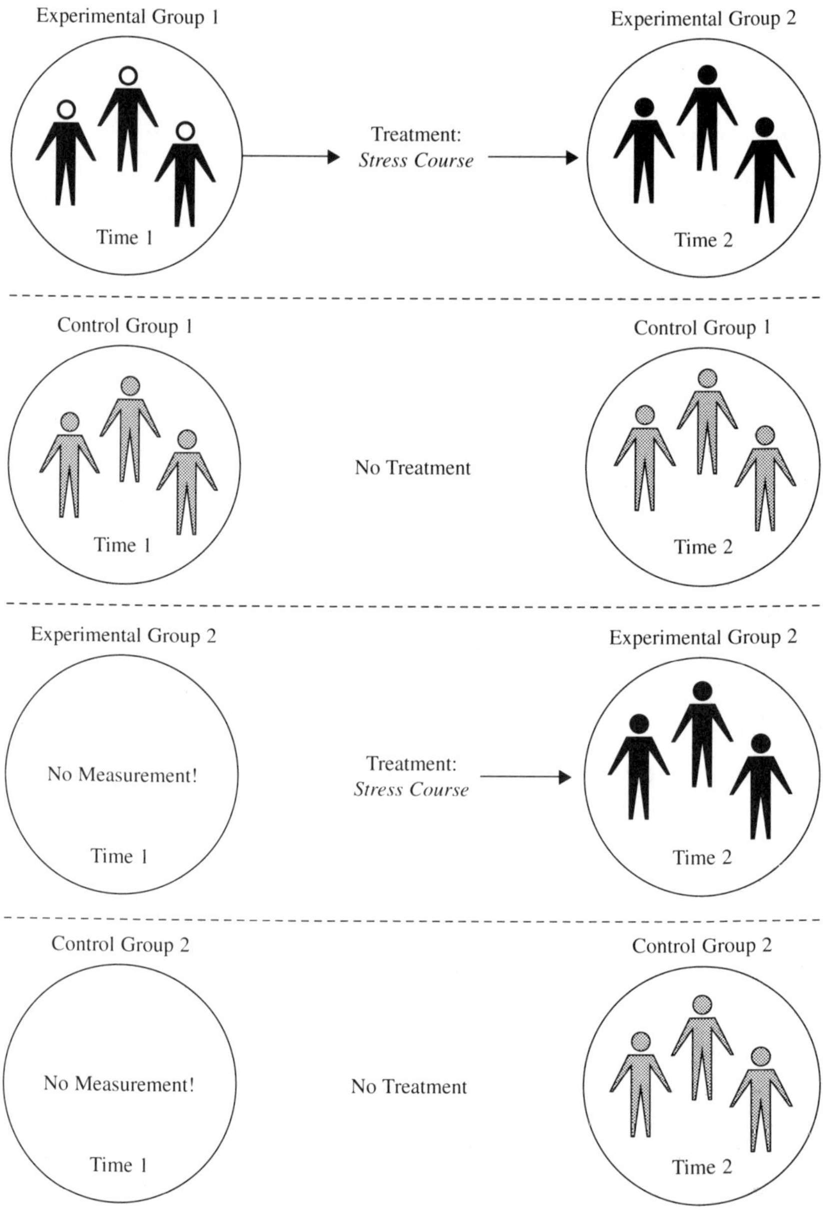

microcomputing for statistical analysis of factorial models has improved the details of these studies. Researchers that conduct experimental designs tend to use these factorial models to get the biggest bang for their research and data collection buck. Instead of studying each independent variable effect on the dependent variable separately, the researcher combines the treatments into a factorial design. The big advantage in factorial designs is that they allow broader generalization because the additional independent variables are added to the model.

Factorial designs and the analysis of variance (i.e., ANOVA) have been developed in the field of psychometrics and psychology. These research designs and analysis approaches have a well-developed history and are used to great benefit in factorial research designs. Figure 6.6 illustrates a factorial model. There are two treatments, or independent variables, a stress reduction class and an exercise program, in this design. The figure shows that a portion of each group of the two types of officers (high and low stress) is given the two treatments. In the factorial model, we can assess which treatment has the best stress reduction effects. Further, we can determine whether the combination or interaction of treatments works better than one treatment alone. The second dimension (high stress versus low stress) also adds another range of possibilities for assessing how the different treatments affect the different stress levels and which individual treatment or combination of treatments reduces stress levels best.

Figure 6.6
FACTORIAL DESIGN

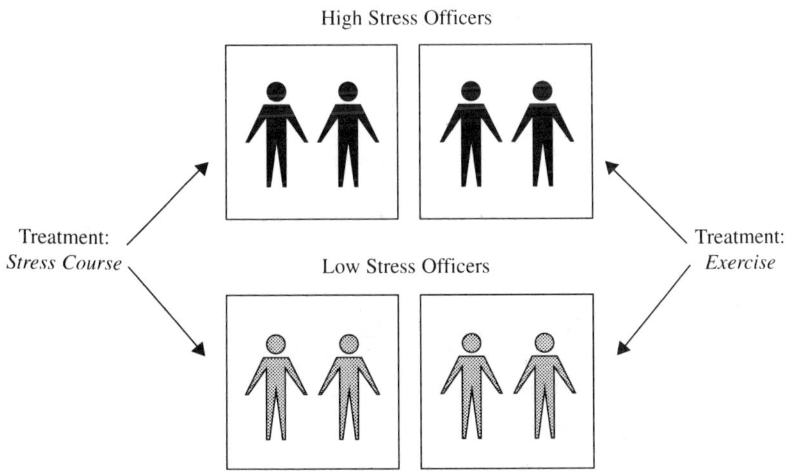

Quasi-Experimental Designs

Researchers have developed additional experimental models because it is not always possible to control external and internal conditions sufficiently to conduct a classical experiment. For example, it is sometimes difficult, if not impossible, to use random sampling in operational criminal justice agencies. Or, experimental designs may be too intrusive. While the *quasi-experimental designs* are not as powerful as the experimental designs, they are more powerful than the pre-experimental designs and those approaches that are less consistent with the classical experimental model. Another aspect of the quasi-experimental design that is attractive for criminal justice researchers is that these designs do not require randomization.

Contrasted Design

Perhaps the biggest limitation in using experimental designs in most criminal justice settings is that cases cannot be randomly assigned. It would be difficult, for example, to randomly assign burglars to prison or probation to determine which correctional "treatment" is more effective. Given that such assignment cannot be done, a researcher that surmises that the effects of prisons on burglars, car thieves and drunk drivers are different would need to adjust the traditional experimental model, because random assignment cannot be completed. The researcher would simply compare the separate groups on the treatment or independent variable of interest to determine whether there are important differences (see figure 6.7).

One method of adjustment of the traditional experimental model is the *contrasted design.* In the contrasted design we select members of different clearly defined groups. For example, burglars are clearly different than drunk drivers or car thieves in terms of the offense they have committed. We then measure the effects of prison, perhaps in terms of the recidivism rates, for each of the groups. In this example, the recidivism rates would measure the treatment effects—the effect of prison.

This design is sometimes problematic, because the groups are likely to be different on many other variables than just their recidivism rates. There are differences in burglars and drunk drivers in that the former group tends to be older, male, and imprisoned in the past (Bureau of Justice Statistics, 1990) whereas the latter group may have higher incomes and not be involved in any other criminal activities. These differences can be controlled by making sure the subjects in each group are similar on the variables other than the independent variable of interest. The biggest benefit of the contrasted design is that it allows us to take preexisting categorical groups and study them in a quasi-experimental design.

Time-Series Design

A *time-series design* is appropriate where we have identified an experimental group but there is no comparison group. Instead of comparing the treatment effects in the time-series design with a control group, we compare the effects over time on the same group. These designs are also important to the establishment of longer term effects of treatments because there are several follow-up measurements. Time-series designs can also be used to establish the future rate of demand on criminal justice services and organizations based on existing series. That is, we can plot a future time-series for a specific jail population to determine the potential future needs.

For example, figure 6.8 shows a potential time-series design. In this quasi-experimental design police officers are given training to improve their

Figure 6.7
CONTRASTED DESIGN EXAMPLE

Burglers

Thieves

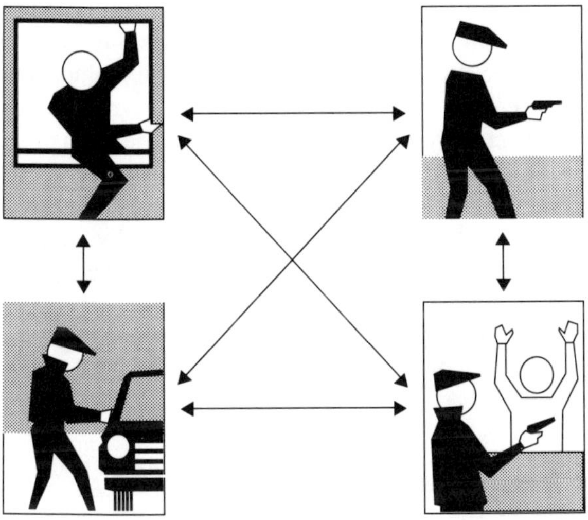

Car Thieves

Bank Robbers

Figure 6.8
TIME-SERIES DESIGN EXAMPLE

Time 1

Time 2

Time 3

Treatment:
Vehicle Pursuit Training

vehicular pursuit driving techniques. The figure shows three follow-up measurements instead of one as in the classical experimental design. If you were a chief of police, you would want to see continual improvements in the ability of officers after such training. If improved driving, and perhaps fewer accidents, did not occur, you might consider adding an additional refresher course for the officers. You would probably want all of your officers who drive vehicles to go through the training because of the liability of the department. Hence, you would not have a comparison group. Therefore, the comparisons over time in the improvement of driving can be accomplished through sequential study of the trained officers.

Time-series designs are not common in criminal justice and criminological research. This may be due to the time and costs of conducting research in criminal justice settings or it may be due to the dynamic nature of the primary study subjects (i.e., offenders or inmates). Perhaps the lack of time-series designs in criminal justice and criminological research is due to the level of statistical sophistication that is needed to conduct time-series analyses. Although each of these reasons is valid, the most likely reason for the lack of time-series designs is that they are difficult to conduct without open cooperation and persistently interested researchers.

There are several other quasi-experimental designs.[3] All of these approaches are useful when there is some reason why we cannot collect a control or comparison group or we cannot randomly assign individuals to the experimental or control groups. While quasi-experimental designs are not as strong as the classical experimental approaches, they are a reasonable compromise to achieve experimental goals of establishing cause and effect.

Validity Problems

One of the issues that must be discussed in connection with experimental designs is the accuracy (validity) of the findings from such models. Experimental designs are used in an attempt to deal with the many problems in conducting cause and effect studies. The following sections describe some of these problems as well as how experimental designs help handle or reduce their effects. In general, the inaccuracy of experimental designs can arise from factors that are external to the research design (i.e., external validity) and that are related to the design itself (internal validity).

External Validity

External validity problems in experiments, and other research approaches, can arise from errors or sampling problems. For instance, suppose you were doing research based on the classical experimental model and you used simple random or systematic processes for assigning cases to the experimental and control groups. If you relied on the systematic method and there were some biases in your list (e.g., every fifth name on the list was a supervisor), then your experiment would have external invalidity. It would be inaccurate because the subjects you brought to the experiment were selected with a systematic bias.

In addition, if you relied on the matching technique, wherein you matched the control and experimental groups on the basis of gender, age, race, and income but failed to match them on other factors, your experiment could suffer from "selection bias"—the control and experimental groups were different before the experiment even began. For example, suppose we selected control and experimental groups of police officers on the basis of gender, race, age, and years of service for a study of police productivity (i.e., number of arrests, convictions from arrests, and so on). Even though the percentages of men and women, different races, ages, and years of service are the same in the control and experimental groups, other factors may not be evenly distributed across the groups. The experimental group could have a higher proportion of officers who serve on the third shift, when most arrests occur, than the control group. There could be other reasons for the differences that were not considered in the selection of members of the control and experimental groups, that is, there could be other sources of external invalidity.

The assignment of subjects to the control and experimental groups should be done with care. If a random technique is used, the list relied upon should be unbiased, and the technique for selection of subjects for each group should be logical and scientific. It is usually easier for a researcher to control for these "selection bias" problems than to control for the sources of internal validity.

Internal Validity

Internal invalidity occurs when the experimental or control subjects are influenced by the research experiment itself rather than by the research treatment or stimulus. The five most common sources of internal invalidity are history, maturation, experimental mortality, instrumentation, and testing.

History. During the course of conducting an experiment, certain events that take place outside of the experiment may influence experimental performance. For example, suppose we are conducting an experiment to reintegrate offenders back into the community through the provision of job counseling and job location services (treatments). If, during the time of our experiment, the economy began to turn toward recession, the effectiveness of our efforts and the treatments would probably be weakened, and results may be tainted by the changes in the economy rather than the effectiveness or lack of effectiveness of our treatments.

The longer the period between the initial measurements (i.e., pretest) and the final measurements (i.e., posttests), the more likely that the effects of history will enter into considerations of the interpretation of experimental results. To counteract the effects of history, experiments use pretests and control groups. The pretests or measurements taken at time 1 help establish the base-line performance, such as the level of employment of the inmates before they were incarcerated. Thus, even if the economy changes there is likely to be some change from the base line established by the pretest measures. The control group also helps to reduce the effects of history in that the control group is not given the benefit of the treatment and in a recession is at an even larger disadvantage than the experimental group.

Maturation. Another problem with experimental subjects, and people in particular, is that they change both physically and psychologically over time. People may mature over the course of a study to the point of influencing the experiment. Suppose you are studying juvenile delinquents from onset of delinquency to their adulthood. You would probably start with youths in their early teens and end up with young adults in their late teens and early twenties. The attitudes of a thirteen-year-old are very different from those of an eighteen-year-old, regardless of the focus of the study. These changes in maturity would influence the results of your experiment.

People also get tired. For example, in an experiment of police training on a computerized firing range, you could not test the officers for four hours straight with no break because there are few who would have the physical strength to complete such a rigorous testing schedule.

Experiments attempt to reduce the effects of maturation by using control groups who also mature. The difference between the experimental and control groups should be attributed to the treatment and not the fact that the study subjects got tired or bored. The effects of maturation are serious and should be considered in making claims of causation in any experimental results.

Experimental Mortality. Study subjects may decide they have had enough and drop out of the study, or may be for some other reason unavailable after the pretest measure for the subsequent follow-up study measurement. One of the key principles in modern research ethics is to not force subjects to stay in an experiment should they decide they no longer wish to participate (see chapter 13). Most ethical researchers, in fact, give subjects the opportunity to withdraw from participation in study at any point, at the subjects' choosing. This validity problem could be very damaging to experimental results should the "dropouts" be significantly different from those who decide to remain in the experiment. The most common way to prevent mortality is to fully inform the subjects before the experiment about the nature and time commitments involved in participation in the study so they can make an informed decision about whether they wish to participate in the study or not. Additionally, some researchers that conduct experiments collect larger samples than is necessary so the data collected over the course of the study will not be as damaged by a few dropouts.

Instrumentation. Changes in the use of measurement instruments (surveys, questionnaires, interview guidelines, and so on) can also influence the accuracy of the experimental data that are collected. Typically, the experimental research design includes provisions for pretesting and posttesting with the same survey. For example, if I were to test your opinions about the death penalty before and after I gave you a lecture sensitizing you to the racial imbalances in executions in the United States, I would have to use the same test before and after the lecture to determine whether my "racial imbalance" lecture influenced your opinions. If I used two different measurement methods, a survey before the class and a discussion about the death penalty after the lecture, the differences in your opinions may be attributed to the use of different instrumentation rather than actual changes in your opinions. Needless to say, in well-designed experimental research, the same instruments are used in the posttests as were used in pretests.

Testing. The effects of testing or measurement may also influence experimental or research results. I consistently track my students performance each time they take a course from me. I have found that students who have taken my courses the most, regardless of their grade-point averages, do better on my tests than those who are taking my class for the first time. Students who learn my test design and approach tend to do better than those who have not had the benefit of prior tests.[4] The invalidity problem of "testing" is that the simple attempt to measure the variables of interest may influence the results of experiments. Subjects may score better because they become skilled at taking your surveys or figure out what it is you want them to say.

One way to reduce the effects of pretesting or testing is to rely on a Solomon four-group or a factorial model. While most of the preexperimental models avoid the pretesting phase, they are not recommended because they suffer from other invalidity problems. In the Solomon four-group design, an experimental and control group without pretests are included in an attempt to measure the effects of pretesting. These nonpretest groups can be compared to the pretested control and experimental groups to assess the effects of testing. Factorial designs also allow one to isolate the effects of testing by including groups that were either not pretested or tested several times. While there are other factors that may influence the validity of experiments, those listed are the most typical and most damaging to the results.

Summary

This chapter discusses and illustrates the most common preexperimental (single group) designs, the classical experimental design as well as the most common variations on that design. The structure of several quasi-experimental designs are also shown. The problems of external and internal validity are explained and discussed.

Main Concepts

single-group experiment
pretest and posttest design
classical experiment
matching
factorial design
contrasted design
validity problems
internal validity
maturation
instrumentation

single group design
posttest only design
randomization
Solomon four-group design
quasi-experimental designs
time-series design
external validity
history
experimental mortality
testing

Discussion Questions

1. Discuss the problems with a single group design as opposed to a simple pretest-posttest design.
2. Why are the single group experimental designs inferior to the classical design?
3. What is the essence of the factorial design?
4. What is the essence of the Solomon four-group design?
5. Which is more problematic for an experiment—the effects of history or subject selection? Why?

Exercises

1. Design a classical experiment to study citizens' attitudes toward the death penalty related to a sensitivity training program (of your design). How will the subjects be selected, what are your validity problems, what is the treatment, and what would you expect to find?

2. Conduct an experiment in class. Pretest the entire class on their opinions about their classmates. Select half the class to leave for twenty minutes. Have the remaining students introduce themselves to each other and talk a little bit about their educational and life goals. Retest the entire group and report the outcome.

7

SURVEY RESEARCH

Learning Objectives

1. To describe the processes of survey construction and administration
2. To provide specific examples of survey questions and guidelines for development
3. To describe interview approaches
4. To discuss telephone interview methods.
5. To provide examples and discuss the advantages and disadvantages of self-report questionnaires, telephone surveys, and interviews

Chapter Outline

Introduction
Self-Report Questionnaires
Questionnaire Creation Guidelines
Format Guidelines
Pretesting
Types of Questions
Closed-Ended Questions
Open-Ended Questions
Contingency Questions
Matrix Questions
Questionnaire Administration
Response Rates
Advantages and Disadvantages of Questionnaires
Telephone Surveys
Telephone Interview Schedules
Selection of Subjects
Computer-Assisted Telephone Surveys
Interview Surveys
Interview Schedules
Structured Interview
Semi-Structured Interview
Limited Structure Interview
Interview Questions
Interview Administration
Summary
Main Concepts
Discussion Questions
Exercises

CHAPTER SEVEN

Introduction

The most typical image students have of research methods is that of the self-report survey; respondents select from among preexisting categories and fill in the requested data. These types of surveys are common data collection tools in sociology and psychology, and they have recently become more common in criminal justice and criminological research. Earl Babbie, who many in the social sciences regard as one of the "fathers" of modern sociological research methods, provides a description of the history of survey research for social science in general. He explains that survey research is based on the experiences of (1) censuses of the population by government, (2) the work of pollsters like Gallup, Roper, and Harris, and (3) the work of academics in university-based research (Babbie, 1989). Many in the academic community have been developing and executing survey research designs for purposes beyond university-based research. Because criminal justice and criminology are fields that came into being rather recently, the scientific bases established by sociology, psychology, and political science for their research methods provide a foundation for scientific studies by criminologists and those who study criminal justice.

There is also a well-documented developmental history of survey research approaches. Yet this documentation has not been applied to criminal justice settings, organizations, or applications even though surveys have been used for over three decades. Thus, while survey research methods have a long history in some fields, they have not been considerate of the specific problems and prospects of criminal justice organizations or research in these agencies or populations. The development of survey research methodologies has not been grounded in criminal justice or criminological topics.

Nevertheless, there have been large-scale national criminal justice surveys. For example, the Bureau of Justice Statistics (BJS) has completed, and continues to conduct, several large scale research surveys of criminal justice agencies and populations. Figure 7.1 provides a partial list of the data sets the BJS has created or is continuing to create on the basis of surveys. Although these data sets represent a considerable effort on the part of the federal government to create useful information about the criminal justice system and its operations, a close examination of the results of these data sets reveals that there are many questions that are unanswered by the data. In addition, many questions remain unasked or are not amenable to survey research.[1]

Given this history in criminal justice, a focus on the application of survey methods in criminal justice settings is important for all students of criminal justice organizations or criminologists. Without a clear understanding of how survey research should be conducted, it is nearly impossible to judge the accuracy or believability of survey research results. One of the best ways to gain a thorough understanding of survey research methods is to examine them in an applied context. An applied knowledge of survey methods is gained through the use and application of these methods.

In my classes I regularly have students design and execute mini-surveys. Students soon find out that writing questions that measure what they want to measure, that are understandable, and that the study subjects will complete is no small task, whether the questions are for interviews, telephone surveys, or self-reported questionnaires. Survey research, whether it involves mailed questionnaires, telephone interviews, or face-to-face interviews, is not as simple as it first appears. There are a myriad of considerations that should be taken into account in the design of a survey, and it is contingent upon the researcher to work out these issues.

The following sections describe mail questionnaires, telephone surveys, and interviews. These are the three most common forms of survey

Figure 7.1

PARTIAL LISTING OF NATIONAL BUREAU OF JUSTICE STATISTICS DATA SETS

National Crime Victimization Surveys, 1986–1990

Law Enforcement Management and Administrative Statistics 1987

National Pretrial Reporting Program, 1988–1989

National Judicial Reporting Program, 1986, 1988

Survey of Inmates of Local Jails, 1978, 1983, 1989

National Jail Census, 1978, 1983, 1988

Survey of Inmates of State Correctional Facilities, 1974, 1979, 1986

Census of State Adult Correctional Facilities, 1984, 1979, 1974

Survey of Youth in Custody, 1987

methods employed in the social sciences. In each section specific guidelines and examples are provided. In addition, the advantages and disadvantages are discussed and explained.

Self-Report Questionnaires

Self-report questionnaires are used to elicit opinions or information from a broad sample of a study population. Questionnaires are typically completed by the subjects of the study without any prompting from the researcher. For example, at the end of the semester, many colleges and universities provide students with the opportunity to evaluate their instructors based on a standardized survey form (SIRS or student instructional rating sheets).

The basic idea in self-reported questionnaires is that the subjects of the study, at least those in the selected sample, provide standardized information or opinions about very specific questions or statements. First, the questionnaires are completed by the study subjects. This is not the case with interviews or telephone surveys. When using these survey techniques, the researcher completes the data collection and may interpret or change these data in the process of recording. The benefit in having the subjects of the research directly participate in the study is that the researcher may be more confident about the opinions or information received, because it comes directly from the study sample.

Second, self-report questionnaires have as one of their chief advantages the ability to cover very large samples and thus to have a better chance of being representative of the population. They are one of the best sources of generalization in social science research, because they can cover broad populations. In order to collect opinions or information from a large sample of the population, compromises must be made. One compromise is to create standardized questionnaire items. The respondents to the survey are typically restricted to categorical response choices on self-report surveys. This is not to say that less structured items are not included on such questionnaires, only that it is less typical for researchers to include open-ended items in a self-report questionnaire. That is the case because the goal of this type of research is to collect more basic information from a representative sample of the population rather than to collect detailed information from a smaller group.

Third, questionnaires focus on specific information or opinions. For example, in an interview a researcher might ask: "How do you feel about the death penalty?" The question requires the subjects to provide more than a yes or no answer. In a questionnaire the same question might be stated as follows:

What is your opinion about the death penalty?
- ___ I favor its use for every inmate.
- ___ I favor its use for every murderer.
- ___ I favor its use for murderers and rapists.
- ___ I favor its use for ______________________. (fill in)
- ___ I do not favor its use.
- ___ I have no opinion about the death penalty.

Self-report questionnaires force the subjects of research into responding in predetermined categories. While telephone surveys can be structured the same way, they are typically more open-ended than self-report questionnaires. The benefits of generalization to a large sample of the population are balanced against the loss in precision of the data collected though the restriction on the study subjects to respond in preset opinion or information categories.

There are three typical types of self-report questionnaires: (1) those given to a group, (2) mailed surveys, and (3) censuses. Questionnaires given to a group are very common in pretesting for more rigorous study. I often use my classes to pretest surveys intended for inmates (the age, race, and gender proportions have been fairly consistent). Additionally, inmates, police officers, judges, and probation officers are also fairly typical groups that have been given questionnaires. One should be cautious about the use of group data. It is appropriate to use a self-report questionnaire on a group of inmates in confinement, for example, but one should not presume from this questionnaire an ability to generalize to inmates, inmates in confinement, or even to inmates in the facility where the inmates one studied are located. Groups are appropriate sources of self-report questionnaires only insofar as they allow researchers to achieve the purpose of the research project at hand. If the goal is generalization, questionnaires are typically insufficient. On the other hand, if the goal is to understand the particular group, to evaluate their opinions, to collect information for administrative purposes, or to pretest a questionnaire, a questionnaire is acceptable. Given this limited roll for group surveys, researchers tend to rely on mailed questionnaires.

Mailed questionnaires are popular in both the social sciences and criminal justice. The questionnaire is mailed to the subjects, and they fill it out at their leisure and return it to the researcher. The biggest problem with self-report questionnaire studies is that response rates may be low, thus influencing the representativeness of the sample as well as the nature and results of the analysis of the data. The advantages of the mailed questionnaire are that it requires much less time than interviewing and it is fairly simple to conduct once the survey is designed. The sample that the researcher wishes to administer the instrument to must be literate and able to provide the opinions or information the researcher wants.

The other common form of self-report questionnaire is the census. One example is the U.S. Department of Commerce, Bureau of the Census decenial census of the population of the United States. This self-report questionnaire, and in some cases interviews and/or telephone surveys, is an attempt to describe the population of the United States. The basic difference between the self-report questionnaires given to groups or samples and the census is that in the census an attempt is made to include the entire population in the study. If we were to do a census of police agencies in the United States, we would send a self-report questionnaire to every local, state, and county police department in the country. Clearly, the costs and time involved in conducting such a census is cost prohibitive—only the Bureau of the Census or the Bureau of Justice Statistics could gather such information.

There are other possibilities for self-report questionnaires that are less common but show promise; these are: (1) home delivery (Babbie, 1989), (2) focus groups, and (3) pretest/posttest evaluations. Babbie describes the use of home delivery of self-report questionnaires as a relatively recent experiment in increasing the response rates. Home delivery involves the use of research workers to deliver and pick up the surveys once they are completed. Both of these features would seem to encourage higher response rates, yet the costs are high and the complexity of completing these studies are increased.

Another possibility for self-report questionnaires is the use of focus groups. Focus groups are common in marketing research, and the National Institute of Justice often uses these groups to define their focus for criminal justice research grants. This technique involves the creation of several homogeneous groups and using self-report questionnaires or interviews with each of these groups. The focus groups are composed of each relevant interest from the population, such as police chiefs, police captains, and police officers. The supposition is that, in total, the individual groups represent the opinions of the target population.

For example, suppose we were to conduct a study of the new "mandatory" sentences for "three time losers." The first step in conducting focus groups is to create several homogeneous groups. We would collect groups of prosecutors, defense attorneys, judges, police officers, probation officers, prison officials, victims rights groups, and citizens. Each group would be interviewed or given the self-report questionnaire. The views of each group can then be assessed. The use of questionnaires can facilitate the reliability and accuracy of the information collected. In addition, the use of questionnaires would not require the members of the focus groups to be present at the study group location to participate in the study. However, if questionnaires are used, the results from the initial questionnaire administration should be redistributed to each focus group for comments.

The third self-report questionnaire is pretest/posttest. In an attempt to impose a quasi-experimental design on questionnaire administration, we can use a pretest/posttest format. For example, in a study of a Life Skills program in a prison I constructed a self-report questionnaire concerning inmates' perceptions and knowledge about certain key life skills for the inmates to complete. On the first day of the course the inmates filled in the questionnaire. On the last day of the class the inmates were asked to fill in the survey again. Any differences between the pretest on the first day of the class and the posttest on the last day can be attributed to the Life Skills program. While this type of evaluation focuses on the internal components of the Life Skills class, it provides bounded information about how much the inmates know, and perceive they know, both before and after the treatment program. Administrating pretest/posttest self-administered questionnaires can be a quick way to create accurate and reliable data, and with the addition of a control group (a group that doesn't get the Life Skills training but is tested over time) it can be made even more valuable.

Questionnaire Creation Guidelines

The creation of questions for questionnaires should be done with conscious effort in anticipation of the future respondents in the study. In general, the questions should be understandable, concise, and clear. Figure 7.2 lists several specific points that should be considered for each question. The application of these guidelines will result in better questions, but they should not be taken out of context with the study one is conducting.

Biased questions are those that respondents may not want to answer because the answers might make them look bad or incriminate them. For example, the following question is clearly biased: *When was the last time you had sexual contact with another inmate?* This question clearly implies that the inmate has had sexual contact with inmates. There is no opportunity for inmates that have had no sexual contacts to respond, because they have had no "last time!" The bias can be removed from this question as

Figure 7.2

GENERAL QUESTIONNAIRE CREATION CONSIDERATIONS

Don't ask biased questions.
Don't ask directional questions.
Don't ask double-barreled questions.
Don't ask offensive questions.
Don't ask questions that subjects can't answer.
Don't use vague wording.

Sources: Hagan, 1989; Baker, 1988.

follows: *Have you ever had sexual contact with another inmate?* Inmates who have had no sexual contacts could respond. However, the second question reduces the precision of the information solicited because it does not ask for the time frame for sexual contact of the inmates as in the biased question. This could be corrected by asking only those inmates who have had sexual contacts when the most recent contact occurred in the form of a contingency question.

Directional questions should also be avoided. These questions suggest the answer that the researcher is seeking. For example, if we were studying a group of police officers who were using a new firearm (9 millimeter as opposed to the traditional revolver) we might ask: *Why do you think the new firearms are better than the revolver for the police in this department?* Officers who respond to this question are asked (directed) to endorse the new firearms over the revolver. How would officers who did not find the new firearms to be better than the revolvers respond to this question? A less directional version of this question is: *Are the new firearms better, worse, or the same as the issued revolver for the police in this department?*

Double-barreled questions ask two or more questions at the same time in a complex format the subjects of the study might find difficult to understand. Suppose we were doing a study of male customers of female prostitutes and asked the following double-barreled question: *When selecting a prostitute do you prefer young women or white women?* Double-barreled questions are two questions in one. We can separate the questions about the age and race of prostitutes to form two separate questions: *When selecting a prostitute, what age do you prefer? When selecting a prostitute, do you prefer white, black, or Asian women?*

Questions should not be offensive. Do not ask questions that are insulting to or critical of the subjects of the study. For example, consider the effect of the following question on a victim of crime: *Why didn't you physically resist the assailant more?* This question may be interpreted as being critical of the crime victim. It may also be directional in the sense that if this question were given to a random sample of citizens it would not allow those who did physically resist (even those who actually killed the assailant) to respond. To understand whether victims physically resisted, without being critical or insulting, we might ask a simple yes/no question and follow it up with contingency questions about the degree or level of resistance. For example: *Did you physically resist your assailant?*

Beware of unanswerable questions. Questions that presume that subjects have a certain level of knowledge when they do not are likely to result in the collection of inaccurate or unreliable information. Even though subjects may not have the presumed level of knowledge they may still answer the question. Suppose we asked a group of average citizens about the crime rates in their home city: *How many inmates are housed in the city jail?* The average citizen is not likely to know the official population rates of their local jail. In fact, most people don't even know where the local jail is located let alone how many inmates it houses.

Vague questions should not be used in questionnaires. Wording should be clear and concise so that subjects may quickly understand the meaning and the response that is requested. An example of a vague question asked of police officers is: *How should police officers process a person that they find when their shift is nearing an end?* The police officers who respond to this question may not know who the question refers to or what is meant by "process a person." This question fails to specify what is meant by the term "find." Subjects cannot respond with any accuracy or reliability because they cannot figure out what is being asked. A good way to determine whether a question is vague or not is to focus on the time sequencing and the subjects. In the example, the time sequencing implicit in the term "process" is not clear. What is meant by "process"? Does it mean "arrest"? Could it also mean "take to a homeless shelter"? This example question also requires the police officers to guess who the subject might be. It could be a homeless person or a drug dealer or a lost child—the information is not provided in the question. A more precise version of this question is: *Are police officers more likely, less likely, or as likely to arrest a person when they are within one-half hour of the end of their shift?*

Consider the questionnaire question design guidelines for each and every question included in the study. Although these guidelines do not guarantee that questions will result in valid and consistent data, the results from surveys that have been "cleaned" of these problems are much more likely to result in better data.

Format Guidelines

In addition to the general guidelines that should be considered for the construction of questions, one should consider the general format of the questionnaire. The physical structure of the questionnaire influences the responses of the research subjects.

First, avoid patterns in the questionnaire that result in a rhythmic response from the study subjects. For instance, in a study of citizens attitudes about the "Clinton Crime Plan" we might ask ten questions about whether more prisons or prison space should be built. The respondents may get in the habit of agreeing with each statement. Figure 7.3 gives an example of such questions.

Because the questions in figure 7.3 are so similar, the respondents may get in the habit of agreeing to all the statements without really reading the questions or because they believe that all the questions are essentially the same and require the same response. The major problem with groups of questions that form patterns, however, is that the questions following the

Figure 7.3
EXAMPLE OF PATTERNED RESPONSE

	Agree	Disagree	No opinion
1. More prisons should be built.	☐	☐	☐
2. Increases in the number of prisons in this country are needed.	☐	☐	☐
3. More prison cells should be made available for offenders.	☐	☐	☐
4. More prisons should be constructed in the country.	☐	☐	☐
5. Each state should build more prisons for criminals.	☐	☐	☐
6. Each county should build more jails for criminals.	☐	☐	☐
7. Each city should build more jails for criminals.	☐	☐	☐
8. More jail cells should be made available for offenders.	☐	☐	☐
9. Increases in the number of jails in this country are needed.	☐	☐	☐
10. More jails should be built.	☐	☐	☐

patterned group tend to be included in the response pattern. For example, if we ask whether more probation sentences should be used, the respondents may agree because they agreed to the earlier questions as a response pattern.

One way to avoid patterns in a questionnaire is to randomize the ordering of the questions. While this would help to remove patterns it may make the questionnaire tedious to complete. Alternatively, it makes sense to place the questions that would most easily be answered first, both to encourage further participation and to give the subjects a sense that the survey is less time consuming than they presumed or that it is easy to complete. Another way to reduce the possibility of patterning is to reverse the ordering of the question. For example, the first question in figure 7.3 asks the respondents to agree, disagree, or have no opinion about whether more prisons should be built. The order of this question could be reversed to state: *Fewer prisons should be built.* In the reverse order format, the researcher would anticipate a "disagree" response rather than an "agree." Judicious placement of reverse-ordering questions can break up sections where the questionnaire respondents may respond in habitual rather than conscious ways.

It is also important to not include irrelevant questions in questionnaires. Not only will these questions add to the costs and length of the instrument, but they are distracting to the focus of the study. For example, I am in the process of designing a study on college students' fear of crime on campus. I have been going through the process of constructing questionnaire items based on the 437 research articles, books, and other documents on fear of crime that I have located to date. I am also interested in studying public knowledge about jails. I contemplated including a question on my three-thousand-subject study of fear of crime on campus on whether the subjects know where the jail is located in their respective communities. The jail location question is irrelevant to the fear of crime on campus study. While the temptation to use the large sample for two purposes is great, I am leaning toward not including the jail location question, because I have too many other, more relevant fear-of-crime questions.

It is also important to make the questionnaire physically appealing. The questionnaire should be readable, neat, and error free. The goal should be to create the best looking questionnaire possible. The more professional the questionnaire, the more likely the respondents will be to return it. Professional printing of questionnaires is both unnecessary and expensive. Most Windows® or OS/2® based word processing programs allow you to create attractive questionnaire designs, including check boxes and outlined contingency questions as well as graphics.[2] In addition, there is a program called Clickbook® by Bookmaker Corporation that creates a booklet-type survey from any Windows-based word processor. Leave plenty of space between the items. In general, maintain one-inch margins on the top, bottom, left, right and at least a double space between each question or item.

Many research methodologists also recommend that questionnaires be kept as short as possible. It is often difficult to keep self-report questionnaires to a reasonable length. This is due, in part, to the need to keep statements or questions in the instrument concise; in order to be concise, one typically includes more items. In my study of fear of crime on campus, I have designed well over one hundred questions on the topic. Given the nature of the sample I will rely upon (working and commuter students) I doubt that many will participate in the study because it would take thirty minutes or more of their limited free time.

Having made the obligatory statement that the survey should be as short as possible, I also believe it important that the questionnaire retain its substance. That is, it should ask the most important theoretical or practical questions in reference to the research purpose at hand. Pretesting the questionnaire on a small group of subjects often gives a good basis for judging the number of questions that can be asked given the method of survey administration.

Finally, the technical aspects, instructions, and return procedures should be kept as simple as possible. For a multiple-choice opinion self-report questionnaire could be as simple as:

> INSTRUCTIONS: For the following items, please mark your opinions from strongly agree to strongly disagree.

In most cases the respondents will not spend a great deal of time with detailed instructions, and researchers will not be present to answer respondents' questions unless the questionnaire is given to a group or focus group. The best instructions, therefore, are those that can be read quickly and understood.

Instructions for returning the questionnaire should also be explicit. There are several choices the researcher has to secure the return of the questionnaires after they are completed: business reply envelopes, stamped envelopes, pick-up, or special envelopes. I prefer business reply envelopes, because I am not charged for those that are not returned. While they are more expensive to use if returned, I have found the level of professionalism they project contributes to a higher response rate, especially in criminal justice agencies and settings. However, Babbie argues that stamped envelopes may be beneficial, because they are more personal than business reply envelopes (Babbie, 1989). Perhaps for questionnaires of college students or citizens this may be the case, but I am more persuaded by the argument that criminal justice organizations and actors are more comfortable with official business reply envelopes. Picking up responses is also a good alternative to the mail, but it is not possible when one is studying a nationally diverse population.

The last format of return—special envelopes—is sometimes appropriate. In a study I conducted in Indiana of citizens' opinions about the correctional sanctions, I used a special survey that had a special cover that functioned as an envelope. The cover had a small adhesive dot for sealing the cover and my address and business reply permission were printed on the outside. I pretested the use of the return cover system on several employees at the university as well as at the local diner where I ate breakfast. Most had no problem figuring out the procedures for return. Although it was a simple matter to refold the six-page questionnaire, some may not have been returned because of the envelope format. The response rate was 55 percent, but I still wonder whether the response rate might have been higher had I used business reply envelopes.

Pretesting

Ideally, questionnaires should be tested before they are used on the study sample. To do this we would use the questionnaire with a small group of individuals who are similar in background and important characteristics to the study population. The idea behind the pretest is to determine if there are any problems prior to conducting the study.

Recently I conducted a pretest of a self-report questionnaire on criminal justice ethics that I was going to complete the following fall semester. I was interested in determining whether criminal justice majors are more likely than non–criminal justice majors to identify appropriate criminal-justice-system actor conduct. I asked one of my colleagues, who was teaching that summer, if I could use her class to conduct my pretest.

She agreed, and I conducted the pretest at the end of a class of twenty students. Each student got the cover letter and all instructions. I informed the students that I would wait for the responses and that they should place their names on their surveys (there was about twenty-five minutes left in the class period and my questionnaire took only about ten minutes to complete by my estimation).[3] One student upon reading the introduction letter and my statement that participation was voluntary got up and left the classroom without filling in his opinions. The remaining nineteen students completed the questionnaire and placed their responses in the envelopes as instructed. I returned one week later as per my arrangement with my colleague to give the students the questionnaire a second time. I thought a week was enough time between the first measurement given the concentrated class scheduling during the summer. Students had classes every day, and the workload was quite intense in an eight-week semester. Given these realities, they would have forgotten my survey of a week before (I know I would have).

The second time I administered the survey in the class, I got eighteen of the original nineteen to complete the questionnaire. Once this pretest data were collected I was ready to assess the validity and reliability of the questionnaire. I assessed the conformance (i.e., correlation) between how the students responded in week one with their responses in week two. I found an overall conformance between the two weeks ($r = .88$). I concluded that the instrument was reliable. However, students tended not to answer certain questions the same way both times. I reworded these questions so as to make them more clear without changing their meaning. Other things to look for in the pretest are skipped questions, questions that everyone answers alike (if everyone says the same thing, the question is not useful), ambiguous answers to open-ended questions, and patterned responses (Baker, 1988).

This process of pretesting a questionnaire may seem a bit like overkill, but it usually leads to an improved questionnaire instrument and allows you to work out the kinks before you collect the data for the "real" study.

Types of Questions

There are several different forms of questions. Most research methods texts and methodologists explain the four typical formats that follow. However, you should not be limited by these typical formats. When you design a questionnaire with a format other than the typical ones, and it works both in terms of the pretest and the purposes of the research, then use it. The best type of questionnaire items are those that illicit the highest responses and understanding by the study participants.

Closed-Ended Questions. One format for questions is called "closed-ended." A *closed-ended question* forces the subject to respond with an opinion or information within a specified listing printed under the question.

I fear being a crime victim when I walk alone at night
___ never
___ sometimes
___ often
___ always

Closed-ended questions must include a range of opinion or information options that are both exhaustive and mutually exclusive. The choices must include every possibility for the opinions or information requested. If we were to ask respondents to indicate their gender, we would have to include the categories of male and female because that is the full range of categories of gender that are available.[4] The list of opinions or information must allow the respondents to select only one most appropriate category. For example, if someone responded "male," he cannot also respond "female."

Open-Ended Questions. Open-ended questions allow respondents to fill in the information requested in their own words. The response will be easier to read if lines are provided. There is a trade-off between closed-ended and open-ended questions. Closed-ended questions provide more concise bits of information, but they tend to get answered. Open-ended questions provide a full range of information or opinion, but they tend to be less likely to be answered by respondents. This is not to say that open-ended items should not be included in the questionnaire, only that many respondents find them too difficult to complete. It's easier to state whether one agrees or disagrees (closed-ended) as opposed to explaining why one believes what one believes (open-ended).

There is no definitive answer to open-ended questions. Each respondent can provide a different answer or opinion. While it is common to see patterns form in the respondents' answers (that is, many respondents agree with one another), this isn't always the case. For example, we could redesign the closed-ended question from the previous section to make it open ended as follows:

How much do you fear being a crime victim? Why?

Contingency Questions. Contingency questions are questions that are dependent upon the responses of the subjects to earlier questions. Contingency questions are created to get at more detailed information. In some questionnaires there can be several levels of contingency. A contingency question example is as follows:

Do you fear crime?
__ no
__ yes (if yes, respond to the following)
Which of the following do your fear most?
being assaulted
being murdered
having property taken
other: ______________________________
(please specify)

Matrix Questions. Matrix questions allow you to ask a series of related questions that have similar types of responses. Patterns can be avoided by requiring some items in the matrix to be coded "agree" and some "disagree" (see question 4 in the example). The advantage of using matrix questions is that you can save considerable amount of space in the questionnaire. In addition, matrix questions are easier for the subjects of the study because they can quickly understand and complete them.

	SA	A	D	SD	NO
1. I fear being a crime victim during the day.	☐	☐	☐	☐	☐
2. I fear being a crime victim at night.	☐	☐	☐	☐	☐
3. I walk with others for safety.	☐	☐	☐	☐	☐
4. I do not fear being assaulted.	☐	☐	☐	☐	☐

Key: SA = Strongly agree; A = Agree; D = Disagree; SD = Strongly disagree; NO = No opinion

Questionnaire Administration

Once the questionnaire has been designed, reviewed, and pretested, the questionnaire can be given to the study subjects. Some methodologists recommend that the questionnaire should be precoded. They believe that numerical codes should be placed next to the response categories. I would recommend against this procedure. While such precoding makes it somewhat easier to take the information from the respondents and make it usable for analysis, it clutters the appearance of the questionnaire, and the benefits from precoding do not outweigh the problem of cluttering up the format of the questionnaire.

To administer a questionnaire the researcher should write a cover letter with instructions for completing and filling out the instrument. It is also important to include an addressed return envelope. The cover letter should concisely explain the purpose of the study. The researcher's identity should also be specified. Baker (1988) suggests two approaches to encouraging participation: (1) egotistical—to help the researcher do science, (2) altruistic—to participate because one is a good person and the researcher needs help (Baker, 1988, p. 172).

The cover letter should be concise and no longer than one page in length. I endeavor to keep my cover letters to three paragraphs. Figure 7.4 shows an example of a cover letter.[5]

Once the questionnaire instrument is mailed, the researcher must consider whether to use follow-up mailings to increase the response rate. There are several follow-up methods that can be conducted: (1) postcards; (2) telephone calls; (3) new questionnaires; and (4) certified mail. Keep in mind, however, that the quality of the responses after the initial mailing can decline.

Figure 7.4

COVER LETTER EXAMPLE

August 21, 1996

Dr. Jeff Senese
Department of Criminal Justice
1234 Baltimore Way
Baltimore, Maryland 11111-1111

Please find enclosed a copy of a questionnaire on the fear of crime. The purpose of this study is to understand the issues of fear of crime in mid-town Baltimore. Your contribution to this study would be greatly appreciated and would help us to design better crime prevention programs for the area.

It should take you only 5 minutes or so to complete this survey, and the responses you provide are important to improving our understandings of how people view the issues in this questionnaire. You are guaranteed complete confidentiality in your responses, and the data collected from this questionnaire will only be reported in an aggregate form.

Thank you very much for your time and efforts in completing this questionnaire. Your participation is both greatly appreciated and valuable to this study. If you have any questions, please feel free to call Dr. Jeff Senese at (999) 999-9999.

Sincerely,

Jeffrey D. Senese Ph.D.

Some researchers send postcard reminders in the second week after the questionnaire has been mailed. These postcards remind and encourage the respondents who have not returned their questionnaires to do so. Postcards are effective in some cases, but the researcher must weigh the costs involved (cards plus postage) and whether they will be effective with the sample involved in the study.

In other cases follow-ups can be done over the telephone. This involves several trade-offs. Telephone calls clearly let the respondents know that you know how to contact them, and this may cause them to feel intimidated or upset. On the other hand, if the researcher presents him- or herself in an appropriate fashion to the subjects in the study, this technique can result in additional responses.

Another obvious way to increase the responses to a survey is to mail another questionnaire to the respondents who have not replied. This is probably the best follow-up method because most respondents who do not return the questionnaire within the first month after the first mailing have trouble locating the instrument. They probably could not complete the survey even if you encouraged responses with postcards or telephone calls.

In some cases the follow-up mailing of the questionnaire can be conducted using certified mail. This technique should be used only in certain circumstances. For example, I have served as a consultant to the American Correctional Association, and they regularly study their membership. The response rates to most of their studies are quite high, but it would be appropriate to send a duplicate questionnaire by certified mail to the nonrespondents in this case. The danger here is that certified mail can be intimidating to the respondents, and they may resent the implication that they did not pay attention to the questionnaire of the initial mailing.

Response Rates

Perhaps the key dilemma in self-report questionnaires is the response rate. The *response rate* is determined by the proportion of the study sample that return or participate in the questionnaire. Several methodologists state that a response rate of 50 percent of the study sample is both typical and acceptable (Babbie, 1989; Baker, 1988; Nachmias and Nachmias, 1981). Certainly a response rate greater than 50 percent should be both welcomed and encouraged. However, the sample collected should be as closely representative of the total sample that one desires to collect from the study population. Some have recommended a 75 percent response rate as a minimum (Bailey, 1978). These percentages are arbitrarily set. Although that percentage cited are certainly reasonable benchmarks for survey response rates, they should not be viewed as absolute requirements. One can learn a great deal from a less-than-stellar response rate data set if the group that does response is representative of the population from which it has been drawn.

One needs to balance the benefits of conducting research on a data set that comes from a low response rate against the generalization strength or purpose of the research.

There are several methods for increasing the response rates on questionnaires. These methods are: (1) follow-ups; (2) remuneration; (3) sponsorship; (4) endorsements; and (5) additional appeals. More than one follow-up mailing is likely to result in a higher response rate. In a study of response rates by Dillman et al. (1974) it was found that by the second follow-up mailing of the questionnaire, an average of 73 percent response rate can be expected. The use of remuneration is sometimes effective. Remuneration can be in the form of money payment or in-kind gifts (e.g., discount coupons at the local supermarket). The problem with what is essentially "paying" respondents is that those who respond may be influenced by this payment in that they will endeavor to respond in the manner in which they think the researcher wants them to respond rather than in the way they might respond without the payment.

Sponsorships and endorsements are also effective response rate enhancers. Sponsorships usually involve the support of the research being made explicit to the point where the sponsor's stationery is used for the cover letter. If we were to study police we might try to get the International Association of Chiefs of Police to sponsor it. Endorsements, on the other hand, could be a specific statement of support from an organization that the study participants are members. In a study I conducted of probation agencies, for example, I was sponsored by the American Correctional Association, and I received an endorsement from the president of the American Probation and Parole Association. Finally, the researcher can make additional types of appeals in follow-up mailings based on logic or encouragement to participate in the study. These additional appeals could involve writing a personal letter to the study subjects with their names printed on the follow-up letter and envelope.

Advantages and Disadvantages of Questionnaires

In summary, there are several advantages as well as disadvantages of self-report questionnaires. The use of this data collection device should be relevant to the study one wants to conduct. Self-report questionnaires are appropriate in situations where researchers clearly understand the information they want to collect and can formulate concise statements or questions to collect the information. On the other hand, questionnaires are inappropriate in situations where researchers cannot clearly define the concepts to be collected or the topic is yet to be defined or where a reasonable sample cannot be collected. An example of a situation where questionnaires would not be appropriate is an AIDS study involving offenders or sexual assault victims in prisons or jails.

The advantages of questionnaires are: (1) they are capable of covering large representative samples; (2) they are relatively less expensive than other forms of data collection; and (3) they allow the respondents to retain their confidentiality and to consider their responses in a comfortable environment.

The disadvantages of questionnaires are: (1) they are based on concise, somewhat simple questions; (2) there are limited opportunities to gain detailed follow-up information about the responses or respondents; and (3) there is a tendency for low response rates. In criminal justice settings there is also a problem with determining who actually fills out the survey. I have been involved in corretions studies where I was uncertain whether the correctional officers filled out the questionnaires or the inmates filled them out. Moreover it is always difficult to determine who fills out questionnaires when the units of analysis are organizations or groups. While these disadvantages are certainly important considerations there are situations where no other research data collection device is appropriate.

Telephone Surveys

Telephone surveys are part questionnaire and part interview. They are part questionnaire because the researcher usually has a structured questionnaire or interview schedule of specific questions. Telephone surveys are also part interview in that the researcher fills in the questionnaire for the respondents and additional questions can be asked and answered. Although early in this century telephone surveys suffered from validity problems because many people did not have telephones, that is not the case today.

The primary reason for conducting a study by telephone is that one can reach a large representative sample of the population. One can conduct a national study by telephone that would not be possible using other methods. The costs per phone call are also relatively low compared to mailed questionnaires. Telephone surveys are also quickly conducted, can be supervised by the researcher, and have low nonresponse rates. Follow-ups for telephone surveys are also a simple matter.

However, there are several problems related to collecting data through the use of telephone surveys. For instance, it is difficult to conduct in-depth or long telephone interviews. Most are between five and thirty minutes in length. The questions on a telephone survey must be concise, much like in questionnaires, and hence, you may collect only simple information. There are also many people who have unlisted phone numbers. These unlisted numbers are as high as 40 percent in some areas.[6] It is also difficult for the researcher to encourage individuals to complete a telephone interview. Respondents who are likely to participate in a telephone survey may be quite different from those that would hang up the phone as soon as they determine that a study was being conducted. And there are devices today that restrict access (answering machines, caller I.D.), and these also tend to reduce response rates.

Telephone Interview Schedules

Telephone interview schedules are in most cases similar to questionnaires and are often computerized. Interviewing components, such as asking the respondents whether they understood the question, can be incorporated into the survey. A telephone interview schedule can use several approaches. The most common approaches are: (1) developmental; (2) semantic differentials; (3) open ended; and (4) forced choice.

In the developmental approach, the researcher asks a general screening question and then follows that screening question with one or more levels of detailed questions. The screening questions are typically closed ended, with categorical responses. The detail questions, however, can be either closed ended or open ended. An example of a developmental approach in conducting telephone interviews with recently released inmates could be as follows:

Do you think you will use drugs in the next six months?

A	B	C
___ I probably will use drugs.	___ I probably will not use drugs.	___ I don't know.
What drug? ___	Why not?	Are you:
How often? ___	___ Rehabilitated	___ Likely to use (go to A)
How will you pay for the habit?	___ Health reasons	___ Probably won't use (go to B)
___ Steal	___ Other: _______	___ As likely to use as to not use
___ Work		
___ Other: _____		

The developmental approach, while focused on concise and simple questions and responses, can be made quite elaborate. You should keep in mind that the telephone survey must be conducted quickly, and if research assistants are used it must not be so complex as to confuse data collection. The developmental method's biggest strength is that it allows you to develop a series of responses. As in the example above, the question attempts to more completely understand why respondents believe they are going to continue or not continue to use drugs.

Another common telephone interview schedule format is that of the semantic differential. The semantic differential is also a form of response category for questionnaires but is particularly well suited to the telephone survey. It is important to make the scale of the semantic differential simple for telephone surveys, because verbal clues to improve the respondent's understanding are not available (you can't show them a list of numbers wherein 1 is "strongly agree" and 10 is "strongly disagree"). An example of a semantic differential question of police officers could be as follows:

> On a scale of 1 = very effective protection to 10 = very ineffective protection, rate your current bulletproof vest equipment.
>
> | 1 | 2 | 3 | 4 | 5 | 6 | 7 | 8 | 9 | 10 |
> |---|---|---|---|---|---|---|---|---|---|
> | ☐ | ☐ | ☐ | ☐ | ☐ | ☐ | ☐ | ☐ | ☐ | ☐ |
>
> Very effective protection — Very ineffective protection

You can also use open-ended or forced entry questions on telephone surveys. The problem with open-ended questions on telephone surveys is that respondents will provide either a brief response or a long verbal dissertation. Even if you ask respondents to list problems or solutions to problems they will tend to supply only one or two (Groves and Kahn, 1979). Forced-entry questions (closed-ended) questions are perhaps the best design. When you use closed-ended questions on a telephone survey more care must be taken that the subject understands the questions before you move on to other questions. Computer-assisted telephone surveys are quite adept at closed-ended questioning.

Selection of Subjects

Telephone surveys differ from the mail self-report questionnaire in the selection of study subjects. Several techniques are available to the telephone research approach that are intrinsic to the fact that telephone numbers are "numerical" and are assigned on geographical and a consecutive basis. The three most common ways subjects are selected for telephone research are (1) telephone directories, (2) random digit dialing, and (3) the use of cross-index telephone directories for stratification.

The use of telephone directories is usually acceptable for most public opinion surveys. However, you should be aware that a large percentage of people may have unlisted numbers. One way to reduce the influence of unlisted numbers on biasing the sample you select is to randomly select an additional proportion of numbers equal to the proportion of unlisted numbers.

In order to use a telephone directory you must set up a logical list of rules as in simple random sampling. First decide whether you will use the entire phone book or just the white pages. I tend to favor using just the white pages of the directory, because businesses are listed in the white pages of many phone books and because the yellow pages have large adds that make the decisions about which number to use more difficult. I would then use the process listed in table 7.1.

Count the total number of pages (phone books I have seen have numbered pages). Let's say that the total number of pages is two hundred. From the population of each directory, I tend to select 25 percent because this is a significant proportion of the population. When the population of two hundred pages is multiplied by .25 (the proportion of sampled pages) I end up with fifty pages. Hence, I would randomly select fifty pages based on the simple random sampling procedure explained in the sampling chapter. Once the fifty pages are randomly selected, I could select one of the four columns per page. This, too, could be done through the use of a random numbers table or computer. Once the columns are selected for each page, I could then randomly select two observations, or phone numbers, per page. The selection of phone numbers from each page would be based on the random numbers table as well as their consecutive location on the pages. For example, if the first number in the random numbers table was a 17, I would include the seventeenth number listed in the selected column on one of the selected pages in my sample. I could continue this process until all one hundred phone numbers were selected.

Although the process of using a telephone directory is tedious, the sample selection is as random as possible. In addition, the consecutive nature of the assignment of phone numbers is irrelevant as is the number of pages that correspond to letters of common last names. The advancements in computer technology should make the selection of samples from directories even more useful. For instance, CD-ROMs can be purchased which have over 70 million residential listings that can be used to create customized samples and even print labels.

Table 7.1

SELECTING A RANDOM SAMPLE FROM A TELEPHONE DIRECTORY

Steps	**Example**
1. Count the total number of pages	200 pages
2. Select pages from a random numbers table	50 pages
3. Count the number of columns on each page	4 columns per page
4. For each of the selected pages, randomly select a column	1 column per page
5. For each column on each selected page, randomly select two numbers based on their location on the page	2 phone numbers per page
6. Continue until the sample is selected	100 phone numbers in the sample

Once the sample has been selected you make a decision about who is to be surveyed once the number is called for the study. The Bureau of Justice Statistics and the Bureau of the Census use what they call the "household respondent," that is, anyone over the age of thirteen who answers the phone will be asked to participate in the survey. While this may not be the best method, age is a fairly typical way to decide who will be interviewed when the survey is conducted. Some have even constructed schemes for randomly sampling the interviewee based on the total number of potential respondents who work or live at the location of the phone number. Whatever process one uses, it should be clear and consistent with the purposes and goals of one's research.

Random-digit dialing does not involve reliance on the use of telephone directories. This technique uses a computer to select the numbers to be called. The areas where the survey will take place are selected, along with the exchange numbers in that area. The computer is then asked for a list of the appropriate size with randomly constructed telephone numbers for the remaining four digits. Random digit dialing is an objective way to select a survey sample. However, you might get numbers in the sample that are not currently active or that have not been assigned, so it is better to generate a slightly larger sample of phone numbers than you actually need to compensate for those that are disconnected or unassigned.

Cross-index telephone directories allow you to stratify the telephone directory selection process. This type of telephone directory lists phone numbers by address or by numerical ordering. Hence, these directories are particularly helpful if you want a stratified sample based on location or separate private and commercial samples.

Computer-Assisted Telephone Surveys

Another issue with regard to telephone surveys is the use of Computer-Assisted Telephone Interviewing, or *CATI*. There have been significant hardware and software developments in the past five years, and there are likely to be similar advances in the next five years, that make the use of computers in such interviewing both valuable and reliable.

In CATI the researcher sits in front of the computer and can proceed through a preprogrammed interview guideline that automatically jumps and skips questions as the responses are recorded. This is a substantial improvement over recording the results of telephone interviews on paper. The researcher can record the data while conducting the interview. Thus, the two steps of recording the interviews and coding the interviews are removed from the data coding process.

Interview Surveys

Interview surveys are qualitative data collection approaches. In both telephone surveys and self-report questionnaires, the results would tend to be counts of the answers of respondents rather than qualitative or narrative information. The choice between the quantitative design of a questionnaire and a qualitative approach in interview surveys should be entirely based on the goals of the research and logic and common sense. Patton (1990) succinctly describes the task of the interviewer as to "find out what is in and on someone else's mind. . . . We interview people to find out from them those things we cannot directly (or discretely) observe" (p. 278).

Good interviews are based on the ability of the researcher to understand the interview guidelines and to complete the interview. In addition, it is important for the researcher to practice the interview procedures in order to be competent in their use. Interviewers also attempt, as much as possible, to reduce the influences or effects of personal viewpoints or mannerisms on the interview situation.

The following sections describe several of the issues involved in interviewing or interview surveys. They describe the three major interview guideline approaches and how to conduct interviews based on these structures.

Interview Schedules

While Patton (1990) suggests that there are three general types of interviewing—conversations, interview guidelines, and standardized—I believe that the most logical and defensible format is the guideline approach. You can learn a great deal from a conversation with those in the know about the issues you are interested in studying. For example, conversations with police officers about community policing will tell you a lot about the topic. However, conversations are free-wheeling, and it is difficult to accurately record conversations. I believe that it is best to impose at last some structure. Similarly, standardized interviews are the application of questionnaires in a verbal context wherein the researcher completes the survey and the subjects are present.

Structured Interview. Structured interview guidelines are a group of questions (and perhaps follow-up questions or probes) upon which the interview is based. In this form of interview guideline, the subjects are all asked the same questions in the same order. The structured guideline differs from the questionnaire, usually but not always, in that the responses are not categorical but open ended. The use of a structured guideline creates more objective information than the other formats in that every subject is asked the same questions in the same order, variation between interviews is minimized, and the interview is focused specifically on issues and doesn't meander like a "conversation."

An example (one which I will carry through to the semi-structured and limited structure guideline models) can be constructed for interviews of judges about their views on inmates' rights to mental health treatment.

Should inmates have access to mental health professionals?
(Probes: *Why or why not? What type of care? How much care?*)

Should correctional staff provide counseling to mentally ill inmates?
(Probes: *Why or why not?*)

Where should mentally ill inmates be housed during trial and sentencing if found guilty?

Every judge is asked these questions in the same order. We could also add probe questions to follow up on and clarify responses to each of the questions. In a structured interview, researchers do not deviate from the questions and probes that they have predetermined for the interview situation.

Semi-Structured Interview. A second approach, semi-structured, removes some of the restrictions involved in the fully structured approach. The semi-structured guideline provides a list of topics to be discussed in the interview. The interviewers are permitted greater flexibility in how they ask the questions as long as the questions are within a particular topical area. I have found this approach to be well suited to exploratory studies. When the knowledge base is limited, one can list what is known and expand the depth of knowledge from there.

An example of the semi-structured interview approach in the study of judges is:

Access to help?
Costs of help?
Who should provide help?
Confinement of mentally ill?

Neither the probes nor the exact wording is the same for each interview. Thus, the researcher has greater flexibility in this approach. The downside is that the reliability across interviews suffers, because each interview is different.

Limited Structure Interview. The last type of interview guideline we will examine here has a limited structure format. The limited structure format interview schedule is certainly the most unstructured of the three types, but it should retain a theoretical or conceptual basis or framework. For example, I would not conduct an interview study of police chiefs' leadership styles without knowing what has been studied in the past. The limited structure format is conducted with very little preparation insofar as the interviews are concerned. Questions are asked and follow-up questions are formulated on the basis of the answers to the initial questions. Researchers conducting this type of research typically have a long history of conducting such qualitative research. Two very good examples of such research can be found in Robert Johnson's (1990) work on the death penalty and Hagedorn's (1988) work on gangs in Milwaukee.

Interview Questions

There are several different types of questions that can be asked in the interview setting. In this section the various types of questions will be defined and examples will be proffered. Figure 7.5 lists the types of questions that can be asked and the subsequent paragraphs give descriptions and examples of each of these questions.

Experience/behavior questions are those that attempt to find out what a person does or has done, or what could have been observed had the researcher been present when the behavior or activity occurred. For example, we could ask correctional officers about their typical days. We could ask them to describe what makes a day in the prison a good day and what experiences lead them to conclude that they have had a bad day. There are several natural follow-up questions, because many officers simply state that a good day is one where "I don't have to write anyone up." An obvious follow-up question that I often ask is, "Why would writing inmates up make your day a bad one?" Basically, experience or behavior type questions are attempts at re-creating the reality or phenomenon of interest so it can be recorded in a systematic interview study.

When we ask subjects opinion/values questions we are attempting to get their thoughts about the topic of interest. This type of question also elicits a value judgment on the part of the study subjects. An example of an opinions/value question of a sample of juvenile probation officers might be, "What do you think is the biggest problem facing juvenile probation officers?" or "If you could do anything with your gang case load, what changes might you make?"

Feeling questions are "aimed at understanding the emotional responses of people to their experiences and thoughts" (Patton, 1990, p. 291). Thus, feeling questions attempt to integrate what the subjects experience and their opinions of those experiences (i.e., the first two types of questions). An example of a feeling question in a study of rape crisis center counselors might include such questions as "To what extent does going to court with victims make you intimidated?" and "Are you usually confident in the claims of victims that they will follow through and help prosecute the offender?"

To determine simple factual information, an interviewer would use knowledge questions. Subjects in studies can clearly state whether they live in the city or county. Many police officers have an understanding about what social services are available for battered women. Inmates typically know

Figure 7.5
INTERVIEW QUESTIONS

1. Experience/Behavior questions
2. Opinion/Value questions
3. Feeling questions
4. Knowledge questions
5. Sensory questions
6. Background/Demographic questions

Source: Patton, 1990.

what rule violations will get them written up in prison. Knowledge questions are an attempt to measure "just the facts."

Sensory questions attempt to measure "what is seen, heard, touched, tasted, and smelled" (Patton, 1990, p. 292). I have toured prisons and jails in fifty different states and counties, and I am amazed by the similarities in smell and sound of many correctional facilities. However, there are significant exceptions, most notably the podular jails, which have carpeting and "regular" furniture. They tend to be less noisy and to smell less "institutionalized." An interesting research study could be conducted asking interviewees if they can identify the sights, sounds, tastes, and smells of institutions to determine if my perceptions are accurate. Such knowledge, beyond satisfying my curiosity, could result in improved environments and the creation of better conditions for the employees of many prisons and jails.

Background/demographic questions can sometimes be answered through observation. One can usually determine the gender of an inmate through observation. Other questions, such as "Are you employed?" can simply be asked. Knowledge questions focus on the research issues relevant to the study, whereas the background/demographic questions focus on "routine" information collection.

Interview Administration

The process of conducting the interviews for a study should be determined prior to the start of the study. Regardless of the type of interview, it makes sense to conduct the interviews in a situation where the researcher and the subject can have privacy. I have, on occasion, conducted interviews with correctional officers while they were at their posts and have found that the officers don't focus on either supervision or the interviews. However, the interviews could not be completed any other way. On the other hand, I have done ride-along interviews with police officers that have worked quite well, although they were time consuming. It is also important to conduct interviews in a one-on-one situation. While focus groups are often conducted as group interviews (consisting of five to ten similar people), groups are difficult to interview because of the interactive influences the individuals may have on one another. Also it is difficult enough to record interview data for one-on-one interviews let alone a group of people.

That brings me to another issue that requires careful consideration and preplanning. Consider how the interview data will be recorded. Several options exist, including taking notes during the interview, using a structured interview form with check boxes for responses, tape recorders, video recording, and writing notes after the interview. I am most comfortable with a combination of recording and note taking when it is possible. I tend to take notes during my interviews and where possible use a micro tape recorder. The use of a tape recorder is somewhat off-putting to many criminal justice subjects (including police officers, correctional officers, and inmates). However, once I have established rapport with an agency and have taken time to learn as much as possible through informal interviews and conversations, I am more likely to be permitted to use a tape recorder.

A final word about interviews—ask factual or demographic questions in the beginning of the interview to make the subject more comfortable. These matter-of-fact questions tend to be much less intimidating than the more substantive questions and can help you build rapport with the subject.

Summary

This chapter has discussed the use of self-report questionnaires, telephone surveys, and interviews. While these are probably the most common forms of data collection devices in the social sciences, they have also been used with increased frequency in criminal justice settings. Evaluation research, or program evaluations, have also increasingly relied on the data from these approaches.

Table 7.2
COMPARISON OF THREE SURVEY METHODS

Characteristics	Questionnaires	Telephone	Interview
Costs	high	low	moderate
Response rate	moderate	low	high
Control of situation	high	low	moderate
Diversity of population	moderate	high	moderate
Heterogeneous population	high	low	high
Detail of information	high	moderate	moderate
Speed	low	low	high

Source: Nachmias and Nachmias, 1981.

Nachmias and Nachmias (1981) provide an informative summary of these three approaches. This summary suggests that each approach is more appropriate in certain types of studies than in others. For example, the questionnaire is well suited to studies involving large samples that could be costly to interview and where one wants to control the responses to specific categories. Telephone interviews are best for collecting data from diverse populations. Finally, interviews are useful where the response rate is extremely important (usually in smaller sample studies) and where one is interested in detailed information.

Main Concepts

self-report questionnaires
closed-ended questions
contingency questions
response rate
telephone interview schedules
interview surveys
semi-structured interview
pretesting
open-ended questions
matrix questions
telephone surveys
CATI
structured interview
limited structure interview

Discussion Questions

1. Which method of surveying would you use to study criminal justice students nationally? Why?
2. How can a telephone surveyor improve the representativeness of those who complete interviews?
3. If you were to study inmates that test positive for HIV, which survey method would you rely on? Why?
4. When would you use a structured interview schedule?
5. Which interview schedule would be most appropriate in a study of judges' biases for sentencing? Why?
6. Which of the three main techniques—questionnaires, telephone surveys, or interviews—is best for collecting accurate data? Why?

Exercises

1. Design a survey research project on one of the following topics: (1) views of the death penalty; (2) opinions about prison treatment; or (3) police officers' views of patrol.
2. Interview another student using an interview schedule that the entire class designs.

8

OBSERVATIONAL DESIGNS

Learning Objectives

1. To describe the particular advantages and disadvantages of observational research designs
2. To provide an understanding for the possible subjects of observational studies
3. To give students an understanding of data collection in observational studies

Chapter Outline

Introduction
Advantages
Direct Collection of Data
Conducted in Natural Settings
High Feasibility
Disadvantages
Reduced Accuracy
Lack of Consistency
Subjects of Observation
Body Language
Spatial Behavior
Language
Extralinguistic Observations
Linguistic Behaviors
Physical Setting
Social Setting
Unobtrusive Indicators
Nonoccurrences
Collecting Observational Data
Timing
Recording Observations
Fieldwork Guidelines
Summary
Main Concepts
Discussion Questions
Exercise

CHAPTER EIGHT

Introduction

Observational studies are not typical in criminal justice and criminological research settings. In fact, the opposite is true. An overwhelming majority of the published research is quantitative in nature.[1] However, there are research projects that cannot be adequately completed on the basis of quantitative data and analyses alone. The preference in the criminal justice research for increasingly sophisticated statistical research approaches may also explain why many practitioners see research as irrelevant. Sophisticated statistical analyses are not what the applied world of criminal justice practice requires to improve its functioning. The fact remains, however, that quantitative questions require quantitative studies and data. Conversely, qualitative studies require qualitative data and analyses. Neither quantitative nor qualitative approaches is intrinsically right or wrong or better or worse. The decision about the general approach is simply a matter of one or the other approach being particularly suited to the research purpose one is interested in pursuing.[2]

The purpose of this chapter is to explain and demonstrate the particular benefits and problems involved in conducting observation-based research. One of the most significant problems with observational designs is that they must overcome the perceptions of those researchers with a more quantitative orientation. Many quantitative researchers view qualitative data collection and studies as invalid or unreliable because these cannot be established directly through statistical testing. Quantitative researchers also make the argument that observational studies are inaccurate because they rely upon "soft-data" that is created by the researcher and not on an objective source such as the Uniform Crime Reports or the U.S. census of the population. While it is true that observational studies rely on so-called soft data (i.e., the results of conversations or interactions), they are not necessarily doomed to invalidity. What the observational research project lacks in objectified and concise measures (e.g., the UCR, or population counts) it makes up for in detailed description and explanations.

A great deal of literature on human perceptions supports the contention that people's behavior or attitudes cannot be either accurately or consistently measured through quantitative measures alone. For example, do you remember the name of the clerk at the store where you get your morning coffee or to whom this text is dedicated? We simply are not very observant beings. There is much we fail to see even though we are looking right at it. However, if I told students to observe the clerk's name tomorrow morning because it will be a bonus question on an examination, their skills of observation would dramatically improve. The conduct of observational studies is similar in that we attempt to concentrate and give full attention to our observations so as not to miss anything that is, or may be, important to the research being conducted.

It is important to keep in mind that quantitative studies suffer from the same accuracy problems as do qualitative ones. For instance, we rely on the U.S. Department of Labor statistics for the reported "unemployment rate" (the proportion of the total available labor force that is not currently working). The Department of Labor however, counts only those who are currently signing up for unemployment benefits, and therefore, excludes all those people who fail to sign up or have used all of their unemployment benefits. Hence, the unemployment statistics measure only those who are actively seeking employment and not those who have given up searching for a job.

In observational designs the researcher endeavors to become a more accurate and consistent observer. Hence, observational designs are based on objective, scientific, and systematic observations by trained observers and are recorded in as much detail as possible. The potential approaches that researchers can take vary from being a full participant to being a complete objective researcher. More specifically, observational designs can be approached by the researcher from the following perspectives: (1) full participant; (2) participant researcher; (3) researcher who participates; and (4) complete researcher. These perspectives place in context the discussions and examples in this chapter and the description of observational designs. These differentiations are important when one considers how much of an observer or participant one will be in the particular research project.

Figure 8.1 shows a model of a *full participant* perspective of conducting observational designs. In the full participant approach the researcher becomes a full participant in the situation under study yet completes the research as a sideline to direct participation within the context of the study site. For the purposes of illustration, the following examples of this perspective assume that we want to conduct a qualitative observational study of a prison cell block. Suppose further that we are interested in studying inmate staff communications.

Figure 8.1
FULL PARTICIPANT

In a full participant perspective the researcher would become a full member of the situation under study as either an inmate or a staff person. Full participation would involve participation in the day-to-day functioning of the prison cell block. The research that the researcher who is a full participant is conducting takes a secondary position to the job at hand whether it be as a correctional officer or an inmate. Generally, the full-participant researcher does not take notes when participating but attempts to reconstruct the notes after the participation has ended for the day. The full-participant researcher also rarely conducts formal interviews, as these would be clearly unnatural, and the research, if it is secret, may be discovered by the study subjects.

Full participation clearly would give the researcher an insider's understanding of communications in a cell block, but would do so through deception and stealth. An example of the full participation (see figure 8.1) would be a researcher who went undercover to study a prison cell block as an inmate. Hence, the researcher is totally immersed in the research situation.

A *participant researcher* is one who would study the research situation, the prison cell block, from the perspective of a researcher, yet would participate in the functional activities in the study situation. The participant researcher participates in the research situation, but research is the priority, not the participation. Recording research notes can also be done in the open, because the subjects are aware of the purpose of the researcher's presence. In the role of a participant, the researcher is physically involved in the research setting yet is cognitively conducting research during his or her experience in the "real world" (see figure 8.2). Thus, the researcher is physically involved in the situation and mentally conducting research.

For example, in an evaluation I was conducting of a vocational program for inmates, I was a participant observer. In this role I was invited to attend the training for the teachers in the vocational program. While the trainer and the teachers were told I was the "evaluation researcher" for the project, they were also told that I was not evaluating the training so much as I was interested in getting a feel for the programs that the teachers were going to deliver to the inmate students. Hence, my participation in the training and the exercises in the training was as a researcher not as a full participant although I still participated in the training experiences and exercises.

The most common perspective in observational studies is that of the *researcher who participates.* The researcher who participates is one who, like the participant researcher, fully discloses to the research subjects that he or she is present to conduct research. Moreover, the researcher who participates attempts to reduce the influence he or she has on the situation by not directly participating. Hence, the researcher who participates is present only to conduct the observational research and not to influence or change the study situation. The focus here is to collect data in the setting of interest without influencing or changing it.

The researcher who participates in research of a prison cell block might study the cell block from an observation window, interview staff and inmates, or occasionally walk through the cell block. The researcher in this perspective is focused more on research goals than on participating, yet views participation in hands-on contact with the setting as important to data collection. Figure 8.3 shows that the researcher in this perspective focuses his or her research attention on the prison cell block but is not physically

Figure 8.2
PARTICIPANT RESEARCHER

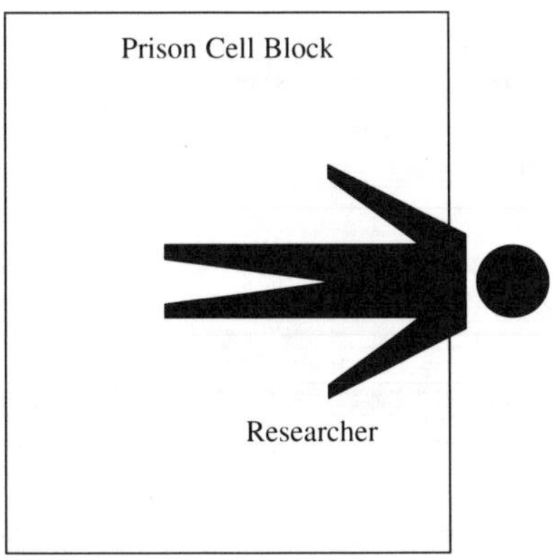

Figure 8.3
RESEARCHER WHO PARTICIPATES

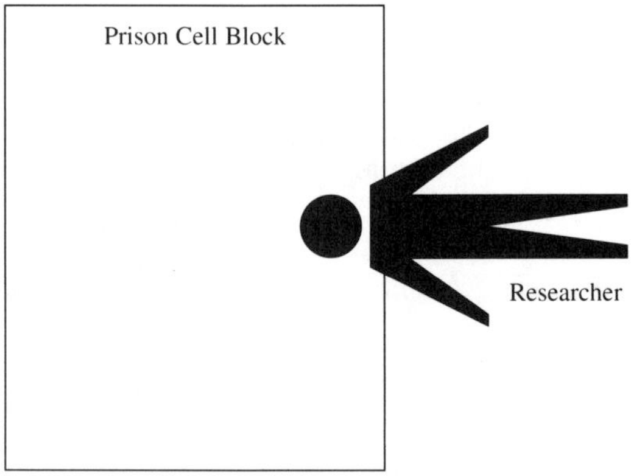

involved in the day-to-day operations of the prison. The mere presence of the researcher influences the setting. However, these influences are assumed to be so subtle as to not significantly change the setting. The researcher in this perspective is an "outsider" who is looking in.

The last perspective in conducting observational designs is that of the *complete researcher.* The complete researcher is totally invested in the research project, and the study situation is merely the context for collecting data. The complete researcher is similar to the survey researcher in that he or she does not get directly involved with the research subjects.

A complete-researcher project of a prison cell block could involve the study of video tapes from security cameras. This study would be based on data that would not influence the cell block situation in any way, because the cameras are already installed in the setting. The observational researcher who takes the complete research perspective endeavors to collect research data but not to change or influence the setting in any way. The complete researcher conducting an observational study is a complete "outsider" (see figure 8.4).

The use of these four perspectives depends in part upon the purpose of one's research and in part on the level of access one can gain to a particular research setting. Before the perspective is decided upon, a fully developed research design should be constructed, and the nature of the research one anticipates conducting should be well thought out.

There are also several other general issues that should be considered when conducting observational designs: (1) whether the observations are done on public, semi-public, or private areas; (2) the type of phenomena that are

Figure 8.4
COMPLETE RESEARCHER

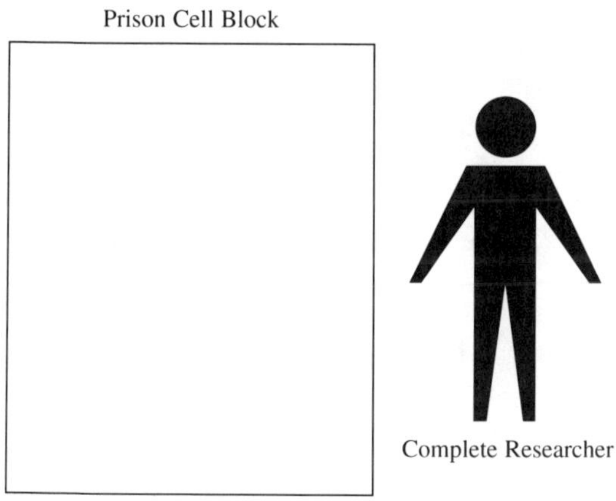

focused on (i.e., characteristics, causes, or outcomes); and (3) the time frame for observations. These issues influence how the observational research and data collection will take place.

The consideration of whether the observations are done in public, semi-public, or private areas is an important one. Public areas are those to which everyone has access. Public areas in criminal justice studies are the lobby of a police station, most adult courtrooms, and the streets surrounding the local jail. Semi-public areas are those with more restricted access, usually linked to a specific purpose. For example, a semi-public area in a police station could be the squad room, where witnesses and offenders might be interviewed. Private areas are those where access is denied to all but authorized and escorted persons. A judge's chambers, for example, are private. It is much easier for you to conduct a "complete researcher" observational study in a public area than in a private setting, because in a public area there are many others present and the presence of the researcher would not be considered unusual. Semi-public settings are most likely to be used by participant-researcher and researcher-who-participates perspectives. These areas are of limited access, and disclosure of the researcher and his or her purpose is usually necessary for access to these research sites. Finally, private areas are more likely to be used for full participant observational studies. For example, you could not study many details of a gang like the Hells Angels without some undercover infiltration of that subculture.

In most observational research, we focus on the characteristics of people, what causes people to behave as they do, or the outcomes of particular behavior patterns. Researchers may look at one or more of these concerns simultaneously. Typically, however, the researcher who conducts observational research would have some sense of the topical focus of the study prior to conducting the data collection and analyses. An example of an observational study of characteristics is a study of inmate communication patterns (with whom they talk and what they talk about). The focus could be on description. A study that focuses on causes would attempt to describe the causes of behavior. For instance, an inmate communicates with another inmate because they are from the same home town or because they are members of the same street gang (communication is due to "free-world" residential proximity).

Finally, a focus on outcomes attempts to explain the result of communications. That is, perhaps those inmates who communicate with many different inmates are less problematic than those who keep to themselves, or vice versa. The point in assessing outcomes is to answer the question of relevance or influence.

Advantages

It is important to understand the distinct advantages and disadvantages of observational research designs so you can make an informed decision about their applicability to the project you are interested in conducting. It is also important to know the advantages and disadvantages so that the strengths of this approach can be included and the disadvantages minimized in the design stage. The sections that follow highlight a few of the *advantages of observational designs.*

Direct Collection of Data

One of the biggest advantages of the observational designs is that they allow the researcher to directly collect data from the research setting of most relevance to the project. For example, rather than relying on the official robbery rates for a particular area of the city, the observational researcher could design a study to directly observe the area and the number and types of robberies that occur at that location. Many researchers presume that the UCR or National Crime Victim Surveys conducted by the Bureau of Justice Statistics provide accurate documentation of crime or victimization. Others refute and criticize these sources. However, these data sets are not based on direct observation of crimes or victimizations but on hearsay evidence from police reports or the victims themselves based on a sample survey.

Observational studies, on the other hand, can directly count and describe the details of every single incident during the observed time frame. Observational studies do not rely on indirect or hearsay sources, but they do rely on the actual observation of the study setting. In fact, observational designs are particularly well suited to collecting detailed data on phenomena or on characteristics directly from the subjects of the study. Survey research and interviews tend to concern the opinions of subjects rather than direct behavior. Similarly, while the use of statistics to analyze data is direct, statistics tend not to be detailed when taken alone (i.e., the crime rate tells us little about who was victimized, how they were victimized, and the costs of victimization).

Conducted in Natural Settings

A second advantage of observational designs is that they can be conducted in "real world," or natural, settings. One of the most damaging criticisms of experimental designs is that they create contrived or fake settings and that the study subjects may behave or perform quite differently in the real world. In addition, it is no small matter to set up an experimental design, especially in operational criminal justice settings where either ethical or legal restrictions prohibit such a research design from being fully utilized. Similarly, surveys or interviews are acquired out of the real world context of the setting about which the researcher is asking questions. This is not to say that surveys, experiments, or interviews are not valid and useful research designs, only that they do not, for the most part, rely on the study setting as it occurs naturally in the real world. If a researcher is asking citizens their opinions about the use of capital punishment, it is probably not crucial that he or she places the study subjects in the setting where capital punishment takes place. On the other hand, an observational study of the process of capital punishment from the perspective of the correctional officers charged with such a duty should be done only in its natural setting, and with an observational approach, because the correctional officers, death row, and the inmates are intricately interrelated. The subtle give and take between inmates and officers would be lost in a survey design, little data exists on such a setting, and an experimental control group may not exist. Hence, in natural settings where the researcher does not wish to alter the phenomena or behaviors under study the researcher can rely on the unobtrusiveness of observational approaches.

High Feasibility

Another advantage of observational designs is that they are workable in many cases where other designs would not be possible. Although the process of creating and conducting an observational design is challenging and requires much more than simply being present in the research setting, it is a process that can be easily engaged in and executed. Statistical studies may require years of mathematical training and experience in the use of mainframe or micro computers. Observational studies, on the other hand, can be conducted by any researcher who understands and can apply scientific research logic.

That is not to say that experience and specialized training is not needed to conduct good observational research, only that is is much more accessible to practitioners and researchers than more quantitative designs, which rely on statistical analyses and numerical data collection.

Observational designs are also feasible when a researcher has limited resources and when population generalization is not the goal of the study. For example, suppose you wanted to determine if a gang supervision unit in probation was effective at reducing re-offending while the offenders are under such supervision. In an observational design you could dress as a gang member and "hang out" in the waiting room of the probation office (complete participant). You might ask the "clients" about any recent offenses they committed. There are no official statistical data sets that would allow you to get this data, so only the observational design would be useful in such a setting.

In summary, observational designs are particularly advantageous where the research one is interested in conducting is done in direct contact with the study subjects, in the real-world settings where the subjects are actors or acted upon, and where it is not feasible or appropriate to collect other forms of data. Observational studies also allow one to collect a great deal of detail about the research setting in the context of the setting and the relevant actors in the study. Even though observational designs have these advantages, they tend to suffer from validity and reliability problems. The following section discusses these issues and some of the possible remedies to reduce these problems.

Disadvantages

The *disadvantages of observational designs* are not necessarily unique to these designs but are problems that must be minimized in most of the research designs explained in this text. In experimental designs the attempt to control these disadvantages is a primary focus. In survey or interview research designs a great deal of effort is made to collect a representative sample and to pretest the data collection devices to reduce errors. The following sections describe the problems one encounters in observational designs in more detail as well as suggestions for reducing the problems introduced by these disadvantages.

Reduced Accuracy

One problem with observational designs is the accuracy of the data, as a reflection of the population, that is collected. Researchers in any research approach are concerned with increasing the accuracy, or validity, of the data that they collect. However, in observational designs, because there is a tendency to collect data from nonprobability samples or small samples, the problem of accuracy is even more pronounced. One obvious result of the limitations in the representativeness, and therefore, the accuracy of the study subjects is that the data collected will be accurate only to describe the sample rather than to address the more general conceptual or theoretical issues at the heart of the purpose of the research project.

For example, suppose a researcher is studying a particular juvenile court process such as adjudication. Suppose further that the researcher is particularly interested in studying the incidents of judicial use of parental language with the juveniles who come before his bench. The data collected from this courtroom may or may not be likely to reflect the incidents and quality of *parens patriae* in the population of all juvenile courts in the United States, or in a particular state, or even in the local jurisdiction where the researcher conducts the study. Hence, the results from such an observational design may or may not be an accurate reflection of the population.

The goal of observational designs is not likely to be an accurate reflection of a population, although that would be nice. More commonly, the primary focus in observational designs is to collect details rather than to generalize to the population. One way to improve the representativeness of observational designs is to use probability sampling. For example, in the study of judges mentioned earlier, the researcher might randomly sample from all the juvenile courtrooms or of all scheduled adjudication hearings for a particular court during a specified time period.

There is also another accuracy consideration on the individual level. Observational studies tend to flow and develop as data are collected and are not based on collecting numerical values or frequencies in categories. For example, suppose the researcher collected data on Friday in the study courtroom and the judge on that particular day made a long speech to one particular juvenile offender in an attempt to counsel her to be a "better girl" and to "listen to your mother." The researcher would record as much as possible about this incident, yet this may not be an accurate reflection of the *parens patriae* attitude because it is an extreme example. In essence, the problem is that in the more open data collection of observational designs the individual variables may contain various meanings and may have been collected differently. These problems are dealt with in the analyses of the results of the observational data collection, but result in a data set that is perhaps inconsistent across the study subjects (adjudications, in this example).

The researcher in the process of conducting an observational study must also maintain a level of attention throughout the collection of data and record information similarly for each area of concern within the research project. This is not as easy as it sounds. For example, in a study of several dozen prisons over a period of several months the researcher may find his or her attention distracted. When I was involved in such a project I found that my notes included many distractions near the end of the project. I was focusing not only on the structure and process of the prison but also on irrelevant issues such as the types of cars in the parking lot and the nature of the library collection.

To improve the accuracy of individual variables across observations of subjects, one can: (1) write more descriptively; (2) use a specific process for recording research notes; (3) record only important information; and (4) use rigorous validation methods.

Writing descriptively involves training yourself to record major details and processes. You would also control the process for recording research notes. In order to increase the accuracy of research notes taken in the observational period, you could expand upon their content by reflection or by transcribing the tapes from a recorder used during the research. Whatever the method for recording research notes, the more structured, detailed, and accurate these notes can be made, the more valid the data will be. In the process of writing descriptively and reconstructing the notes, unimportant information should be excluded. Validation using rigorous statistical or logical methods could also be applied to the data that were collected to test for the validity of the observational data.

Lack of Consistency

Another problem in observational design is lack of consistency over the course of the research project. For example, the collection of data on the first day of the observational project may be different from data collection on the last day because researchers may develop their techniques more fully over time or they may get tired. To improve the consistency of data recording use a pretest recording sheet and do not change it throughout the course of the observational study. While this would improve the consistency of the data, it may not allow the observational researcher flexibility in the "process" of collecting data. Once again, the true value of observational studies is not collecting the same data from each study subject but creating a detailed and complete understanding of the behavior or phenomenon under study.

Subjects of Observation

Once you determine the particular perspective of your observational study (i.e., full participation to complete observer) you should consider the types of data you want to collect. There is a broad range of possibilities for the subject, from directly observable behaviors like a police "frisk" to more subtle and indirect indicators like police officer body language. The subjects of observational studies are akin to types of variables that the researcher collects. The observational data types that follow also provide additional definitional context for the nature and qualities of observational research. Hence, in the following sections several of the possible subjects of observations are discussed and examples of appropriate variables within each type are given. In practice, most researchers would collect several different types of observations, but in the following sections the discussion will attempt to focus on each type individually so as to make the explanations more clear.

Body Language

Some claim that as much as 90 percent of our communications are nonverbal, and *body language* is one prominent form of such communications. Body language consists of physical gestures and expressions used to communicate or emphasize verbal communications. Body language, therefore, includes facial expressions, hand gestures, and general body positioning. The researcher who intends to collect data on body language would focus on the body language as if he or she were watching a silent movie.

For example, if you have ever watched President Clinton give a speech you may have noticed that he slammed his fist on the podium during his speech. He was using body language to emphasize his verbal points. You could view several of his speeches to determine when he pounds his fist and then study other politicians to see if this is a universal body language for that group. Politicians are interesting subjects for observational studies of body language, especially during their campaigns, because they attempt to use body language in various ways to get people to vote for them. They often rely on consultants who instruct them in the proper use of body language in their speeches.

An example of a criminal justice observational study that could focus on body language is interactions of police officers and citizens. One way to approach the police for such a study would be to ask if the researcher could ride along with the police officers in a patrol car. The researcher in such a study could be a participant observer or a researcher who participates, depending on whether he or she felt comfortable about revealing the true research purpose to the individual police officers. The researcher would then carefully observe and systematically record the body language of the police officers and citizens in every encounter that the researcher observed. The researcher would also be likely to record descriptive factors of the police/citizen encounters, such as the location, the gender and race of the citizens and officers, whether there was an arrest, and so on. The researcher might then be capable of investigating whether the police interact with different categories of citizens differently. For instance, the researcher may focus on the use of body language to communicate with alleged offenders versus that used with witnesses or victims. Officers are likely to use a more forceful body position with alleged offenders (i.e., they will place their hand on their firearm) than they would with victims or when on service calls. This type of research would not be possible in a questionnaire study because the officers and citizens would be less likely to remember the details of the encounter or may not be willing to report their behaviors.

Spatial Behavior

Spatial behavior is a special case of body language. It is a subtle data collection approach and is appropriate for the complete observation perspective. Spatial behavior is linked with cultural values. In Arabic countries a very small space is required for normal conversations. When I was in Morocco, for instance, I observed Arab men having a conversation almost nose-to-nose while they were holding hands. On the other hand, in the United States a conversational distance of between four and five feet is expected. Spatial behaviors are measured by distances and positioning in space of two research subjects.

For example, in the police ride-along observational study in the body language section, I discussed the observation of police/citizen encounters. If researchers were interested in spatial behaviors of the research subjects they might estimate how close the officer gets to victims as opposed to offenders. Officers who desire to remain nonthreatening and help victims would be likely to maintain a distance of four to five feet. Conversely, when an offender is arrested the officers would have to get close enough to place their hands on the person. The analyses of the spatial behaviors of citizens and police could include assessing whether there are differences between spatial behavior for men or women (officers and/or citizens). The study of spatial behaviors could help improve our general understanding of different cultures and their interactions with police.

Language

Perhaps the most common observational focus when observing people is their use of *language,* what is said by the study subjects and within what context they said it. A focus on spoken words is perhaps the most apparent way to study an observational approach. Language would be an appropriate focus in full participation, participant researcher, and researcher who participates perspectives.

The researcher who focuses on language, however, can look at the explicit and implicit content of the language. The explicit content is what is stated. For example, if researchers were interested in the *explicit content* of inmate statements they would record the inmate's statement, for example: *"Inmates should do their own time."* The researcher would not attempt to analyze the meaning of this statement if the focus is explicit but would attempt to determine how many inmates felt this way about doing time. On the other hand, if researchers were interested in the implicit content of language they would attempt to interpret the meaning of the inmate statement about doing time. That is, the researchers might surmise that the statement that inmates should do their own time means that inmates should not bother other inmates or perhaps that they should not cooperate with the staff to make their time easier. The implicit focus on language would obviously require more detailed contextual data collection than the explicit approach, but there would certainly be more details in the data.

In addition to the focus on language in general, or the explicit or implicit content, there are two other categories of language that can be the focus of observational studies: extralinguistic and linguistic behaviors.

Extralinguistic Observations. Extralinguistic observations are those outside of the meaning, either explicit or implicit, of the spoken word. As the term "extralinguistic" implies, these subjects of observations are outside of the language context. For example, in a study of a courtroom work group (i.e., the judge, prosecutor, defense attorney, defendant, jury, or witnesses) we could look at the extralinguistic behaviors, such as who communicates to whom and what language they use in these communications. The judges would be more likely to use legal jargon with the attorneys than they would with the witnesses. The lawyers would also use very different language when they were communicating with the jury than they would with the judge. In essence, the extralinguistic observations are those noncontent patterns of speech that researchers are interested in collecting and including in the research data.

Linguistic Behaviors. Another noncontent aspect of language that can be used as the basis for observational studies are *linguistic behaviors.* These are all noncontent aspects of speech that attend the verbal language. Several linguistic behaviors can be measured, such as tone of voice, volume, cadence, and so on. These linguistic behaviors are similar to the extralinguistic ones in that they are very subtle measures of language. A criminal trial would be an interesting context in which to study these behaviors and could improve one's understanding of the give-and-take that is the "adversarial" process in the trial courts in the United States.

Physical Setting

Another subject of observational studies can be the *physical setting* of the study. The data relevant to the physical setting may include the amount of space that is available, how the space is utilized, and other characteristics of the physical setting, such as the lighting, temperature, or acoustical qualities. An observational study of the physical setting of a research project could be done from any perspective, from full participation to complete researcher.

An example of a study of physical space in criminal justice is examining several different jail cell blocks to determine if the differences in physical space are related to differences in the assaults-on-staff rates or stress levels. In such a study we could select a podular cell block, a remote supervision cell block, and a linear cell block from a particular jail to observe. We could then measure three variables: (1) the noise in each area; (2) the lighting; and (3) the size of the space that is available for each inmate. Then we could correlate these factors with the level of stress that is apparent in inmate-staff interactions. In this case the perspective is that of complete researcher. These three variables could be quantitative in measurement (i.e., noise = number of decibels, lighting = number of lumens, and space = number of square feet per inmate). This study of physical space could also be done by a full participant who either worked in or lived in each of the three cell blocks and recorded incidents of stress and the appearance of each physical structure.

Studies of physical settings are usually accompanied by other types of data collection. The collection of physical data is a good way to document and establish the context for the observational study.

Social Setting

A focus on the *social setting* under study could also be the subject of data collection in observational studies. Social settings can produce rich data for the observational researcher. The focus on social settings involves assessing the relationships and interactions between the subjects within their particular social roles or societal norms.

For instance, we could conduct an observational study of the social setting of a juvenile halfway house. The house parents have certain roles relative to the residents at the house. House parents make sure that the house runs in an efficient and appropriate manner. They ensure that the residents are fed and clothed and that they attend counseling and school. The house parents' role is administrator of the halfway house situation. Conversely, the juvenile residents are responsible for conforming to the house rules and, in some cases, formulating these rules.

The study of the social setting might involve the inclusion of language, body language, or even spatial variables. However, the focus is different than in these individual subjects of observation in that the researcher is interested in establishing a systematic and accurate description of the interactions and context of social situations and settings. The observational researcher that desires to conduct research on the social settings in a study can conduct this type of data collection from any of the four perspectives depending upon the level of access to the study situation. However, it is arguable that in order to get at the more subtle issues and variables involved in studying the social setting of a situation the researcher would probably have to be more of a participant than not.

Unobtrusive Indicators

Another approach to observational studies is to rely on *unobtrusive indicators,* measures that can be gathered without the research subjects' knowledge. For example, in a study on mentally ill inmates in jail that I conducted, I reviewed the psychologist's files and case notes. I observed these unobtrusive measures of case history and progress without the inmate subjects' knowledge. The most common sources of unobtrusive measures are official agency records. The police, courts, and correctional facilities all have official records of one sort or another that can be used for observational purposes.

In correctional research a common focus is on officer incident reports (Flanagan, 1980, 1983; Marquart, 1986; Senese, 1992). These reports are widely criticized as being inaccurate and inconsistent (see Wooldrege, 1991). While there is no doubt that the official records that correctional officers create have validity and reliability problems for some research purposes, they are not necessarily worse than direct observational study data or interview data. In fact, the official records are perhaps the most precise measures of the organizational culture of a prison or jail than anything that could be created by a researcher.

Direct observations and interviews are not the best ways to obtain valid and reliable data in operational settings. Because researchers are outsiders they are likely to misunderstand phenomena even though they are engaged in direct observations of the setting. If they are direct participants this is less likely to be the case, but even in these situations full participant researchers must do the operational job, and they may not have the time to fully and accurately record their observations. Similarly, when researchers do correctional officer interviews it takes considerable time and effort to develop rapport and trust before the interviews will be successful. They cannot expect to go into a correctional setting and immediately learn all there is to know without earning some level of trust. Researchers who conduct one-shot interviews in corrections, of either inmates or staff, should presume their data to be problematic at best and downright delusional at worst.

How is one to know whether the unobtrusive or observational data are worth anything? One way is to compare the official records with interview or observational records to determine if there are consistencies or inconsistencies. If the data from observations, interviews, and the unobtrusive data yield similar conclusions and findings, then one can assume the data are valid and reliable. For example, in a study of "Use of Force Reports" I conducted in a large prison system I corroborated my unobtrusive official reports with officer interviews, inmate interviews, observational studies, and reviews of use-of-force video tapes. There was a remarkable consistency between the factors I was looking at across all of these different sources.

For example, most use-of-force incidents in the sample of official reports are inmate-on-inmate fights. This finding was also found in the interviews with staff and inmates as well as on the video reviews. In sum, unobtrusive measures can help provide information as well as validate qualitative observations.

Nonoccurrences

Another focus of observational study can be *nonoccurrences,* those situations where we presume something should happen but it does not. These nonoccurrences could be relevant to the goals of a particular program or could be situational variables. For instance, in a vocational training program for inmates the goals of the program are to facilitate the inmates' employment upon release from prison. When former inmates in such a program do not get jobs, then that is a significant nonoccurrence. The situational nonoccurrences can be other aspects of the study situation or setting that the researcher identifies as important. For example, in a recent study that I conducted of a prison setting in which I collected observational data, I found it significant to note that I did not see one female correctional officer on the open yard, yet there were several male officers. In fact, this pattern was found in ten of the twelve prisons I studied in the same state. This finding might be very important to someone studying the differences in duties and attitudes of correctional officers in a particular state. This observation is an important nonoccurrence in my observational study of several types of prison layouts and supervision patterns.

There are occasions when what does *not* happen is perhaps more significant than what does actually occur. For example, if we decided to "cane" people as a criminal punishment for shoplifting and there was no change in the rate of shoplifting, that nonoccurrence would be a more important, and interesting, finding than if caning had reduced shoplifting. It may also be important to note whether the nonoccurrences are the result of mistakes, deceptions, accidents, or misstatements.

Collecting Observational Data

In collecting observational data it is important to keep in mind that the data collection should be systematic and structured. Even in a study that involves full participation one should structure and systematize the data one collects. For example, if I were to conduct a full participation study of the interpersonal dynamics of a criminal court jury, I would not take research notes during my service on the jury but would reconstruct my "observational data" when I went home each evening. I would make the data structured in that I would place all my observations of a certain type of interpersonal dynamics (i.e., communications) in one file folder. I would also systematically construct a range of file folders for each of the interpersonal dynamic types that I am interested in studying. Researchers should treat such data as methodically as they do more quantitative data. The following sections attempt to further clarify the issue of timing in collecting observational data as well as the physical recording of such data. In the final section, several guidelines are provided for conducting fieldwork in criminal justice settings.

Timing

A key issue in conducting observational studies is the *timing* of the data collection, that is, when the data will be collected. There are two polar choices with variations between these extremes (see figure 8.5).

Researchers can collect observational data at a single point in time. For example, we could observe each courtroom in a researcher-as-participant study of jury interpersonal dynamics on one day. The advantage of observing juries on one day is that we would have time to study several different juries in several different courtrooms, thereby increasing the validity of our data. The disadvantage is that the day we select to study may be very different from the typical day or there may be limited opportunity to study interpersonal dynamics; hence, the reliability of our data may be weak.

The polar alternative to conducting observations on one day at one point in time is to collect observations from many points in time. For example, in the jury study we would sit-in and conduct our research from the public gallery each day court is in session for the entire court calendar (usually three to four months). We could end up with a much better feel for how jury members interact with one another and others in the courtroom from such a study orientation. Our focus, however, is likely to be on one jury because of the time and material constraints of measuring observations every day for three months. Hence, the amount of detailed data collection would improve, but our ability to generalize from this data would be substantially weakened.

What should we do to resolve the issue of timing? That all depends upon the purpose of the study and the data collection needs at hand. If our purpose is generalizing from our observations, then it is more important to

Figure 8.5

RANGE OF TIMES FOR DATA COLLECTION

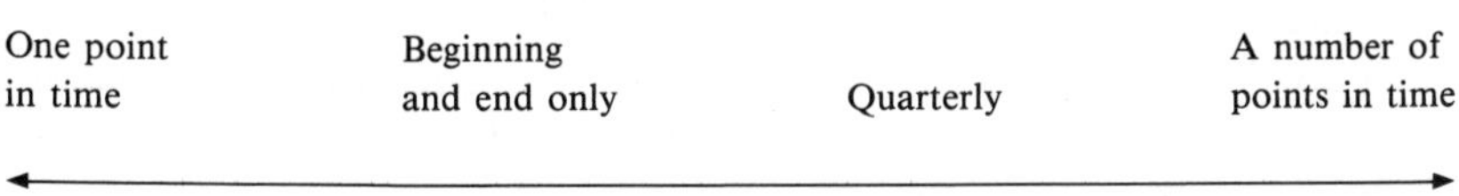

include a broader range of subjects, which necessitates a single-point-in-time focus. On the other hand, if we are interested in studying, in depth and as full participants, behaviors or phenomenon, we would be more likely to rely on multiple observations or multiple time periods.

Whichever time frame you select you should understand that there are validity and reliability trade-offs and that the approach you select should give you the best possible data with which you can address your research questions or hypotheses.

Recording Observations

There are several options for *recording observations.* Technological advances are likely to increase the number and quality of the options that are currently available. It is important to keep in mind, however, that none of these recording methods is intrinsically correct or incorrect; some are better in certain circumstances or research settings. The main recording methods are: (1) field notes; (2) reconstructed notes; (3) tape recording; (4) video tape recording; and (5) records study. These techniques can be used alone or in combination.

Field notes are taken in the research setting while the researcher is actively conducting the research. Full participants would not take field notes because they would have a job to do (i.e., functioning as a full participant first and a researcher second) and because their research purpose might be discovered by others in the research setting. However, for participant researchers, researchers that participate, and complete researchers, recording field notes is the most common form of data collection in observational studies.

I often supplemented my quantitative studies with field notes from observational contacts with agencies where I have done research. For example, in a study of a jail population forecast that I was asked to conduct, I set up a meeting with the warden of the jail and requested a tour of the jail so I could get a "feel" for how the operation was conducted. During that two hour tour and meeting I took extensive notes on what the warden said as well as several of my own observations about the conditions in the jail. These qualitative field notes were invaluable in writing up my quantitative forecast of the jail population.

The key advantage of field notes is that they are the records or observations made during direct contact with the research setting under study. However, it is difficult in some situations to take notes (e.g., in an open cell block with inmates). It is also difficult to write down observations quickly.

Because researchers that conduct full participation research cannot normally take notes during participation, they usually rely on reconstructed notes to create data for their studies. This is not to say that the other perspectives do not use reconstructed notes, just that it is more common in full participation studies.

Reconstructed notes are created after the researcher participates in the research setting. For example, a researcher who decides to study the roles and functions of police in the guise of a police officer would reconstruct his or her notes when completely through with participating as a police officer, usually after each shift. The reconstructed notes would be written on the basis of some structure and logic with regard to the research purpose.

The primary advantage of reconstructed notes is that they allow the researcher to fully participate or observe the research setting without the distraction of writing notes or controlling some recording device. In addition, reconstructed notes can be more completely developed in the creation process; that is, the researcher can fill in his or her reactions and speculations in addition to facts and observations during the reconstruction process.

Conversely, reconstructed notes may not be as accurate as recording notes directly during participation. Even in a systematic observational study it is likely that the researcher will forget some of the details in the situation. It is also difficult to reconstruct notes from an entire observational session (e.g., an eight hour shift) directly following that session, which is one of the primary ways to create such data.

Another option that is sometimes available is tape recording observations or observational settings. Some jails and prisons can provide sound records for their cell blocks, and these could be used as observational data in an unobtrusive sense. In an observational/interview study I conducted last year I asked officers whether they minded if I recorded my observations and our interviews. When they gave me permission, I used the tape recorder. There were a few officers that did not give me permission to use the recorder, so I took notes in these situations. But because I had taken the time to develop a good rapport with many of the jail staff over several months, I had no problem recording the interviews.

Tape recording is the best method when one is in settings that are not conducive to note taking. For example, I once conducted an evaluation of K-9 patrol officers on the third shift for a sheriffs' office. Since the shift began at midnight and did not end until 6:00 A.M. it would have been very difficult to take notes—it was dark and it's difficult to take notes in a moving police car. I received permission from the sheriff to tape record my interviews. I also asked each officer whether it was all right to record the interview.

Tape recording is also advantageous when the research setting is rich with observations and it is difficult to keep up with the setting through written notes. Recording also allows one to collect more information than might otherwise be possible.

The major problem with tape recording in observational studies is that it may affect the subjects. Even if they consent to the use of the tape recorder, they may respond in a different manner than they might otherwise. In my study of sheriffs I did not believe this to be the case, because I was present in the agency for about three months, and most of the officers already knew who I was before I conducted interviews. I also gave each officer several chances to refuse the tape recording of my ride-alongs. In other settings, tape recording is not so benign. For example, in a study of correctional officers' reactions and actions directed at the administration in their facilities, it is unlikely that the officers would agree to tape recording. If they did they would probably alter their behaviors or protect their language.

Another problem with tape recording is that voice records are not organized for analysis. One must transcribe sound records into printed or computerized versions. The process of transcription is not only expensive but also time consuming.

Finally, some researchers may attempt to use a tape recorder by stealth. Besides the obvious ethical problems (see chapter 13) with collecting such detailed information without the subjects' knowledge, there may be a legal violation of the right to privacy. When using sound recording of qualitative data, have the subjects sign an informed consent form that gives them sufficient information so that they can decide to allow or not allow this form of recording.

There is currently a revolution in the development of sound recording in the micro-computing environment with a proliferation of both sound recording and enhancement technologies. The improvements in tools for assessment will undoubtedly lead to more frequent use of this type of records in direct proportion to its accessibility.

Another modern observational data collection technology is video tape recording. For example, we could study the use of correctional officer teams against disruptive or assaultive inmates through studying video tapes of such incidents. We could also record interviews on video tapes and collect the data at a later point in time. Video taping technology has developed to the point where it is affordable, accurate, and portable, which means it can be appropriate for a variety of research settings and particularly in observational studies.

The key advantage of the use of video taping is that it is a multi-media record of the observational setting. Because it includes both visual and sound records it is a more complete source than sound recording alone. Video recording also allows the researcher to go back and review the data during the data coding stage. This could improve the accuracy of the data coding as well as the understanding of the observational situation or setting.

Video recording suffers from many of the same disadvantages as sound recording in that it may not be possible in many settings, because the subjects may be unwilling to allow its use. There is also no doubt that video recording against a person's will is a violation of privacy and research ethics. Even more troubling, however, is the fact that video records are only as good as the ability of the person using the video camera. Even in situations where the person conducting the video recording is a professional videographer there are limits to what can be captured by this recording device. Video records are fallible and can be quite deceptive if created from certain angles in poor lighting and without considerable forethought.

The last form of observational record that could be relied upon are records. While records are technically not observational data, they can be observed in addition to more traditional observational records of situations or phenomenon. If we want to study a cell block in a state prison, we might review the official records to supplement or prepare for our research.

The use of records in observational studies could also be more broadly defined. For example, we could decide to study the graffiti that inmates leave on the institutional furniture to determine what such a record means. Are inmates writing their wives'/husbands'/significant others' names on the furniture? Are there any gang signs or symbols in the graffiti? The observation of such "records" could produce interesting data for the jail administrator as well as the observational researcher.

The advantages of the use of physical records is that they can be the only direct data in an observational study. If the physical records are consistent with the observational record, then the validity of the study is increased. Another advantage of physical records is that they are readily available and are not time dependent like much observational data.

The key disadvantage with physical records is that they may not be available or that they are only superficial measures of the phenomena under study. For the complete researcher it makes sense to collect physical records. On the other hand, the true purpose of the full participant who is conducting research might be revealed should he or she attempt to collect physical records or official records.

Fieldwork Guidelines

Fieldwork, or observational studies, should proceed in as logical a fashion as quantitative or qualitative studies. The general goals of the observational researcher are to collect objective data in an unbiased way and to address the research questions or hypotheses of interest.

There are a few specific guidelines that can improve the focus and conduct of observational studies. First, researchers should have a clear understanding of the research perspective they are taking and of the potential benefits and costs involved in approaching different problems with the different approaches. A researcher who decides to pursue a full participation perspective should understand that once his or her identity is revealed, further research from that perspective may not be possible. Similarly, a complete researcher may look through an observation window into a jail cell block every day for a month, but he or she would not necessarily understand what it is like to serve time in that jail or prison. Each of the four perspectives has particular advantages and disadvantages, and these must be considered prior to conducting any research. In addition, researchers must balance the ideal perspective with what is possible in the real world of criminal justice settings. For example, while being locked up with inmates in a jail would give a researcher a good perspective on what it is like to be an inmate, few correctional organizations would be willing to risk the liability problems such a study would create.

The process of data collection in the observational study should be based on thought and the research purpose. The nature of observational data can range from unstructured reconstructed notes to highly structured counts of occurrences in the particular research setting. You should keep the research purpose in mind when deciding what data to collect. The data that is ultimately collected should be relevant to assessing the research purpose or questions.

Summary

This chapter has explained the particular advantages and disadvantages of the observational research designs. The directness and the context of observational studies lend themselves to detailed data collection, yet the data is representative of a population only insofar as the studied settings are representative of that population. There are several subjects of observational study ranging from body language and verbal language to nonoccurrences. Each is particularly appropriate in different observational research designs. Last, it is important to keep in mind the timing and recording techniques involved in observational designs.

Main Concepts

advantages of observational designs
researcher who participates
complete researcher
body language
language
linguistic behaviors
social setting
nonoccurrences
recording observations
full participant
participant researcher
disadvantages of observational designs
spatial behavior
extralinguistic observations
physical setting
unobtrusive indicators
timing

Discussion Questions

1. What are the particular advantages and disadvantages of each of the researcher perspectives?

2. Can criminal justice research settings be adequately studied from an observational perspective?
3. How can we increase the advantages of observational studies or at least decrease the disadvantages?
4. Which subject of variation is most appropriate in a study of police officers? Why?
5. In a jail what level of data collection (both timing and recording) makes the most sense? Why?

Exercise

Form into small groups of two to four people. Conduct an observational study of the Criminal Justice Department and other department offices. Observations should be made of specific activities such as phone calls, visits, and conversations. Each group should observe a separate department office, and then the groups can compare their observations.

9

SECONDARY ANALYSIS OF DATA

Learning Objectives

1. To describe the concepts and approaches involved in the analysis of existing data
2. To discuss the main federal sources of existing data and the particular advantages and disadvantages of each source
3. To describe the Inter-University Consortium for Political and Social Research

Chapter Outline

Introduction
Data Set Selection
Creating a Subset
Federal Data Sources
The Uniform Crime Reports
Problems with the UCR
Appropriate Uses of the UCR
The National Crime Victimization Survey
Limitations of the NCVS
Appropriate Uses of the NCVS
The National Criminal Justice Data Archive
National Data Archive
The ICPSR
Archival Holdings
Special Programs
Secondary Analyses of Existing Data
Summary
Main Concepts
Discussion Questions
Exercises

CHAPTER NINE

Introduction

The use of secondary data analyses is common in criminal justice and criminological research. This is due in a large part to the financial support and data collection efforts of the federal government through the Office of Justice Programs and, in particular, the National Institute of Justice and the Bureau of Justice Statistics. The Federal Bureau of Investigation also regularly collects massive amounts of data that are particularly relevant to criminal justice research topics through the Uniform Crime Reporting program. Given that so many data sets exist, it is important to discuss their use for various criminal justice research projects. The purpose of this chapter is to describe the types of data that are available as well as the contexts for secondary analyses.

Secondary data analysis is research that relies on data that have been collected for some other purpose or that are collected by someone other than the researcher. For example, while the Uniform Crime Reports are collected primarily for administrative purposes, they are also relevant to criminal justice research questions and analyses. Secondary analyses attempt to (1) address questions that the original data collection may not have imagined or intended, (2) to incorporate several different data sets to increase the power of explanation or to address more complex research questions, and (3) to examine longitudinally collected large-sample data to better define and describe trends in criminological phenomena.

Secondary analyses are frequently performed for criminal justice and criminological research questions. For example, in the Bureau of Justice Statistics (BJS) data set "Survey of Youth in Custody, 1987," data were collected on 277 variables from a representative sample of youths that were incarcerated throughout the United States. The purpose of the data set was to allow for a description of youths in custody. However, in a recent secondary analysis of that survey, the research focused on identifying the patterns of youths that specialize in violent crime and their distinguishing characteristics to determine whether they are similar or dissimilar to youths that do not specialize in violent crime. Whereas the BJS intended this data set to describe youths in custody, it also provided data to address the additional question about whether youths specialize in certain crimes and the explanation of specialists versus nonspecialists. This is just one example of the myriad studies and questions that can be addressed through a secondary analysis.[1]

Secondary analysis can also involve the use of multiple data sets. The incorporation of two or more data sets is an approach that can substantially increase the explanatory power of analyses that rely on one source of data. Such an approach can allow the researcher to pursue questions that either data set could not address when examined alone. This approach can be used for criminal justice data sets or it can bring in data from outside the fields of criminal justice or criminology. An example of the former type of secondary analysis is to conduct a comparative study of jails, prisons, and youth correctional facilities relying on the Bureau of Justice Statistics studies "Survey of Inmates of Local Jails," "Survey of Inmates of State Correctional Facilities," and "Survey of Youth in Custody." While the variables for these studies may not be identical, there are a sufficient number of them that are. Interesting comparisons of the populations and the criminal histories of the inmates in the three types of facilities could be conducted with these data. The beauty of such a secondary analysis is that the data for all three studies are based on nationally representative probability samples, which reduces the problems of unreliability and invalidity. In addition, the samples are large and there is a good number of different variables, giving the researcher many potential measures. Once again, it was unlikely that the Bureau of Justice Statistics was contemplating such an integration of the data sets they collect; otherwise, they would be more compatible. But they are sufficient for such secondary analysis uses.

On the other hand, researchers can also marry criminal justice data sets with non–criminal justice data sets to address secondary research questions that may not be possible with the criminal justice data alone. In my doctoral dissertation I incorporated jail population data with social service data (i.e., welfare rates, food stamp rates, and so on) and labor statistics (i.e., employment, civilian labor force). The data that I relied on for my study were collected by the Michigan Department of Corrections, the Michigan Department of Social Services, and the U.S. Department of Labor. The integration of these three data sets allowed for a much broader research focus on the relationships between local incarceration, employment, and welfare cycles than could have been possible with the criminal justice data set alone. The data were already collected by the listed agencies, so the cost of data collection was substantially less than it could have been considering that I was looking at ten years of monthly data for several variables and locations. Many data sets and secondary research questions can be addressed with either local data or national data. This integration approach is limited only by the researcher's imagination and the form of the data that are collected.

An example of the use of secondary analysis to conduct assessments of the trends might examine the populations of jails across the United States. In this case we could rely on the National Jail Census of 1978, 1983, and 1988 conducted by the Bureau of Justice Statistics. Aspects of these data sets that could prove interesting are assessments of the populations of urban versus rural jails and whether there are regional differences in the jail populations. There are also a series of national jail surveys that could allow researchers to conduct secondary analyses of the mental health of jail inmates and changes in inmates' criminal histories over time. The use of preexisting data sets to address time series questions is particularly advantageous. Few researchers have the budgets to collect such data over time nor can many devote the time and energy to the collection of such large scale studies.[2]

Data Set Selection

The process of *data set selection* for a secondary analysis should be driven by the purpose of the research. While there are data sets that lend themselves to exploratory data analyses, studies that have a strong conceptual and/or theoretical foundation will be easier to conduct. Suppose that we gained access to a data set on the fear of crime. In an atheoretical approach we could look at the data for anything interesting (i.e., relationships, groupings of fearful people vs. the nonfearful, and so on). However, we would still be required to reconstruct or create a conceptual basis for our exploratory study after the fact and attempt to retrofit whatever we might find to the analyses we stumbled upon. There is also a chance that what we found through our data exploration may already have been found by other researchers. If this is the case, we have wasted our time on the secondary analysis.

If we studied the fear of crime literature before going to the data set to conduct our analysis, we would be in a much better position to describe what the data show in reference to our research questions and what is already known. We would also approach the data analysis more systematically and logically rather than through hit-and-miss exploration. While there are cases where exploratory analyses of existing data are required, the formation of a conceptual basis for such studies should be undertaken before one "plays" with the data. The idea here is that one should have a clear and supportable idea about the type of questions one wants to address before conducting any analyses.

To select an appropriate data set for a secondary analysis, the researcher should consider (1) the purpose of the research, (2) the research population, and the (3) feasibility of access and use of the data. First, the purpose of the research should be considered when selecting the existing data to conduct a secondary analysis. There are essentially three purposes for research: description, explanation, and exploration. There are differences in the data and the analysis approaches for addressing each of these general purposes. For example, when conducting a descriptive study of law enforcement agencies a researcher would be interested in data that are representative of the population of such agencies. The data should allow for as accurate a description as possible. The Uniform Crime Reports may not be a good source of descriptions of law enforcement agencies, although this is certainly one source that should be considered. More appropriately, a researcher might select the Bureau of Justice Statistics Law Enforcement Management and Administrative Statistics data to describe law enforcement in the United States. The data one selects should be appropriate to answering the general research questions the researcher wants to address.

The research population should be considered when selecting the data set for a secondary analysis. If a researcher wants to generalize to the population of inmates in jails in the United States, then data from one jail or one state is probably not sufficient. While local or state data would certainly be viable for secondary research, it would be a fallacy to suggest, based on data analysis findings, that it would apply to the entire country. As a general rule of thumb, the secondary analyses are generalizable only to the populations from which the data were collected by the primary researcher. It is also important to note that whereas descriptive and explanatory research tends to have population generalization as a goal, exploratory studies are more typically concerned with developing improved conceptualizations.

Creating a Subset

A common approach in secondary analysis is *creating a subset* that includes only those variables that are pertinent to the research question at hand. This was more necessary in the past, because many computers, both mainframes and microcomputers, had more restrictive memory limitations, and extremely large data sets were less manageable than they are today. The technical considerations in manipulating and handling extremely large data sets are much less of a barrier now. Yet, many universities and criminal justice system computers cannot handle large data sets, and therefore a concentration on only relevant variables and a smaller data set may be necessary.

Another reason for creating a subset of data is that the researcher is relying on several sources for the data in the project, and the data codebook can be simplified through the exclusion of unnecessary variables. For example, if the researcher were interested in the relationship between social conditions and criminality, he or she might select variables from social service agencies (welfare rates, food stamp distributions), community agencies (housing value, vacancy rates, population density), and criminal justice organizations (crime rates, calls for service, jail population). It is usually easier to create a new data subset than to try to directly integrate data from disparate sources. Most computers can handle both creating a subset of data and dealing with the original data. However, the former is much more easily accomplished than is the latter.

Federal Data Sources

The Uniform Crime Reports

The *Uniform Crime Reports (UCR)* produced by the Federal Bureau of Investigation are the oldest continuous criminal justice data set available in the United States. Many researchers, the media, and some administrators rely on the UCR as a primary source for data on crime rates. The UCR coverage includes 98 percent of the total population of the United States. Hence, the crime statistics the UCR reports are as close to population values and as nationally representative as criminal justice data sets get. The primary objective of the FBI in collecting and reporting crime statistics through annual Uniform Crime Reports is to create a reliable data set for criminal justice administrators for operational and managerial activities (UCR, 1993). However, the UCR not only has become a key research and criminal justice indicator but has also achieved the status of a leading social indicator akin to the Gross National Product.

Having given the UCR such accolades I would be remiss if I did not mention the problems associated with the use of the UCR in research and administration. Even though the FBI, in consultation with the International Association of Chiefs of Police and the National Sheriffs' Association, has implemented many quality assurance standards and controls on the reliability and validity of the data the UCR reports, there are persistent data limitations.

The UCR is complied through voluntary cooperation by over 16,000 law enforcement agencies throughout the United States. There are two general methods of reporting to the FBI. The first involves direct reporting by police departments to the FBI of crime statistics. This is not as common as the second method of indirect reporting to a state-level UCR program agency (usually housed in the state police organization). There are currently forty-two state-level UCR organizations. The state-level UCR programs impose quality assurance requirements on the local agencies and are able to more directly assist local law enforcement agencies in their administrative and operational questions regarding their crime rates.

The FBI collects information on (1) Index Crimes (Part I crimes), (2) known offenses, (3) cleared offenses, and (4) Part II crimes. The Index Crimes are recorded by the number of the most serious offenses that are known to have occurred. These are typically reported in rates per 100,000 people in order to make them comparable across various population areas in the United States. The Index or Part I Crimes are murder, nonnegligent manslaughter, forcible rape, robbery, aggravated assault, burglary, larceny-theft, motor vehicle theft, and arson. These are usually the primary media focus when crime rates are reported on television or the newspapers. Part II crimes are all other crimes not classified as Part I crimes with the exception of traffic offenses. Cleared offenses are those where someone was arrested, charged, and turned over to court prosecution or cleared by exceptional means (e.g., the police pursue an offender in a high-speed chase and the offender is killed).

The UCR is currently undertaking a massive redesign effort to make the crime statistics more reliable and valid as well as to improve their utility for police administrators and researchers. The focus in this redesign has been on developing an incident-based reporting system wherein data will be collected on each crime incident for over twenty different crime categories. In addition, the National Incident Based Reporting System (NIBRS) will collect incident, victim, property, offender, and arrestee information. There are currently only four states that report NIBRS data: Alabama, Idaho, North Dakota, and South Carolina. It is likely that the full implementation of these data collection systems will be completed within the next decade or two, but there remain both logistical and operational difficulties associated with implementing these systems. However, substantial political and technical problems need to be overcome before nationwide NIBRS is a reality.

Problems with the UCR. While there are certain situations where the UCR is "the only game in town," there are flaws in the current reporting system. The FBI takes as many precautions as practicable to ensure that the data they collect is reliable. However, a focus on collecting consistent records does not mean that such records will be accurate. It is important to note that the FBI assigns the final responsibility for data submissions to the contributing law enforcement agencies. While this gets the UCR program "off the hook" it suggests that there can be unforeseen problems in data.

One of the greatest limitations of the UCR is not what it tells us but what it does not tell us about crime. There are many crimes that do not come to the attention of law enforcement or that are solved or "cleared" through arrest. Hence, the UCR reports only what is known and not the total amount of crime in society. Even for crimes that are well reported there are gaps in the UCR reports. For example, murders tend to be reported because there is a body, yet there are murders that never get "cleared" and others that do not get discovered. Law enforcement agencies rely on citizen reports to gain knowledge about crimes, and it is probable that there are many crimes (even Part I crimes) that the public fails to report to the police.

Another problem with the UCR is that the definitions for offenses are state specific. Each state in the United States has its own penal code defining crimes and punishments. While the UCR has exerted great efforts to universalize the definitions they rely upon, there is no doubt that there are inconsistencies in reporting from the state UCR programs or the individual police departments. There is always something lost in the translation, and such errors are no doubt present in the UCR given the large number of jurisdictions that report and the differences in the criminal law across the United States.

An additional problem with the UCR is related to the reporting process itself. The person who completes the UCR at the police department level may have been assigned to a desk job involuntarily. Many people in law enforcement select policing as a career because they are interested in serving the community on the street. Placing such an individual in office duty is likely to result in a less than thorough focus on desk tasks. Even though the state UCR programs are assigned to review departmental reports, they have no control over the staff who are assigned to record such information. This source of error should be recognized in the UCR.

Appropriate Uses of the UCR. While the UCR has its problems, as do most large-scale data sets, it is the most appropriate data in many cases. In fact, there are situations where it is the only available data set. When the choice is between a less-than-perfect data source and not studying an important research question I for one would prefer to conduct the study. There are three general areas where the UCR appears to be particularly appropriate. These are when one is interested in conducting (1) research on crime at the national level, (2) comparative studies, and (3) studies of crime over time.

If you are interested in a national-level study of criminality, there is virtually no other source than the Uniform Crime Reports. While the National Crime Victimization Surveys claim to be representative nationally, they are based on a sample of less than 1 percent of the population, whereas the UCR is based on police reporting from over 95 percent of the law enforcement agencies across the country. There are no other data sets that allow you to make national, regional, or state level comparisons. Therefore, the UCR is clearly indispensable for this type of research.

A second appropriate use of the UCR is for comparative studies. While there are many data sets that would allow you to compare one area with another, few are nationally representative. For example, if you were interested in assessing where homicides are the highest in the United States, there would be little choice but to use the UCR. These comparisons may also be based on time. That is, there are few, if any, data sets that would allow you to study crime rates for a particular area or state over time that have been in existence since the 1930s. While the UCR has problems its use can be appropriate if the researcher recognizes its limitations. Clearly, there are other uses where the UCR is appropriate beyond those listed here.

The National Crime Victimization Survey

The *National Crime Victimization Surveys (NCVS)* have been conducted since the early 1970s. This is the second largest household survey program conducted by the federal government (BJS, 1993). The NCVS provides victimization data on both personal and household victimization. The data are collected by the U.S. Bureau of the Census for the Bureau of Justice Statistics. The NCVS asks large samples of the population about their victimization and goes beyond the coverage of the UCR in that it asks questions about the kinds of crimes and victims, the characteristics of crimes, the impacts on victims, as well as whether the crime was reported to the police. In fact, one of the most distinct advantages of the NCVS is that it allows for an estimate not only of crimes reported to police but also of those that are not reported. The NCVS includes the crimes of rape, robbery, assault, burglary, personal and household larceny, and motor vehicle theft, which makes it comparable to the UCR for these crimes.

The NCVS is based on a sample of citizens of the United States and usually includes a very large sample. For example, in 1992, about 166,000 interviews were conducted in 84,000 households (BJS, 1993, p. 36). Another important aspect of the NCVS studies is that the response rate has been consistently high (over 90 percent).

The design for sampling households is based on a panel design. Panel designs include the same units of analysis over time. The selected households stay in the sample for about three years and are interviewed seven times during their participation in the study (each interview is considered a panel). This design is robust and allows for a clear bounding of the victimizations that people may report, that is, the victimization within the three-year study can be tracked within that period and not over the course of the respondents' entire life. This establishes a clear time frame for when victimizations occur.

The NCVS data collection procedures are based on an interview design. The interviews are conducted on a structured format. The field representatives interview everyone in the household over twelve years of age. The interview begins with a brief screening questionnaire to assess whether any crimes have occurred in the past six months. If any crimes are reported, detailed follow-up questions concerning the time, place, and occurrence are asked. While all of the initial interviews are conducted in person by a census field representative, the six remaining interviews are conducted by telephone.

Recently, the National Academy of Sciences and the BJS engaged in active redesign and improvement of the NCVS. In particular, the "screening" approach has been improved, and new questions on rape and family violence have been added to the interview guideline. Another innovation is the use of computer assisted interviewing. While computer-aided telephone interviewing (CATI) is being phased in, the use of computer-aided personal interviewing (CAPI) is being reviewed.

The NCVS is a valuable asset to criminal justice research in that it provides information that cannot be obtained from the UCR. The primary value of the NCVS is that it includes reported and unreported crimes as well as detailed information about each criminal incident that is reported. However, as is true with the UCR, there are certain limitations to the use of the NCVS. The following section describes a few of these limitations.

Limitations of the NCVS. While the NCVS creates valuable information about victimization in the United States, it has limitations due to the nature of sampling, interviewing, and subject participation that cannot be easily dismissed. One problem with the NCVS is that it is sample based. Theoretically all samples are inaccurate to some extent. That is, no sample exactly represents the population from which it has been drawn, even if it is large. The chances of the sample being accurate increase as the sample size increases, relative to the population. The NCVS sample is, at most, 166,000 respondents and is claimed to represent 255 million citizens in the United States. Even though the UCR fails to measure unreported crimes, its coverage of the U.S. population is more nearly complete than the NCVS. Moreover, the NCVS sample is not a probability sample—it's a quota sample. Therefore, there are additional problems with the representativeness of such sampling.

Another potential problem with the NCVS is that it is conducted by interviewers. Whenever interviewers interact with study subjects there is likely to be some influence on the data collected. While the Bureau of the Census hires and trains professional and capable field representatives, the process of interviewing may produce data that are different from the true case (interviewers influence the data collection). The influences of the interviews are varied as well because the first interview is conducted in person (face-to-face interviews tend to introduce more bias than telephone interviews). An additional problem is the fact that the six follow-up interviews are conducted by telephone. Telephone interviews do not result in the quality and quantity of information that could be collected by observation or face-to-face interviews. In addition, the level of interaction between respondents and interviewers reduces the ability of interviewers to ask quality probe questions.

Another limitation of the NCVS is that it is based on the reported victimization of subjects. Hence, it depends on the memories and willingness of respondents to report what happened to them. Even though the NCVS is bounded by the six month intervals, the possibility that respondents may not remember being victimized between interviews must be recognized as a potential problem. In addition, the NCVS requires that respondents perfectly understand the questions being asked of them. Given the diversity of the citizens in the United States it is difficult to argue that all questions will be understood similarly by all people from our many subcultures. Although these three limitations of NCVS data are important, there are few national data sets that collect such consistent and reliable information as the NCVS.

Appropriate Uses of the NCVS. Having pointed out several potential limitations to the NCVS data, it is important to also point out that it is the only national data set that concerns victimization. Therefore, there are research situations where it is the only appropriate data set.

The NCVS is particularly well suited to studies involving victim policy issues. For example, the women who do not report their being raped to the police could be compared to those who actually report rapes to determine what differentiates the two groups of women. Such a study could contribute to the improved handling of victims of rape so as to increase reporting and to assist in the reduction of rape victimizations.

Victim surveys are also well suited to studying crime control, victim's rights, gun control, school crime, and domestic violence, to mention a few of the topics (BJS, 1993, p. 2). The NCVS has shown that nearly two-thirds of all crimes are reported to police. It has also shown that crime has decreased since the 1980s. In terms of different types of victims it has shown that blacks are more likely than whites to be victims, that persons under twenty-five, males, and that those that live in central cities are most likely to be victimized. It has also shown that violent crimes are more likely to be committed by strangers and that victim and offender in a crime tend to be of the same race.

In sum, the NCVS has addressed several important issues about crime incidents and the nature of victimization that could help us form policy as well as drive additional theoretical explanations and solutions. Thus, the NCVS has distinct benefits, as does the UCR, and the researcher should recognize the particular data that is included in each and the requirements of the research questions being posed.

In the 1990s secondary data analysis is not restricted to the UCR and NCVS. Several other specific studies have been collected and provide a large range of types of data for secondary studies. The following sections provide general descriptions and examples of these data sources.

The National Archive of Criminal Justice Data

The Bureau of Justice Statistics in the U.S. Department of Justice sponsored the creation of the *National Archive of Criminal Justice Data (NACJD)* in 1978 and housed this collection at the University of Michigan's ICPSR. The reason for the creation of the archive, and its continued mission, is to facilitate and encourage criminal justice research and the sharing of data resources. In addition, the NACJD provides machine readable data and SPSS source codes.[3] The criminal justice archive also provides training and technical assistance for those wishing to use their data. The only drawback with the NACJD is that it exclusively focuses on quantitative data sets. There are many ways to conduct research, and the quantitative approach is simply one method that is well suited for some purposes but poorly suited for others. Figure 9.1 lists the several types of data collections that are housed at the national criminal justice archive.

The goal of the NACJD makes both economic and research sense. Many of the federally created data sets have been considerable economic investments. For example, imagine the cost of conducting 10,000 or more interviews, each lasting thirty to sixty minutes. It would be a poor return on such an investment if the data were used only once and not made available to others who might use the data. On the research side of this issue, some researchers may be able to combine data sets that might not otherwise be combined to produce evidence for inventive basic research or for policy recommendations. For example, when I was in graduate school a professor I did some work for was studying juvenile delinquency. Because she was interested in creating the most reliable and accurate data about delinquency, she endeavored to collect data from several federally funded studies that had been done in the past. Instead of relying on a sample of a few hundred juveniles, she created a data set with thousands of juveniles. The strength of her generalizations and the range of variables were much improved. This and other creative research approaches, as well as large data set research, could not take place without a framework like the NACJD.

National Data Archives

The main depository for social science data in the United States is located at the University of Michigan in the *Inter-University Consortium for Political and Social Research (ICPSR)*. Most, if not all, of the results of the major data collection efforts conducted or funded by the federal government are housed at the University of Michigan. The basic purpose for collecting data sets in this national archive is to facilitate additional studies of these data sets, thereby gaining additional information and value for the investments in these large-scale data collection efforts. The following sections describe the structure of the ICPSR, its general holdings, and specific criminal justice holdings. The NACJD is also housed at the ICPSR Archive.

Figure 9.1
TYPES OF DATA COLLECTIONS AT THE NACJD

1. Attitude surveys	8. Delinquency
2. Community studies	9. Government response
3. Corrections—Adult	10. Corporate behavior
4. Corrections—Juvenile	11. Official statistics
5. Court case processing	12. Police
6. Courts	13. Victimization
7. Criminal justice system	14. Drug use and crime

The ICPSR

The Inter-University Consortium for Political and Social Research has served social scientists around the world for more than thirty years. The basic goals of the ICPSR are (1) to be a "central repository and dissemination service for machine readable social science data," (2) to provide basic and advanced statistical training, and (3) to collect resources that facilitate the use of advanced computing technologies by social scientists (ICPSR Guide, 1994).

The ICPSR was founded as a partnership between the Survey Research Center and the University of Michigan and twenty-one universities throughout the United States. In 1993, the ICPSR had over 370 college and university members in the United States and abroad. In fact, the data sets that are collected at the ICPSR concern social phenomenon and studies from over 130 countries.

The ICPSR can provide data on several different formats, including magnetic tapes, micro computer diskettes, and CD-ROMs. The most common form of data distribution is magnetic tapes. These tapes are the preferred data storage vehicle for data sets on mainframe computers where the user needs to move a data set from one computer to another. While these tapes are clumsy and require expert assistance to use, they can store extremely large data sets and are quite reliable. Most mainframe system operators can easily download a data set from a magnetic tape. The ICPSR also distributes a few of its data sets on diskettes and CD-ROM, but these are limited in choice. However, the ICPSR has recently made available a CD-ROM on Crime and Justice data sets (1992) and Victimization data (1993).

Archival Holdings

The content of the archive contains machine-readable records of attitudes and social phenomenon from the full rasnge of the social sciences, not just in criminal justice or criminology. The archive has data sets for economic, sociological, historical, demographic, political science, and psychological studies. Recently there has been expansion of the archive to include data sets for "urban studies, education, electoral behavior, socialization, foreign policy, community studies, judicial behavior, legislators (national, state and local), race relations and organizational behavior" (ICPSR Guide, 1994). One of the largest data sets housed at the archive is the U.S. Census, which covers the entire history of the censuses done in this country (1790 to present) as well as all of the roll call votes in Congress (both House and Senate) from 1790 to the present.

The data sets are obtained from (1) scholars, (2) public agencies, (3) private agencies, and (4) governmental agencies/organizations. In addition to the National Criminal Justice Archive the ICPSR houses the National Archive of Computerized Data on Aging.

Special Programs

The ICPSR conducts and facilitates several special programs to further the use of their data sets and help social science researchers. The ICPSR runs a summer training program in quantitative methods every summer. The summer program covers a broad range of methodologies but focuses on quantitative analysis methods. The summer program emphasizes developing researchers' skills in conducting computer-based secondary research that utilizes the ICPSR holdings.

The ICPSR has also maintained a Consortium Data Network (CDNet) since June 1986. The CDNet allows users to order data sets, to access data bases for on-line reference to ICPSR holdings, to access ICPSR data, and to send and receive electronic mail from the ICPSR staff.[4] Eventually, the CDNet will have the capability to allow users to download machine readable data sets directly through the Internet and FTP (File Transfer Protocol).

The ICPSR has developed several informational data bases, primarily for accessing information about the holdings of the ICPSR (ICPSR GUIDE, ICPSR VARIABLES, and ICPSR ROLLCALLS). However, one data base contains extensive information about references to published and unpublished materials bearing on survey research methods (SMIS).

Secondary Analyses of Existing Data

The secondary analysis of existing data is preferred by some because much of the technical work has been completed by the original researcher. The primary researcher has taken the time, and assumed the expense, of collecting the data and coding it in a machine readable form and is likely to have conducted many of the preliminary analyses. Hence, much of the ground work for further studies is already available for secondary data sets. There are also situations where the federal government has funded the collection of a data set and there is little research conducted on that data other than a summary descriptive report. For example, the Bureau of Justice Statistics regularly conducts the National Jail Survey but produces only a summary descriptive report of the data. Such a data set is ripe for secondary analyses. Similarly, the Bureau of the Census reports only the data they collect by certain geographic areas. The Bureau of the Census does not conduct extensive research on the data they collect. Although most sources of secondary analysis have well-developed data sets there are certain considerations that must be undertaken prior to conducting further studies. In the following sections several issues regarding secondary data analyses are discussed: (1) data coding and secondary data sets and (2) missing values.

Data coding is the process of turning observations or raw statistics into a machine readable format. Data coding is basically the process of establishing a road map to the data. It allows a researcher to determine the location of each statistic in the overall data set. For example, suppose that a researcher wishes to create a data set. A possible data coding plan is shown in figure 9.2.

For most preexisting data sets the primary researcher has established a data codebook to convert their observations into a computer readable format. In fact, the ICPSR and the NACJD provide very detailed codebooks of all of the data sets that are available to criminal justice researchers. If one is creating a subset of someone else's data, it is a good idea to write a codebook for that subset. The crucial information that must be included in the subset are the column locations and the names of the variables (see figure 9.2). However, it is also helpful, because of the way computers are able to label and process data, to include data abbreviations and an identification code that is unique to each case in the study, so that any errors can be quickly located.

Figure 9.2
DATA CODEBOOK PLAN

Columns	Variable	Abbreviation
1–2	Identification Code	ID
3–11	Population	POP
12–17	Unemployed Persons	UNP
18	Region 1 = North, 2 = South	REG
19–25	Number of Inmates	NOI
26	Security Level 1 = Maximum, 2 = Medium 3 = Minimum	SECL

Another important issue is the existence of missing values. Given the large scale of the federal data collection efforts there are cases where the subjects are unable to answer. For example, in the National Jail Survey there are questions about the mental health of inmates. Many inmates do not answer these questions, and the BJS codes these as missing. It is exceedingly difficult to include variables such as this in studies. Before utilizing a secondary data source, one should be certain that there are enough cases with sufficient data.

Summary

Secondary data analysis is the reuse of data that already exists. This type of analysis can be accomplished through using data for a purpose other than originally intended, through combining data sets for a new purpose or through the assessment of variables and indicators over time. This chapter describes the Uniform Crime Reports, the National Crime Victims Survey, and the national data archive at the University of Michigan. The many sources of criminal justice data provide possibilities for many important additional studies of criminal justice topics and issues.

Main Concepts

Uniform Crime Reports (UCR)
data set selection
UCR problems
National Crime Victimization Surveys (NCVS)
limitations of the NCVS
National Archive of Criminal Justice Data (NACJD)
creating a subset
uses of the UCR
uses of the NCVS
Inter-University Consortium for Political and Social Research (ICPSR)

Discussion Questions

1. What is the coverage of the UCR and the NCVS?
2. What is the best data source for studying crime over time? Why?
3. What does the ICPSR do?
4. What is NIBRS? How is it an improvement over the current UCR?
5. What improvements have been proposed and implemented for the NCVS?
6. Which sources of secondary analysis are most believable? Why?

Exercise

Form into groups of two or three. Propose secondary data analyses for the following situations.

1. Combining two or more criminal justice data sets.
2. Examining social phenomena over time.
3. Combining two or more criminal justice and non–criminal justice data sets.

The research design for each of these secondary data analyses should include a rationale for the purpose of the secondary research and the compatibilities, and potential incompatibilities, of the data you propose to use.

10 BASIC DESCRIPTIVE ANALYSES

Learning Objectives

1. To demonstrate which statistical analyses are appropriate with particular types of data
2. To discuss applied interpretations of descriptive statistics
3. To facilitate the ability to match data, statistical techniques, and interpretations to appropriate research questions and purposes

Chapter Outline

Introduction
Basic Graphical Displays
Frequency Tables
Charts
Bar Charts
Pie Charts
Line Charts
Central Tendency: Averages
Mode
Median
Mean
Central Tendency: Variation
Index of Dispersion
Range
Standard Deviation and Coefficient of Variation
Relationships
Association
Spearman's Rho
Pearson's Product Moment Correlation Coefficient
Summary
Main Concepts
Discussion Questions
Exercises

CHAPTER TEN

Introduction

Descriptive analyses are usually the first data analyses in research studies in criminal justice or the other social sciences. A researcher is first interested in what the data look like as a group rather than as individual observations of the people, places, or things that he or she is interested in studying (see chapter 12). Descriptive analyses are akin to the analyses done by a medical doctor before he or she prescribes treatment. The doctor takes your temperature, measures your blood pressure, checks your heart rate, and so on. The doctor collects several descriptive measures of your body systems in order to get a "feel" for your overall health and to determine whether more complex, costly, and time-consuming tests are necessary. Descriptive analyses give a researcher a "feel" for the data and establish a basis for undertaking further, more complex analyses if these are necessary or of interest to the researcher.

While this chapter focuses on statistical descriptive analyses, you should not get the impression that descriptive analyses must be quantitative. For example, if you were conducting an observational study of the behaviors of prostitutes in a redlight district, you could "describe" the sample of prostitutes—there are twenty female and two male prostitutes, most seem to work on the street and out of a flop-house hotel, and so on. The descriptive portions of a qualitative study are often the richest findings. However, you should not presume that the only way to approach description is through conversion to statistics. Qualitative studies could be analyzed by combining like cases and qualitatively describing the trends and themes in the data (see chapter 12). Descriptive analyses, whether they be quantitative or qualitative, are basic to the analysis of data in that they create a general picture about the study subjects in particular with reference to the variables that were collected.

Quantitative descriptive analyses are generally less understood by students. They tend to be covered in a non–criminal justice/criminology statistics course that is less relevant to the unique problems and perspectives in our field. Also, the applied emphasis of this text requires an interpretative emphasis rather than a computational one. The following sections discuss and provide examples of basic graphical displays of data, averages, variation, and relationship measures.

Basic Graphical Displays

Often the beginning point in a descriptive analysis is a graphic display of the data. This is done because researchers presume that a picture is worth a thousand words. While most contemporary microcomputers create graphic displays through the use of programs such as Microsoft Excel or Lotus 1-2-3, you should pay particular attention to the types of data required for each of these figures as well as the interpretations of the display.

The researcher's basic choice in graphic displays is between tables and figures. Often researchers present the most complex statistics in tables. You may skip over the tables when you read research articles, but you will miss much of the "meat" of an article and perhaps misunderstand it if you do so. Tables are summaries of the analyses that have been conducted and can facilitate your understanding of the research. Therefore, you should take the time to read tables and make some effort at understanding them. A process model for interpreting descriptive or more complex tables is as follows:

1. Read the title of the table to get a sense of its content. Many authors tell you the variables and the types of analyses they have used in the title.
2. Look at the major subheadings of the columns and rows in the table. These tell you what the statistics within the table refer to.
3. Look at the numbers in the table. Sometimes authors explain the numbers in the text of the research report or paper, but you may also be able to understand them by simply reviewing the table.
4. Ask your instructor about statistics you do not understand. Your instructor should be able to help you interpret the table (or at least tell you where you could find additional information).

With a bit of concentration and effort most tables are understandable. The following sections provide examples of tables and graphs.

Frequency Tables

The most common descriptive analyses presented in tabular form are frequency tables. These tables range from simple to complex. The most basic form presents only the number of observations in each category (see table 10.1).

In frequency tables the numbers of observations in the study are simply presented. Thus, in table 10.1 the number of different levels of security staff are listed and summed. This table is an improvement over the raw data—a list of all 313 participants in the study and their security levels. But it provides only basic information about the numbers of jail staff in each security level. Table 10.1 indicates that the jail staff is mostly composed of correctional officers rather than supervisors. Within the supervisory ranks there are clearly more line supervisors (sergeants) than any other level (lieutenants and captains). On the basis of table 10.1 further analyses may be conducted of the types of correctional officers. How many of the officers are male? How many are female? How much experience do the officers have? What are the duties of the captains? In sum, a simple *frequency distribution,* as illustrated in table 10.1, is a beginning descriptive analysis that forms the basis for study.

In a more complex frequency distribution, further analyses are presented in order to more fully describe each category. A more complex form of frequency distribution is presented in table 10.2.

Table 10.1

NUMBER OF SECURITY STAFF IN GILDER COUNTY JAIL

Level of Staff	Number
Officers	234
Sergeants	65
Lieutenants	10
Captains	4
Total	313

Table 10.2

FREQUENCY TABLE OF SECURITY STAFF IN GILDER COUNTY JAIL

Level of Staff	Number	Percent	Cumulative Percent
Officers	234	74.76%	74.76%
Sergeants	65	20.77%	95.53%
Lieutenants	10	3.19%	98.72%
Captains	4	1.28%	100.00%
Totals	313	100%	100%

Table 10.2 shows that three-fourths of the security staff consists of correctional officers. It also shows that one-fifth of the security staff are sergeants (first-line supervisors). Hence, most inmate management is done by correctional officers, who as a percentage of all security employees outnumber their immediate supervisors (sergeants) by a ratio of more than three to one.

Frequency tables can also be done on grouped data. Grouped data are data that are summaries of more discrete categories. For example, in tables 10.1 and 10.2 the categories of officers, sergeants, lieutenants, and captains represent security employees and could be combined into one "grouped" category labeled "security" (see table 10.3). Furthermore, if you were to construct a frequency table about all the employees in the jail you might wish to group the data by security employees, treatment employees (psychologists, social workers), maintenance staff (plumbers, electricians), medical staff (nurses, doctors), and others (volunteers, computer operators). Grouped data further summarizes the absolute number of categories in the data. Often the grouping of data can provide a more useful summary of the data. For instance, in table 10.3 the summary is based on more general categories of employees of the jail rather than on specific categories. You should be careful when grouping individual data, as the number of grouped categories reduces the complexity of the individual data. Instead of having fourteen or fifteen types of employees, you may categorize employees into five or six groups of categories, which may result in an overly simple reduction. For instance, if you form two groups according to the variable "age"—over twenty-one years and under twenty-one years—much meaning is lost. But if you were looking at illegal drinking by minors, you might be interested only in these two general categories. The size of the grouped categories also relates to the precision presented in the table (the larger the groupings of individual categories, the less precision). The visual organization of the table is also important.

Table 10.3

FREQUENCY TABLE OF EMPLOYEES IN THE GILDER COUNTY JAIL

Level of Staff	Number	Percent	Cumulative Percent
Security	313	75.97%	75.97%
Treatment	75	18.20%	94.17%
Maintenance	8	1.94%	96.11%
Medical	13	3.15%	99.26%
Others	3	0.73%	99.99%
Totals	412	99.99%*	99.99%*

*These do not sum to 100% due to rounding errors.

Frequency tables can have more than one variable. These tables are referred to as bivariate and multivariate tables. Bivariate tables have two variables, and multivariate tables have more than two variables. An example of a bivariate table (security level employees and gender) is shown in table 10.4. Tables that have more than two variables list the subcategories under the column headings (see table 10.4). Multivariate frequency tables often contain a great deal of information and require close attention to detail when interpreting them.

The bivariate and multivariate tables can also include percentages, cumulative percentages, and other relevant statistics. It is apparent that these tables can become quite complex as more variables and descriptive statistics are added.

Charts

There are a multitude of charts and figures that can be used to present data. Software for microcomputers allows you to easily create charts (such as Lotus 123®, Excell®, MS-Works®). These programs are flexible in terms of the types of data that can be used and labeling the charts, as well as the number of different types of charts they produce. The three most common types of charts are bar charts, pie charts, and line charts.

Bar Charts. A bar chart of the staff levels is illustrated in figure 10.1. *Bar charts* typically use nominal or ordinal variables. They can also be used for interval and ratio variables that have been converted into nominal or ordinal categories. The interpretation of bar charts is based on the relative size of each of the bars. Larger bars indicate a higher frequency of occurrence. There are other forms of bar charts where the bars begin at the left and move to the right, multivariate bar charts (for example, gender at each staff level would have to be represented by bars), and other, more esoteric bar chart designs.

Table 10.4

FREQUENCY TABLE OF SECURITY EMPLOYEES AND GENDER IN THE GILDER COUNTY JAIL

	Gender	
Level of Staff	**Males**	**Females**
Security	300	13
Treatment	25	50
Maintenance	8	0
Medical	7	6
Others	3	0
Totals	343	69

Figure 10.1
BAR CHART OF SECURITY LEVEL BY GENDER

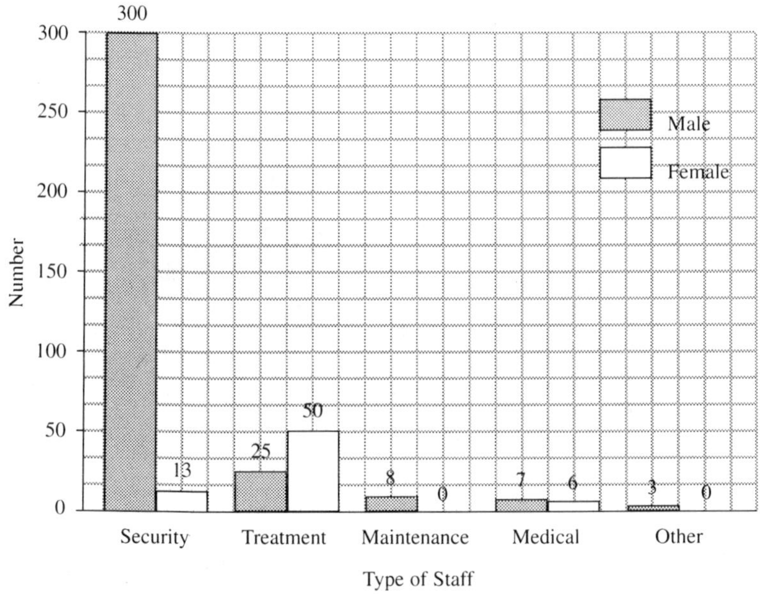

Pie Charts. A pie chart of the staff levels is illustrated in figure 10.2. *Pie charts* show the relative dispersion of cases for each category for a variable that generally has fewer than five categories. Figure 10.2 shows that a pie chart for the staff level variable clearly demonstrates that the largest proportion of staff is employed in a security position. Pie charts are a very effective way to communicate the relative proportions of attributes of a nominal or ordinal variable because most people readily understand the concept of percentages.

Line Charts. A line chart of the number of employees in the jail is shown in figure 10.3. *Line charts* are usually used to show a time-series variable such as numbers of employees over time. It is also common to see time points along the horizontal axis and relative values along the vertical axis. Line charts plot the corresponding points of observations on the horizontal number scale and the vertical number scale, and these data points are joined together with a solid line. The term "scattergram" refers to a special kind of line chart where the points have not been joined together by a line. There are also line charts with more than one time-series displayed.

Figure 10.2
PIE CHART OF SECURITY LEVEL

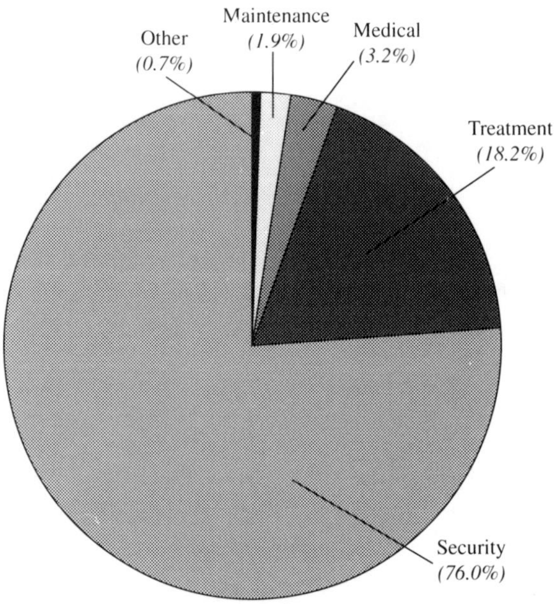

Central Tendency: Averages

In order to clarify basic descriptive statistics, the measures of averages and the measures of variation will be described separately. The issue of central tendency is important in the initial descriptive analyses of research because more complex analyses are often dependent upon certain central tendency characteristics. *Central tendency* can be defined as the common characteristics of a variable for a sample. For example, the average age of a sample of inmates is thirty-four years. The central tendency measure for age is therefore thirty-four. The averages in central tendency are mode, median, and mean. These statistics are indicators of the most common point in the data that one is analyzing. There are three averages because of the different types of precision in the data (nominal, ordinal, interval, and ratio levels of measurement). Each type of data has a "most appropriate" measure of average based on the level of precision.

Mode

The *mode* is the most frequently occurring number in the distribution. The mode is the simplest measure of central tendency and is, therefore, not viewed as an overly precise or informative measure of average. In addition, the mode is the only measure that is appropriate for the nominal level of measurement (categorical variables). This is the case because nominal level variables cannot be mathematically manipulated. There is no rank order and no way to compute a mathematical average. For example, if a police officer driving a paddy wagon counted the numbers of different types of offenders he transported to the city jail, he could get the results shown in figure 10.4. Based on these data you could not sum the numbers of incidents and divide by the total to produce a meaningful "average" (see figure 10.5).

Figure 10.3
LINE CHART OF STAFF OVER TIME

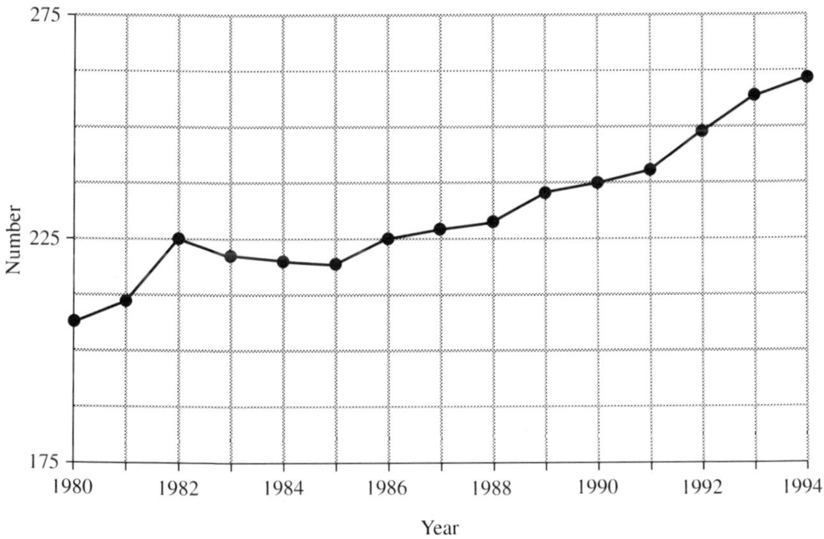

Figure 10.4
MODE

Types	Number
Drunks	12
Drug sales	5
Theft	11
Disorderly	7
Other	2

Figure 10.5
MODE

Types	Number
Drunks	12
Drug sales	5
Theft	11
Disorderly	7
Other	2
Total	37
	37 ÷ 5 = 7.4

The statistic 7.4 in figure 10.5 has no meaningful interpretation relative to the types of inmates that the officer transported to the jail. That is, the statistic 7.4 says nothing about the "average" type of offender the officer transported.

The mode is typically determined through inspection, that is, you select the most frequently occurring category of a nominal variable. For example, assume that you have collected the political affiliation of ten judges in your state (see figure 10.6). Through inspection of the political affiliations claimed by the judges you determine that the most frequently occurring one is Republican, or category 1.

While the mode is a useful calculation, and the only calculation of average available for nominal variables, it provides the least amount of information of the three average measures. However, the mode can be found for any level of measurement as long as the variable is measured at the nominal level. It is important to note that variables can have one mode or they can be multimodal. That is, there can be situations where there is more than one mode. In these cases, the mode is less useful. For instance, there could be four Republican judges and four Democrat judges, in which case the variable would be bimodal.

Median

The *median* is the middle-most value in a distribution of values. It is the point in the distribution of values at which 50 percent of the scores fall below and 50 percent of the scores fall above. In order to calculcate a median you must have at least an ordinally measured variable. The median can be one of the values in a distribution (if the distribution has an odd number of values) or may fall between two values in a distribution (when there is an even number of values in the distribution). Some statisticians refer to the median as the fiftieth percentile.

The median is determined through four basic steps (see figure 10.7). First, the values in the distribution must be rank ordered—that is, they must

Figure 10.6

POLITICAL AFFILIATION OF JUDGES

Subjects	Ideology Category*
Judge Jones	1
Judge Smith	1
Judge Wesson	3
Judge Kaster	1
Judge Stern	1
Judge Richard	1
Judge Hertz	1
Judge Holmes	2
Judge Buher	2
Judge Stalone	2

*Republican = 1; Democrat = 2; Other = 3

Figure 10.7

CALCULATING THE MEDIAN: ODD NUMBER

Subjects	Age	Rank
Jack	12	12
Alicia	13	12
Joe	12	12
Wayne	14	13
Ilene	15	13
Patricia	13	13
Alice	12	14
Karen	13	15
Gina	17	17

Step 1: Rank data (reorder values from low to high)

Step 2: Odd $(9 + 1) \div 2 = 5$

Step 3: 5th position

Step 4: Median = 13

Interpretation: Half of the sample is younger than 13 and half of the sample is older than 13

be placed in consecutive order from lowest value to highest value. Second, the median position in the numerical array, or rank order, must be located. This is done in two ways depending on whether there is an odd or even number of ranks. If there is an odd number, the median position is determined by adding 1 to the number of values and dividing that sum by 2 (see figure 10.7). If there is an even number of values, the median position is found by dividing the number of values by 2 and adding 1 to that product (the median is positioned between the two position values) (see figure 10.8). The third step is to count from either the top or the bottom of the distribution the number of positions. If the distribution is odd in number, the median value is defined by position. If the distribution is even, the median is between two positions. The fourth step is used on the even number of values distributions. If there is an even number of values, add the two values that correspond to the calculated position values and divide by 2. The median in a even distribution is *between* two position values.

Mean

The *mean* of a distribution of scores is the mathematical or arithmatic average. The mean is the first average measure that is numerical in both calculation and definition. While the mean is the most commonly used measure of average, it has stringent data requirements. The data must be at least interval level (i.e., crime rates, incarceration rates, and so on). The mean is determined by adding all the values in the distribution and dividing that sum by the total number of values (see figure 10.9).

The mean is useful for both descriptive and inferential purposes. In fact, the mathematical proofs for the mean are the basis for many more complex inferential analyses. At the same time you should interpret the mean

Figure 10.8

CALCULATING THE MEDIAN: EVEN NUMBER

Subjects	Age	Rank
Ginana	13	12
Jack	12	12
Alicia	13	12
Frank	12	13
Wayne	14	13
Ilene	15	13
Patricia	13	14
Alice	12	15

Step 1: Rank data

Step 2: Even 8 − 2 = 4th
(8 − 2) + 1 = 5th

Step 3: 4th and 5th positions

Step 4: Median = (13 + 13) ÷ 2 = 13

Interpretation: Half (50%) of the sample is younger than 13 and half of the sample is older than 13.

Figure 10.9

CALCULATING THE MEAN

Subjects	Age
Jack	12
Alicia	13
Joe	12
Wayne	14
Ilene	15
Patricia	13
Alice	12
Karen	13
Kyle	13

Step 1: Add ages of each subject = 117

Step 2: Divide sum by number of subjects = 104 ÷ 9 = 13

Step 3: The product of step 2 is the mean (mean = 13 years)

Interpretation: The mean age is 13 years.

cautiously because it is influenced by extreme values and the sample size. For example, assume that five cities have murder rates as follows: city 1 = 12, city 2 = 56, city 3 = 45, city 4 = 3, and city 5 = 21. The mean is 27.4. However, if city 2 were removed, the mean would be 20.25, which is a rather large difference. When there are extreme values, the median is a more accurate measure of average.

Central Tendency: Variation

In addition to the basic indicators of averages, statisticians have constructed indicators of the shape of the distribution. Where the mean provides a common valve for the entire distribution, the variation indicators give you a sense of the overall range of values. Not only is this crucial to many statistical analyses, but also it provides additional descriptive information about the statistical values that have been obtained from the people, places, or things you are studying. In fact, if there is little or no variation, there is no need to conduct further study. If everyone scores an 80 percent on a job performance test, there would be no need to study this issue. Moreover, there would be little to look for if different groups (men, women, old, young) did not perform differently on the test. All criminal justice and criminological research eventually boils down to a description and/or explanation of the variation of the distribution of scores on a variable. Because we are examining the distribution of scores, variance can be modeled (through probability theory). Probability theory allows us to use samples as reasonable representations of populations and to better understand our research queries. Because variance can be modeled, we can make inferences about the amount of variance we believe may be found in similar situations.

Index of Dispersion

The *index of dispersion* is a measure of the amount of variation in observations across categories of a nominal variable. It can be calculated only for a nominal level variable, or one that is assumed to be measured at the nominal level. The smallest value the index of dispersion can take on is zero, which indicates that there is no variation across the categories (this usually happens when the observations are concentrated in one category). The largest value it can take on is 1, which indicates there is the maximum possible distribution of values across the categories (the observations are distributed evenly across all the categories) (see figure 10.10). The value of the index of dispersion will be between 0 and 1.

An example of an index of dispersion where there is a great deal of concentration (e.g., less dispersion across the categories) is illustrate in figure 10.11.

Figure 10.10

CALCULATING THE INDEX OF DISPERSION

Categories	f	f^2
Murder	4	16
Rape	11	121
Assault	79	6,241
Robbery	45	2,025
Other	10	100
	149	8,503

Step 1: Square the frequencies in each category.

Step 2: Substitute values in the formula and calculate.

Formula: $d = \dfrac{k(n^2 - \Sigma f^2)}{n^2(k - 1)}$

Where: k = number of categories
n = number of cases
f = frequencies in categories

Example:

$$d = \frac{5(149^2 - 8{,}503)}{149^2(5 - 1)} = 68{,}490 \div 88{,}804 = .7712$$

Interpretation: The calculated value is near 1; therefore, there is a large dispersion across the categories of violent offenses.

Note: The capital sigma (Σ) requires that we summarize all the values to the right of the symbol. In the index of dispersion in this example, we must add all the f^2 numbers to get the value of 8,503.

Figure 10.11

CALCULATING THE INDEX OF DISPERSION

Categories	f	f^2
Murder	1	1
Rape	0	0
Assault	79	6,241
Robbery	0	0
Other	0	0
	80	6,242

Step 1: Square the frequencies in each category.

Step 2: Substitute values in the formula and calculate.

Formula: $d = \dfrac{k(n^2 - \Sigma f^2)}{n^2(k - 1)}$

Where: k = number of categories
n = number of cases
f = frequencies in categories

Example:

$$d = \frac{5(80^2 - 6{,}242)}{80^2(5 - 1)} = 158 \div 25{,}600 = .0061$$

Interpretation: The calculated value is near 0; therefore, there is a little dispersion across the categories of violent offenses.

Range

The *range* is also a simple measure of variation. The range can be calculated only for ordinal, interval, and ratio level variables. It cannot be calculated for nominal values because it requires an order in the categories; that is, one category must be larger than another variable category (male and female, for example, as categories, cannot be ranked) (see figure 10.12). Because the range can be calculated for ordinal level variables, range is more precise than the index of dispersion in theory, but not in most actual cases, due to the range's ability to use a higher level of measurement. However, in calculating the range you simply identify the "range of values" in a distribution. Calculation of the range is easy unless there are a great number of observations in the distribution of values, in which case it becomes more tedious.

While the range is a valid measure of the degree of variance, you should be careful in its application. First, the range is not comparable across distributions (or variables) because it is based on the values in the distributions (or variables) rather than some standardized scale like the index of dispersion. Distributions that have larger scales will have larger ranges. For example, the range in homicide rates will typically be a small number because there are relatively few homicides, whereas the range of larcenies is much larger because there are more of these. Second, the range is influenced by extremely large or small values in the distribution for which the range is being calculated. Hence, it may not always reflect the actual degree of variation in the distribution of scores. For instance, if Jill's age (figure 10.12) were sixty-five years, the new range would be forty years. For most of the people in the distribution that range is too large. Hence, you should use caution when interpreting and comparing the range across distributions.

Figure 10.12

CALCULATING THE RANGE

Subjects	**Age**
Jill	34
Jack	32
John	31
Joan	30
June	29
Jerry	27
Jon	31
Jeff	33
Jeni	28
Julie	26

Step 1: Find the high value.

Step 2: Find the low value.

Step 3: Subtract the low value from the high value and add 1.

Example:
Step 1: Jill is 34
Step 2: Julie is 26
Step 3: $(34 - 26) + 1 = 9$ years

Interpretation: The ages of the subjects vary by 9 years.

Standard Deviation and Coefficient Variation

The standard deviation has a mathematical meaning and interpretation:

> The standard deviation is the square root of the arithmetic average of the sum of the squared deviations around the mean in a distribution. (Lutz, 1983, p. 117)

More simply stated, the *standard deviation* standardizes the measure of variance by using the mean as the reference point. This measure of variation is the amount of differences (statisticians call these "deviations") of the individual values in the distribution from the mean value. Hence, it is unlike the unstandardized value produced in the range calculation. While the standard deviation is not directly comparable across distributions, it can be used for either descriptive or inferential purposes.

The standard deviation for the age of the sample of ten juveniles is completed in three steps (see figure 10.13). First, the age for each child is squared (multiplied by itself) and then both the original ages and the squared ages are summed. These values, along with the number in the sample (n), are applied to the formula. It is important that the "order of operations" be followed with these calculations. That is, all of the inner-most parentheses must be completed prior to second level parentheses and brackets, and all multiplication and division must be done before addition and subtraction. For example, the inner-most parenthesis requires us to square the sum of the ages $(\Sigma)^2$ which results in a value of $83^2 = 6{,}889$. Next, we divide the value of 6,889 by our sample size of 10 which produces a value of 688.9.

Figure 10.13

CALCULATING THE STANDARD DEVIATION

People	Age	Age²
	X	X^2
Bill	10	100
Bob	9	81
Beau	7	49
Brian	10	100
Bryan	9	81
Bran	7	49
Bonnie	8	64
Betty	6	36
Bobby	11	121
Brad	6	36
	83	717
	ΣX	ΣX^2

Step 1: Square the individual values.

Step 2: Sum the squared values.

Step 3: Apply the formula.

Formula: $s = \sqrt{[(\Sigma X^2) - ((\Sigma X)^2 \div n)] \div n - 1}$

Example: $s = \sqrt{[(717) - ((83)^2 \div 10)] \div 10 - 1}$

$s = 1.7669$

n = number in sample

The calculation within the brackets can now be completed $[(\Sigma^2) - (\Sigma)^2 \div n]$ resulting in the following: $717 - 688.9 = 28.1$. This value is then divided by 9 ($n - 1$ or $10 - 1 = 9$) which results in a value of 3.1222. Finally, the square root of 3.1222 is calculated resulting in the standard deviation value of 1.7669. The standard deviation is similar to the mean in that it is a purely mathematical measure. The interpretation of the standard deviation age is that it is 1.7669 years.

The standard deviation can be calculated only for interval and ratio level variables. The standard deviation is a basic building block for many of the more sophisticated inferential analyses. The standard deviation describes the unit deviation from the mean. For example, if the mean weight of the inmates in a prison is 165 pounds and the standard deviation is found to be 15.78 pounds, you could interpret the amount of variation around the mean weight based on the expected normal distribution. That is, 68 percent of the inmates should be between 1 standard deviation above the mean (i.e., 180.78 pounds) and 1 standard deviation below the mean (i.e., 149.22 pounds) if the distribution of weights are normally distributed. In addition, probability theory allows you to predict that 95 percent will be between ±2 standard deviations, and 99 percent will be between ±3 standard deviations.

The sensitivity of both the range and the standard deviation to the values observed in the distribution under study creates the need for a more standardized or universal measure of variation. The *coefficient of variation* is such a universal measure. The coefficient of variation is based on the standard deviation and mean values. The coefficient of variation is superior to the standard deviation because it considers, simultaneously, both the central tendency and the deviations from the mean. Therefore, the coefficient of variation is more readily comparable across different variables and samples than is the standard deviation.

A demonstration of the calculcation of the coefficient of variation is shown in figure 10.14. As the example demonstrates, the coefficient of variation is simply the standard deviation divided by the mean and that product multiplied by 100. This creates a standardized measure (a percentage) of the variation in the distribution.

The interpretation of the coefficient of variation also considers, or takes into account, both the average value and the distribution of values. For example, the coefficient of variation in figure 10.14 is interpreted as follows. The ages in the sample distribution vary by 21.29 percent around the mean age of 8.3 years.

Relationships

Association

Researchers are often interested in describing whether variables are related. That is, they want to describe how similar or dissimilar two or more variables or measures are to one another. At the most basic level, *association* describes the joint occurrence of two variables (Lutz, 1983). For example, a question that can be addressed on association could be: "What is the joint occurrence of gender and opinions of the death penalty?" In this situation you may be interested in describing the opinions of men and women (and their differences) toward the use of the death penalty. The goal in statistical description of the association between the variable "gender" and the variable "opinion" toward the death penalty is to precisely, concisely, and quantitatively describe the pattern. For example, suppose that we studied 100 people of various genders about their opinions toward the death penalty and the patten shown in figure 10.15 resulted, which generally appears to show that men are in favor of the death penalty and women are against it. This pattern clearly demonstrates a relationship, yet we cannot get a precise measure of that association through mere inspection of the two variables. On the other hand, we may get a pattern of response shown in figure 10.16. Although we can see no differences in opinion by gender, we cannot

Figure 10.14

CALCULATING THE COEFFICIENT OF VARIATION

Step 1: Calculate the standard deviation.

Step 2: Calculcate the mean.

Step 3: Compute the coefficient of variation.

Formula: CV = (standard deviation ÷ mean) × 100

Standard deviation = 1.7669 (from example 10.13)
Mean = 8.3
Coefficient of variation = (1.7669 ÷ 8.3) × 100 = 21.29%

Interpretation: The ages of subjects in our sample vary by about 21.29% around the mean age of 8.3 years.

Figure 10.15

OPINION ABOUT THE DEATH PENALTY

Gender	In favor	Against
Men	50	0
Women	0	50

Figure 10.16
OPINION ABOUT THE DEATH PENALTY

Gender	In favor	Against
Men	25	25
Women	25	25

precisely state an indicator or simple number that documents the lack of association in this case. The reason statistics are used instead of just observations of the numbers is because the contrast between the two variables, or the patterns of relationships or associations is usually not as clear as in these two examples. The most common measures of association for nominal level variables are the chi square and the Cramér's V.

The most common statistic of association between two categorical or nominal level variables is the chi square. The *chi square* basically compares the differences in the observed frequencies with what could be expected if their is no association (see figure 10.17). That is, when we conduct a study, we observe certain data. If the study is a survey, the survey responses are observed values for the sample under study. On the other hand, if the study is an observational study, the qualitative notes or observations are the "observed" data for the study subjects. The chi square measures the observed data against a "no relationship" standard. The expected values reflect this "no relationship" standard against which the observed data are compared. The larger the differences between what is observed for the study subjects and what would be found if no relationship existed, the larger the chi square value. The two main limitations for the chi square are that we have at least twenty subjects in the study and that the expected values for each cell be greater than five. The chi square also should not be used in comparative studies of two samples, because it is bounded by the number of cases and the scale of the variables in each sample.

The data indicate that there is a weak relationship between the two variables. As long as the chi square is greater than zero, some association is present. Hence, we can immediately determine whether or not an association between two variables exists through the use of the chi square statistic. In addition, the chi square statistic can be compared to its maximum possible value (the minimum is always zero) in order to determine the relative strength of the association (as shown at the bottom of figure 10.17). However, a comparison of chi square values across cross-tabulation tables of different sizes cannot be done because the sample sizes will influence the values. Chi square values are not standardized measures of association.

While we can generally state that the larger the coefficient is, the greater the association, these values cannot be compared for dissimilar cross-tabulation tables. The *Cramér's V* is a more universal chi square based statistic because it considers both the size of the chi square value and the maximum possible value it can take on. For example, a Cramér's V calculation for the chi square between gender and opinions about capital punishment is shown in figure 10.18.

The Cramér's V can be found for any size cross-tabulation frequency table. Its value range is always between 0 = no association to 1 = perfect association. Researchers often attach arbitrary verbal labels to the levels of association and correlation coefficients. While such a scheme is listed in

Figure 10.17

CHI-SQUARE ASSOCIATION

Number	Name	Opinion
1	Joe	Favor
2	Patricia	Favor
3	Annette	Not favor
4	Brian	Not favor
5	Bill	Favor
6	Roberta	Not favor
7	Frank	Favor
8	Max	Favor
9	Pat	Favor
10	Robert	Not favor
11	David	Favor
12	Robin	Favor
13	Gina	Not favor
14	Gianna	Not favor
15	Fran	Favor
16	Kathy	Not favor
17	Angel	Not favor
18	Alicia	Not favor
19	Alice	Favor
20	Mary	Favor
21	Lisa	Not favor
22	Amye	Not favor
23	Pete	Not favor
24	Chris	Favor
25	Harry	Favor

Example Calculations

Summary table

	Male	Female	
Favor	8 a	5 b	13
Not favor	3 c	9 d	12
	11	14	25

Formula: $\chi^2 = \Sigma[(f_o - f_e)^2 \div f_e]$

$f_e = (\text{row} \times \text{column}) \div \text{total}$

Chi square calculation:

a = $(8 - 5.72)^2 \div 5.72 = .9088$
b = $(5 - 7.28)^2 \div 7.28 = .7141$
c = $(3 - 5.28)^2 \div 5.28 = .9845$
d = $(9 - 6.72)^2 \div 6.72 = .7735$

Chi square = 3.3809

Maximum Value = $n(k - 1) = 25$
Minimum Value = 0

Interpretation: There is a weak association between gender and opinions about the use of the death penalty.

table 10.5, you should understand that association and correlation coefficient interpretations should be based on the context of the data being examined. That is, if you find a .36 association between AIDS and a cure, you would be likely to assume a strong association. Conversely, if a researcher finds a .62 association between gender and age of criminal justice workers one may wish to assume that to be low or only weak because one would expect a stronger value.

Spearman's Rho

The most commonly used statistic for association between two ordinal level variables is the *Spearman's Rho* correlation coefficient. Basically, Spearman's Rho compares the maximum possible value of the squared differences across

Figure 10.18

CRAMÉR'S V

Minimum V = 0; Maximum V = 1

Formula: $V = \sqrt{\chi^2 \div [n(k - 1)]}$

From figure 10.17, the chi square = 3.3809, and n = 25, k = 2

$V = \sqrt{3.3809 \div [25(2 - 1)]} = .3677$

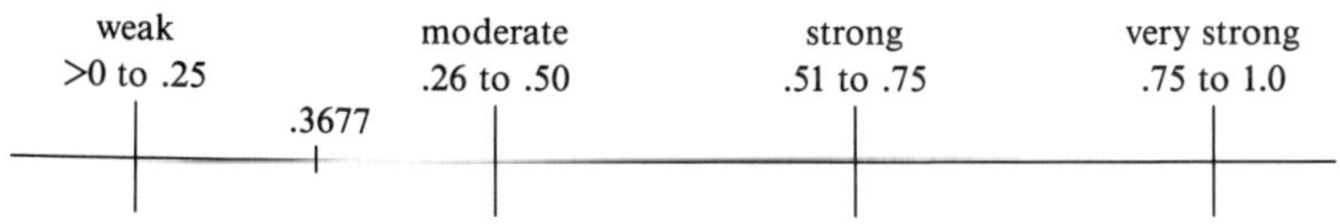

Table 10.5

RULES OF THUMB FOR RELATIONSHIP MEASURES

Statistic Value*	Interpretation
0.0	No relationship
.01 to .30	Weak relationship
.31 to .50	Moderate relationship
.51 to .70	Strong relationship
.71 to .99	Very strong relationship
1.0	Perfect relationship

*For Spearman's rho and Pearson's r these can be interpreted as either ± values.

the two variables. The Spearman's Rho allows you to demonstrate not only whether or not an association exists, but also its strength. In addition, it can take on negative or positive values. Hence, the association can be negative or positive. When a relationship is positive, the values are moving in the same direction (i.e., either they are both increasing or they are both decreasing), and when the relationship is negative, the values of the two variables are moving in opposite directions. Figure 10.19 shows the calculations involved in Spearman's Rho.

Figure 10.19 shows an example of the Spearman's Rho that demonstrates a very strong positive relationship between the rank officers had at their academy and the number of arrests they made as police officers (ranked). One aspect of the calculation of Spearman's Rho that is not mentioned is when the two ranks tie (see figure 10.20). In that case you must take the mean of all the tied ranks. This rank would be assigned to all officers that tied on their number of arrests (in order to compute the differences for the Spearman's Rho formula).

Figure 10.19

SPEARMAN'S Rho (r_S) ASSOCIATION

Arrests Rank	Academy Rank	D	D^2
1	2	−1	1
2	1	1	1
3	3	0	0
4	5	−1	1
5	7	−2	4
6	6	0	0
7	4	3	9
8	8	0	0
9	10	−1	1
10	9	1	1
	Σ's	0	18

Minimum $r_s = 0$
Maximum $r_s = \pm 1$

Formula:

$$r_s = 1 - [(6\ \Sigma D^2) \div (n(n^2 - 1))]$$

$$r_s = 1 - [(6*18) \div (10(10^2 - 1)]$$

$$r_s = 0.8909$$

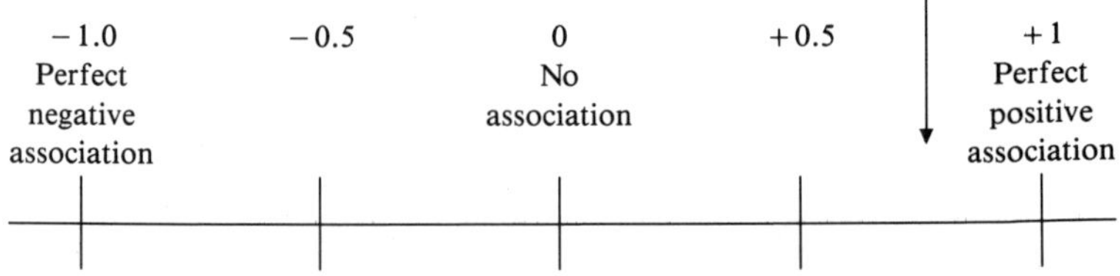

Hence, the association between arrest ranks and academy rank appears to be very strong and positive.

Figure 10.20
HANDLING TIED RANKS

If the ranks for the 3rd, 4th, and 5th observations are tied, that is, all three of these officers had the same number of arrests, then a single average rank would be assigned to each observation based on the following calculation:

$$(3 + 4 + 5) \div 3 = 4$$

So, all three cases would be given a rank of 4.

Pearson's Product Moment Correlation Coefficient

The final descriptive statistic that will be discussed and demonstrated is the Pearson's product moment correlation coefficient, or *Pearson's r,* for short. It is common to label the statistical measures of association between two interval or ratio level variables "correlation" (Lutz, 1983, p. 191). However, the basic idea remains the same as with association. We are only attempting to identify similarities and differences in the response patterns of the subjects of a study for two variables. When there is no correlation between two interval or ratio variables, the Pearson's r is equal to 0. When the two variables are perfectly positively correlated, their Pearson's r will be +1. When the two variables are perfectly negatively correlated, their Pearson's r will be −1. However, one does not typically get values in these three extremes (0, +1, or −1). Most of the time, the Pearson's r is much less clear. One final point that bears mentioning is that the Pearson's r is a symmetrical measure of interval or ratio correlation. That is, it doesn't matter which variable one selects as x or y for computational purposes—the same statistical findings will result. An example of Pearson's r is shown in figure 10.21. This example shows that as juveniles get older, they seem to have fewer arrests. It is important to note, however, that the description of a sample of only five juveniles, whether based on a random sample or not, should be suspect (it is used here only to demonstrate the computations).

Summary

This chapter outlines the most basic descriptive approaches taken in criminal justice and criminological research. The coverage is by no means comprehensive. There are many more descriptive statistics that have not been illustrated in this chapter. Most other, more specialized statistics are used for dealing with different data problems (i.e., nonparametric data, association between a nominal and ordinal variables, and so on). While it might be instructive to cover the whole range of basic statistics, the focus of this

Figure 10.21
PEARSON'S r CORRELATION

	Age X	Arrests Y	X^2	Y^2	X×Y
	11	5	121	25	55
	12	4	144	16	48
	13	6	169	36	78
	14	4	196	16	56
	15	3	225	9	45
Σ's	65	22	855	102	282

Minimum r = 0
Maximum r = ±1

Formula:

$$r = \frac{n(\Sigma XY) - (\Sigma X)(\Sigma Y)}{\sqrt{[n(\Sigma X^2) - (\Sigma X)^2][n(\Sigma Y^2) - (\Sigma Y)^2]}}$$

$$r = \frac{5(282) - (65)(22)}{\sqrt{[5(855) - (65)^2][5(102) - (22)^2]}}$$

$r = -.5547$

Hence, the association between age and number of arrests for this sample appears to be strong and negative.

text is to provide a general sense for the accepted research methodologies. Hence, only basic statistical indicators have been covered in this chapter. Specifically, this chapter has presented, and discussed the graphical and tabular display of data, the basic measures of central tendency, and several indicators of the variation in a distribution. Finally, a demonstration of association and correlation was provided.

Main Concepts

central tendency
mean
index of dispersion
standard deviation
chi square
Spearman's Rho
association
frequency distribution
bar charts
mode
median
range
coefficient of variation
Cramér's V
Pearson's r
pie charts
line charts

Discussion Questions

1. Why do we not use the same measure of average (mode, median, and mean) in every situation?
2. What is the use of the measures of averages to the street-level police officer?
3. Do the measures of variation differ in giving us a "feel" for the distribution of data? Why or why not?
4. What is the difference between positive and negative relationships? Can you give an example of each?
5. What do you know after you have calculated all the relevant descriptive statistics?

Exercises

1. Construct a frequency distribution for the data in figure 10.4.
2. The following numbers represent the values assigned to the political party choices for a sample of fifteen correctional officers (where 1 = republican, 2 = democrat, and 3 = independent). What is the average political party choice?

   1, 1, 1, 2, 2, 3, 2, 2, 1, 2, 2, 3, 3, 1, and 1
3. How much variation is there in the political party choices of the correctional officers in exercise 2 above?
4. Assume you are the departmental planning officer. The chief hands you his ranking of the shift commanders: 1, 4, 3, 7, 8, and 11. He asks you to summarize the data so he can incorporate it into a report. Which descriptive statistics can be used? What is the result of your calculations?
5. What is the correlation between temperature and crime rates in the following cities?

Cities	Temperature	Crime Rates
Gotham	12	9
Atlantis	15	10
Babylon	20	25
Cumulus	30	5
Nebulus	11	5
Mira	15	30

11

BASIC INFERENTIAL ANALYSES

Learning Objectives

1. To demonstrate several basic inferential quantitative data analysis tests
2. To provide a structured and routine procedure and demonstrations of such a procedure for conducting single sample tests
3. To provide a structured and routine procedure and demonstrations of such a procedure for conducting two-sample tests
4. To provide basic guidelines for higher-level statistical analyses and tests

Chapter Outline

Introduction
The Process of Inferential Testing
Hypothesis Setting
Criterion Selection
Test Statistics
Making a Decision/Interpretation
Single Sample Tests
Proportions Test
Means Test
Chi Square Test
Two-Sample Tests
Independent t-Test
Dependent t-Test
Mann-Whitney U Test
Wilcoxon T Test
Chi Square Test
Multiple Sample Tests
ANOVA
Kruskal-Wallis H Test
Summary
Main Concepts
Discussion Questions
Exercise

CHAPTER ELEVEN

Introduction

Inferential statistical analyses are based in probability theory. This entails the testing of sample values against what we could expect in the long run (i.e., population value estimates). For instance, let's say we collect salary data from a random sample of 125 police officers and determine that their average salary is $27,000 per year. Inferential analyses would allow us to estimate whether this sample salary is an accurate representation of the "true" salary of all police officers in the population of police officers in the United States. Inferential analyses allow researchers to answer theoretical or policy questions using sample data. This means that inferential analyses allow us to make generalizations to populations based on sample data. Whereas, the descriptive analyses discussed in chapter 10 allowed us only to describe our sample data, inferential analyses allow us to make general statements about the population from which the sample is drawn. In a study of correctional officers' stress, for example, we could study the blood pressures of a random sample of 1,500 correctional officers as our measure of the level of stress. If we found that correctional officers in our sample have higher than normal blood pressures we could infer that that would be the case for the population of *all* correctional officers. Inferential analysis allow researchers to study research questions and hypotheses in simple and complex studies. In fact, inferential analyses are the heart of modern statistical analysis techniques in the social sciences.

The basis for the generalization from sample values to populations is probability theory. Since probability theory is a lengthy topic, we cannot discuss it here in depth. Instead, we will focus on the practical use of statistical tests and probability tables.

The way an applied statistician uses probability theory in most criminal justice and criminological statistical analyses is as a set of assumptions about how sample values should behave relative to their populations. Therefore, in most inferential tests in criminal justice research projects, we would compare the results from a sample and then calculate a statistical test value with the theoretical values for the population listed in probability tables. The decision in most social science research would be simple and focused on rejecting or retaining the null hypothesis. The null hypothesis is a simple statement of no difference between sample values or variables. This concept is demonstrated in the examples that follow.

Given that population values are not directly observable, we rely on probability theory to give us estimates of how the population should behave in the long run. The assessment asks the question: What would be the probable outcome if we were using population data? Statisticians have created empirical expectations about how population values should behave and have collected these in what are known as probability tables.[1] In statistical analyses we generally make inferences about population values based on sample statistics, and statistical test values are compared to the population estimates in the tables. Most computer-based statistical programs (SPSS-PC®, Minitab®, or Systat®), however, calculate exact probability estimates rather than tabled population values. Exact estimates are preferred to the tabled values, because they are more precise.

Inferential statistics (tests that use sample data) are, however, only estimates of the true population values and behavior. Therefore, there is always a chance that our inferences about the population from our sample data are incorrect. For example, there are over 19,000 inmates in the prisons of the state of Maryland. If we were to study a random sample of 500 inmates on recidivism, it is likely that our relatively small sample of 500 inmates would not exactly represent the full population of 19,000 inmates. Fortunately, probability sampling allows us to claim that the sample theoretically represents the population. The following sections provide details about the process of inferential testing. These sections are followed by examples of the most commonly employed statistical tests.

The Process of Inferential Testing

The *process of inferential testing* is based on a structured and logical approach to assessing the statistical test values in reference to the population parameters. While the process is structured, it is not without limitations. Hypothesis testing is simple and focused and generally considers only simple questions. The researcher must still link the individual hypothesis tests into a coherent meaning for the study purposes or to drive policy relevant decisions. It is also important to note that the process of inferential testing must be undertaken with care. That is, the number of variables, the units of analysis about which the data are collected, and the level of measurement of the variables all influence the type of test that is appropriate to the comparisons of the sample and population data. The decision about the appropriate test must be based on the consideration of all three of these key elements.

The following sections detail the basic steps or considerations in the process of inferential testing. The major aspects that change in various inferential test situations are the *test statistics* and the probability distributions (tables) that are used. It is also important to note that the most crucial consideration in the testing of hypotheses is usually the level of measurement of the data. Before inferential testing can be undertaken one must have a very clear understanding of the different levels of measurement and the types of tests that are appropriate at these different levels (see chapters 1 and 2). There are tests that are most appropriate for nominal data, ordinal data, and interval and ratio data.

Hypothesis Setting

The first step in inferential testing is to set the expectations for the test that one is undertaking. In this step the researcher attempts to set up the research questions in such a way that the sample statistics can be compared to population values to address the substantive queries he or she is interested in. Thus, hypothesis setting is the crucial first step to conducting statistical tests.

Hypotheses should be created based on literature and/or decision needs. In the traditional research process (see chapter 1), the theory that the researcher relies upon provides the conceptual framework on which speculations or hypotheses can be made. *Hypothesis setting* is the process of turning the speculations the researcher has as well as the concepts in the literature into concrete variable relationships or connections.

In figure 11.1, the process of setting a *research hypothesis* is illustrated. Suppose that we are interested in studying the relationship between crime and the economy, because we believe that (1) when the economy is in a recession there might tend to be more people unemployed and (2) that a certain portion of these unemployed people would commit crimes for income. In the circle on the left in figure 11.1 the concepts that we took from the literature and logically formulated are shown. Gary Becker (1968) found a relationship between crime rates and unemployment rates, and therefore we should include both concepts in our study.[2] It makes sense that the number of employers (i.e., opportunities) should be included in our study. The formulated hypothesis in the righthand circle in figure 11.1 shows a research hypothesis that was derived from the listing of concepts and the theory of Becker (1968).

We generally have three choices in stating the research hypothesis. These choices are (1) to state a relation, (2) to state a difference, or (3) to state a direction. Figure 11.1 is an example of stating a relationship between unemployment and crime rates. The research hypothesis in this case states that there is relationship between two variables, crime rate and unemployment rate. Another common form of research hypothesis is to state a difference. For example, we might state the *difference hypothesis* as shown in figure 11.2. In this case, the hypothesis is stated in terms of differences rather than a relationship. In this example we are interested only in whether there is a difference in the crime rates based on the number of police. If we were to study a random sample of, say, one hundred communities with this research hypothesis, the focus would be on assessing whether the different towns with different size police forces would have different numbers of crimes. If a significant difference were found, we would probably want to know what influenced that difference and perhaps the relationship between the number of police officer and crime rates. But these are follow-up questions

Figure 11.1
HYPOTHESIS SETTING

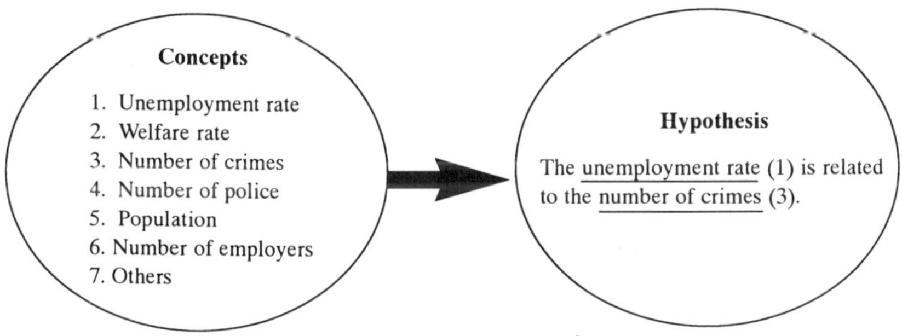

Figure 11.2
DIFFERENCE HYPOTHESIS EXAMPLE

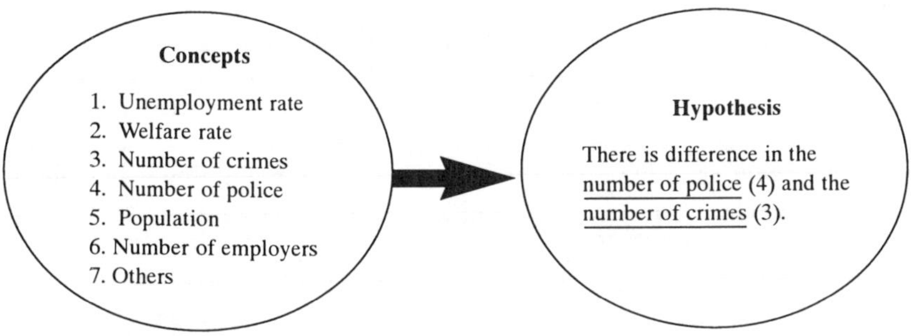

to the basic research hypothesis in this case of differences between the two variables.

Hypotheses can also be stated in a directional context. In figure 11.3, the example from figure 11.2 is made into a directional research hypothesis. In a *directional hypothesis* the researcher states the nature of the interaction between the two variables. Hence, in the example in figure 11.3 the research hypothesis is stated in terms of the number of police and the number of crimes. This hypothesis speculates that the more police a community has, the higher the number of crimes. Directional hypothesis tend to have greater explanatory power than nondirectional hypotheses (i.e., relationship or difference hypotheses). The reason directional hypotheses tend to be the most powerful is because they state a very specific situation with respect to the sample values. They are also compared to more precise population probability values because they are stated in terms of magnitude rather than simply "differences/no differences" or "relationship/no relationship."

So far, I have been discussing only the research hypothesis. However, there is another hypothesis that must be stated in order to conduct statistical testing of sample values against the supposed population parameters (i.e., tabled values). This second hypothesis is called the *null hypothesis.* In inferential testing we test the null hypothesis, not the research hypothesis. While both the research and null hypotheses should be stated prior to the conducting of any tests, *only* the null hypothesis is tested.

The null hypothesis is the converse of the research hypothesis. The research hypothesis is the research question that is driven by the purpose of the research, and as such it should be set prior to stating the null hypothesis. The research hypothesis is the speculation that we would like to support or refute with the statistical analyses. For example, a research hypothesis might be: As unemployment increases, the crime rate will increase. However, the research hypothesis is inexact and cannot be tested directly. That is, we have no idea why, as unemployment increases, crime increases, from these two variables, even if we find a relationship between the two. Conversely, the null hypothesis can be directly tested with our sample statistics, and we can either accept or reject it. For example, a null hypothesis for this example might be: There is no relationship between unemployment and crime rates. The null hypothesis is similar to the research hypothesis in that it is a speculation that is based on the research hypothesis and literature or logic. However, the null hypothesis is an exact possibility.

The null hypotheses in table 11.1 reflect exact possibilities that can be tested, whereas the research hypotheses do not. For example, we can precisely determine whether there is or isn't a difference between the number of police and the number of crimes (the null hypothesis), but even if we found that there was a difference (we found support for our research hypothesis), our research hypothesis test doesn't explain why that is the case. The

Figure 11.3
DIRECTIONAL HYPOTHESIS EXAMPLE

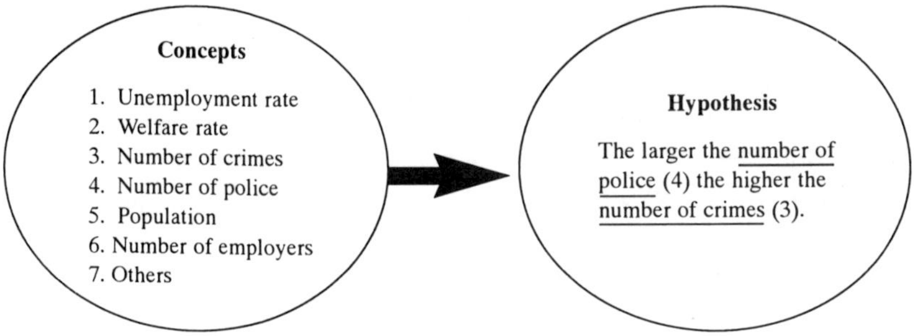

Table 11.1
NULL HYPOTHESIS EXAMPLES

Research Hypotheses	Null Hypotheses
There is a relationship between the unemployment rate and the number of crimes.	There is no relationship between the unemployment rate and the number of crimes.
There is a difference in the number of police and the number of crimes.	There is no difference in the number of police and the number of crimes.
The larger the number of police the higher the number of crimes.	The larger the number of police the smaller the number of crimes.

null hypothesis is the one that is tested through the comparison of the sample statistics to the population probability values. This is the case because they are exact possibilities, whereas the research hypotheses are not.

To clarify this idea, consider the first hypothesis pair in table 11.1. The research hypothesis states that there is a relationship between unemployment rates and the number of crimes. We can use sample data to determine whether such a relationship exists. But the sample statistics are merely estimates of the true relationship in the population. Hence, we cannot directly test the research hypothesis, because we cannot collect the actual population values. On the other hand, the null hypothesis is an exact possibility that we can test. We can use the population probability values to establish that the unemployment rate is not related to the crime rate (or is related). That is, we do not need to collect all population values to establish whether the null hypothesis situation is believable or not. The estimates of the population values are enough, in comparison to the population probability values, to clearly establish whether the sample values we found are believable, and hence, the null can be directly tested. This is not the case with the research hypothesis. Even if we find support for our research hypothesis we have no idea, based on statistical testing alone, why it is supported.

The process of hypothesis testing is a logical "trick" that researchers use to test their speculations or research questions. The null hypothesis is the only one tested and is presumed to be true for the testing purposes. If the null hypothesis is rejected, based on the comparisons of the sample values with the population probabilities, then the researchers presume they have found evidence to support their research hypothesis. This is an extremely important stream of logic. Researchers never directly test their research hypothesis but only reject or retain their null hypothesis. The support for the research hypothesis is therefore indirect at best. Based on this logic they should *never* presume that their research hypothesis has been proven, accepted, or otherwise directly supported based on statistical testing because that can *never* be the case. They can merely reject a tested null hypothesis and by inference find evidence that shows that the research hypothesis is simply more tenable or believable.

There is a possibility that the decision about the null hypothesis, since it is based on sample data, is inaccurate. This is due to the fact that the statistical test values that we compare to the population parameters are merely estimates of the "true" population values. The two types of errors are commonly known as TYPE I and TYPE II errors. *TYPE I errors* are those that are committed when the researcher rejects a true null hypothesis. For example, suppose the researcher states as the null hypothesis that there is no difference between recidivism rates for male and female inmates. A TYPE I error would involve rejecting this null hypothesis and would cause the researcher to inappropriately attribute indirect support for the research hypothesis. Researchers attempt to reduce this type of error through improving the precision of the criterion selection. That is, researchers improve the precision of the population parameter estimates by making them more conservative.

TYPE II errors are those situations where the researcher retains a null hypothesis that is in fact untrue. This is clearly problematic as the researcher has actually found indirect support for his or her research hypothesis but, because of the population parameter estimate, he or she failed to reject the null hypothesis. Without getting into a very detailed discussion of the theoretical and mathematical reasons for these errors, we can reduce the possibilities of both types of errors through increasing the sample size in the study. In addition, TYPE I error can be reduced through increasing the precision in the population value estimates, and TYPE II error can be reduced through decreasing the precision in the population value estimate. Criterion selection, or population value estimates, is where the researcher conducting inferential tests balances the precision of the test considerations to reduce both TYPE I and TYPE II errors.

In summary, the process of writing hypotheses is shown in figure 11.4. The three steps involved in constructing reasonable research hypotheses presume you have identified a relevant theory or decision need as well as the concepts you need to conduct hypothesis tests. The construction process begins with a consideration of the type of hypothesis that you require in relation to the theory. Second, the research hypothesis is stated, which considers the type of hypothesis as well as the variables or groups involved in the study. Last, the null hypothesis is stated as the converse of the research hypothesis.

Criterion Selection

The next step in the process of conducting basic inferential analyses is to determine the comparative population value estimates and the amount of decision errors that we are willing to tolerate. The criterion selection is based on a specific *level of significance* for the decision about the null hypothesis. Calculations conducted with microcomputer-based programs provide a direct estimate of the level of significance of the test being conducted. There are, however, listings of population probability values in the form of statistical tables in most statistics text and listed in the tables throughout this chapter.

The three most commonly employed criterion levels of significance are .10, .05 and .01. The use of .10 is rare in criminal justice and criminological research, but where the study is exploratory it is commonly used. The value of .10 means that researchers are willing to retain the null hypothesis 90 percent of the time. We should have confidence in the decision about

Figure 11.4

STATING HYPOTHESES

Step 1:
Consider the type of hypothesis needed (i.e., relationship, difference, or directional).

Example: Difference

Step 2:
State the research hypothesis considering the variables and/or groups.

Example: There is a difference in the recidivism rates for male and female inmates.

Step 3:
State the null hypothesis as the opposite of the research hypothesis.

Example: There is no difference in the recidivism rates for male and female inmates.

the null because it would be rare to reject it, that is, we would make a mistake in our decision about the null only 10 percent of the time. It is much more common for researchers in criminal justice and criminology to use the .05 level of significance or criterion. The .05 level is a good compromise between TYPE I and TYPE II errors. We feel comfortable with being correct in our decision about the null 95 percent of the time and are willing to risk being incorrect in that decision only 5 percent of the time. The .01 level of significance is used in sophisticated studies or those inferential analyses where theory is well developed or there has been quite a bit of study.

The criterion selection stage of inferential testing involves setting a level of significance, determining the type of hypothesis, and locating an appropriate population probability estimate. For example, if we were to test the following hypothesis set (see figure 11.5).

There has been some research on recidivism, but little comparing men and women; therefore, we would select .05 as our level of significance. The type of test in the example is a difference hypothesis, so the test would be nondirectional and the value we select would be a nondirectional value. Finally, because the recidivism rate is at least an interval level variable (we would have to have the recidivism rates for men and women to conduct the proposed tests), we would use an independent t-test.[3] Hence, we would have to consult a probability table that is appropriate for an independent t-test (i.e., student's t-table).

Test Statistics

There are hundreds of statistical tests of inference. What this chapter provides is a description and examples of the most commonly employed statistical inference tests. However, it is important to keep in mind that there are many tests that are not covered here.[4]

The statistical test portion of inferential analyses is where we calculate the sample statistic to compare to the probability value that was obtained in the criterion selection section. There are three major considerations in selecting the most appropriate test for testing the research hypothesis at hand. These considerations are: (1) the level of measurement of the data, (2) the number of variables or groups, and (3) the type of hypothesis at hand. Usually, the most crucial consideration in selecting the appropriate test is the level of measurement of the data. The reason there are hundreds of inferential tests is because researchers may be confronted with having to test several variables or groups that are measured at various levels of measurement or there are combinations of levels of measurement. The different tests adjust for the precision that is intrinsic to each level of measurement and the research situation at hand. Researchers generally have a choice between (1) making all variables the same level of measurement when they collect the data or through conversion after the data are in hand or (2) using test

Figure 11.5
CRITERION SELECTION

Research Hypothesis:
There is a difference between recidivism rates for male and female inmates.

Null Hypothesis
There is *no* difference between recidivism rates for male and female inmates.

Table 11.2
STATISTICAL TESTS OF INFERENCE

Test Name	Variables	Level of Measurement	Parametric
Proportions test	one	interval+	yes
Means test	one	interval+	yes
Single chi square test	one	nominal	yes
Independent t-test	two	interval+	yes
Dependent t-test	two	interval+	yes
Mann-Whitney U test	two	ordinal+	no
Wilcoxon T test	two	ordinal+	no
Two chi square test	two	nominal	no
Analysis of variance F test	three or more	interval+	yes
Kruskal-Wallis H test	three or more	ordinal+	no

statistics that can handle variables of different levels of measurement. I have found that the multiple level of measurement tests are required only when there are very subtle differences in the variables or groups, and therefore it usually makes more sense to convert the variables that I am using into the same level of measurement.[5] Table 11.2 shows the tests that will be demonstrated in this chapter and the situations wherein they are most appropriate. These tests will allow you to conduct virtually any test at any level through conversion of levels of measurement, that is, included are tests at the nominal, ordinal, and interval/ratio levels of measurement.[6]

Making a Decision/Interpretation

The final step in inferential data analysis is to compare the sample statistic with the population probability value to determine whether the null hypothesis should be retained or rejected. It is important to note that the decision is always made about the null hypothesis, because that is the hypothesis that we test when we compare our sample values to the probability or long-run outcomes. The most we can say about the research hypothesis is that it is indirectly supported, because we have "rejected" the null hypothesis. Table 11.3 shows the only two possible decisions we can make as regards the null hypothesis.

In this case (table 11.3), if the test statistic is a reasonable population parameter estimate, we would retain the null hypothesis. That is, there is no evidence that males and females have statistically different recidivism rates. While there is no statistically significant difference as indicated by the comparison of our test value with the population probability values, it is important to recognize that we may have committed a TYPE II error.

In the case where we reject the null hypothesis (the righthand column of table 11.3), we would have found statistical evidence that the male and female recidivism rates are not the same. Thus, we presume that, when the sample test values are not consistent with the population probability values, there is a difference. In this case we could be making a TYPE I error in that we are rejecting a true null hypothesis. This type of error is more serious than a TYPE II error as in the retention decision. That is, if we retain a false null hypothesis, we simply have no evidence to support our research hypothesis; but if the null is rejected when it is in fact true, we could report support for their research hypothesis when in fact no empirical support exists.

Another important distinction for inferential testing is whether the test statistic is parametric or nonparametric. While all statistical tests assume

Table 11.3
NULL HYPOTHESIS DECISION EXAMPLE

Example: There is no difference between male and female recidivism rates.

Retain Null Hypothesis	*Reject Null Hypothesis*
Sample statistic is consistent with the population probability value. There is no evidence the sample is different from the population, and hence male and female recidivism are presumed to be similar.	Sample statistic is inconsistent with the population probability value. The sample is different from the population, and hence we presume that male and female recidivism are not the same.
TYPE I Error:	*TYPE I Error:*
Nonexistent	We could be rejecting a true null due to the precision of our decision criteria.
TYPE II Error:	*TYPE II Error:*
We could be retaining a false null due to sampling inaccuracy.	Nonexistent

that the data are collected from a random sample, some tests have additional requirements for their use. In general, the *parametric tests* are considered to be more powerful than *nonparametric tests.* That is, the parametric tests are more accurate with respect to making decisions about the null hypothesis and minimizing TYPE I and TYPE II errors. The cost of this superior power, however, is specific and rather stringent data requirements.

Parametric tests require data that have known population characteristics. That is, before these tests can be used, researchers generally conduct other empirical tests to make certain that the data are consistent with the assumptions required for this level of statistical testing. Parametric tests generally require that the data be normally distributed, random, and homogeneous (i.e., have similar variation). In sum, the parametric tests are more powerful and hence are preferred over the nonparametric tests, but there are fairly strict requirements for the data we observe.

Now we are ready to examine examples of the inferential tests that can be used in criminal justice and criminological research. For each of the following tests we will move through the four steps just discussed in order to provide concrete examples of each test and application.

Single Sample Tests

The first set of inferential tests that we will examine are known as *single sample tests.* These tests are not commonly used in criminal justice and criminological research, because we tend to focus on multivariate research situations and because there are more complex quantitative tests to handle such situations. However, the single sample tests are quite useful. In particular, single sample tests are particularly appropriate in (1) making policy relevant decisions, (2) conducting preliminary exploratory analyses, and (3) testing sample representativeness.

An example of using a single sample test to make an operational decision might involve the use of a known population parameter to determine whether a study agency is different or the same as the population of all such agencies. Data indicates, for instance, that the national average percentage of inmates that are classified as maximum security is 10.2 percent (Camp and Camp, 1993). Suppose the head of the Department of Corrections in the state of Maryland determined that the average percentage of maximum security inmates for his state, based on a sample of prisons in his state, is 12.2 percent. We could use a single sample test to determine whether the difference in the national and state averages is significant or statistically important. The head of the Department of Corrections could then use such information to make policy relevant decisions about increasing or decreasing the percentage of maximum security inmates in his state's prison system.

Single sample tests could also be used to conduct preliminary or exploratory tests of the sample data. For example, suppose that a researcher was interested in studying juvenile delinquents in a particular jurisdiction. She was particularly interested in the most serious offenders, (those with five or more current and/or prior offenses). Upon collection of frequency data the researcher determined that the seventy-five juveniles in the sample committed a total of 325 offenses of various types. As a preliminary step, she could determine whether there was an empirically (measurable) significant difference in the sample across seven crime categories. She could compare the test statistic from the sample with the distribution of scores across all categories over the long run.

Single sample tests could be used to compare the sample data relative to known population parameters to determine whether the sample is empirically representative. The students in an advanced criminal justice studies class at the University of Baltimore were given the task of conducting a fear-of-crime survey on a random sample of students at the university. They collected a sample of 127 students out of nearly seven thousand students. The average age of the students in the sample was 23.94 years of age. In order to assess the accuracy of the sample, I collected the official population statistics from the Office of Institutional Research at the university. While we looked at the gender, race, and town of residence of the students in the sample in comparison to the entire student population, the example here focuses on age. The average age of students at the university (as given by the Office of Institutional Research) was 27. We could then use a single sample test to compare the average ages of students in the sample collected with the population parameter from the Office of Institutional Research to determine whether the sample is accurate.

Having laid the preliminary ground work for the single sample tests the following sections provide examples of three common single sample tests. The first two tests are parametric tests; the third is nonparametric. There are other single sample tests, but these are the most typical. The examples just given will be used so you can see how they would play out in an actual inferential test situation.

Proportions Test

Before conducting the proportions test, one should be certain that the parametric assumptions are met. This test compares a summary percentage for a sample with that of a known population value. The population values can be taken from national level statistical studies such as the Uniform Crime Reports or through referencing the Criminal Justice Sourcebook.

The example is the comparison of the percentage of maximum security classification in Maryland with the national average. The national average percentage of inmates classified as maximum security is 10.2 percent (Camp and Camp, 1993). In Maryland the percentage of maximum security classification that is available is 12.2 percent across twenty-six institutions. The head of the Maryland Department of Corrections would like to argue, for example, that the percentage in Maryland is higher than the national proportion.

Step 1: Set the Hypotheses. The first step in the analysis is to set the research and alternative hypotheses. The research hypothesis is driven by the administrator's need for decision-based information. The research and null hypotheses are as follows:

> *Research Hypothesis:* The proportion of maximum security cell space in the United States is 10.2 percent.
>
> *Null Hypothesis:* The proportion of maximum security cell space in the United States is *not* 10.2 percent.

Step 2: Select the Criteria. Once the hypotheses are set, we are ready to determine the criteria for a probability value and to set up the comparison between the sample value and the potential population value. Assume that the administrator uses the most common level of significance. The test is a nondirectional one, and therefore a nondirectional value should be used. Given that the sample of the Maryland institutions was randomly selected (sixty-one of the seventy-seven correctional institutions were selected), we can use a standard normal curve to find the population probability to compare to our calculated sample statistic. However, prior to consulting the table we should be certain that the data are normally distributed. This is determined through making certain that the number in the sample times the population parameter, and its inverse, are both greater than 5.

Formula 11.1: $61 \times .102 = 6.222$

Formula 11.2: $(1 - .102) \times 61 = 54.77$

The population proportion ($10.2\% \div 100 = .102$)

The value for formulas 11.1 and 11.2 both produce statistics that are greater than 5, and therefore we can assume that the normal distribution (use a z table) is appropriate. (If either of these values is less than 5, then we would not use the single sample proportions test.) There is no need to consult the z table, however, because if the level of significance is .05, the critical probability value for the population is 1.96. That is, for nondirectional tests that use a .05 level and are large samples (i.e., >30 units of analysis), the critical population probability value that we compare our sample statistic to is ± 1.96. For directional tests at the .05 level, the critical z value is either $+1.65$ or -1.65 depending upon the direction of the value proposed in the research hypothesis. It is easier to remember these values and apply them for every test than to look up the same value each time one conducts a test. A summary of z values that are most commonly used is listed in table 11.4.

The basic approach here is to calculate a test value based on the sample data (proportions, in this case) and to compare that value with the critical z value (i.e., the population probability value). If our calculated sample statistic is greater than +1.96 or less than −1.96, then we would reject our null hypothesis. Conversely, if our calculated sample statistic is less than ±1.96, we would retain the null hypothesis. The value ±1.96, therefore, is our decision criterion for the null hypothesis.

Step 3: Calculate a Test Value. The sample of sixty-one Maryland prisons has an average proportion of maximum security classification area of 7.44 percent (61 × .122 = 7.44%). That means that 92.56 percent of the prison system has cell space that is classified in some level other than maximum security. In addition, we can see that the national percentage of maximum security and the Maryland percentage differ by 2 percent. Is this difference large enough to reject the null hypothesis and thereby to infer that Maryland's percentage is similar to the national percentage? If the value is significantly different (based on our comparison of our test value with the population probability), then we would reject the null hypothesis because either the percentages are actually different or the amount of sampling error in our sample is so great that we should not retain the null hypothesis. Formula 11.3 is used for a large sample proportions test.

Formula 11.3: $Z_{pt} = (p - P) \div \sigma_p$

Where:

p = sample proportion

P = population proportion

σ_p = standard error of the proportions $\sigma_p = \sqrt{(P \times Q) \div n}$

P = proportion of maximum security nationally

Q = proportion not maximum security (1 − P) nationally

Figure 11.6

SINGLE SAMPLE PROPORTIONS TEST

$$\sigma_p = \sqrt{(\underset{P}{.102} \times \underset{Q}{.898}) \div \underset{n}{61}} = 0.03875$$

$$z_{pt} = (\underset{p}{.122} - \underset{P}{.102}) \div \underset{\sigma_p}{0.03875} = 0.5161$$

Table 11.4
CRITICAL z VALUES

Level of Significance	Directional	Critical z Value
.01	no	±2.58
.05	no	±1.96
.10	no	±1.65
.01	yes	+2.33 or −2.33
.05	yes	+1.65 or −1.65
.10	yes	+1.29 or −1.29

Step 4: Decision and Interpretation. The decision as regards the sample value is made through a comparison of the sample statistic (z_{pt} = 0.5161) with the population probability estimate (z = ±1.96). When the test statistic is between −1.96 and +1.96, the null hypothesis is retained. Conversely, when the test statistic is outside of this range we would reject the null hypothesis. We could interpret this finding as follows:

> There is no statistical evidence that the proportion of maximum security cell space in the United States is not 10.2 percent.

The administrator of the Maryland Department of Corrections may then take this information as indicative of a similarity between Maryland and what is done nationally. The administrator may then argue for more maximum security cell space because Maryland requires it. He would need more analysis to establish why he needs it, but at least this single sample result could support such an argument. On the other hand, the administrator may argue that Maryland doesn't require more maximum security bed space because it is consistent with the national average.

Means Test

Another approach to single sample testing can involve the use of means. The comparisons here would be similar to the proportions example (i.e., a comparison of sample statistics with population probability estimates) but would rely on means instead of proportions or percentages. The means test assumes that the data are normally distributed (i.e., bell shaped or symmetrical), that over the long run the sample means will accurately represent the true population mean, and that the data are randomly and independently obtained.[7]

Suppose we have a random sample of the ages of 127 college students from the University of Baltimore. The sample is presumed to be normally distributed because it is not skewed and because when we graph it, it appears to be symetrical and bell shaped. Suppose we are interested in testing whether our sample has a lower average age than the population of University of Baltimore students. The average age for our sample is 23.94 years with a standard deviation of 2.00 years, whereas the average age for all students at the university is 27 years. In a study of fear of crime on campus, the use of the age variable is crucial, because much of the literature indicates that older people tend to fear crime more than younger people do, and if our sample is skewed towards younger students, then it may be biased. If there is a significant difference in the sample average age and the population average we might consider increasing the sample size or examining other key fear-of-crime variables, such as gender, to determine how damaging the difference between the population and sample is to the representativeness of the sample.

The four-step process that was used with the proportions test will be used for this inferential analyses as well. Notice that the only differences in the various tests in this chapter are the probability distributions that are used to determine the population probability comparison values and the tests. The general structure of the questions remains the same.

Step 1: Set the Hypotheses.

Research Hypothesis: The average age of students at the University of Baltimore is less than 27 years.

Null Hypothesis: The average age of students at the University of Baltimore is 27 years or more.

Step 2: Select the Criteria. This is an example of a directional test. We presume that students are younger, on average, than the known population parameter based on the sample average we have computed. Since the test is a directional test, we are required to use a directional population probability estimate. If we use a .05 level of significance (meaning we will make errors about our decision about our null hypothesis about 5 percent of the time) we would have a critical z population probability estimate of 1.65. To determine whether this estimate is positive or negative, we need only refer to the research hypothesis. When the population is presumed to be less than the actual value, the sign is negative, and conversely, when the population value is presumed to be greater than the actual value, the sign is positive. Because we presume in this test that the average age is less than the population parameter of 27 years of age, the critical value in this case is −1.65.

Step 3: Calculate a Test Value. The next step is to calculate a test value to make our comparison between the sample and population estimate. This test involves three steps: (1) calculating an estimated standard deviation (see formula 11.4), (2) calculating a standard error (see formula 11.5), and (3) calculating the test value (see formula 11.6). In the example, formula 11.4 would be calculated as shown in figure 11.7.

Formula 11.4: $s = \sqrt{(\text{Sum of the ages}^2)} \div (n - 1)$

Formula 11.5: $\sigma_m = s \div \sqrt{n}$

Formula 11.6: $z_m = (\text{sample mean} - \text{population mean}) \div \sigma_m$

The standard error of the means that is estimated from the calculated "s" is shown in figure 11.8

Finally, the test statistic can be calculated through formula 11.6, which involves the comparison of the sample value with the population parameter controlling for the standard error estimate (see figure 11.9).

Figure 11.7

ESTIMATED STANDARD DEVIATION

24.5, 25, 20, 27, 27, 24, 21, 21, 27, 29, 22, 24, 21, 25, 21, 25, 21, 26, 24, 24,
24.5, 24, 21, 28, 23, 24, 24, 22, 25, 22, 23, 24, 22, 24, 24, 25, 24, 24, 25, 25,
24.5, 25, 26, 27, 26, 24, 21, 24, 26, 30, 24, 25, 24, 26, 24, 21, 23, 25, 24, 22,
24.5, 24, 24, 29, 23, 22, 24, 25, 22, 21, 26, 25, 24, 24, 22, 20, 23, 26, 25, 25,
24.5, 23, 26, 27, 25, 23, 23, 20, 22, 22, 25, 27, 25, 24, 22, 25, 23, 26, 22, 21,
24.5, 25, 25, 21, 21, 24, 21, 20, 22, 25, 22, 24, 24, 26, 24, 23, 24, 27, 21, 21,
23, 24, 25, 24, 25, 26, 27

$s = \sqrt{(73{,}276.5)} \div (127 - 1) = 24.1155$

(73,276.5: sum of the squared ages; 127: n)

The sum of each of the 127 values squared is 73,276.5

Figure 11.8

STANDARD ERROR OF THE MEANS ESTIMATE

$\sigma_m = 24.1155 \div \sqrt{127} = 2.1399$

(24.1155: s; 127: n)

Figure 11.9

CALCULATION OF THE SAMPLE STATISTIC

$z_m = (23.94 - 27) \div 2.1399 = -1.4299$

(23.94: sample mean; 27: population mean; 2.1399: σ_m)

Step 4: Decision and Interpretation. The calculated test statistic for the sample is −1.4299, and the critical probability value for the population is −1.65. Because the calculated value for the test statistic is greater than the critical population probability value, we must retain the null hypothesis. There is no statistical evidence that the average age of students at the University of Baltimore is less than 27 years of age. That is, our sample, even though it produced an average age of 23.94 years, is not statistically so unusual that we would not find such a result. Hence, the sample appears to represent the population, at least insofar as the age variable is concerned.

Chi Square Test

The final single sample test that we will consider in this chapter is the chi square test. The chi square test is a common nonparametric test and can be applied to nominal level data. As was explained in chapter 10, the chi square test has descriptive properties. It also has an accompanying probability distribution that makes its use in inferential analysis feasible. The chi square test assumes that the data are randomly and independently obtained, but it does not require that the data be normally distributed or that the background populations be homogeneous. That is, the chi square test can be used in many more situations than the more demanding parametric tests.[8] Although nonparametric tests such as the chi square are not as precise as the parametric tests, they provide reasonable estimates of the population probability values and are well accepted by statisticians and researchers.

The chi square test can be used to determine whether there is a relationship or no relationship in one variable, two variable, or multivariate tests. The focus here is on the univariate situation, although later in this chapter a bivariate inferential chi square test will be shown. Suppose a researcher is interested in determining whether there is a relationship between the types of crimes that a sample of juveniles commit. Suppose further that a sample of seventy-five juveniles resulted in 325 different violent offenses across seven types of violent crimes. If there is no relationship, the juveniles will commit an equal number of offenses across the seven categories; on the other hand, if there is a relationship across the seven categories, there would appear to be a patterning in the types of offenses they commit. The following section illustrates a test of such a situation.

Step 1: Set the Hypotheses. A *relationship hypothesis* are stated in terms of the relationship of the variables that we are interested in testing. In a single sample chi square test we are testing an observed sample against the expected values if there were no association. If there were no association between the frequencies of the types of crimes the juveniles commit, then all 325 offenses would be equally distributed across the seven categories (i.e., there would be exactly 46.43 offenses in each of the seven types [325 ÷ 7 = 46.43]). In fact, many statisticians refer to this form of the chi square test as a goodness of fit test (Lutz, 1983, p. 322). The goodness of fit is a measure of how well the frequency data in the various categories of violent crimes fit the "no relationship" situation. The further the sample data are from the no relationship situation, the more significant the difference.

Research Hypothesis: There is an association in the frequencies of types of offenses committed by violent juvenile offenders. That is, violent juveniles tend to commit one violent crime in a higher proportion than other violent crimes.

Null Hypothesis: There is no association in the frequencies of types of offenses committed by violent juvenile offenders. That is, violent juveniles tend to commit all types of violent offenses in equal proportions.

Table 11.5

CRITICAL CHI SQUARE VALUES (.05)

Degrees of Freedom*	Chi Square Probability Values
1	3.841
2	5.991
3	7.815
4	9.488
5	11.071
6	12.592
7	14.067
8	15.507
9	16.919
10	18.307
11	19.675
12	21.026
13	22.362
14	23.685
15	24.996
16	26.296
17	27.587
18	28.869
19	30.144
20	31.410

*Degrees of freedom = the number of categories − 1 (for the single sample example, the degrees of freedom are 7 − 1 = 6). When the df is > 20 the value can be estimated with the following formula:

$\chi^2_{cv} = [1 - (2 \div (9\times df)) + 1.96 \times \sqrt{(2 \div (9\times df)}]^3$

Step 2: Select the Criteria. The second step, as was true in the other examples, is to select the population value to compare to the sample test value. While there are fewer parametric requirements for the data, it must be collected on the basis of a random sample. The number of cases must not be too large or too small (Lutz, 1983, p. 324). This is because the chi square distribution performs poorly on extremely small ($n < 20$ cases) and large samples ($n > 1{,}000$ cases). While there are techniques to adjust the chi square for small sample sizes, when the size of the study gets below twenty research subjects, there are problems with the way the probability values for the population chi squares behave. That is, the sample values from extremely small samples tend to be less likely to behave as a chi square probability theory would have them behave over the long run.

In terms of conducting this test, we could use a .05 level of significance and 6 degrees of freedom ($n - 1$) to find a population estimate of the association between the sample test value and the population parameter. The population estimate value is therefore 12.592. This population value can be compared to the sample test statistic to make a decision about the null hypothesis. The next step is to calculate the test statistic.

Step 3: Calculate a Test Value. The calculated test statistic compares the actual observed values to the expected values if there were no relationship. The formula for the chi square test is formula 11.7.

Formula 11.7: Chi square

$$x^2 = \Sigma\ [(f_o - f_e)^2 \div f_e]$$

Where: f_o = the observed frequencies in each category

f_e = the expected frequencies in each category ($\Sigma f \div$ the number of categories)

Σ = sum of the formula for each category of the variable

Step 4: Make a Decision/Interpretation. In this case, our calculated value is 269.81, and the population probability value is 12.592. Hence, there is a statistically significant relationship in the distribution of the types of offenses that the sample of serious juvenile offenders committed. Since the null hypothesis is rejected, we presume that we have found evidence to support the research hypothesis. While we only tested the null hypothesis, if it is rejected we have established at least implied evidence that the research hypothesis situation is possible.

In sum, the single sample tests certainly have utility insofar as we are interested in testing single samples. It is also clear that single sample situations are rare in the criminological or criminal justice literature. Even in

Figure 11.10

SINGLE SAMPLE CHI SQUARE TEST

Categories	f_o	f_e	$f_o - f_e$	$(f_o - f_e)^2$	$(f_o - f_e)^2 \div f_e$
Murder	12	46.43	−34.43	1,185.43	25.53
Rape	56	46.43	9.57	91.58	1.97
Robbery	125	46.43	78.57	6,173.24	132.96
Assault	18	46.43	−28.43	808.26	17.41
Sex offenses	12	46.43	−34.43	1,185.43	25.53
Simple assault	90	46.43	43.57	1,898.34	40.88
Maiming	12	46.43	−34.43	1,185.43	25.53
	325				Chi square = 269.81

Observed from the sample of juveniles.

No relationship would divide the 325 offenses equally across the 7 categories (325 ÷ 7 = 46.43)

The sum of the use of the chi square formula for each category of juvenile offense.

the last example above that assesses whether the data fit a no relationship model or not is quite unfulfilling in terms of helping to develop useful information about the similarities and/or differences in such a group of offenders. For example, the example study of the relationship has not elaborated on the several demographic (age, race, residence) or criminological (prior arrests, prior incarcerations, types of past offenses) that could help to explain the relationship between the current offense categories for different types of juveniles.

The following sections move in this direction. They consider tests where we have two variables or groups to test simultaneously. Although this is not multivariate it can be used to formulate much more realistic analyses and tests. Typically, the two-sample test level is where most criminal justice and criminological researchers will begin their inferential analysis.

Two-Sample Tests

The study of quantitative variables is commonly done through the comparison of two variables or groups. For example, are the differences between arrest rates and imprisonment rates significant? Are male recidivism rates different from female recidivism rates? Such questions can certainly be made directional. That is, are arrests rates higher when the imprisonment rates are higher? Is female recidivism lower than male recidivism? The point here is that the comparisons for two-sample tests can focus on important research or policy-level comparisons for various variables.

As was true of the single sample tests, there are many *two-sample tests.* Here we will consider only the most common tests and those that will allow you to conduct analyses with any level of measurement. Keep in mind that there are many other tests that allow you to test two variables, and two variables with different levels of measurement, that will not be illustrated in this chapter. (See Kanji, 1993, or other, more advanced social science statistics texts. Consult with your instructor should you be interested in advanced analysis sources.)

The tests that are demonstrated here can be used in most situations through the conversion of the levels of measurement of the two variables into the highest common level of measurement. For example, suppose we have two variables: gender (males and females) and the number of arrests. Gender is clearly a nominal level of measurement in that we only know that the two possible genders are different. Men or women cannot be ranked on the basis of their gender alone. On the other hand, the number of arrests is a ratio level variable in that it differentiates the people in the study by the kind of arrests, the rank order of their arrests, and the magnitude of their arrests, and it is possible that some of the people in our study may have no arrests. The highest common level of measurement is the nominal level, because we cannot move the gender variable up to a ratio level measurement (or any other level for that matter), but we can bring the ratio variable down to a nominal level.

Five specific tests will be demonstrated in this chapter. These tests and their requirements are listed in table 11.6. There are generally three considerations in deciding which of these five tests to apply to various research situations: (1) the level of measurement; (2) the parametric assumptions; and (3) the time frame of the measurement of the two variables.

The issue of the parametric assumption was not discussed in the section on the single-sample tests because I generally discount the applicability of those tests and believe that the level of measurement can drive the use of the particular tests and decisions in a single sample context. However,

Table 11.6
TWO-SAMPLE TEST CONSIDERATIONS

Test	Level of Measurement of the Variables	Assumptions	Time
Independent t-test	Interval/ratio	Parametric	One
Dependent t-test	Interval/ratio	Parametric	Two
Mann-Whitney U-test	Ordinal+	Nonparametric	One
Wilcoxon T-test	Ordinal+	Nonparametric	Two
Chi square	Nominal	Nonparametric	One

it is important in two-sample tests and in *multiple sample tests* to clearly understand where parametric and nonparametric tests are appropriate. Your goal should be to use parametric tests whenever possible, because they tend to lead to better decisions about the null hypothesis in that they reduce TYPE I errors better than nonparametric tests. Nevertheless, you should not view the nonparametric tests as invalid. They are well accepted and have a sound basis in probability theory.

There are three key parametric assumptions about the data that you have collected that should be satisfied prior to using these tests. Otherwise, the nonparametric alternative tests should be used if the parametric assumptions are not met. These assumptions are: (1) the selection of observations is random; (2) the population variances of the variables are similar; and (3) the data are normally distributed.

In order to collect data that are random we have to rely on probability sampling procedures. These techniques are no guarantee that the data will be randomly selected, but most researchers assume when they rely on simple random sampling or other probability-based sampling techniques that the data they obtain are random.[9] This is generally an acceptable assumption given the basis for probability sampling. Besides, the randomness assumption is not as crucial as the normality assumption.

The second parametric assumption, that the population variances are similar, can be tested through sample estimates. In a two-sample situation we could simply calculate the variance for each of the two samples and compare them. If they are significantly different we would not have met this parametric assumption. Homogeneity (similarity in variances) can be tested through simply forming a ratio of the larger variance to the smaller variance and comparing that calculated "F" value to a population probability value for an F distribution (see Lutz, 1983; or Elifson, Runyon and Haber, 1990) (see figure 11.11).

Figure 11.11

F TEST OF HOMOGENEITY

Ages of male and female offenders

Males: 25, 24, 12, 13, 14, 16, 20, and 21 ($n = 8$)

Male Variance (s^2_{males}) = 25.5535

Females: 26, 23, 13, 15, 17, 22, and 22 ($n = 7$)

Female Variance ($s^2_{females}$) = 22.5714

F probability value = 4.21 (Hinkle et al., 1994, p. 618)

F Test = 25.5535 ÷ 22.5714 = 1.1321

Since the calculated F value (1.1321) is less than the F probability value (4.21), the population variances are homogeneous (similar).

The final assumption, and the most crucial one, is that of normally distributed data. The parametric tests make the general assumption that the data that are collected conform to a normal distribution. This assumption assumes that the distribution is symmetrical in physical shape. The basic idea here is that data behave in a predictable way and that the sum of the squared deviations around the mean are a minimum. That is, this assumption requires that 68 percent of the observations be between one standard deviation above and below the mean, 95 percent between two standard deviations above and below the mean, and 99 percent within three standard deviations above and below the mean. The extent to which the actual data differ from this theoretical distribution is the extent to which it is non-normal.

Normality can be assessed through inspection of the standard deviations and the percentage of the samples that conform to the normal distribution, through assessment of the skewness of the samples, through using a statistical normality test, or through the use of probability paper. Probability paper is a graphic display of normality that is not used today, given the existence of normality "tests." The closer the samples are to the normal curve distribution about the mean (see figure 11.12), the more normal the sample distributions. The "closeness" of the samples to what should be found if the distribution is normal can be determined through mere inspection. That is, we could study whether 68 percent of the scores in the distributions fall between one standard deviation above (+1s) and below (−1s) the mean. We can alco calculate a skewness value to determine how normal the sampling distribution is empirically. Positive skewness values indicate a leaning of the distribution away from the normal distribution toward the high end of the distribution, and negative values indicate leaning toward the low end. A skewness value of zero shows that the distribution is perfectly normal (a rare occurrence in criminal justice and criminological research). As a rule of thumb, whenever the skewness of the distribution is greater than +2.00 or less than −2.00, you should consider this sufficient evidence that the distribution is not normal.

Formula 11.8: Skewness

$$S_k = (3 \times (\text{mean} - \text{median})) \div \text{sample standard deviation}$$

The final method for determining normality is through statistical testing. A common test of normality is the Kolmogorov-Smirnov normality test, but there are others. Basically, these tests assess the deviation of the samples from what would be expected if they were normally distributed. The larger the difference between the sample and normality, the higher the probability that the sample distributions are not normal. This test can be conducted on many statistical programs including SPSS, so I will not provide

Figure 11.12
NORMAL CURVE

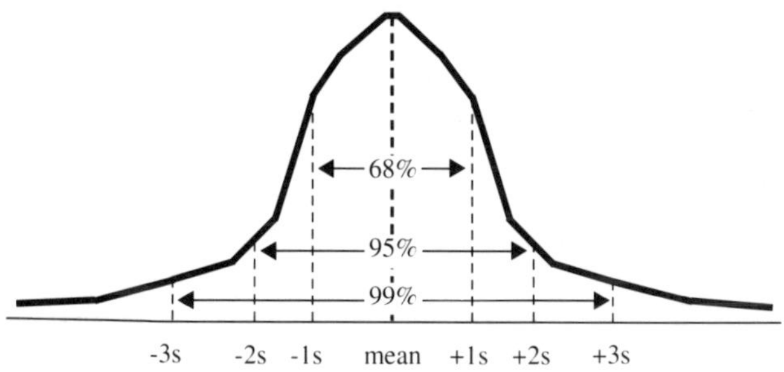

a detailed example here. Suffice it to say that empirical testing of the normality is based on probability theory, and therefore less individual judgment is involved in making the normality decision.

After meeting all of the normality assumptions the parametric tests can be used. If the normality assumptions are not met, then the nonparametric alternatives should be used, because the data do not conform to the normal distribution. The nonparametric tests generally assume randomly selected data but little else, and their population probability distributions are generally more flexible as regards the other assumptions of parametric tests.

Independent t-Test

In the independent t-test we are testing the two mean values of the sample against each other (either as differences or directionally). Suppose, for example, that researchers for the American Civil Liberties Union (ACLU) are working on a discrimination case and are examining the wages paid to male and female inmates. The ACLU believes that it can statistically support its position that female inmates are paid less on average than are male inmates. The researchers, in an effort to test this presumption, collect two small samples.

The parametric assumptions have all been met by the data that have been collected by the ACLU researchers. Hence, the data are measured at the interval level of measurement, the samples are simple random samples of a prison population, the background populations are similar because the samples are homogeneous ($F_{calculated} = 1.53$, $F_{critical} = 3.07$), and the data are normally distributed (e.g., the skewness for the male sample is -1.53, and the skewness for the female sample is 0.237). Therefore, we can proceed with the parametric independent t-test.

Step 1: Set the Hypotheses

Research Hypothesis: The average wage paid to the male inmates is greater than that paid to female inmates.

Null Hypothesis: The average wage paid to the male inmates is less than or the same as that paid to female inmates.

The research hypothesis in this case is driven by the ACLU researchers' need to make an initial assessment of the average wages paid to male and female inmates. In other situations they would construct the research hypothesis on the basis of past research and logic. In the previous example, if past research studies showed that juveniles tend to commit fewer offenses as they get older, that finding should be considered when one constructs a research hypothesis that states that while older juveniles commit fewer crimes than younger juveniles, the older juveniles commit more serious offenses on average. The point is that we can use prior research to improve the research hypothesis in terms of not repeating what others have already found and to more appropriately explore the details of the research situation.

Step 2: Select the Criteria. The second step is the selection of the tabled value for the comparison of the sample test statistic. Because we are using a t-test, we have to use a t probability distribution to obtain the population probability value. Table 11.7 shows the t probability values for both directional and nondirectional tests. The only value that we need to select, the appropriate probability value, is the degrees of freedom for the test. The degrees of freedom is calculated based on the sample size and formula 11.9.

Formula 11.9: $n_1 + n_2 - 2 =$ degrees of freedom

In the example we have been working on we have the following data:

Male inmates' wages: \$1.25, \$1.23, \$1.45, \$.56, \$.86, \$.99, \$.98, \$1.27, \$1.25, \$1.22, and \$.96

Female inmates' wages: \$1.13, \$.67, \$.89, \$.98, \$1.45, \$1.24, \$.45, \$.98, and \$1.25

The degrees of freedom for our test is 11 (males) + 9 (females) −2 = 18, and the population probability value for our directional hypothesis is 1.734. Now that we have set the hypothesis and selected the decision criteria, we need to calculate a test statistic.

Table 11.7
CRITICAL VALUES FOR T TESTS

Degrees of Freedom	Directional Tests	Nondirectional Tests
1	6.314	12.706
2	2.920	4.303
3	2.353	3.182
4	2.132	2.776
5	2.015	2.571
6	1.943	2.447
7	1.895	2.365
8	1.860	2.306
9	1.833	2.262
10	1.812	2.228
11	1.796	2.201
12	1.782	2.179
13	1.771	2.160
14	1.761	2.145
15	1.753	2.132
16	1.746	2.120
17	1.740	2.110
18	1.734	2.101
19	1.729	2.093
20	1.725	2.086
21	1.721	2.080
22	1.717	2.074
23	1.714	2.069
24	1.714	2.064
25	1.708	2.060
26	1.706	2.056
27	1.703	2.052
28	1.701	2.048
29	1.700	2.045
30	1.697	2.042

Step 3: Calculate a Test Value. The calculated test value for the t-test involves several estimates. First, a measure of the combined variance in the two groups or samples must be calculated. This variance is then converted into a combined standard deviation measure (called the standard error for samples), and then the test value can be calculated. Each of these steps is demonstrated in the following sections. The formula for the combined variance is formula 11.10, the standard error formula is formula 11.11, and the t-test formula is formula 11.12.

Formula 11.10: Pooled Variance

$$s^2_{pooled} = [(n_1 - 1)s^2_{one} + (n_2 - 1)s^2_{two}] \div n_1 + n_2 - 2$$

Where: n_1 = number of subjects in sample 1.
n_2 = number of subjects in sample 2.
s^2_{one} = variance of sample 1 (standard deviation squared)
s^2_{two} = variance of sample 2

Formula 11.11: Standard Error

$$\sigma_{standard\ error} = \sqrt{s^2_{pooled}\ ((1 \div n_1) + (1 \div n_2))}$$

Formula 11.12: t-Test

$$t = (mean_{one} - mean_{two}) \div \sigma_{standard\ error}$$

The calculcations of the sample value for this example are listed in figure 11.13. The test value that we would compare to the population probability value is 0.7081. This is our estimate of the ratio of the differences in the means of males and females relative to their combined standard variation that will be used to make a decision about the null hypothesis.[10]

Step 4: Make a Decision/Interpretation. Based on the calculated sample value of 0.7081 and the critical value of 1.734, the null hypothesis will be retained. There is no evidence that the difference in the average wage paid to male inmates ($1.09) and female inmates ($1.00) is statistically different from what could be expected in the long run. More appropriately there is no evidence for the ACLU researchers that the wages paid to male inmates are significantly higher than those paid to female inmates. There is no support for the research hypothesis.

Dependent t-Test

The dependent t-test is appropriate when we are interested in testing the differences or direction in means of a small sample over time. Dependent

Figure 11.13

INDEPENDENT T-TEST

$$s^2_{pooled} = [(11 - 1).0622 + (9 - 1).0955] \div 11 + 9 - 2 - 0.077$$

$$\sigma_{standard\ error} = \sqrt{0.077\ ((1 \div 11) + (1 \div 9))} = 0.1247$$

$$t = (1.0927 - 1.0044) \div 0.1247 = 0.7081$$

t-tests are common in experimental designs, because the whole point in the experimental design is to measure treatment effects on the experimental group over time.

Suppose we have a program to increase the weights of smaller inmates so that they can engage in more effective self-protection. Much of the prison literature documents that smaller, weaker inmates are often the victims in prison violence. Hence, an experimental program to reduce prison violence that has as its goal to increase the physical size of a group of smaller-than-average inmates would make sense. We collect the following data (weights in pounds) both before and after our physical training program for a random sample of smaller inmates:

> Before the program: Jack: 145, Joe: 156, Jim: 142, Bill: 132, Bob: 133 and Frank: 160
>
> After the program: Jack: 155, Joe: 158, Jim: 162, Bill: 147, Bob: 133 and Frank: 165

Step 1: Set the Hypotheses

> *Research Hypothesis:* The physical training program increases the inmates' weights.
>
> *Null Hypothesis:* The physical training program does not change, or decreases, the inmates' weights.

The hope of the program designers is that the inmates will gain weight over the course of their program participation; therefore, this hypothesis is directional. The dependent t-test will provide an estimate, based on sample data, about the research hypothesis.

Step 2: Select the Criteria. The criteria for this test are determined through reference to the t-test critical values table (see table 11.6). The degrees of freedom for dependent tests is determined by subtracting 1 from the sample size (6 people in the weights study − 1 = 5 degrees of freedom). In referring to table 11.6 under the directional test column and 5 degrees of freedom, we find that the population probability estimate is 2.015. Since the test is directional, we should use −2.015.

Step 3: Calculate a Test Value. The first step in calculating the sample test value is to make certain that the parametric assumptions are met for the data. The data were drawn from a random sample of the prison population, so we can assume randomness. The ratio of the larger variance to the smaller variance is 1.033 ($F_{\text{test value}}$), and the comparable probability value is 4.28 ($F_{probability\ value}$). The background populations are assumed, based on this ratio, to be homogeneous, because the calculated value is less than the probability value. In terms of normality, the skewness for the weights at time 1 is 0.3039, and the skewness at time 2 is −0.8100. The data appear to be normally distributed. Hence, the use of a parametric test is appropriate.

The formulas for the dependent t-test are shown in formulas 11.13.

Formulas 11.13: Dependent t-Test

a. $\sigma_d = \sqrt{[\Sigma\ (d - d_m)^2] \div (n - 1)}$

b. $S.E._d = \sigma_d \div \sqrt{n}$

c. $t_d = d_m \div S.E._d$

The mathematical operation here is to sum the individual differences in the scores over time. This calculation relies on the sum of the squared deviations about the main ideal as its basis. Hence, for the example the calculated test value is shown in figure 11.14.

Step 4: Make a Decision/Interpretation. Since the calculated sample test value (−2.72) is less than our population probability estimate (−2.015), we reject the null hypothesis.[11] The inmates in the program appear to have gained weight over their participation in the program. We have certainly not proven or established this weight gain as a fact. We have demonstrated only that given our sample estimates of the population it is less likely that their weights decreased or stayed the same.

It is important to keep in mind when interpreting the results of such probability tests that even though there is a statistical significance, that may not be practically significant. The average increases in the weights of the small sample of inmates may not increase their ability to protect themselves, because the theoretical link between physical size and self-protection may be an erroneous assumption.

Mann-Whitney U Test

The Mann-Whitney U test is the nonparametric alternative to the independent t-test. As such, the Mann-Whitney U test assumes that the data are collected from random samples and two independent samples or variables. The Mann-Whitney U test should be used when the data are shown to be nonhomogeneous or not normally distributed. Although it is affected by tied scores across the two variables, it is still a good alternative to the independent t-test. Another advantage of the Mann-Whitney test is that it can also be conducted on ordinal-level data. As is true of proportions, means, and t-tests, there is a comparable population probability distribution that can be used to compare sample test U values with those that should occur in

Figure 11.14
DEPENDENT T-TEST EXAMPLE

Time 1	Time 2	difference (d)	$d - d_m$	$(d - d_m)^2$
145	155	$145 - 155 = -10$	$-10 - (-8.67) = -1.33$	$(-1.33)^2 = 1.77$
156	158	$156 - 158 = -2$	$-2 - (-8.67) = 6.67$	$(6.67)^2 = 44.49$
142	162	$142 - 162 = -20$	$-20 - (-8.67) = -11.33$	$(-11.33)^2 = 128.37$
132	147	$132 - 147 = -15$	$-15 - (-8.67) = -6.33$	$(-6.33)^2 = 40.07$
133	133	$133 - 133 = 0$	$0 - (-8.67) = 8.67$	$(8.67)^2 = 75.17$
160	165	$160 - 165 = -5$	$-5 - (-8.67) = 3.67$	$(3.67)^2 = 13.47$

The d_m is the mean of the differences:
$(-10) + (-2) + (-20) + (-15) + (0) + (-5) = -52$
$d_m = (-52) \div 6 = -8.67$

$\Sigma(d - d_m)^2 = 303.34$

$$\sigma_d = \sqrt{[303.34] \div (6 - 1)} = 7.7889$$

$$S.D._{d} = 7.7889 \div \sqrt{6} = 3.1798$$

$$t_d = -8.67 \div 3.1798 = -2.7266$$

the long run. The Mann-Whitney U test is calculated in a much different way than the t-test or the other parametric tests in that it is not based on the assumption that deviations from the mean value are a minimum. The Mann-Whitney U test, the Wilcoxon T test, and the chi square test focus on sample values that compare what is collected in the data with what could be expected.

An example of a Mann-Whitney U test could be conducted for Department of Corrections researchers studying the prices of commissary goods in two similar prisons. The inmates have been complaining about the high cost of the various goods sold in the prison stores and have threatened to initiate a costly class-action law suit if the matter is not given serious attention. The director of the Department of Corrections asks the researchers to determine whether there are significant differences in the prices inmates pay for commissary items. The researchers decide to take a random sample of the prices of six commissary items in two typical prisons in the state. The data for the two prisons are as follows:

Voorhees Prison: $1.35, $2.37, $1.44, $1.40, $1.46, $1.45
(mean = $1.57)

Adam Lane Prison: $1.32, $1.33, $1.42, $1.34, $1.36, $1.43
(mean = $1.37)

Because the researchers are interested in the strongest possible test for determining whether these data are different, they assess whether the independent t-test is appropriate (i.e., whether the parametric assumptions have been met by this data). First, they draw random samples of the prices of six similar goods from each of the two prisons and are satisfied with the representativeness of the sample. Second, they determine that the prices of goods in the Voorhees Prison are not influenced by the prices in the Adam Lane Prison. The test of homogeneity, however, results in a lack of homogeneity of the background populations ($F_{calculated} = 69.1167$, $F_{critical} = 4.28$). While the data appear to be normally distributed because the skewness measures for both prisons are within an acceptable range (Voorhees Prison skewness = 1.00, and Adam Lane Prison skewness = 1.279), the researchers, to be on the safe side, decide to use the Mann-Whitney U test to conduct the requested analyses.

Step 1: Set the Hypotheses

Research Hypothesis: There is a difference in the costs of commissary goods in the Voorhees and Adam Lane Prisons.

Null Hypothesis: There is no difference in the costs of commissary goods in the Voorhees and Adam Lane Prisons.

Step 2: Select the Criteria. The criteria for the Mann-Whitney U test can be determined through the referencing of a population probability table of Mann-Whitney U values, but the normal distribution (arguably the most accepted probability distribution) can be applied after the fact to test the calculated U value. I prefer this method, because most Mann-Whitney probability tables are a complex series of subtables, and we have already discussed the use of the z values for the normal probability distribution. The critical Mann-Whitney value is calculated and then added to formula 11.14.

Formula 11.14: Mann-Whitney U Test

$$z_U = U - 0.5(n_1)(n_2) \div \sqrt{[(n_1 \times n_2) \times (n_1 + n_2 + 1)] \div 12]}$$

If the calculated z value, based on the calculated U test value, within the range of ±1.96, then the null hypothesis is retained; otherwise, it is rejected. For the example that follows, the critical value calculation is:

$$z_U = [5 - 0.5(6)(6)] \div \sqrt{[[(6 \times 6) \times (6 + 6 + 1)] \div 12]} = -2.082$$

Since the calculated z value based on the Mann-Whitney U test statistic is outside of the z value range of −1.96 and +1.96 on a normal probability distribution, we should reject the null hypothesis. But we're jumping the gun here. Let me show how we got the value of U = 5.

Step 3: Calculcate the Test Value. There are two parts to the calculation of the Mann-Whitney U test value. First, the data must be organized into a summary table of ranks, and second, the summary values of the ranked data are applied to formulas 11.15a and 11.15b to determine the two U test values for each sample. The estimated U test value that is used for the comparison to the population probability value is the smaller of the two values. The summary rank is shown in table 11.8. The next step is to calculate the two Mann-Whitney U test values and select the smaller of the two for our comparison (and calculation) with the population probability estimate. Formulas 11.15a and 11.15b are used for the Mann-Whitney U tests.

Table 11.8

SUMMARY RANK

Ordered Values	Rank	Prison
$1.32	1	Adam Lane
1.33	2	Adam Lane
1.34	3	Adam Lane
1.35	4	Voorhees
1.36	5	Adam Lane
1.40	6	Voorhees
1.42	7	Adam Lane
1.43	8	Adam Lane
1.44	9	Voorhees
1.45	10	Voorhees
1.46	11	Voorhees
2.37	12	Voorhees

R_1 = Sum of ranks for Voorhees prison
(4 + 6 + 9 + 10 + 11 + 12) = 52

R_2 = Sum of ranks for Adam Lane prison
(1 + 2 + 3 + 5 + 7 + 8) = 26

Formulas 11.15: Mann-Whitney U Tests

a. $U_{\text{sample one}} = (n_1 \times n_2) + (0.5 \times n_1) \times (n_1 + 1) - R_1$

b. $U_{\text{sample two}} = (n_1 \times n_2) + (0.5 \times n_2) \times (n_2 + 1) - R_2$

Step 4: Make a Decision/Interpretation. Because the calculated value of the Mann-Whitney U test results in a calculated z_u value of -2.08, the null hypothesis is rejected. That is, if we obtain a calculated U test value of greater than $+1.96$ or less than -1.96, then the null hypothesis should be rejected. It appears that there is a statistically significant difference in the price of commissary goods in the study prisons. On average, the inmates in the Voorhees Prison pay $1.58 for their commissary goods, whereas the inmates in the Adam Lane Prison pay $1.36 on average. The differences between the two prisons are statistically significant. That is, the differences in the average costs are not due solely to sampling error but are estimated, based on a normal probability distribution, to be important.[12]

Wilcoxon T Test

The Wilcoxon T test is the nonparametric alternative to the dependent t-test. That is, when the data do not meet the parametric assumptions, the Wilcoxon T test can be used because it is nonparametric, and the requirements for such tests are less stringent than those for parametric tests. Both the Mann-Whitney U test and the Wilcoxon T test can be used for large or small sized samples.

The Wilcoxon T test could be used, for example, by a police academy training officer who is interested in studying firing range scores of police officers after they took a specific training program that should improve their shooting scores. The training officer believes that the training in shooting should make the shooting scores of the cadets increase. The training officer collected data before and after the training sessions for a sample of eight cadets (table 11.9).

Ideally, we would like to use a parametric test, but the data fail two of the most important parametric assumptions. That is, while the data are

Figure 11.15

MANN-WHITNEY U TESTS

$U_{\text{Voorhees Prison}} = (6 \times 6) + (0.5 \times 6) \times (6 + 1) - 52 = 5$

$U_{\text{Adam Lane Prison}} = (6 \times 6) + (0.5 \times 6) \times (6 + 1) - 26 = 31$

Therefore, Mann-Whitney U test value = 5

Table 11.9
SHOOTING SCORES

Cadets	Before Training Scores	After Training Scores
Alicia	10	61
Joe	7	47
Frank	9	13
Max	10	12
Ryan	15	14
David	12	15
Glenn	8	65
Chris	9	15
	$\text{Mean}_{\text{before}} = 10$	$\text{Mean}_{\text{after}} = 30.25$

collected from randomly selected police cadets, they are not from homogeneous populations ($F_{\text{calculated}} = 86.16$, $F_{\text{critical}} = 3.79$) and the after-training scores are not normally distributed (skewness = 2.029). Given that the parametric assumptions have not been met, the Wilcoxon T test is the most appropriate test in this case.

Step 1: Set the Hypotheses

Research Hypothesis: The shooting scores of the police cadets is higher after the shooting training program than before the program.

Null Hypothesis: The shooting scores of the police cadets is lower or the same after the shooting training program.

Step 2: Select the Criteria. Setting the criteria for the Wilcoxon T test is similar to the Mann-Whitney U test in that it can be based on probability tables for the Wilcoxon test or through reference to the normal distribution. I prefer to use the normal distribution because it cuts down on the need to consult multiple tables and complex tables. Formula 11.16 is used to calculate the critical z value for the Wilcoxon T test.

Formula 11.16: Calculating z Value

$$z_T = T - 0.25\ (n)\ (n + 1) \div \sqrt{[[n(n - 1)\ )2n + 1)] \div 24]}$$

Step 3: Calculate a Test Value. The calculation of the Wilcoxon T test value involves the ranking of the scores for each time period while retaining the time period identification and summing the ranks for each time period. Table 11.10 demonstrates the calculation of the Wilcoxon test value.

Table 11.10
WILCOXON T-TEST EXAMPLE

Cadets	Before	After	Differences	Ranks	B>A	B<A
Alicia	10	61	−51	7	—	7
Joe	7	47	−40	6	—	6
Frank	9	13	−4	4	—	4
Max	10	12	−2	2	—	2
Ryan	15	14	1	1	1	—
David	12	15	−3	3	—	3
Glenn	8	65	−57	8	—	8
Chris	9	15	−6	5	—	5
Wilcoxon calculated value = 35 (larger of the two R's)					$R_1 = 1$	$R_2 = 35$

Step 4: Make a Decision/Interpretation. The calculcated critical z value for a calculated Wilcoxon T test value of 35 is:

$$z_T = 35 - 0.25\ (8)\ (8 + 1) \div \sqrt{[[8\ (8 + 1)\ (2 \times 8 + 1)] \div 24]} = 2.38$$

Hence, there is a significant difference between the before-training and after-training periods. There is evidence to support that the training is coincident with improvements in the shooting range scores of police cadets.

Chi Square Test

The final two-sample test that will be demonstrated is the chi square test. The chi square two-sample test can be used with nominally measured variables, and therefore can be applied in many research situations. The chi square test is a nonparametric test. Although it is not necessarily a nonparametric alternative to the independent or dependent t-tests, it can be used when the data fail to meet the parametric assumptions or the data are nominally measured.

The example, below, is an attempt to determine whether inmates favor or disfavor male and female corrections officers. An important issue in correctional practice since the early 1980s has been the introduction of opposite-sex correctional officers in both male and female facilities. We may presume that some inmates treat opposite-sex officers differently than same-sex officers. Male inmates may view the female officers as inappropriately assigned to oversee them. Conversely, the male inmates may treat female staff with more respect than male staff because they are women. In a study of thirty randomly selected inmates, the following data were collected:

Male Officers		**Female Officers**	
Favored	*Not favored*	*Favored*	*Not favored*
Bill	Albert	Sally	Mauren
Rob	Fred	Krista	Linda
Frank	Glenn	Melly	Alicia
Max	Ryan	Jo	June
Al	Brandon	Harriet	Carol
John	Shawn	Sue	Ann
	Jack		Annette
	Joe		Betty
			Geane
			Dee

Step 1: Set the Hypotheses.

Research Hypothesis: There is a difference in the opinions of inmates about correctional officers based on the officers' gender.

Null Hypothesis: There is no difference in the opinions of inmates about correctional officers based on the officers' gender.

Step 2: Select the Criteria. Because we are interested in testing a nondirectional or difference hypothesis, the critical value should be a nondirectional one. The selection of the population probability estimate for the two-sample chi square test is based on formula 11.17 and looking up the value in table 11.5.

Formula 11.17: Degrees of Freedom for Two-Sample Chi Square

$$\text{df} = [\text{number of rows} - 1] \times [\text{number of columns} - 1]$$

Since in the example data we have two categories of the row variable (favor, don't favor) and two categories of the column variable (male officers, female officers), the calculation of the degrees of freedom formula would result in a degrees of freedom of 1 ($[2-1] \times [2-1] = 1$df). Hence, the critical population probability value at 1 degree of freedom that we will use to compare our sample chi square calculation result with is 3.841.

Step 3: Calculate a Test Value. Before we calculate a test value, the raw data from the data table should be summarized into a two-by-two summary table (table 11.11). The next step is to calculate the expected values (table 11.12) for each of the four cells in the summary table. The expected values are those that should be found if there were no relationship or difference between the two variables (formula 11.18).

Formula 11.18: Expected Values

$$f_e = (\text{row total} \times \text{column total}) \div \text{total sample}$$

Finally, the calculations of the chi square test values are shown in the calculations table (table 11.13) and is based on the use of formula 11.19.

Formula 11.19:

$$\chi_2 = \Sigma\ [(\text{observed frequency} - \text{expected frequency})^2 \div (\text{expected frequency})]$$

Step 4: Make a Decision/Interpretation. Since the calculated chi square test value is only 0.0894 and the population probability value is 3.841, we should retain the null hypothesis in this example. Therefore, there is no statistically significant difference in the opinions of inmates about correctional officers based on the officers' gender.

Multiple Sample Tests

In addition to two-sample tests listed and demonstrated there are multiple sample or group analyses. These tests can be parametric or nonparametric. Researchers use parametric tests at this multivariate level, however, much more commonly. In terms of the use of parametric multivariate tests the most common set of techniques are labeled "Analysis of Variance" or ANOVA based techniques.

The analysis of variance at the multivariate level examines the differences between the means of each of the three or more groups. This comparison, however, is based on the deviation of the three or more groups about that mean rather than an actual test of the means themselves. The research hypothesis in ANOVA designs is always a nondirectional difference statement, and the null hypothesis is a statement of similarity. To be more specific, the comparisons of the deviations from the means of the scores is done through looking at the between-group variation and within-group variation. Between-group variation compares how much variation there is in each of the three or more groups in comparison to each other, whereas within-group variation assesses the individual group variation.

The ANOVA test calculates the differences between the means of each of the three or more groups as a ratio to the total variation in the three or more groups. Hence, the ANOVA test is similar to an independent t-test, but its calculation is complicated because the additional group scores must

Table 11.11
DATA SUMMARY

	Male officers	Female officers	Total
Favor officers	6	6	12
Don't favor officers	8	10	18
	14	16	30

Table 11.12
EXPECTED FREQUENCIES

	Male officers	Female officers	Total
Favor officers	5.6 (12 × 14) ÷ 30	6.4 (12 × 16) ÷ 30	12
Don't favor officers	8.4 (18 × 14) ÷ 30	9.6 (18 × 16) ÷ 30	18
	14	16	30

Table 11.13
CHI SQUARE CALCULATIONS

	Male officers	Female officers
Favor officers	.0286 $(6 - 5.6)^2 \div 5.6$	.0250 $(6 - 6.4)^2 \div 6.4$
Don't favor officers	.0191 $(8 - 8.4)^2 \div 8.4$	.0167 $(10 - 9.6)^2 \div 9.6$

Chi Square Test Value = .0286 + .0250 + 0.0191 + .0167 = 0.0894 be included. The basis of the population values is a series of probability distributions that are referred to as "F" distributions (after Ronald A. Fisher, their inventor). The example that follows shows a simple one-way example of the analysis of variance.

ANOVA

The use of the analysis of variance can be demonstrated in much the same way as were the single- and two-sample tests. The example in this situation concerns the behavior of inmates recently booked into a jail facility. Suppose we are interested in the adaptation abilities of individuals to jails. That is, how quickly do people adapt to the routine procedures and operations to become manageable inmates. Both theoretically and operationally it would be helpful to understand more about how long it takes for inmates to adjust to correctional confinement. Theoretically, this could drive the development of a more operationally based theory of inmate subcultures. On the other hand, if an administrator finds out that it takes only twelve hours on average for people to adjust to a jail facility he or she might confine individuals to a special area during this key adjustment period to facilitate a smoother transition into the facility.

In order to conduct an analysis of the adjustment of inmates, a random sample of four inmates from the population of inmates in the study facility was selected and the inmates' adjustment scores were collected. The adjustment scores are a function of the number of complaints the new inmates have, staff assessments about adjustment, other inmates' assessments, and the number of incidents involving the inmates. The adjustment scores are assumed to be both parametric and measured at the interval level. That is, they are from a randomly drawn sample, are homogeneous, and are normally distributed. Admittedly, a sample of only four inmates is rather small, and in no way would it be viable for an actual research study of the nature of inmate adjustment in the study jail or corrections. However, it is sufficient for demonstration purposes given the complexity of the calculations involved in an ANOVA analysis and the focus here on the process, or method, of analysis of variance testing. The data collected are shown in table 11.14.

Step 1: Set the Hypotheses. The research and null hypotheses are nondirectional for these tests, at least in a main-effects model such as a one-way ANOVA demonstrated here. That is, the means are presumed to be different for the research hypothesis or similar for the null hypothesis.

> *Research Hypothesis:* There is a significant difference in the adjustment of inmates across the four time periods.
>
> *Null Hypothesis:* There is no significant difference in the adjustment of inmates across the four time periods.

Table 11.14
ANOVA DATA

Subject	4 hours	12 hours	20 hours	28 hours
David	36	37	44	71
Joey	22	46	76	76
Joseph	21	45	63	50
Al	24	26	47	61
Sum	103	154	230	258
Mean	25.75	38.5	57.5	64.5
Standard Deviation	6.94	9.26	14.89	11.50

Step 2: Select the Criteria. The second step is the selection of the relevant comparison population probability value. The selection of this value involves the calculation of a between-groups and within-groups degrees of freedom (formulas 11.20a and 11.20b). Once the degrees of freedom values are determined, the population probability value is then located in an "F" distribution table (see Lutz, 1983; Fitzgerald and Cox, 1994).

Formula 11.20

a. $df_{\text{between groups}} = a - 1$
b. $df_{\text{within groups}} = a\ (s - 1)$

where: a = the number of groups
s = the number of subjects in each group

For the example we are working on, that means that we have 3 degrees of freedom for the between groups side (4 − 1 = 3) and 12 degrees of freedom for the within-groups equation (4(4 − 1) = 12). A nondirectional test for 7 and 12 degrees of freedom is 2.92. As was true of the other tests, if the calculated sample value is less than this population probability value, we should reject the null hypothesis; otherwise, we should retain it.

Step 3: Calculate the Test Value. The calculation of the test value for the ANOVA test involves the calculation of three sum of squares values, two mean squares values, and an "F" ratio based on the mean squares calculations. Because of this level of complexity, ANOVA is typically conducted on a microcomputer or mainframe computer system. If the sample sizes are much larger than the one demonstrated here, it would take a considerable amount of time to complete the computations. The formulas for finding the three sum of squares values are formulas 11.21a, 11.21b, and 11.21c.

Formulas 11.21

a. Sum of Squares Total: $\Sigma (x_i - \text{mean}_{TOTAL})^2$

Where: x_i = individual scores
mean_{TOTAL} = total mean across all groups

b. Sum of Squares Between: $\Sigma [n_1 (\text{mean}_{SAMPLES} - \text{mean}_{TOTAL})^2]$

Where: ni = number of subjects in each group
$\text{mean}_{SAMPLES}$ = mean in each group

c. Sum of Squares Within: $\Sigma x^2_1 + \Sigma x^2_2 + \Sigma x^2_3 + \ldots \Sigma x^2_k$

Square and sum each score for all subjects in all groups.

The formulas for finding the mean squares and the F ratio (the test statistic) are formulas 11.22a, 11.22b, and 11.22c.

Formulas 11.22

a. Mean Squares Between Groups:

Sum of Squares Between Groups ÷ degrees of $\text{freedom}_{between}$

b. Mean Squares Within Groups:

Sum of Squares Within Groups ÷ degrees of freedom_{within}

c. F Ratio:

Mean Squares Between Groups ÷ Mean Squares Within Groups

The computations for the example are shown in figures 11.16 and 11.17.

Step 4: Make a Decision/Interpretation. Because the calculated value of the F test statistic is 10.2699 and is greater than the estimated population probability value of 2.92 (see Step 2 above), we reject the null hypothesis that the average adjustment scores are the same at each time period. There is evidence that there is a statistically significant difference in the means for the four time periods. That is not to say that the means are statistically increasing, as they appear to be (because we have not tested that condition) only that they are statistically different from one another on a probability basis. There are several additional tests that may be engaged in to determine whether the means are increasing or decreasing, but these are clearly beyond the scope of this text.

Figure 11.16
SUM OF SQUARES

$mean_{TOTAL}$ = (103 + 154 + 230 + 258) ÷ 16 = 46.56

Sum of Squares Total (SST)

4 hours	12 hours	20 hours	28 hours
$(36 - 46.56)^2 = 111.51$	$(37 - 46.56)^2 = 91.39$	$(44 - 46.56)^2 = 6.55$	$(71 - 46.56)^2 = 597.31$
$(22 - 46.56)^2 = 603.19$	$(46 - 46.56)^2 = 0.31$	$(76 - 46.56)^2 = 866.71$	$(76 - 46.56)^2 = 866.71$
$(21 - 46.56)^2 = 653.31$	$(45 - 46.56)^2 = 2.43$	$(63 - 46.56)^2 = 270.27$	$(50 - 46.56)^2 = 11.83$
$(24 - 46.56)^2 = 508.95$	$(26 - 46.56)^2 = 422.71$	$(47 - 46.56)^2 = 0.19$	$(61 - 46.56)^2 = 208.51$
1,876.96	516.84	1,143.72	1,684.36

Sum of Squares Total = 5,221.88

Sum of Squares Between (SSB)

$SSB = [4(25.75 - 46.56)^2] + [4(38.5 - 46.56)^2] + [4(57.5 - 46.46)^2] + [4(64.5 - 46.56)^2]$

$= 1{,}732.22 + 259.85 + 478.73 + 1{,}287.37$

Sum of Squares Between = 3,758.17

Sum of Squares Within (SSW)

4 hours	12 hours	20 hours	28 hours
$(36 - 25.75)^2 = 105.06$	$(37 - 38.5)^2 = 2.25$	$(44 - 57.5)^2 = 182.25$	$(71 - 64.5)^2 = 42.25$
$(22 - 25.75)^2 = 14.06$	$(46 - 38.5)^2 = 56.25$	$(76 - 57.5)^2 = 342.25$	$(76 - 64.5)^2 = 132.25$
$(21 - 25.75)^2 = 22.56$	$(45 - 38.5)^2 = 42.25$	$(63 - 57.5)^2 = 30.25$	$(50 - 64.5)^2 = 210.25$
$(24 - 25.75)^2 = 3.06$	$(26 - 38.5)^2 = 156.25$	$(47 - 57.5)^2 = 110.25$	$(61 - 64.5)^2 = 12.25$
144.74	257.00	665.00	397.00

Sum of Squares Within = 1,463.74

Figure 11.17
MEAN SQUARES AND F RATIO

Mean Squares Between = 3,758.17 ÷ 3 = 1,252.72

Mean Squares Within = 1,463.74 ÷ 12 = 121.98

F Ratio = 1,252.72 ÷ 121.98 = 10.2699

Kruskal Wallis H Test

The Kruskal-Wallis H test is the nonparametric alternative to the ANOVA tests. While the chi square test (as shown in the two-sample example) can be applied to multivariate situations, the H test is more powerful and produces decisions close to those of the analysis of variance. The H test is also specifically constructed to handle studies of three or more variables. The population probability tables for the Kruskal-Wallis H test is the same as the chi square distributions (see table 11.5).

Suppose, for example, that the state Department of Social Services is interested in determining whether there is a significant difference between the average number of new arrests of offenders who have participated in its programs for substance abuse, intensive supervision, and employment counseling. Each program is run independently of the state, but there are insufficient numbers of clients (offenders) to conduct a parametric ANOVA based analysis. The data for this example is listed in figure 11.18; these are the number of arrests offenders have had after participating in the programs. The Kruskal-Wallis H test follows the same basic logic that we have been using on all of the tests in this chapter. Once again, the only alterations are that the formula for the H test value changes and that the population probability distribution for the sample statistic is the chi square table (see table 11.5).

Step 1: Set the Hypotheses. The hypotheses are constrained in the same way as those for the analysis of variance in that they should be difference

Figure 11.18
NEW ARREST DATA

Substance Abuse Counseling	Intensive Supervision	Employment Counseling
1	4	5
2	5	4
3	6	2
1	7	2
2	4	2
4	3	3
—	2	1
—	1	1
—	6	—

and no difference statements. The following demonstrate that idea and testing using the nonparametric H test.

> *Research Hypothesis:* There is a difference in the number of new arrests that offenders have after participating in substance abuse counseling, intensive supervision, or employment counseling.
>
> *Null Hypothesis:* There is no difference in the number of new arrests that offenders have after participating in substance abuse counseling, intensive supervision, or employment counseling.

Step 2: Select the Criteria. The Kruskal-Wallis test follows a chi square probability distribution for the population values. The use of the chi square probability table requires that we have the degrees of freedom for the test situation. The degrees of freedom is calculated by taking 1 from the number of groups in the study situation ($df = k - 1$). Hence, there are three study groups in the example data (above) so 3 − 1 results in a degrees of freedom value of 2. The resulting population probability value (located in table 11.5) is 5.991. We can compare this population probability value with the sample H statistic from the sample values.

Step 3: Calculate a Test Value. Calculating the H test value involves two steps. First, the values must be ranked from low to high (because the Kruskal-Wallis test requires ordinal values, the interval data must be converted to the ordinal level [table 11.15]). When there are tied ranks, the mean of the tied ranks is assigned to each score that ties. Second, the ranks are applied in the Kruskal-Wallis H test formula (see formula 11.23).

Formula 11.23:

$$H = [12 \div (n(n + 1))] \times [\Sigma((\Sigma R_i)^2 \div n_i)] - [3(n + 1)]$$

Once the ranks have been assigned the next step is to compute the H test statistic. The calculation of the H test statistic for the example data is shown in figure 11.19.

Step 4: Make a Decision/Interpretation. Since the calculated H test value based on the sample data is 4.9891 and the critical population probability estimate from the chi square table is 5.991, the null hypothesis is retained. There is no statistically significant differences in the number of new arrests for the three programs. Basically, this shows that no program is inherently better at preventing new arrests after offenders go through such programs. That is not to say that the programs do not have other impacts.

For example, the employment counseling, even though it doesn't significantly reduce new arrests any better than abuse counseling or intensive supervision, may allow the offenders to support their families. The abuse counseling may even reduce the potential number of arrests that the offenders may have engaged in had there been no program participation. The point here

Table 11.15

RANKING OF SCORES

Group	Original Scores[a]	Ranked Scores[b]	
Abuse Counseling	1	3	
Abuse Counseling	1	3	
Intensive Supervision	1	3	Add tied ranks: $(1+2+3+4+5) \div 5 = 3$
Employment Program	1	3	
Employment Program	1	3	
Abuse Counseling	2	8.5	
Abuse Counseling	2	8.5	
Intensive Supervision	2	8.5	Add tied ranks: $(6+7+8+9+10+11) \div 6 = 8.5$
Employment Program	2	8.5	
Employment Program	2	8.5	
Employment Program	2	8.5	
Abuse Counseling	3	13	
Intensive Supervision	3	13	Add tied ranks: $(12+13+14) \div 3 = 13$
Employment Program	3	13	
Abuse Counseling	4	16.5	
Intensive Supervision	4	16.5	Add tied ranks: $(15+16+17+18) \div 4 = 16.5$
Intensive Supervision	4	16.5	
Employment Program	4	16.5	
Intensive Supervision	5	19.5	Add tied ranks: $(19+20) \div 2 = 19.5$
Employment Program	5	19.5	
Intensive Supervision	6	21.5	Add tied ranks: $(21+22) \div 2 = 21.5$
Intensive Supervision	6	21.5	
Intensive Supervision	7	23	

a. Place all of the original scores in all of the groups in an ordered array while retaining group membership.

b. A rank must be assigned to each observation in each group. Averages are used for ties as shown.

Figure 11.19
H TEST EXAMPLE

Sum of substance abuse counseling group ranks = 52.5 R_1

Sum of intensive supervision group ranks = 143 R_2

Sum of employment counseling group ranks = 80.5 R_3

$$H = [12 \div (23(23 + 1))] \times [[(52.5)^2 \div 6] + [(143)^2 \div 9] + [(80.5)^2 \div 8]] - [3(23 + 1)]$$

$$H = 4.9891$$

is that the finding is limited only to the number of new arrest variable, and there are likely to be other explanatory variables.

Summary

This chapter has provided detailed explanations and demonstrations of the most common inferential analyses used in criminology and criminal justice. These analyses, while basic, should provide you with the tools necessary to conduct many analyses of both theoretical and practical questions in criminal justice. The descriptive analyses in chapter 10 only allow us to describe the sample that we have obtained. The inferential analyses in this chapter allow us to generalize to the larger population from which the sample is drawn.

The single-sample tests allow us to compare an individual variable, whether it is parametric or nonparametric, to some known population value. These tests include the single-sample proportions test for comparing a sample proportion to a known population proportion, the means test for comparing a sample mean to a population mean, and the chi-square test for assessing the distribution of observations across the categories of a nominal variable.

The two-sample tests included both parametric and nonparametric tests. The parametric tests have much higher data expectations and generally require data that are normally distributed. These tests include the two-sample proportions test, the independent t-tests, the dependent t-tests, and the z-test. The proportions test allows us to compare the proportions of two samples on some variable. The independent t-tests allow us to compare two independent variables or groups. The dependent t-test is used in situations where we take two measures of the exact same sample over time and desires to assess whether there is a statistical difference. Last, the z-test is similar to the independent t-test in that it compares two groups or variables but is dissimilar in that it is used when we have a large sample (greater than thirty cases).

The comparable two-sample nonparametric tests (Mann-Whitney U, Wilcoxon T, and chi square) are used when the data are not normally distributed or the samples relied upon are not based on probability methods. The Mann-Whitney U test is the nonparametric alternative to the independent t-test and z-test in that it allows us to compare two variables or groups. The Wilcoxon Test is the nonparametric alternative to the dependent t-test. Finally, the chi square test can also be used on two samples and is the only test available when we have nominal level variables.

Main Concepts

process of inferential testing
concepts
relationship hypothesis
research hypothesis
TYPE I error
stating hypotheses
test statistics
nonparametric tests
retaining the null hypothesis
two-sample tests
hypothesis setting
difference hypothesis
directional hypothesis
null hypothesis
TYPE II error
level of significance
parametric tests
rejecting the null hypothesis
single sample tests
multiple sample tests

Discussion Questions

1. What are the advantages and disadvantages of the traditional hypothesis testing process?
2. How do you decide which single-sample test to use?
3. How do you decide which two-sample test to use?
4. A researcher is interested in determining whether her sample is representative. She would be most interested in which kind of tests to determine whether her sample of police officers were representative of the population of all police officers?
5. If you were interested in looking at the effects of prison programs and employment counseling on a particular group of inmates, which test should you use? Why?
6. What does the ANOVA F test do with data that the Kruskal-Wallis H test does not? Which is better? Why?

Exercise

Form into small groups of three or four people. From a list of criminal justice variables, such as the following, describe a single-sample, two-sample, and multisample test for the group of variables. Explain your rationale for selecting the tests and what you hope to find through conducting these tests.

1. Unemployment rate for each state in the United States
2. UCR crime rate for each state in the United States
3. Number of inmates per 1,000 of population for each state in the United States
4. The percentage of the population in poverty for each state in the United States
5. The number of people per 1,000 on food stamps for each state in the United States

12 BASIC QUALITATIVE ANALYSES

Learning Objectives

1. To describe several qualitative data analysis techniques
2. To discuss and illustrate content analysis
3. To discuss and illustrate case study analysis
4. To discuss and illustrate several computer-based qualitative analysis program techniques

Chapter Outline

Introduction

Interview Data Analysis Approach

Observational Study Data Analysis Approach

Theoretical Approaches to Qualitative Analyses

Qualitative Analysis Process

Data Investigation

Data Aggregation

Data Meanings

Content Analysis

Content Analysis Defined

The Process of Content Analysis

Case Studies

Reasons for Case Studies

Case Study Defined

Case Study Data Analysis Example

Computer-Based Qualitative Analyses

The Ethnograph

DYNAKWIC

Summary

Main Concepts

Discussion Questions

Exercise

CHAPTER TWELVE

Introduction

While there is a rich tradition of qualitative research in criminal justice and criminology, there have been few methodologically instructive discussions of qualitative data analysis. This is rather surprising given that "data" are neither intrinsically nor exclusively quantitative. One of the reasons there have been few discussions of qualitative data analysis is the perception of a lack of clarity in the approaches to qualitative analyses. That is, there are no comparable probability tables that can be used with qualitative analyses as there are for quantitative studies. Although qualitative data can be converted into percentages or other descriptive measures, such a process does not accommodate the complex and rich nature of the qualitative data. Hence, researchers that want to analyze qualitative data must approach it differently than they would if it were numerical in nature.

Qualitative researchers suggest that a crisp set of analytical procedures comparable to those for quantitative data has not been created because qualitative data is presumed to be

> *private* (when one returns from the interaction of the field of the interview, on sits alone, thinks and writes), *mysterious* (drawing on intuition, cognitive leaps, on patterns of concepts that emerge), *idiosyncratic* (with each researcher assumed to analyze data her/his own way), and to some degree *simplistic* (because these procedures are so mechanical and boil down to nothing more than underlining, shuffling paper, rereading, and cutting and pasting). (Conrad and Reinharz, 1984, p. 6, emphasis added)

Hence, qualitative data, by its very nature and the process of collecting it, is somehow incapable of using some set of predetermined procedures as is the case with quantitative data analyses. While there is certainly a degree of truth to the unclear analysis problems in qualitatively based research projects, there are general guidelines that can be applied to qualitative data analyses. In addition, there are several computer-based qualitative analysis programs that are nearly as structured as those for quantitative analyses.

The purpose of this chapter is to help students to accept Michael Patton's challenge to make sense of massive amounts of qualitative data, to reduce its volume, to identify patterns, and to construct a framework for communicating the essence of what qualitative data analyses can reveal (Patton, 1990, p. 372). This is clearly a challenge, because there are "few agreed-upon canons for qualitative data analysis, in the sense of shared ground rules for drawing conclusions and verifying their sturdiness" (Miles and Huberman, 1984, p. 16). This chapter presents several procedural guidelines that can be followed in qualitative data analyses. Although I make no claim to being intrinsically correct in my approach to such analyses, I believe that the processes and examples demonstrated are logical and are based on the scientific principles. An unfortunate reality of qualitative data analyses is that such data analyses and approaches are dependent upon the ability of the researcher and upon his or her experience, training, capabilities, and intellect (Patton, 1990). This chapter presents a few model qualitative data analyses so that at the very least students have a starting point for conducting such analyses or understanding how such analyses are done.

I would be remiss if I did not bring us back to the debate between qualitative and quantitative researchers at this point in the text. Many quantitative researchers believe that everything can be measured and that qualitative research is nothing more than a preliminary step on the way to measuring quantitative variables. Similarly, qualitative researchers believe that the true richness of behaviors and attitudes cannot be measured through the simple counting and summarizing conducted by quantitative researchers, and that counting does little for understanding. There is a grain of both truth and falsehood in each of these extreme positions. Quantitative research is clearly appropriate for quantitative questions (i.e., those that ask aggregate and generalization questions), whereas qualitative research is much better suited to asking and answering process and rationale based questions. Figure 12.1

Figure 12.1

QUALITATIVE VERSUS QUANTITATIVE QUESTIONS

General Study Issue: Inmate control by correctional officers

Qualitative Foci	Quantitative Foci
1. Why do inmates need to be controlled?	1. How many inmates are controlled?
2. What is the process for controlling inmates?	2. What is the most frequent situation where officer control is needed?

provides examples of the different questions that researchers of the two types of approaches might pursue.

The qualitative focus of the question of controlling inmates through correctional supervision is show in the right-hand column of figure 12.1. A qualitative researcher might ask why inmates need to be controlled or what the process for controlling inmates looks like. The qualitative researcher might study inmate control through conducting interview studies that detail the statements of correctional officers and inmates about why they think control procedures are needed. Observational studies of prisons where the researcher might be disguised as either an inmate or an corrections officer would also allow the researcher to address the question of the process of controlling inmates as well as why inmates need to be controlled albeit for only a limited sample. If we consider the qualitative side of this general research issue, it is clear that there are few if any data sources that allow researchers to clearly and accurately describe why inmates need to be controlled or the exact process for controlling inmates.

The quantitative data sources for this general research issue could range from institutional incident reports, to officer and inmate surveys, to official use of force records.[1] These quantitative records are often questioned by qualitative researchers as being of suspect validity. These criticisms are based on the fact that correctional officers do not write up every inmate interaction (Poole and Regoli, 1983). However, because the qualitative approaches (i.e., interviews or observational studies) cannot collect wide statistically random samples, they are a poor basis for addressing the extent of the number of inmates that require officer controlling or the frequency of different types of situations (e.g., inmate fights, cell extractions, and so on) where inmates need to be controlled. Quantitative data is more appropriate in these cases. In addition, there is no reason to believe the qualitative researchers are not just as inaccurate in their perceptions of situations they observe as are the officers reporting on incidents. There are certainly political and organizational pressures on correctional officers that influence how they fill in the official records, but ideological and research issues also influence the qualitative researcher.

It is important to note that the examples in figure 12.1 appear to be more consistent than inconsistent. That is, most researchers would want to know not only how many inmates are controlled but also the process for controlling them. Both quantitative and qualitative research are strengthened by incorporating components of each approach. In addition, the more consistent the data, both quantitative and qualitative, the more evidence we have for the validity of our measures in general.[2] The general debate over quantitative and qualitative approaches is a bit less heated as most of the more contemporary researchers, while typically retaining a preference for one or the other, will use both approaches in the same research project.

The next several sections discuss common approaches to qualitative data collection in criminal justice and criminology as well as a few more general theoretical issues about the nature and conduct of qualitative data analyses.

Interview Data Analysis Approach

According to Patton (1990), there are two basic decisions about analysis of data from interviews. The first choice is *case analysis.* Basically, the case analysis approach is one wherein the researcher focuses on each interview as a separate case study. That is, each case is fully described and interpreted. The focus of the researcher in these individual case analyses is to identify critical events, grouping phenomena, and so forth. For example, if you were to study several hundred interviews of police officer attitudes toward domestic violence cases, each case could be subject to case analyses to identify who the officers supported in the domestic violence situations—the wife or the husband.

On the other hand, the study of interviews can be based on a *cross-case analysis* (Patton, 1990). If a structured interview guideline is used for the interviews, then it is somewhat easier to conduct cross-case analyses. That is, if the data collection instrument for the interviews is similar across all interviews, then it's more likely that specific variables can be assessed across several cases. For example, if I were to conduct interviews with the passengers on a commuter train about their perceptions of safety, I could begin the analysis with a description of the types of people who participated in the survey or perhaps when the participants ride the train. The basic idea in the cross-case approach is to define the patterns of experiences or attitudes that the riders of the commuter train relate to the interviewers. The cross-case analysis is much closer in approach to quantitative analyses in that the general results across the cases are the focus of the analyses in both cases. It is dissimilar in the sense that qualitative data tends to be based on units of analysis from something other than a large probability sampling.

Observational Study Data Analysis Approach

A major alternative to the interview study in qualitative studies is the observational study. There are several potential sources for the analysis of observational study data. Patton lists the options shown in figure 12.2. These *observational strategies* are neither exhaustive of all the possible types that could be used nor mutually exclusive of one another. There are other approaches, although these are the most common strategies, and researchers will often use several of these strategies simultaneously.

The strategy of chronology entails a detailed description over time of the observational data. For example, suppose we were going to observe inmates in a particular cell block for a study about officer-inmate interactions. In a

Figure 12.2

PATTON'S STRATEGIES FOR ANALYZING OBSERVATIONS

1. Chronology
2. Key events
3. Settings
4. People
5. Processes
6. Issues

chronology strategy, we would tell the "story" of our observational study from beginning to end. This would require that our observations be recorded with time labels and be conducted or take place over some time period. Let's suppose we observed inmates in the particular cell block from June through December in eight hour shifts three days a week. We might begin by telling our initial reactions to the cell block environment, for example, "the cell block appears to be a very noisy and clinical environment." Toward the end of our observational period we might see more clearly that the cell-block is a mini-society wherein the inmates and staff interact on a regular and "normal" as well as "friendly" basis. A chronology strategy is a simple approach to describing how the obvious institutional corrections environment functions. The more subtle nature of most correctional environments can be discovered if the chronology is detailed enough.

Another strategy for analyzing observational data is to focus on key events. A focus on key events would involve a focus on the major events that occurred during the observational study. For example, if we were observing the cell block we could describe major events such as inmate-on-inmate fights, officers being assaulted, or any other such major happening in the course of our observational studies. We could also focus on events that are outside of the routine functioning of the cell block as key events. That is, we would probably not consider the addition of a new officer to a cell block along the lines of a major event as described above, but that may certainly influence the types of observations that are subsequently collected and may thus turn out to be a key event.

Observational data analyses can also focus on the description of various "places, sites, settings, or locations" (Patton, 1990). This focus on various settings of the observational data can provide a context for how different behaviors may or may not be present in a variety of settings. In our example of the observational study of an inmate cell block, for instance, we could follow the inmates to the dining halls, exercise yards, and visitation areas to observe how they interact with the staff and others in these areas. Inmates that are loners might not welcome the opportunity to engage in the typically unstructured activities involved on the exercise yards, whereas they might really look forward to visits from their families and friends. Analyses based on the various places and settings can lead to significant insights about how inmates react in different contexts.

Patton's final three observational strategies are similar in that they suggest different approaches based on people, processes, and issues. These three seem to go together in that they suggest different units of analysis for observational studies. The focus on people is an individual unit of analysis, whereas processes are typically group-level phenomena, and issues are more general questions at an organizational level. Our observational data analysis could focus on detailed descriptions of individuals within the cell block under study. We could describe, for instance, inmate Fortunato Saviano in as much detail as possible, from his criminal history to his heritage as an Italian American. In a study of inmate and officer interactions, our observational data about "people" could lead to interesting insights about such phenomena as inmate-inmate assaults and how individuals fit into a cell block situation.

Processes are more general levels of observational data collection. In this case we might focus our attention on the process of gang membership in the cell block under observation. We could observe who associates with the gang members and how the gang recruits new members, how it controls the cell block, or how decisions are made.

Although the majority of qualitative studies in criminal justice and criminological studies are either interviews or observational, there are certainly cases where other approaches are used (i.e., content analysis, document analysis, and so on). While this section gives you an impression about some of the focuses that the qualitative researcher may take in terms of data analyses, it does not exhaust all the possible approaches that can be taken. The following sections provide a description of the approaches to data collection and analyses for qualitative data. because I believe applied approaches are generally easier for students to understand and are more useful in research and criminal justice practice. There are, however, more general theoretical frameworks for conducting qualitative data collection and analyses. The following section describes several of these theoretical approaches.

Theoretical Approaches to Qualitative Analyses

Theoretical approaches to qualitative data analysis basically involve three modes: (1) thick description, (2) grounded theory, and (3) analytic induction. *Thick description* provides data that give the researcher a sense for the details of the people, places, or processes under study. Such level of description would allow the researcher a level of information about the attitudes and feelings of those under study. The attempt here is to give the data a level of specificity that would have the ability to measure "walking in the informants' shoes" (Geertz, 1983). For example, the data necessary for a thick description of inmate Saviano would involve collecting data on his behaviors and statements as well as his attitudes, beliefs, and viewpoints in addition to the views and attitudes others have about him. In sociology, thick descriptions are also known as ethnography, wherein the researcher attempts to render a "true to life" picture of what people say and how they act to let people's words and actions "speak for themselves" (Taylor and Bogdan, 1984, p. 124).

The *grounded theory* approach to qualitative studies is one in which researchers direct their attention to developing theory or concepts (Glaser and Strauss, 1967). In the grounded theory approach the researcher attempts to discover theories, concepts, and even hypotheses and propositions directly from the data rather than from some assumptions or beliefs that he or she has in mind before conducting the research.

Glaser and Strauss suggest two ways to conduct grounded theoretical analyses of qualitative data. The first approach is an integration of data collection and analysis. That is, the researcher simultaneously codes and analyzes data to develop concepts and theories. For example, if you observed an inmate helping a correctional officer to control a belligerent inmate, you could theorize that inmates sometimes help staff control other inmates. This concept (i.e., idea) might be refined the next time that an officer attempts to control a belligerent inmate and a second inmate did not help because the inmate being controlled was from a different racial group.

The second approach to the grounded theory framework is the use of theoretical sampling (Glaser and Strauss, 1967). Theoretical sampling involves the selection of new cases on the basis of their potential to help further explain a theory or concepts that have already been developed. In an observational study of inmate gangs, for example, if we found that gang members tended to avoid all one-on-one interactions with staff we might purposely select situations to observe where known gang members were placed in close proximity to staff members to observe and record their interactions.

The last major theoretical approach to qualitative data analyses is labeled *analytic induction* (Cressey, 1953; Denzin, 1978; and Katz, 1983). Unlike the grounded theory approach, where theories and concepts are discovered, the analytic induction approach attempts to verify theories and propositions based on qualitative data. This can be done, according to analytic induction theorists (Denzin, 1978; Katz, 1983) through the predetermination of the phenomenon to be explained, the formulation of hypotheses, and then the collection of qualitative data. The data are then used to substantiate, refine, or reject the theoretical propositions until one has examined a large number of cases and has produced a supportable explanation. In the cell block observational study, we could formulate a theoretical framework that states that inmates with longer sentences will tend to commit more serious infractions than other inmates (Flanagan, 1980; Jones, 1986) and proceed to collect qualitative data that supports and refutes this proposition until we understood the nature of the infractions committed by inmates that have longer sentences. The final section of the introduction to this chapter on qualitative data analysis attempts to set a general process that can be applied to specific qualitative analyses. This process should be viewed as an ideal, as each researcher and research situation would likely require some modification of, or additions to, this process.

Qualitative Analysis Process

The processes and procedures for conducting quantitative analyses are fairly routine (see chapters 10 and 11). This is not the case with qualitative analyses. However, a general structure or typical process is nonetheless relevant to the analysis of textual or qualitative data. The following subsections describe the process for conducting qualitative data analyses relying on textual data from the narrative section of official use of force reports.[3] The data are shown in figure 12.3. The two cases listed in figure 12.3 will be used to illustrate the process of conducting qualitative data analysis. Keep in mind, however, that a researcher would likely have several more cases when conducting a qualitative analysis, not these two narratives alone. In addition, such textual examples as these are not the only type of qualitative data that can be applied to this process. That is, the process of qualitative data analysis that is demonstrated here is applicable to interviews, observational notes, video tapes, audio tapes, and other forms of qualitative data collection. This is the case because once the qualitative data have been collected, one of the preliminary steps is to convert the data into textual records (see figure 12.3). Whether the researcher has interview or observational notes or sound recordings, these raw data are converted or transcribed into textual formats for analysis. This is very similar to the process of coding quantitative data and is usually required if a researcher is going to use any of the computer based qualitative data analysis programs that are available.

Data Investigation. The first general step in conducting qualitative analyses is to investigate the data collected. This involves four procedures: (1) reading and rereading the data; (2) take notes on reading the data; (3) establishing groupings of the notes; and (4) reviewing literature for similar groups and additional grouping categories. In essence, the first stage involves creating a complete and thorough understanding of the data collected. This is a necessary first step, because a researcher often spends a great deal of time "in the field" collecting qualitative data (weeks or months), and may find it difficult to remember all of the data collected. The data investigation step helps the researcher to refresh his or her memory about the qualitative

Figure 12.3
USE OF FORCE NARRATIVES

Case 1

On October 1, 1992, at approximately 2:45 p.m. while assigned to Starr Dormitory as Housing Officer, Inmate X #161907 refused to obey a direct order to remove her clothing to be strip searched before being placed in Confinement. She refused several orders made to her. I placed my left hand on Inmate X's left wrist and placed my right hand on her left shoulder while Captain A was trying to cuff her right hand. In the process Inmate X went down and I went down on top of her. My left hand was removed from her left wrist and with the fingers of my left hand I grasped her left collar bone. After her right hand was cuffed I released her collarbone and forced her left hand behind her back with both my hands to be handcuffed. We then assisted Inmate X from the floor by placing my left arm under her right armpit. My left hand was then placed under the cuffs and my right hand was placed on her left shoulder. Moments later I removed my right hand from her left shoulder to the clothing on her right shoulder pulling her in a backward motion to help in assisting in getting her to her cell.

Case 2

At approximately 11:15 a.m., on July 19, 1992, while assigned to Housing Unit 3, I heard a loud noise coming from the B-side of the Unit. I responded to room 19B and observed inmates Y #162058 and Z #161546 engaged in a physical altercation. I ordered both inmates to separate, to no avail. I again ordered both inmates to separate, they again did not comply. At this time I separated the inmates by pulling Inmate Y away from Inmate Z and placed him in an adjacent room. Control room was notified and Sgt. B and Officer C arrived and handcuffed both inmates, at which time they escorted them out of the Housing Unit. All resistance and use of force ceased when the inmate was placed in the empty room.

---

data that has been collected and how it fits or doesn't fit with the existing literature on the topic.

The procedure of reading and rereading the qualitative data (i.e., case-level data) is simple enough, albeit time consuming. I typically read all of my qualitative data, once it has been collected, straight through (at one sitting, if possible) to get as clear a picture of the overall breadth of the data. Following my initial read through, I conduct a second review wherein I take notes about general themes and categorize characteristics that may be relevant across all of the cases. For example, in the examples in figure 12.3 I might create the categories "Type of staff involved," "Results of situation," and "Reason for situation." These categories would be the basis of establishing groupings for the qualitative data. While there are clearly several other categorization factors in the data in figure 12.3, we'll assume that the categories that have been identified are the primary interest in the study purpose. Thus, we will concentrate on these factors across the systematic sample of 1,400 narrative reports. The last procedure in the initial investigation of the data is to read and/or reread the literature as regards the research purpose or goals of the study and particularly those that are relevant to the categorization factors. For example, Goetting and Howser (1986) state that the results of control situations are "a major concern in the field of corrections" and that the "management of institutional order in terms of inmate conformity to prison rules" is paramount. When the interview data is searched in regard to the category "Results of situation" we would record incidents where the inmates did not conform to prison rules (i.e., Case 1 in figure 12.3) as opposed to inmate-on-inmate fights (Case 2 in figure 12.3). The literature also suggests that inmate-on-inmate fights are very common (Camp and Camp, 1991; Johnson, 1987). We should therefore classify our "Reason for situation" as fights and nonfights to determine where else force may be used besides fights. Another study suggests that "prisoners are less likely to impute legitimacy to the bases of social control in the prison than is typical of a person in other spheres of the society" (Cloward, 1975, p. 20). Hence, we could consider our category "Type of staff involved" to determine whether there are differences in legitimacy based on the type of staff involved in these incidents. In sum, the data investigation portion of the qualitative analysis attempts to establish as many links to the literature and the data that have been collected as are possible.

Data Aggregation. A typical next step in the process of qualitative data analysis is to create aggregations of the data. In this step, the researcher (1) assigns labels to each of the groups, (2) codes all of the cases in the data set, and (3) assesses what has and has not been found. In data aggregation, the established categorizations from the data investigation are assigned labels. For example, each of the three aggregation categories from step one (i.e., "Type of staff involved," "Results of situation," and "Reason for situation") could be assigned the following labels: "Staff," "Results," and "Reason." The procedure of assigning labels to the categories is not always as simple as shortening the category labels. The point to keep in mind in creating and assigning labels to each of the groups is that the label be as descriptive of the category as possible and as much a summary indicator as is feasible. The assignment of labels in this manner helps in understanding the general characteristics of the data as a whole.

Following the establishment of category labels the researcher codes all of the cases in the data set. The researcher applies the established labels to the textual data for each of the cases in the entire data set. For instance, I would apply the three established labels (e.g., Staff, Results, and Reason) to all of the 1,400 cases of use of force narratives in the sample, taking additional notes and classifying each of the cases based on the categorizations and the information gleaned from the current research literature. Figure 12.4 shows how this would be done for the cases in figure 12.3.

Once all of the cases have been coded for all of the categorization labels, the researcher then attempts to conduct an assessment of what has and has not been found. In the simple two case example, we have found that there appears to be no particular illegitimacy assigned to different staff levels and that there is no difference in such assignment based on the type of incident or the result of the incidents. Clearly, this data is simplistic given the purpose of this example to demonstrate the process of qualitative data analysis. In an actual qualitative analysis the researcher typically deals with not only more data but usually a more developed system of categorization and labeling. Many of the computer-based qualitative data analysis programs and procedures that will be discussed assist qualitative researchers in searching for their data for such complicated labels and categories and help them aggregate the results of such assessments.

Data Meanings. The final step in qualitative data analyses is to investigate the meanings of the results of the aggregation step. In this step the researcher attempts (1) to consider theoretical or research meanings as well as (2) to consider other influences on the data. In considering the theoretical or research meanings of the data analyses, the researcher would reconsult the literature and/or review the purpose of conducting the research. For example, the literature suggests that the majority of inmate situations requiring staff response are inmate-on-inmate fights. If, in the study of the 1,400 narrative reports, we found that to be the case, we might state that there

Figure 12.4

CODING THE CASES

Case 1

Staff. An officer and a captain used force and there is no evidence that either was resisted more than the other.

Results: After a refusal to obey an order and an initial struggle with the inmate, she was placed on the floor, cuffed, and conformed to orders.

Reason: Nonconformance to rules.

Case 2

Staff. Two officers and a sergeant, but there was no difference in resistance.

Results: After initial command there was compliance. No evidence of differential resistance.

Reason: Inmate on inmate fight.

is a consistency between our study and the literature indicating that the data set in our study is, on its face, valid. We might also go back and attempt to relate the aggregate findings to our research purpose. If our purpose was to differentiate the theoretical content of use of force situations for male and female inmates, we would be able to explain our categorization results for the male incidents and female incidents, perhaps highlighting the similarities and differences in the staff handling of these two general types of inmates.

Another final qualitative data analysis procedure is to consider other influences on the data. At this stage, the researcher attempts to deal with any problems with the data. He or she explains the limitations and potential influences and attempts to debunk or discount these as influencing the results of the study. For example, the 1,400 narrative reports on the use of force in the study vary with respect to the level of detail and construction across the nearly thirty prisons from which they were drawn. Hence, the difference in male and female handling may not be a function of the qualitative differences in handling but be due to reporting realities in the different prisons. That is, in some prisons there are full-time incident investigation officers and in others the staff that uses force fills in the narrative report. We could discount this influence by stating that we have collected a large number of incidence report narratives and that the influence of the report writer will be balanced in that we have similar numbers of officer and investigator created reports. Unfortunately, large samples are not typical in most qualitative research due largely to the costs in creating such a data set. In addition, given that the goal of our project is to examine the organizational function as regards use of force reporting we might go back and add the category "Who filled out the report" and the label "Reporter" and recode all of our cases to determine whether this has an influence on the types of other considerations in the data.

The process for conducting qualitative data analyses is listed in figure 12.5. It is important to keep in mind that this is merely a guideline for qualitative analysis and that actual qualitative data analysis may require additional steps, the researcher's creativity, and most of all a considerable amount of patience and time. In the end, however, the analysis and reanalysis of qualitative data is important beyond measure for certain research questions and contexts.

The analyses described here are not necessarily the "best" approaches in every qualitative study, but they do provide a range of approaches for such analyses and as such provide a good range of examples of qualitative data analysis. Qualitative analysis is an ongoing process throughout the data collection stage of research (Taylor and Bogdan, 1984) and as such there is less of a clear distinction between collecting data and attempting to determine the means or themes in such data.

Figure 12.5

SUMMARY OF THE QUALITATIVE ANALYSIS PROCESS

Step 1: Data Investigation

Part 1: Reading and Rereading
Part 2: Notes on Rereading
Part 3: Establishing Groupings
Part 4: Reviewing Literature

Step 2: Data Aggregation

Part 1: Create Categories
Part 2: Create and Assign Labels
Part 3: Code and Assess Meaning

Step 3: Data Meaning

Part 1: Theoretical/Research Meanings
Part 2: Other Influences

Content Analysis

Content analysis is a specific example of qualitative data analysis. While qualitative researchers have identified at least six general types of qualitative research designs the general qualitative analysis process can be applied to each, with some modifications. Content analysis is one of the general approaches to qualitative study[4] but is also a specific and commonly employed example in criminal justice. In fact, there are dozens of content analyses of law enforcement issues, criminological topics, correctional studies, and other such qualitatively based studies. In fact, these studies range from studying the effects of cameras in the courtroom (Alexander, 1991) to content analyses of statements about policewomen's handling of domestic violence (Homant and Kennedy, 1984), to the study of human relations training for correctional personnel (Groeneveld and Brian, 1985) and studies of criminal justice texts (Tunnell, 1993). The following sections provide examples of this useful technique.

Content Analysis Defined

A *content analysis* is the analysis of the content of the records of communications. Content analyses can be conducted on the results or records of any contemporary form of communication—written, video, sound, and electronic communication as well as police or correctional officer reports or any records of conversations. Content analyses can also be conducted on books, journals, newspapers, magazines and any other form of written material that a criminal justice researcher chooses to analyze from this methodological approach. With the advent of modern video recording technologies and the pervasive nature of television and surveillance equipment there are many sources for content analyses. Even more modern forms of content analyses have used electronic mail systems (i.e., E-mail) to investigate the content of communications (see Workman, 1992). Suffice it to say there are few means of communication between individuals, groups, or organizations that do not create some record. Table 12.1 lists several content analyses in criminal justice and criminology.

Content analyses can be used to determine the blatant and underlying meanings within these various forms of communications. The idea behind content analyses is that they are less intrusive into the lives of the study subjects and they eliminate the possibility of the researcher influencing the study subjects as in interview or observational studies. In addition, a qualitative researcher can conduct a study of a much larger, and more random, sample when they rely on content analysis rather than interviews or observations, because regularly kept records of communications (newspapers, magazines) are much more readily available.

Table 12.1

LITERATURE EXAMPLES OF CONTENT ANALYSIS

Author/Source	Subject
Cavender and Bond/*Sociological Inquiry,* 1993	"An analysis of 'America's Most Wanted' and 'Unsolved Mysteries' "
McGahan/*Canadian Police Journal,* 1992	"Public Awareness of Policing Initiatives"
Crouch and Damphousse/*Sociological Spectrum,* 1992	"Newspapers and Antisatanism"
Rapaport/*Law and Society Review,* 1991	"The Death Penalty and Gender Discrimination"
Liska and Baccaglini/*Social Problems,* 1990	"Crime in the Newspapers"
Carey/*Probation and Justice* by McAnany, Thompson, and Fogel, eds., 1984	"The Professionalization of Probation"
Greene and Bynum/*Journal of Criminal Justice,* 1982	"Television Crooks"
Heal and Ekblum/*Police Studies,* 1981	"Coping with Public Demand: A Challenge for Police Management"

The particular advantage of content analysis is that it is much less time consuming than interviews or observations and can, therefore, allow for much larger samples to be collected. One of the key ways to reduce both TYPE I and TYPE II errors is to increase the representativeness of the sample, and the best way to do that is to increase the size of the group under study. Another particularly important advantage in conducting a content analysis is that we can study the results of communications over time to look for changes in either meaning or form. For example, we could study the local newspaper for crime stories to determine whether they have increased in accuracy over the course of several years. Such a study would be very difficult to conduct if it were based on interviews or observations. However, content analyses are limited in the sense that they must focus on the results of communications that have been recorded. Hence, where there is no evidence of communications, there can be no content to analyze. In addition, the process of analyzing qualitative data is only as accurate and helpful as the categorizations and labels that the researcher sets. There is certainly no guarantee that the categories that a particular researcher defines and uses to investigate and aggregate the qualitative data are intrinsically accurate or even helpful relative to theory or the research problem under study. Be that as it may, content analyses is a valuable approach to the qualitative analysis of the records of communication.

The Process of Content Analysis

The process of conducting content analysis is multifaceted and consists of pre–data collection, data collection, and data analysis stages. It is important that all stages be appropriately integrated for the analysis process to be as effective as possible. The process of conducting a content analysis is listed in figure 12.6.

The first step, constructing a research question, involves a process similar to that used in quantitative research. That is, the researcher searches the literature for what is known about the topic of interest and builds on that knowledge to create a viable research problem. For instance, one study in the literature on content analyses of newspapers reports that "bias newspaper reporting may create and define a broad public awareness of crime that is substantially different from the 'reality' portrayed in official crime statistics" (Smith, 1984).[5] Hence, we can develop a research question from the idea that newspapers are biased and do not portray official statistics accurately. In the example study developed here the research question is that the likelihood of accuracy increases as the depth of the crime story coverage increases. In addition, the most important crime stories should be most accurate. Hence, our research question could be stated: *As crime coverage increases, the accuracy of reporting increases.*

Figure 12.6
THE PROCESS OF CONTENT ANALYSIS

Step 1: Construct a research question.

Step 2: Develop definitions of important concepts.

Step 3: Select a sample.

Step 4: Conduct qualitative analysis.

Following the construction of the research question the important concepts and variables needed for studying this question must be defined and delimited. For example, we need to agree on how each article will be defined (i.e., crime story, foreign policy story, economy story, and so on) and how we will specifically focus the research. Because we are going to look at "the most serious" crime stories, we will look only at the front page of the newspaper. Editors of newspapers generally assign what they consider the most important stories to the front page, and therefore, if a crime story is found on the front page it is considered important (at least as the editor perceives it).

Our research question also requires that we deal with the concept of the amount of coverage given to particular articles and crime articles. There may be several ways to measure the amount of coverage given to crime articles. That is, we can measure the square inches of the front page that is devoted to crime stories or the percentage of the entire front page that is so dedicated. We could also measure whether there are pictures, given that a picture tends to draw readers' attention more readily than text and increases the importance, or at least the prominence, of the article. To summarize, lets assume we will measure the concepts of crime stories and their importance and accuracy through the collection of seven specific variables: (1) day; (2) crime story; (3) square inches; (4) percent of page; (5) lead story; (6) crime pictures; and (7) accuracy of story.

Before we get to the collection of data, we need to decide on the type of sample that we will rely on for data collection. Any of the probability or nonprobability samples would be appropriate for sampling in content analysis. But, as was true with quantitative analyses, the more accurate the sample, the more likely the resulting data will be representative of the population of all newspaper reports. Let's suppose that we are going to rely on simple random sampling to select the front pages from our study newspaper. The first step is to decide the time period that will be included in the population sampling frame. That is, we need to decide which days will be included in our study or the time period to which we would like to generalize. Suppose for this example that we decide to randomly select one month out of twelve months of daily papers as the sampling frame. We could then select our sample as shown in figure 12.7.

The use of simple random sampling requires that we list all of the days in the randomly selected month. In the left-hand box of figure 12.7 the thirty days in the selected month (i.e., the population sampling frame) are listed. In the center box of figure 12.7, a random numbers table is shown. (Most statistics text have such tables listed in their appendices or you can use a hand calculator to select sample elements.) In order to use the random numbers table, we first decide on the sample size. In this case we have decided to sample six days. We have also decided that the day number is the day label for selection purposes (i.e., if we get the random number 15, we include the fifteenth of the month in the study sample). In addition, we have decided to select a random starting point in the table by looking away and placing a pencil point on the random numbers table. The pencil landed outside the table but was closest to the 9 in the first row, as indicated. Given that there are two digits, at most, for the sampling frame days, we must select two digit numbers from the random numbers table. Starting with the random number 98, we proceed to select two digit numbers until we have a total of six sampling elements or study days.[6]

We can now read the six front pages for the days we have randomly selected and measure our seven variables (the sample is small only because this is a demonstration—an actual sample would be much larger). The data should be measured prior to the analysis steps. However, considerations of the meaning and simple analyses of the data as we collect it are certainly

Figure 12.7
SIMPLE RANDOM SAMPLE OF NEWSPAPERS

Sampling Frame				Random Numbers							Selected Sample
					↓	↓	↓				
day 1	day 11	day 21		19	61	27	84	30	11	66	1. day 27
day 2	day 12	day 22		39	**14**	37	74	00	28	00	2. day 14
day 3	day 13	day 23		64	75	68	**04**	57	08	74	3. day 6
day 4	day 14	day 24		92	90	**15**	18	78	56	44	4. day 15
day 5	day 15	day 25		03	55	**19**	00	70	09	48	5. day 19
day 6	day 16	day 26	start →	98	88	46	62	09	06	83	6. day 4
day 7	day 17	day 27	↓	**27**	36	98	68	82	53	47	
day 8	day 18	day 28	↓	59	**06**	67	59	74	63	33	
day 9	day 19	day 29	↓	91	64	79	37	83	64	16	
day 10	day 20	day 30	↓	83	60	59	24	19	39	54	

part and parcel of the qualitative study approach. The data we collect from our sample is shown in table 12.2. The variables in content analysis can be anything from textual (i.e., the type of story) to numerical (i.e., the percentage of the front page that is taken up by the crime story). However, the analysis of the content tends to be the focus rather than quantitative analyses of the numerical variables.

The final step in conducting the content analysis is to analyze the data we have collected. The qualitative data analysis process can be used to assist us in this task. We can begin the process by conducting an investigation (Step 1) of the data that we have collected. We could read and reread each front page to learn more about the crime stories and perhaps add additional data variables to our data collection sheet shown in table 12.2. As we read the newspaper, these additional categorizations could form the basis for establishing groupings. For example, we might classify certain days as "slow" crime days, whereas other days are "large" crime days, when crime stories dominate the paper. This may also influence the degree of accuracy of the crime stories in that large crime days would tend to have more detail than slow days. It is also important at this point to review the literature for additional conceptual assistance in our data investigation. This is an important step because it will reduce our chances of ignoring meaningful concepts as well as reduce the likelihood that we will simply repeat the errors of the past.

Following our investigation of the data, we would create clear categories for the newspapers that we have studied. That is, we would complete the process of aggregation (Step 2) or summarize the basic and implied content of each sample element (i.e., newspaper article). We could assign the following labels to the newspaper reporting of crime stories:

1. Inaccurate: crime reports are inaccurate
2. Mixed inaccurate: crime reports are more inaccurate than accurate, but there is some element of accuracy

Table 12.2

DATA FOR CONTENT ANALYSIS EXAMPLE

Day	Crime Stories	Square Inches	Percent of Page	Lead Story	Crime Pictures	Crime Story Accurate
27	1	59.50	19%	Crime	No	No
14	1	42.00	13%	Politics	No	No
6	2	108.00	35%	Education	Yes	Yes
15	2	117.00	38%	Politics	No	Yes
19	2	59.75	19%	Science	No	No
4	1	20.81	7%	Politics	No	No and Yes

3. Mixed accurate: crime reports are more accurate than inaccurate, but there is some element of inaccuracy
4. Accurate: crime reports are accurate

The process of aggregating the data would continue until we have created all of the conceptually relevant categories we believe we need and have assigned labels and coded all of the cases in our sample.

The last step in the analysis of the content of the newspaper articles is to determine the meaning of the data (Step 3). We look at our research question and determine whether we have shown that as crime coverage increases the accuracy of reporting increases or whether some other phenomenon is occurring. The data investigation stage requires that we know our data as well as the complete set of conceptual, theoretical and practical considerations that are part of our research focus. The investigation step of qualitative data analysis requires creativity as well as experience.

Another important consideration in the data investigation stage is to recognize the limitations of the data. There are several limitations in the data in this example. First, the data were taken only from one randomly sampled month in the year. There may be seasonal fluctuations in the coverage of crime stories or multiyear fluctuations (such as election cycles) that may have biased the sample. In addition, it is quite difficult to get a good sense for crime coverage from merely six copies of one newspaper. Other approaches to the study of the content analysis rely on counting words, for example, counting the number of times the words "serious crime" were used in a newspaper. Hence, there may be additional categories and codings that have not been included in this example. All that we can do is the best possible job of investigation, aggregation, and determining the meaning of the data and present it in an honest and ethical manner. It is up to future researchers to refine and/or refute current findings.

Case Studies

The use of case studies in sociology and psychology has a long and rich history. Case studies have been conducted in criminal justice and criminological settings since the inception of these disciplines as separate areas of study. It is important, however, to note that although case studies are a very common qualitative method, they do not have to be exclusively concerned with qualitative data. In fact, an integration of quantitative and qualitative data would substantially improve the overall effect and information included in the case study approach, and such data are commonly included.

Reasons for Case Studies

There are several reasons for conducting case studies. First, there may be little known about the topic, and as a preliminary step, the researcher trades the ability to generalize with an in-depth focus on one or two representative cases in order to fully develop an understanding and conceptualization of the topic he or she is interested in studying. For example, Felkenes and and Schroedel recently conducted a case study of minority women in policing in Los Angeles, California. One aspect of this issue that they were particularly interested in understanding was how minority women and majority women differed and were similar in their decisions to enter the police service (Felkenes and Schroedel, 1993). There are few studies (quantitative or qualitative) of this issue, and their study of a very large urban area with large numbers of female employees would clearly allow them to form a sound conceptual basis for addressing their research questions and to contribute to a broader conceptualization that could be used in future research.

Another reason for conducting case studies is to examine unusual cases, that is, situations where there are successes or failures (Patton, 1990). For instance, in a study of gangs on probation and parole that I conducted, I found that a few agencies were particularly adept at handling such "clients" in their case loads and in controlling these offenders, at least during their probation and parole sentence. Unfortunately, there is little research on gangs in community correctional settings. Hence, a case study can provide information about why and how a program was successful that would not otherwise be available. We could also conduct a separate case study of the agencies that were unsuccessful with gang probationers. In particular, we could attempt to describe what the agencies were unsuccessful with, and how the individual gang members were handled and progressed throughout the sentence. The goal in this case might be to define points during the sentence where the probation and parole agencies failed or could apply more appropriate programs or sanctions to reduce the failures.

Yet another reason to conduct case studies is because they are manageable and provide much detailed information than more probability based data collections. There are researchers in criminal justice and criminology who believe that any study that relies on numerical data is inherently invalid. While this perspective is rather narrow minded, there is something to be said for the in-depth investigation of a situation or setting before conducting quantitative or qualitative analyses.

Case Study Defined

Case studies are in many situations observation-based studies of particular units of analysis. In general, case studies are a better context for observations than is any other particular method (Baker, 1988). However, case studies are different from other kinds of qualitative or quantitative research in that they focus specifically on either one unit of analysis or a small group of a particular unit of analysis. Case studies are limited in terms of their sampling because of this specific focus. Random sampling, or other probability sampling techniques, are rarely used in case study research. The researcher conducting a case study generally relies on cases to be studied that are felt by the researcher to represent the research problem he or she is concentrating on in the study. Simply defined, *case studies* are (1) exhaustive, (2) methodical, and (3) in-depth data analyses about particular groups or individuals of interest.

Case studies are exhaustive in the sense that they rely on the collection of information about all aspects of the study group or individuals. For example, if we were to conduct a case study of a particular jail facility, we would collect information about the facility from those who work there, those who reside there, as well as the police, courts, and social service agencies that have contacts with the facility. Every source of relevant information would be included through either observation or interviews.

Case studies are methodical in the sense that they might start with a focus on the internal actors of the jail and then systematically include all individuals that are identified by these actors to have an impact on the facility. Being methodical might entail the collection of very specific bits of information, specific observations, or interview questions as sources of data from individual perspectives.

Case studies are in-depth in that they attempt to "leave no stone unturned." That is, the researcher in a case study pursues any relevant source of information as a data source. Another aspect of being in-depth involves the study of the case under research in more than one time period to get a more complete sense for the phenomenon under study. (Chapter 8 describes in detail the approaches to observational studies. These techniques and procedures are essentially identical for case studies.)

Case Study Data Analysis Example

A case study might be done on a particular program approach or situation. For example, I am serving as an evaluation researcher for a program for prison inmates in which life skills training, vocational education, and post-prison employment counseling are components. The idea in this program is to teach inmates how to find, keep, and be successful in legitimate employment. The life skills training is the initial phase of the program wherein program staff help inmates work through a life plan for their eventual employment and help them write a resume and cover letter as well as learn how to conduct themselves at interviews. The vocational training is given to the inmates in the first phase of the project at the Maryland Occupational Training Skills Center in the Maryland Department of Corrections. The vocational programs are various and include printing, carpentry, auto mechanics, and office skills. They are offered to all inmates in the program by training staff. The final component or phase of the program involves the program office in the Baltimore metropolitan area, which assists inmates in finding employment and serves as a point of contact for employment and counseling and interviews.

The program in Maryland has several sister programs across the United States, but none are replicas of it.[7] I am conducting a case study because the program managers and Department of Corrections want to know as much as possible about the program and its participants as possible. I am collecting both quantitative and qualitative data, but in this example I will focus on the analysis of the qualitative data I have obtained.

The qualitative data I have collected are from interviews with teachers and program managers as well as observational studies of inmate classes and vocational training sessions. The qualitative data is at this point based on unstructured formats and research notes, because I am most concerned with collecting as much information as possible. That means that I write down anything and everything that the program manager relates in our interviews as well as everything I can observe during the classroom time. At the present time I have well over one hundred pages of unstructured research notes that need to be analyzed.

In the data investigation step (Step 1) I will read and reread these notes in an attempt to understand the potential groupings that can be imposed on this data set. While I am collecting data I am amassing the literature on vocational education, life skills, and employment as contributors to ex-convict success. After I sit in on classes with inmates I generally fill in additional observations about the experience and reread the notes. However, in terms of the first step of data investigation, this process would have to be done when all of the observations have been completed.

In the next step of the analysis of the qualitative data I would create categories, assign labels, and code all of the cases in the data set. For example, suppose I identify a group of observations that whenever the teacher focuses attention on relevant problems, the inmates seem to perk up and contribute to the learning experience and conversations. I would then go through all of my notes on individual classroom visits (fifteen visits) to determine whether this is a typical response to certain examples. In the third step, determining the meaning in the data, I could then impose either a theoretical meaning from the literature or answer research questions for the program evaluation that will allow the program to be modified and improved.

The influences that I may or may not have on the observational environment should also be recognized, as well as the fact that one of the program managers is a former student of mine. The point here is that the process for conducting qualitative data analysis can be applied to many different types of qualitative studies to make the process of analysis much more logical and structured.

The following section describes a few of the more popular computer qualitative analysis programs and approaches. Computers can greatly assist in collecting qualitative and quantitative data in a much less time consuming way. There are other qualitative data analyses types that are not covered here. For example, some researchers attempt to understand records based on their content in a numerical sense. A researcher may query jail inspections for the past fifty years and measure how correctional officers were variously referred to as "guards" or "screws" or some other term. Computer programs exist that can establish counts of each of the terms that one wishes to identify.

Computer-Based Qualitative Analyses

There are essentially three approaches to the use of computers in qualitative data analyses (Brent, 1984). Most computer applications focus on one of these three types of applications. The first involves the creation and analysis of field notes. In this approach the researcher uses the computer to create mechanical records similar to hand-written notes. The computer facilitates the reading and rereading as well as grouping and coding activities involved in the analysis of this data.

The second general approach is to use text processors as assistants in qualitative data analysis (Brent, 1984; Hessler, 1983). Programs such as The Ethnograph (Seidel, 1983) are examples of such text-based analysis programs. While these programs generally assist in the manipulation and study of unstructured text, researchers must impose their own categorizations and labeling on the data and code it in the form that is required for the program to work. These limitations are tolerable, however, because of the abilities of text analysis programs to increase the speed of qualitative data analysis. Text processors most closely mirror the traditional "cut and paste" approach of qualitative researchers. That is, qualitative researchers who do not use text processors complete the task manually. Once copies of the field notes are made, they are cut into identifiable categories and pasted together based on groupings, and sense is made of these reconstructions of the original field notes. Many data-base management programs can also be placed in the text processing category.

The third general approach is the use of knowledge-based or artificial intelligence systems. These are the newest developments in qualitative research. The idea here is that we can program computers to conduct complex tasks that were once thought to require human intellect alone. There is no reason why data investigation, aggregation, or data meaning could not be done by a complex and well-programmed computer. This is not to say that human creativity or logic can always be modeled, but only that the more structured parts of analyses of qualitative data may be amenable to structured or unstructured computer-based programming. Although there have been amazing developments in the area of artificial intelligence for many applications, such an approach in qualitative data analysis lies in the future.

The Ethnograph

The Ethnograph is a computer-based text analysis program. The general purpose of the program is to manage some of the more mechanical tasks of qualitative data analysis, thus allowing the researcher to concentrate on the data meaning step of qualitative data analyses. The Ethnograph requires four basic steps: (1) input—the qualitative or textual data need to be put into a computer text file[8]; (2) the data need to be numbered—that is, each line of text needs to be assigned a number so that specific labels can be searched for by line numbers; (3) the file is then categorically defined based on researcher-created categorizations and labels; and (4) certain sections of the data are placed in an output file, based on specific labels.

An example of data is shown in figure 12.8. In this example, interviews with various probation officers about a gang prevention program case study are shown. The data must be coded in columns 3 through 44 and the grouping labels are flush with the left column, as shown in figure 12.8. The notes for the interviews are placed in a single file for analysis. This approach requires a considerable amount of time and effort to get the raw data notes or reports into a textual format. However, the whole point of using The Ethnograph is that it is much faster than the paper shuffling that is done in noncomputerized textual analysis. The designers of The Ethnograph have designed it to conform as much as possible to the manual format.

The category codes in this case (i.e., DIR, PO1, and PO2) structure the research notes on Asian gangs into groups based on the type of staff that was interviewed. The second step, numbering, is shown in figure 12.9. After data input and numbering, the researcher attempts to sort through the numbered file to find additional categorizations and labels. Once the file is numbered, the researcher can attempt to impose additional categorizations on the numbered list that could help further clarify the meaning of the data. For example, each probation officer and the director all say something about an aspect of Asian gang members management. We could then create another grouping code based on this categorization and insert it into the file as shown in figure 12.10.

The creation of the additional categorical groupings of "SIZ = statements about the size of the gangs" as well as the more general category of "MAN = statements about management of Asian gangs" can be accomplished automatically with The Ethnograph program. The bottom line is that the program facilitates the sorting and categorization of qualitative and textual data.

The final step in using The Ethnograph is to create output to assist you, as the researcher, in determining the meaning of the data in reference to your theory and/or research questions. The Ethnograph program can print only those sections of text you ask it to produce so you can focus your analysis of the textual data. In sum, The Ethnograph is a data assistant that will "cut and paste" various pieces of textual data. It is not a substitute for qualitative data analysis process but an augmentation. While The Ethnograph is helpful and a real time saver, it does not "conduct" textual analysis. The DYNAKWIC program, explained next, is an actual text analysis program that allows researchers to examine the content of textual files.

Figure 12.8
ETHNOGRAPH DATA SET

ID:
-QR09
Interview with staff of Gothlam County
gangs unit
May 12, 1993

+COMBINED INTERVIEWS OF
JUVENILE AND ADULT STAFFS

DIR: There are certain groups that consistently require additional attention more than others. For example, we have seen a dramatic increase in the numbers of Asian gangs.

POl: The problem with Asian gangs is that they tend to be very secretive and if you are not an Asian the people in the community tend to support the gang members over us.

PO2: I haven't seen that many Asian gang members, but I just started to look for them. Now if you are talking about Hispanic or Black gangs there are thousands of those folks.

POl: The Asian kids also tend to victimize their own.

DYNAKWIC

Another example of a qualitative data analysis computer program is DYNAKWIC. This program, and others like it, allow researchers to conduct rather complex text analysis. That is, the *DYNAKWIC* program is used to locate the contexts of one or more key words in a selection of texts. For example, suppose we were interested in examining how criminal justice personnel are portrayed in a selection of newspaper articles. We could use this program to search for and list each and every context where the word "police" or "guard" is used in the entered text. This program, and others like it allow researchers to isolate key words or phrases, compare word frequencies, and

Figure 12.9

NUMBERED ETHNOGRAPH DATA SET

```
 1  ID:
 2  -QR09
 3    Interview with staff of Gothlam County
 4    gangs unit
 5    May 12, 1993

 6  +COMBINED INTERVIEW OF
 7    JUVENILE AND ADULT STAFFS

 8  DIR: There are certain groups that
 9    consistently require additional attention
10    more than others. For example, we have seen
11    a dramatic increase in the numbers of
12    Asian gangs.

13  PO1: The problem with Asian gangs is that
14    they tend to be very secretive and if you
15    are not an Asian the people in the
16    community tend to support the gang
17    members over us.

18  PO2: I haven't seen that many Asian gang
19    members, but I just started to look for them.
20    Now if you are talking about Hispanic or
21    Black gangs there are thousands of
22    those folks.

23  PO1: The Asian kids also tend to victimize
24    their own.
```

Figure 12.10
ETHNOGRAPH DATA SET

```
1  ID:
2  -QR09
3     Interview with staff of Gothlam County
4     gangs unit
5     May 12, 1993

6  + COMBINED INTERVIEWS OF
7     JUVENILE AND ADULT STAFFS

8  DIR: There are certain groups that
9     consistently require additional attention
10    more than others. For example, we have seen      Size
11    a dramatic increase in the numbers of
12    Asian gangs.                                            Man

13 POl: The problem with Asian gangs is that
14    they tend to be very secretive and if you
15    are not an Asian the people in the
16    community tend to support the gang
17    members over us.
```

examine the style or themes in written text. DYNAKWIC is simpler to use than The Ethnograph in that all it requires is ASCII text, whereas The Ethnograph has several formatting requirements and restrictions.

Other text analysis tools for computers are on the market, and it is likely that with advances in CD-ROM technologies and read-right versions that can handle nearly 400 megabits of text there will be more advanced text analysis software for qualitative analyses. In addition, there have been several advances in the use of artificial intelligence in computing, and once the complex procedures are worked out a qualitative analysis program similar to SPSS will be available in the next decade or two. Another trend that is likely to dramatically assist in the qualitative analysis of textual data is the use of voice entered data. The technology currently exists that allows us to enter data verbally, but it is still somewhat crude and not reliable. However, improvements in the functioning of voice recording are likely, and this will assist the use and analysis of qualitative data and its analysis.

Summary

This chapter presents a logical process for conducting qualitative data analyses wherein the researcher builds the analysis of the data into the collection process and the literature and research problem under study. The process involves the investigation of the data once collection is completed, an aggregation or grouping process, and the considerations of the meanings in the data relative to the research question and/or literature. Content analysis and case study research designs are also presented, and typical qualitative data analysis and examples of each are demonstrated. Finally, two computer approaches to the analysis of qualitative data are presented (The Ethnograph and DYNAKWIC), illustrating the text manipulation and text analysis approaches to qualitative data analysis.

Main Concepts

qualitative versus quantitative
cross-case analysis
thick description
analytic induction
data aggregation
content analysis
computer-based analysis
DYNAKWIC
case analysis
observational strategies
grounded theory
data investigation
data meanings
case studies
The Ethnograph

Discussion Questions

1. Describe the differences between interview data and observational data.
2. Describe how you would analyze television crime shows such as "Real Stories of the Highway Patrol" using the qualitative analysis process.
3. What are some of the content analyses related to criminal justice topics that you could conduct?
4. Discuss how you would conduct a case study of police handling of domestic violence cases.
5. What does The Ethnograph do that DYNAKWIC does not, and vice versa?

Exercise

Form small groups (two or three students) and conduct an observational study of the campus. Report on your analysis of your observations based on the qualitative analysis process. One purpose of your study might be to study students on campus as potential crime victims. For example, you can watch how people walk on campus. Do they carry their "stuff" out in the open or in a backpack? Do they pay attention to those around them? Do they make eye contact with others? Be prepared to discuss your findings as well as your use of the qualitative process when you return to class.

13

RESEARCH ETHICS

Learning Objectives

1. To describe and provide examples of the basic ethical agreements for conducting social science research
2. To describe the Federal Code of Regulations
3. To explain the nexus between the legal requirements and the ethical agreements

Chapter Outline

Introduction
Basic Ethical Agreements
Research Should Be Harmless
Participation Should Be Voluntary
Researchers Should Be Honest
Research Results Should Be Reported Fairly
Approaches to Protecting Research Subjects
Professional Codes of Ethics
Government Regulations
Legal Intervention
Self-Imposed Morality
Legal Protections of Human Subjects
Exempted Research
Review of Research
Prisoner Research
Summary
Main Concepts
Discussion Questions
Exercise

CHAPTER THIRTEEN

Introduction

Up to this point, we have been concerned with the applications and use of scientific principles and procedures for conducting research in criminal justice and criminology, and the technical aspects of conducting samples or descriptive analyses. However, these scientific constraints are not the only ones to which research must be held. There are also other considerations besides conforming to scientific principles that should be considered by researchers. This is especially true when the researcher is dealing with human subjects.

Earl Babbie rightly suggests that beyond the scientific constraints on research and researchers there are administrative, political, legal, and ethical constraints (Babbie, 1989). The administrative constraints are practical ones. That is, some research is simply too expensive to conduct. For example, if a researcher wanted to conduct a mail survey with three follow-up mailings of a ten-page survey for a sample of 40,000 inmates, the costs would likely be in excess of $50,000.[1] A sample of only 40,000 may sound like a large number, but it represents at best only 5 percent of the total prison population.[2] Hence, the amount of resources certainly will constrain the type of research that can be conducted. The statement that "time is money" is also applicable to the idea of administrative constraints. Recently, I was involved in two national level research grants that required travel throughout the United States. I taught six courses, published a few articles, and wrote several research grant proposals. I barely had time for my wedding in August, let alone take on any more research projects. Active researchers in criminal justice, mostly faculty in criminal justice and criminology, are typically limited to what they can accomplish given their primary responsibility to their students and their own sense of how much they would like to accomplish, not to mention the pressures from family and friends to "have a life" beyond work.

The second type of constraints on research and researchers are political. These are in part similar to the administrative constraints and in part very different. Political constraints are similar to administrative constraints in that they typically are unrelated to the quality of the project or the interest of the researcher but are more contextual to the environment that the researcher works in. The political constraints are also very different in the sense that they can be imposed upon the researcher and can seriously limit, or kill, a research project. Political constraints can emanate from the administrative hierarchy of a university or from those in charge of the research site or situation.

An example of political constraints that can be imposed by a university is a situation that I was involved in. A colleague and I developed a fear-of-crime-on-campus survey.[3] We proceeded to pretest the survey in several of our classes and revised the instrument each time to improve its validity and reliability. Once we were confident that the instrument was a good one we requested permission from the chief academic officer of the university to conduct the survey. He was very concerned about the potential for our survey information being made public. He believed that we should not conduct the survey because it might make others fearful. His concerns were real. Although we assured him that our study would not reveal any individual responses and that survey research is generally considered to be quite benign,[4] he felt that the project should not proceed, because he did not want to see the image of the university damaged by the creation of a data set on the fear of crime.[5] Conversely, there can be political constraints on research based on the research site itself. For example, a jail administrator may not allow access to files because they are confidential or because he or she believes that you will publish your results in the local newspaper and make the administrator look bad. The point is that when political constraints are imposed on research or reseracher s it is likely to be due to reasons beyond the research itself.

Another constraint on research is in the category of legal constraints. Research on researchers' views about legal constraints shows that most researchers want to exercise self-control rather than "suffer" external legal control (Longmire, 1991; Toch, 1981), but that desire does not remove such constraints. In addition, the only way to prevent violations of the basic ethical agreements according to some is to be able to impose legal sanctions. In this chapter, I will discuss one of the most comprehensive legal constraints imposed on social science research in the form of the Code of Federal Regulations (Article 45, Part 46, 1993). Although many view the legal constraints imposed upon researchers as limiting, the constraints also provide protections for individual researchers that are not available in their absence. That is, if a university reviews a researcher's project and gives it approval (i.e., the subjects are sufficiently protected and ethical agreements have been maintained and insured), then the researcher is protected from redress insofar as the responsibilities are on the university policy and procedures used to review projects where human subjects are involved. Another legal consideration, and perhaps constraint, is the fact that researchers' subjects are not entitled to the same protection that marital partners or clergy are entitled. That is, researchers can be compelled to reveal their sources.

The final constraints, and the topic of this chapter, are ethical constraints. Ethical constraints involve the considerations of basic moral constraints in conducting research. These moral constraints are imposed upon researchers in a variety of ways but are based on a set of basic ethical agreements. The following sections describe these constraints and provides examples.

Basic Ethical Agreements

The *basic ethical agreements* are general and informal guidelines that most ethical researchers attempt to maintain. These basic agreements are above and beyond the scientific requirements for conducting well-designed and executed research projects. Although some researchers view these arguments as placing unnecessary constraints on the conduct of valuable research, they provide basic protections to research subjects that are morally grounded and justified. This is necessary because the "scientific life" rarely provides a barrier to unethical conduct (Braswell, McCarthy, and McCarthy, 1991, p. 277). That is, scientists (even social scientists) might be so involved with the research that they fail to recognize the dangers to the subjects participating in the project.

The current ethical agreements have been developed over time, largely because of several particularly bad experiences where the subjects of research have been adversely affected, and even harmed, by the research process. For example, there is an infamous criminal justice study wherein some subjects were assigned the role of inmates and others were given the role of guards and a "simulated prison" was set-up (Zimbardo, 1963). The research subjects in this case experienced strong emotional and psychological harms as a result of this experiment, and it had to be stopped before its completion. In another notorious experiment, research subjects were asked to deliver increasing strengths of electrical shocks to experimental confederates in order to test their obedience to authority (Milgram, 1963). The research subjects in Milgram's experiment also experienced psychological harms as a result of their participation in the study. In addition, it has been common, historically, to use inmates as experimental subjects that often lead to physical harms. There are other less extreme examples of unethical research where the studies may have actually done more harm than good. Due to these cases where researchers have done damage to research subjects, and perhaps because of government regulations and stipulations placed on grant moneys, several ethical agreements have been developed. Researchers have also developed these guidelines because they are interested in being ethical and do not formulate research projects to purposely harm people or the subjects of their studies but to address important research questions. The following subsections of this chapter describe these basic ethical agreements.

Research Should Be Harmless

First and foremost, researchers agree that research should not physically, psychologically, socially, or economically harm the subjects of research. As is true of other agreements listed here, this basic guideline is not an absolute requirement. To not harm study subjects physically is fairly apparent; however, there are certainly times when physical harm is the only means to conduct studies. For example, suppose a researcher is interested in studying the similarities and differences in the musculature of male and female police officers in order to better design firearms for each gender. The researcher believes that hand strength is a key issue in the use of handguns and that an individual's musculature is a key determinant of hand strength. Suppose further that the researcher's approach is at the muscular and cellular level. In order to study the type of muscle in the male and female officers in such a study, the researcher would have to cause an intense amount of pain (albeit short term) in order to take appropriate muscle samples. The justification would likely be that the need for the muscle tissue samples and the better designed firearms would outweigh the one-time pain caused by taking muscle samples from volunteer police officers.[6] Conversely, if the taking of muscle samples caused permanent damage or there were other ways to study firearm redesign at the muscular level without taking muscle samples, then such a study would be unnecessarily harmful to the study subjects and probably should not be conducted.

The agreement that studies will not cause psychological harm is related to insuring that the mental state of the subjects is preserved or reconstructed to the prestudy state of health. That is, the study should not cause emotional or psychological damage to the study subjects. A study such as the obedience to authority experiments by Milgram (1963) is an example of a study that caused psychological harms. The bottom line is that the researcher should be sensitive to the psychological level harms and should leave the study subjects as they were found or provide a means for them to get back to the same psychological health as when they began their study participation. It is clear that there are times when a researcher wants to study the effects of psychological harm. For example, how could researchers study how police officers make decisions when they are under duress unless they place the officers under duress and studied decision making in such situations. Once again, if the results of the study outweigh the potential harms it seems the lessor of the two evils to go forward with the study, but that may not always be the case, and such a consideration should be made in each research situation. The protection of the study subjects should be a priority and any harms should be minimized or reduced after the study is completed.

Social and economic harms are even less specific than physical and psychological harms. Social harms might involve the harm done to an inmate who participates in a study on AIDS when the other inmates in his cell block are told, or find out, that he has this disease. The inmate with AIDS without a doubt would suffer social harms because of the research. The other inmates might decide to discontinue any associations with the inmate because he has AIDS or his otherwise friendly cell mate might decide to ignore him. Social harms are those that affect relationships or standing in a community whatever the community might be, and researchers should strive not to cause such harms. Economic harms are similar to social harms, although the harm in this case is monetary whereas social harms involve subjects' relationships and interactions with others.

In extreme cases where the value of the research is great and harm cannot be avoided, the subjects should be given the opportunity to return to their preparticipation state. The researcher should build this into the research costs and design. However, research should be conducted on the basis of doing as little harm as is absolutely necessary. The reduction of harm to study subjects is perhaps one of the best reasons for imposing legal constraints on researchers to be certain that research subjects are not harmed. Although most researchers in criminal justice and criminology prefer to police their own ethical standards in their research (Longmire, 1991), examples such as the Milgram and prison simulation studies demonstrate that we are not as critical as we need to be to protect the subjects of research.

Participation Should Be Voluntary

A second key ethical agreement is that the subjects of research voluntarily participate in the research. This is an important corollary to the agreement of doing no harm to research subjects. In those cases where harm is necessary, the research subjects can decide, based on their own free will, whether they want to participate in the study. If we give research subjects the right to decide whether they want to participate in the research, even though they know it may cause them harm, that is more ethical than causing harm and not giving the subjects an opportunity to refuse to be in the study. In most professional codes of ethics, as they apply to research, there is some statement that supports the principle that study subjects voluntarily participate in the research. In addition, the legal codes tend to provide detailed criteria for insuring voluntariness in participation. That is, the legal codes (and particularly the Code of Federal Regulations, Article 45, Part 46) provide detailed criteria for helping researchers formulate questions to insure that the research subjects have been given enough information on which to base their decision to participate in studies.

There are situations, however, where it would be difficult, if not impossible, to get research subjects to agree to participate in a study. For example, if we wanted to study attitudes of correctional officers about one another in an observational design, it would be difficult to ask everyone in the jail to voluntarily participate in the study and still be able to conduct an observational study where people will not change their behaviors because they know they are under study. Staff would certainly treat us differently than they normally would have because they know we are watching them. A simple guideline to determine whether voluntary participation should be secured before the study seems to make sense to me in this regard was offered by McCarthy (1991). She suggests that if the behaviors being studied are those that would have occurred even if the study had not taken place or occur in public view that the requirement of voluntary participation should be relaxed. This does not relinquish the responsibility of researchers from fully disclosing the study after it has been conducted and for researchers to protect the identities of the study subjects. McCarthy only suggests that if the subject or actions to be observed could be readily viewed without permission that it makes less sense to ask for permission.

There are three different techniques, used alone or together, that a researcher can use to encourage participation, and all three involve the protection of the identity and responses of the study subjects. First, the researcher can guarantee the research subjects anonymity. *Anonymity* occurs when the researcher is totally unable to match a particular respondent's answers with their names or identifiers. For example, suppose we were to study the fear of crime on campus and handed our survey out during registration when students stand in long lines to sign up for classes or pay their tuition, and then we had someone else collect the responses. There would be virtually no way of identifying individual surveys with the people who filled them in, and hence subjects could be guaranteed anonymity.

Sometimes it is not possible to guarantee anonymity. In this case, we could give our research subjects a guarantee of confidentiality. *Confidentiality* means that the researcher could in fact identify the people who made specific responses to the fear of crime survey but promises the study subjects not to reveal their names in conjunction with their responses. For example, if I were to mail the fear of crime on campus survey to a random sample of students and made three copies of their names for follow-up mailings, I would promise to destroy their mailing labels and remove their names from their surveys upon the completion of my final mailing and data collection.

Another way to protect the subjects' identity and thereby encourage their voluntary participation is to acquire an *informed consent* from each study subject. Securing informed consent involves telling the research subjects, in some detail, about the research project, its goals, and the extent of subject participation and asking the subject to indicate, given that information, that they would still be willing to participate in the study. An example of informed consent in studying fear of crime on campus might involve an interview-based study wherein each subject is told (before being interviewed) about the goals, methods, and the extent of participation required and asked to sign a release form prior to the interview.

Even if informed consent or the enticements of anonymity or confidentiality are used, they are no guarantee that the subjects are free to make a decision about whether they should participate or not. For example, I regularly ask students in my classes to fill out survey instruments (for pretesting purposes only) and clearly state that they do not have to participate (both in writing and verbally), yet I typically get a 99 percent response rate. Students may believe that I would somehow link their lack of participation in my surveys to grades no matter how many times I tell them otherwise.[7] I consistently worry that I am not giving students an opportunity to participate in my survey pretests because of the differential power that exists between a faculty and students.

The issue of the lack of ability of study subjects to make a decision about whether they will participate or not is even more crucial when the study subjects are children or inmates or other vulnerable groups. Inmates may participate in studies because they believe the parole board will see such participation as favorable or helpful to them, even when they are told otherwise. In addition, if inmates are given cigarettes for their participation, it would be difficult for them to turn down participation, given the value of cigarettes in the barter system in many prisons (Kalinich, 1980). Again, the legal codes have specific guidelines that deal with vulnerable groups (such as inmates, children, or pregnant women) to extend extra precautions to protect them from harm and to ensure them the opportunity to voluntary participation. One of the problems with voluntariness in participation is that those who understand the research and still decide to volunteer to participate may be somehow different from those who decide not to participate. The issues of doing no harm and relying on voluntary participation also point to the more subtle agreements that researchers treat study subjects honestly and fairly.

Researchers Should Be Honest

Another ethical principle is that researchers should be honest about their identity, the purpose of their research, and the nature of the study subjects' participation in the project. The agreements of being honest are much less certain than the issues of doing no harm or ensuring voluntary participation. The first issue of honesty is the matter of the *researcher's identity* as presented to the study subjects. In an evaluation study that I conducted of a vocational education in a state prison, I repeatedly told both the program staff and inmates in the program that I was an outside researcher that was specifically hired to evaluate the effects of the program. Because I had no reason to believe that the program staff or inmates would, or could, alter the data that I was collecting, I had no reservations about full disclosure about my identity. On the other hand, consider if I were to conduct observational studies about the inmate programs. I might not be as open, at least before I conducted the research, as I would be with a more qualitatively driven study. Revealing one's identity in an observational design might well influence how the inmates and staff behave during observation.

Along with the revelation of his or her identity, the researcher should give the subjects some sense of the purpose of the research. This is important in terms of the consideration of voluntariness. That is, it would be difficult to argue that the subjects of the study agreed to participate if the researcher does not tell them at least something about the purpose of the study. For example, suppose that I told the program staff and inmates in the program evaluation that I was a hired evaluation researcher but did not tell them what it was I was evaluating. Not only would they likely be very suspicious of my purposes but they might alter their behaviors even more than they would have had I told them something about the purpose of the study. Conversely, there are situations when the researcher could limit the amount of information presented to the subjects about the purposes of the research. In these cases, however, the researcher should debrief or tell the study subjects the true purpose of the research once the research is concluded.

Another issue related to being honest to the study subjects and extending the ability to make free choices to participate in research is to explain to the research subjects the nature and extent of their participation. I was involved in a study in which researchers conducted in-depth interviews with correctional officers and inmates. We told them that the interview was conducted for a research project and that it involved several specific questions about certain situations in the prison. We also told them that their participation involved only one interview, and that we would not share any information from individual interviews with any of their supervisors or colleagues under any circumstances. Once again, it is not always easy to get into the details of the nature and extent of participation in the study. Study subjects themselves are not always interested in the details but only in the amount of time it will take to participate. Often, researchers will add the considerations of the nature and extent of participation in the informed consent form.

Research Results Should Be Reported Fairly

The last basic ethical agreement is to present the findings with a sense of *fairness.* Research reports should include the limitations, contrary findings, and any changes or re-analyses. The researcher should describe the limitations of the sample that he or she has collected. Suppose, for example, that two researchers studied the recidivism rates for the same prison, and the first researcher reports the rate of recidivism for the prison is 33 percent. He definitively states that his research shows that one-third of the inmates that are released from the prison return to prison. His research report goes on to further describe the sample and the characteristics of the recidivists and nonrecidivists in his study. At no time does he honestly and scientifically present the type of sampling he used or any of the potential limitations that are involved in his study.

By way of contrast, a second researcher reports that the recidivism rate for the same prison is 34 percent. She, however, fully discloses that her sample is a systematic sample of all inmates present in the prison on July 1, 1992, and for whom current records are available. She fully explains how the sample may have been influenced by the record keeping at the prison and the fact that some inmates moved out of the study state and she does not have access to the out-of-state records. In addition, she explains that she selected a 10 percent sample of the 873 inmates present on the study date (i.e., 88 inmates) and that six files where missing and another five had been destroyed in a riot at the prison, resulting in a total sample size of 77 inmate records. On the basis of this, and perhaps additional detailed explanations, we can clearly make rational and reasonable assessments about the worth and believability of the researcher's study in the second case. The first researcher presented limited details about his sample, which makes it very difficult to assess whether there were problems with his sampling or analyses or any other aspect of his study.

I often look at research reports and articles that skirt the problems of their research designs or analyses as somewhat suspect. It makes me uncomfortable to base my studies on what I see as superficial explanations of the problems of research. All research has limitations, and these should be recognized and fairly presented. The nature of studies in social sciences, and in criminal justice research in particular, is that problems cannot be avoided. Researchers are obligated to explain and describe the limitations in as much detail as possible so those who read their research can make up their own minds about the value of the research.

Approaches to Protecting Research Subjects

There are basically four general approaches to ensuring that research subjects are protected from research and researchers. The idea of protecting research subjects is intertwined with the basic ethical agreements that were stipulated in the previous sections. Thus, if it is important to protect research subjects from harm, then there should be a way to ensure that study subjects do not get harmed. The four approaches that follow may be used alone or together to ensure that the general agreements are followed by researchers.

Another point that should be mentioned prior to the discussion of these approaches is the almost exclusive focus in most social science research on the protection of "human" subjects. There is little mention of other units of analysis, in particular, groups or organizations, as study subjects in this consideration. While the political limitations of studying, say, a police precinct would restrict what harms could be caused by a research study, it is important that researchers consider the ethical agreements as applicable to units of analysis other than people.

Professional Codes of Ethics

Professional codes of ethics are standards that certain fields have set for themselves to guide the behaviors of their memberships. The medical and legal professions have extensive and well-developed codes of ethics guiding everything from the fees they charge to issues of client confidentiality. Yet, we all hear of situations where doctors may have conducted unnecessary procedures for money and lawyers may have overcharged clients. In the research community Babbie (1989) lists the Code of Professional Ethics and Practices of the American Association for Public Opinion Research. This code lists several of the ethical agreements in the field of public opinion research. These codes on the ethical conduct of research are similar in that they list the ethical agreements as described here and usually list a few specific considerations that are relevant to the field of study that has promulgated the code. While Longmire (1991) and others in the field of criminal justice and criminological research believe that there is a need for such a code and that it could increase the ethical conduct of research, I do not put much faith in the listing of rules of conduct when there is no monitoring or consequences for not following the code. It certainly would be helpful, from a public relations standpoint, for criminal justice and criminological researchers to have a professional code of research ethics. But in terms of preventing unethical research, such codes are like having the fox guard the chickens. Besides, I doubt very much if a useful code beyond restatements of the general ethical agreements could be agreed upon by the Academy of Criminal Justice Scientists of the American Society of Criminology.[8]

Government Regulations

The second major approach to making sure that the subjects of research are protected from research and researchers is the use of *governmental regulations.* These regulations have increased in number and breadth with the increases in federal funding for criminal justice research in the form of the National Institute of Justice grants or other such federal funding sources. The two most common sources for protective regulations for studies involving the protection of human subjects are the Office of Management and Budget protections and the Code of Federal Regulations, Article 45, Part 46. The government regulations articulate the protections that are implied and stated in the basic ethical agreements described earlier. The regulations also require a somewhat more complex structure than professional codes or self-imposed morality to ensure that the subjects of research are protected. The U.S. Department of Health and Human Services (the lead agency for the Federal Code of Regulations requirements) has the duty of establishing whether federal grantees are in compliance with the federal regulations and has set up the Office for the Protection of Research Subjects, which reviews agency and university policies on the protection of human research subjects. These codes focus on considerations of the basic ethical agreements and can require that research not be conducted until it is in compliance with such regulations. While the process of securing approval for a research project based on the government regulations is daunting, the researcher can be sure that once it is completed the research he or she is conducting is in compliance with the basic ethical principles, at least from a legal standpoint.

Legal Intervention

Another approach to ensuring that researchers comply with the basic ethical agreements is for study subjects to use legal redress. Researchers need to be aware that if they harm study subjects and have not forewarned the subjects of such harm or have not acquired informed consent, the researchers may be liable for their actions. In addition, researchers who reveal information that was guaranteed to be confidential could be the defendant in a suit for slander or libel. One thing that is clear, researchers are likely to avoid practices that would lead to their being named in a lawsuit. It is also important for researchers to recognize that the United States has become the most litigious society that has ever existed. Hence, it behooves researchers to be certain that ethical policies and procedures are relied upon and that the procedures are defensible. The possibility of legal intervention is another reason why I believe the government regulation approach is superior to professional codes of ethics. If one follows government regulations there is a much more sound legal basis for stating that the research is ethical as opposed to following professional codes of ethics where there is no arbitrator, no controls, or no review of research.

Self-Imposed Morality

The final approach that I will discuss is the use of *self-imposed morality*. Researchers by and large attempt to be ethical in conducting their research simply because it is the "right thing to do." This morality is based on the general ethical agreements of doing no harm, voluntariness, and being honest. The scientific perspective also places researchers in a mind-set wherein they try to be as objective as possible and to collect as impartial information and data as is possible. Hence, researchers understand that if individuals are deceived or harmed, the data may be tainted by the effects of the experience. Thus, a distortion will present itself in the data rather than a realistic depiction of the issues under study. The problem with self-imposed morality is that some researchers, like others in society, may not have a strong sense for the basic ethical agreements, and even if they do, they may not understand how their research violates them. For instance, recently the head of a research institute told me that he rarely gives research subjects information about the studies the institute researchers conduct and that there are no reviews of the "ethical" agreements as I explained them to him. While he justified their approach because they conduct telephone interviews and have no time to tell the subjects about the studies, the point remains that this otherwise ethical person and well-qualified researcher does not understand the basic meaning of the ethical agreements that researchers espouse. For the reasons cited in this section I tend to believe that the government regulation approach is the only one wherein the researcher is provided with clear guidelines and controls on unethical or harmful studies. The following sections describe some of the policies and procedures in such regulations.

Legal Protections of Human Subjects

The following sections describe some of the protections provided by the *Code of Federal Regulation (CFR)* as administered by the U.S. Department of Health and Human Services. Most, if not all, universities and research institutes engage in a consideration of the ethical standing of research based on this governmental regulatory policy. In addition, the National Institute of Justice, the main source for criminal justice and criminology research funds, relies on the CFR regulations for all of its research grants. While some academic researchers are strongly opposed to the idea that government regulations should be imposed on their research, the current reality is that if universities and researchers receive federal research grants they must conform to the government regulations as stipulated in the CFR. I also believe that those who do not understand the practice of applying the government regulations might claim that the regulations are "dramatic evidence of the failure of associations (i.e., ASC and ACJS) to convince the public that their members are to be trusted as individuals or that the associations are to be trusted to control them" (Reynolds, 1979, p. 103). Yet criminal justice and criminology are not well-regulated by their national associations, because membership, while helpful and interesting, is neither mandatory nor necessary to conduct research on criminal justice topics. Moreover, there continue to be no professional codes of ethics for criminal justice and criminological researchers, and there are also persistent and current examples of potentially unethical practices in research. I do not want to suggest that the CFR is a panacea and that all problems as regards unethical research practices will be solved by these regulations, only that it is the best available approach at this time and one that is required for most large-scale funded research in criminal justice and criminology.

Exempted Research

The CFR begins with a discussion of *exempted research,* research that should not be subjected to the regulations. That is, there are some research designs that are intrinsically not in violation of the basic ethical agreements. This is so when a few of the agreements are met and when there is clearly no potential for harm to the subjects of research. Research that is done in common research settings, research that is unobtrusive, and research on existing data do not require review.

Research in common research settings is typically related to research in educational institutions. Therefore, research conducted in established or commonly accepted educational settings involving normal educational practices, such as research on instructional strategies, research on effectiveness, or the comparison among instructional techniques, curricula, or classroom management techniques (CFR Article 45, Part 46, §46.101 (b) (1)) are exempted from the regulations in the CFR. That means that if the Department of Criminal Justice or Criminology at your university wants to compare how much students learn in lecture classes as opposed to seminar format courses, such a project is not subject to the review process. Researchers in such a project should uphold and maintain the basic ethical agreements, but the more extensive review process provided for in the CFR is not necessary.

Second, projects involving unobtrusive research techniques are also not considered as applicable to the CFR policies and review procedures. Examples of such unobtrusive techniques according to the 1993 version of the CFR are (1) research involving the use of survey procedures, (2) interview procedures, and (3) observation of public behavior unless the human subjects can be identified directly or indirectly through identifiers linked to subjects and any potential disclosure of their responses outside the research could reasonably place the subjects at risk of criminal or civil liability or be damaging to the subjects' financial standing, employability, or reputation (CFR Article 45, Part 46, §46.101 (b) (2)). Hence, in a study where no identifiers that can be linked to the study subjects, as in the first fear-of-crime example, there is no need to apply the CFR policies and procedures. However, as is true of research in common research settings, it is always required that the researcher conform to the basic ethical agreements. Because I am cautious about my research and consider myself to be ethical, I regularly subject my surveys, interviews, and observational studies to the CFR review policies just to be certain that I provide protections for the subjects of my research.

Research on preexisting data, documents, records, pathological specimens, or diagnostic specimens, if these sources are publicly available or if the information is recorded by the investigator in such a manner that subjects cannot be identified, directly or through identifiers linked to the subjects, are clearly excluded from the review process required in the CFR (CFR Article 45, Part 46, §46.101 (b) (4)). For example, given that the National Crime Victims Survey is preexisting data, there is no need to reconsider the protection of those human subjects, especially since there are no identifiers linked to subjects and no one in the Bureau of Justice Statistics knows who was included in the study.

In sum, the government regulations embodied in the CFR allow certain research to be completed without any review and depend upon either professional codes or ethics of the researcher's own morality, or both. However, the CFR also assumes that the legal restrictions on unethical research be considered in that all research that is exempt from the review process must comply with all federal, state, and local statutes and regulations that provide additional protections for human research subjects (CFR Article 45, Part 46, §46.101 (e)).

Review of Research

The basis for the *review of research* is an *Institutional Review Board (IRB)* composed of a group of reviewers to whom research projects are presented before they are conducted. If a project does not conform to the basic ethical agreements, it will not receive approval from the IRB. Projects can, and often are, modified by the IRB to ensure the protection of research subjects. The IRB is made up of individuals who are qualified to review research projects and usually includes four or five faculty members of diverse backgrounds (i.e., not from the same department), a lawyer, and a member that is not associated with the university (i.e., a local citizen or a business leader).

The procedures for review of research are conducted by the IRB in specific reference to a local university policy for reviewing research projects. These procedures lay the ground rules for submission of a project to the IRB review process for new and continuing research, the decision categories assigned by the IRB, and the specific documents and information that must be provided to the IRB. However, depending on the nature of the research, additional materials may be required at the discretion of any of the IRB members. First, the researcher is required to present a summary of the research he or she intends to conduct to the IRB. This can be done in writing or in the form of a presentation to the IRB. At this time, the researcher must document the specific activities and aspects of the project that will protect the voluntariness of the subjects and reduce any unnecessary harms.

Most of these initial reviews are conducted with a particular focus on the means of collecting data (i.e., the survey instrument, questionnaire, observational design, or other such method for gleaning data from the research subjects).

The focus of the IRB review is on the consideration of risks to the subjects of the research project. Specifically, the considerations of the risks to human research subjects will be based on the subjects' voluntariness of participation, the harm to research participants, considerations of anonymity or confidentiality of research participants, and the researcher's identity. The researcher must make clear that the research subjects are not required to participate, can withdraw their participation at any time during the course of the research, and can retroactively withdraw their participation. The researcher must assure the IRB (through the presentation of consent forms or other evidence) that the research subjects' participation in the research is voluntary.

The IRB also reviews whether the research harms the subjects. Research should not injure the people being studied whether they volunteer or not. In particular, in any cases where the researcher, for example, asks the research subjects to reveal information about their deviant behaviors, unpopular attitudes, self-evaluation, or demeaning personal characteristics, the amount of harm to the subjects should be minimized. This also encourages survey researchers to have their studies reviewed by the IRB to make certain that the project does not harm the subjects. At this point of the review process, it is the responsibility of the researcher to explain how harm will be minimized. However, the IRB can make further recommendations as well as impose changes on the researcher that further minimize the harm to research subjects. The IRB members usually recognize the fact that no research is completely harmless. That is, when a researcher conducts a study there is an intrusion into the lives of the subjects and hence "harm" to the research subjects, no matter how minimal. The basic job of the IRB is to make certain that any harms (physical, psychological, economic, or otherwise) in research be minimized to every extent possible.

Perhaps the most important way to ensure protections for subjects is through the granting of research subjects anonymity for confidentiality. In fact, the most important concern in research is the protection of the identities of the human research subjects. The deliberations of the IRB concerning the anonymity or confidentiality of the subjects is, therefore, crucial. Research subjects can be protected from many harms through the guarantees of either anonymity or confidentiality. At this point, the researcher who guarantees anonymity is responsible for documenting how he or she will provide research subjects with such an assurance (through providing the IRB with the actual informed consent form to be used or through any other means that the IRB deems acceptable). Researchers who guarantee only confidentiality must provide clear and uncontroversial evidence that the research subjects' identities will not be revealed outside of the context of the research for any purpose to any party. Typically, research that does not grant the study subjects either anonymity or confidentiality in their responses will not be approved (i.e., will be deemed to be in violation of the CFR regulations).

Another important consideration in the IRB review process is the revelation of the researcher's identity as well as the nature of the research. It is ethical to reveal to research subjects the nature of the research and the researcher's identify prior to conducting the research. While some research must temporarily hide the identity of both the researcher and the true purpose of the research, such deception must be absolutely necessary for the conduct of the research. The IRB considers whether the purpose of the research and the researcher's identity should be disclosed prior to the project or after the completion of the research project. In each and every case it is the researcher's responsibility to make it clear to the IRB how the researcher subjects will be informed of the researcher's identity and the true purpose of the research.

The end result of the IRB review of potential research objects involves the approval of the project, recommendations for changes to further protect the subjects, or disapproval of the project. Research does not have the approval of the IRB and must be redesigned to conform to the recommendations of the IRB if the researcher still wishes to conduct the research as an employee of the university.

In sum, the IRB considers (1) whether the risks to subjects are minimized (CFR Article 45, Part 46, §46.111 (a) (1)); (2) whether the risks are reasonable considering the potential benefits of the research (CFR Article 45, Part 46, §46.111 (a) (2)); (3) if the selection of subjects is equitable (CFR Article 45, Part 46, §46.111 (a) (3)); (4) if informed consent or its equivalent has been sought from each prospective subject or the subject's legal representative (CFR Article 45, Part 46, §46.111 (1) (4)) and has consent been documented (CFR Article 45, Part 46, §46.111 (a) (5)); (5) whether the research design makes adequate provisions for monitoring the data collection to ensure the safety of subjects (CFR Article 45, Part 46, §46.111 (a) (6)); (6) whether there are adequate provisions to protect the privacy of the subjects (CFR Article 45, Part 46, §46.111 (a) (7)); and (7) whether, when the subjects are particularly vulnerable to coercion or undue influence (i.e., children, prisoners, the mentally ill, etc.), there are additional safeguards provided to protect these research subjects (CFR Article 45, Part 46, §46.111 (a) (7) (b)).

The CFR also requires that, once research is approved, it periodically be reviewed during its conduct. Typically, research that is approved must be re-reviewed each and every academic calendar year. While research projects can be reviewed on an ongoing basis upon the recommendations of the IRB in increments of less than one year, this tends to be rare in criminal justice and criminological research projects. The continuing review of research requires that the IRB monitor the data collection stage of the research to make sure that it conforms to their recommendations and that there are no problems with the protections given to the research subjects.

Another particularly attractive aspect of the CFR review process is the requirement that reviews of research must be based on records. Hence, if there are any legal problems related to the research (i.e., a subject sues a researcher for supposed harm done to him) the records of the university policy on human subjects research and the IRB review could well save the researcher as well as the university a great deal of money not to mention provide clear documentation of the consistency of the research with accepted ethical practices. The IRB records are maintained by the IRB chairperson and are retained for a period of seven years after the scheduled completion of the research project.

One of the key aspects of the CFR is securing informed consent, and the following sections describe this process in some detail. The IRB may approve a consent procedure that does not include or that alters some or all of the following elements of informed consent. The IRB may also waive the requirements to obtain informed consent provided it finds that the research is (1) a study of public benefits, (2) the researcher could not practicably conduct the research with informed consent or an alteration thereof, (3) there is minimal risk to subjects, (4) subjects will be provided with the information after their participation, and/or (5) there is no violation of federal, state and local laws (CFR Article 45, Part 46, §46.116 (c) (d) (e) and (f)). Informed consent documentation must be provided by the researcher in the form of a written consent document, a written form of the orally stated informed consent, or a statement about how subjects will be granted informed consent (CFR Article 45, Part 46, §46.117 (1) and (2)). The IRB can waive written consent forms, especially in cases where the only link between the subjects and their responses is the consent form itself (CFR Article 45, Part 46, §46.117 (2) (c)). In essence, informed consent requires the researcher to state the purposes of the research, describe the benefits and risks, provide treatment recommendations, ensure confidentiality, make a statement about compensation, specify a contact person or agency, provide voluntary participation, and any other provisions that the IRB or researcher deems necessary to protect the research subjects.

A statement that the study involves research, an explanation of the purposes of the research and the expected duration of the subjects' participation, a description of the procedures to be followed, and identification of any procedures which are experimental (CFR Article 45, Part 46, §46.116 (a) (1)) should be provided in informed consent. The rationale here is that if a subject knows little about a research project, then it is difficult for that person to make an "informed" decision about participating or not participating in such a study. It is also crucial that the researcher provide an open description of any reasonably foreseeable risks or discomforts to the subjects. Clearly, subjects of research need to understand the potential for harm if they are to truly be voluntary participants.

Researchers should provide a description of any benefits to the subject or to others that may reasonably be expected from the research. Subjects can be encouraged to participate in the study to benefit others. For example, I recently broke my ankle and was asked to participate in a study on muscle atrophy (i.e., shrinking) after having a cast on my leg for an extended period of time (eight weeks). The study researcher did not pay me for my participation, and there were no direct benefits to me. However, if they can make the transition from cast to no cast easier and faster for those who break bones, then the results of such research could clearly be beneficial to many others. The researcher should make clear the benefits to the subjects that may result from their participation.

Researchers should also describe appropriate alternative procedures or courses of treatment, if any, that might be advantageous to the subject (CFR Article 45, Part 46, §46.116 (a) (4)). For example, if the researcher is providing an educational program wherein he or she tests the reading comprehension of the subjects, then it would be ethical to provide information about programs to improve the comprehension of the study subjects (this could be provided *after* the study has been completed).

Informed consent must contain a statement describing the extent, if any, to which confidentiality of the records identifying the subjects will be maintained, as well as the compensation for participation. In studies involving more than minimal risk, an explanation about compensation and whether any medical treatments are available if injury occurs (and, if so, what they consist of) or where further information may be obtained should be fully described. In addition, the researcher should provide a statement about whom to contact for answers to pertinent questions about the research and about subjects' rights to ensure that the researcher is held responsible for study subject participation. Finally, a statement to the effect that participation is voluntary, that refusal to participate will involve no penalty or loss of benefits to which the subject is otherwise entitled, and that the subject may discontinue participation at any time without penalty or loss of benefits to which the subject is otherwise entitled. (CFR Article 45, Part 46, §46.116 (a) (8)) should also be included in the informed consent instrument.

Prisoner Research

There are additional considerations of the application of the CFR when the subjects of research are prisoners. In fact, there are limits on the types of research that can be conducted on inmates or prisoners. Research on biomedical or behavioral issues is permitted when it involves (1) studies of the possible causes, effects, and processes of incarceration, and of criminal behavior, provided that the study presents no more than inconvenience to the subjects; (2) studies of prisons, jails, or other correctional facilities as places of incarceration provided the study presents no more than minimal risk and no more than inconvenience to the subjects; (3) investigating conditions particularly affecting prisoners as a class of people; and (4) studies of practices that are accepted and innovative and have a reasonable probability of improving the health or well-being of the subjects (CFR Article 45, Part 46, §46.306).

When doing research on inmates the possible benefits of research participation for inmate subjects should not be so great as to remove their ability of making an informed consent decision about whether they should participate in the research. For example, suppose you want to conduct a study on food; a sample of inmates would eat fast food, another sample a home-cooked food diet, and a third, the prison food. The inmates in the fast food group (McDonalds, Burger King, Taco Bell, and so on) as well as the home-cooking group (food actually prepared by a "good" cook) would be hard pressed to refuse participation given the taste and nature of most prison food. The selection of research subjects should also be fair to all inmates and be free from arbitrary intervention by the correctional facility administration or staff. Each inmate should have an equal chance to be in the fast-food or home-cooking groups. It is also important to present the informed consent information in language that can be understood by the subject population. Another important component of informed consent is the inclusion of an assurance that parole boards will not take the research participation into account in deciding whether the inmates should be paroled; otherwise, why would an inmate refuse to participate?

Summary

This chapter has described and given examples of the basic ethical agreements for conducting research that is harmless to the subjects, in which subjects voluntarily participate, that is honestly conducted, and that treats the results fairly. There are four ways in use to consider the basic ethical agreements: professional codes of ethics, government regulations, legal intervention, and self-imposed morality. However, because of the legal and governmental realities that currently exist, a code of federal regulations is the preferred approach to ensuring that ethical research is conducted and that research subjects are protected. The last sections of the chapter provide a detailed discussion of the issues involved in the considerations of the Code of Federal Regulations (CFR). The CFR provides detailed instructions for the protection of human research subjects. These include the research that is exempted from this law as well as detailed review procedures based on the existence of an Institutional Review Board (IRB). The key consideration of the IRB is the risks to human subjects who participate in the research. Researchers should endeavor to balance scientific considerations with ethical agreements.

Main Concepts

basic ethical agreements
harmlessness
fairness
confidentiality
professional codes of ethics
governmental regulations
Code of Federal Regulations (CFR)
exempted research
prisoner research
Institutional Review Board (IRB)
voluntariness
honesty
anonymity
informed consent
legal intervention
self-imposed morality
review of research

Discussion Questions

1. Why is the ethical agreement for voluntariness so important?
2. Why is the ethical agreement for harmlessness so important?
3. Compare and contrast the four approaches to ensuring that the ethical agreements are maintained.
4. What are some of the advantages and disadvantages to securing informed consent?
5. Describe how you would gain informed consent for a study of police officers.

Exercise

Form small groups of three or four people. Discuss the four approaches to guaranteeing that ethical agreements are maintained and decide which approach to use for one of the research situations listed below. Present a summary of your group's procedures and rationale for the approach.

Research situations:

1. Victims of rape
2. How police officer handle mentally ill citizens
3. Jury deliberation content
4. Correctional officer stress
5. Inmate deviance while in the prison

14

LIBRARY RESEARCH IN CRIMINAL JUSTICE AND CRIMINOLOGY

Chapter Objectives

1. To describe the most common approach to conducting library research
2. To discuss the use of the most common reference sources

Chapter Outline

Introduction
Topic Selection
Preparation
Reference Locator Sources
Criminal Justice Abstracts
Criminology Penology and Police Science Abstracts
Criminal Justice Periodical Index
Criminal Justice Abstracts on CD-ROM
Main Concepts
Discussion Questions
Exercise

CHAPTER FOURTEEN

Introduction

Criminal justice and criminological research often has as its intellectual and practical basis the work of others. Traditional research, as explained in chapter 1 follows a logical structure wherein researchers interested in a current topic begin their study with a thorough investigation of what is known about the topic they are interested in studying. This investigation will likely be based on library sources such as journals, books, or documents where most criminal justice and criminological research is reported. While we do not always have to follow the traditional process of research, there is always a point in developing a research idea or project where we are forced to consult with the existing knowledge base.

For example, suppose a jail administrator is interested in studying the "cyclical" nature of his jail's population because he wanted to better allocate his personnel to meet the high demand portion of the cycle while not wasting personnel resources when there is a "lull" in the population. He could proceed to analyze his data without looking at the literature and he may come up with a reasonable empirical solution. The production of such an empirical solution would be based on the administrator's talent as a researcher. Not all of us are that talented, nor do we always have the time to conduct complete or extensive research projects.

However, if he had searched the literature for studies which examined "cyclicity" in jails or prisons, while there is a limited literature, he would have found that there are several articles that have studied the nature of correctional populations over time (see Senese, 1991, for example). He may have been able to make his personnel allocation decision based on past research rather than repeating what has already been done. In addition, he would have found that there are differences in the male and female populations cycles and that his personnel would have to be differentially allocated based on these differences.[1] It is unlikely that many jail administrators are very concerned with being consistent with the development of academic or theoretical knowledge, as are most academic researchers, but they have practical knowledge to offer that could greatly improve the current knowledge base, so if the administrator could help inform academic researchers, the knowledge base would be that much more accurate.[2] He may have been able to develop a more in-depth understanding of jail population changes or cycles over time than just an overall idea about the male and female populations, and such knowledge would help other jail administrators and academic researchers. If he had looked at the current literature before doing his study he would have found that his question, while based in the literature, was a logical extension of what is already known. He may have also used the literature to more fully develop the type and quality of the research that he anticipated conducting. In sum, consulting the current knowledge base helps improve the overall quality and results of research.

There are five reasons for conducting library studies of a research topic before conducting an empirical analysis. The following sections describe these reasons. The five specific reasons for conducting a library search of the current knowledge are: (1) to save limited research resources; (2) to develop a better research idea; (3) to link current research with tradition or the knowledge base; (4) to allow logical departures from tradition or the knowledge base; and (5) to help construct the conceptual framework upon which the current research can be built.

It is important to most people that they don't waste their time. For example, my wife and I determined that we needed to get our lawn cut. We regularly ask one of the young boys in our neighborhood to cut our lawn and we pay $20 for the job. When I got home one evening I asked James to cut the lawn the next day and prepaid him the $20. My wife had already asked Sam, another neighbor, to cut the lawn and had prepaid him. The next day our lawn was cut twice! As in research that doesn't consult the knowledge base, we wasted our valuable resources. While we only wasted $20, the researcher that doesn't consult preexisting knowledge may waste months of research efforts or dozens of hours of time. Moreover, research cannot be conducted on every topic or every detail of every topic. One way to focus research on the most necessary and appropriate issues is to conduct research in the library about what is known before conducting your research.

Studying the literature before conducting research also allows the researcher to develop a better research idea. Suppose your father is a police officer, and he tells you how the citizens "hate" the police. He also tells you that you know nothing about the "real world" and that "research smesearch—I know how the citizens view the police!" You decide not to argue with your father but to conduct a research project for class on the topic of public opinion about the police in your city. Your father's knowledge about public opinion is based on his twenty some years of experience dealing with people in specific areas of the city. It is not based on a representative sample of the city's population nor is it based on the public opinion research knowledge base, which shows that citizens generally hold favorable attitudes about the police. In a search of the literature you find an article by Linguanti and McIntyre (1992) in the *Canadian Police College Journal* that presents a questionnaire for conducting a public-opinion-toward-the-police study. You conduct a study based on a random sample of 100 citizens and find out that 80 percent of the sample believe the police are doing a good job. Your father's knowledge about policing and his opinions about how the public view the police are not objective or based on current knowledge about the topic.

Studying the current knowledge also allows researchers to link their current research with tradition or the knowledge base. For example, suppose we are interested in studying domestic violence, particularly in what the public wants the police to do in such situations. We could search the literature and find articles such as one published by Breci and Murphy (1992) entitled "What Do Citizens Want Police to Do at Domestics: Enforce the Law or Provide Services?" published in the *American Journal of Police* to help us understand what is traditionally done and what is known about the issue. Otherwise, our research would be exploratory.

Once we know what is known about a topic, we can make logical departures from tradition or the knowledge base. There is currently a large knowledge base on prison and jail overcrowding. There are virtually hundreds of articles about the topic. In a recent departure from that knowledge base Klofas, Stojkovic, and Kalinich (1992) attempted to develop an overall index of the amount of overcrowding for prison and jail administrators as well as researchers. Their index is a logical departure from the literature and was based on an extensive search of what is currently known about the topic of overcrowding. Klofas and Stojkovic logically derived their index from the current knowledge base and added additional concepts that they believe logically fit in a crowding index.

Last, but certainly not least, the search of current literature allows us to construct the conceptual framework upon which current research can build. It would be difficult for anyone to conduct a study about prisoner's rights and how they affect prison operations, for example, without a thorough understanding of prisoners' rights and prison operations. There is no way that most researchers can develop their conceptual basis for such a study without consulting the literature on both topics. While an administrator in an agency or a lawyer who initiates lawsuits may have the necessary knowledge to formulate ideas about the topic, they would not have a sufficient knowledge base to study the topic from a researcher's perspective because they have limited experiences and opinions. A thorough search of the literature before conducting research provides the researcher with a complete list of the concepts that are important to the topic they intend to study as well as lists of variables and potential methodologies that would have to be invented had the literature not been consulted.

In the end, the current literature should be consulted—and must be consulted eventually. It makes sense to build this component into most research projects whether they are for making operational decisions or developing the knowledge base. Research without a firm base is more likely to be wasteful and inaccurate than research with such a grounding in the current knowledge. The following sections discuss the issues of selecting a researchable topic and how to prepare to begin a search of the library. Next, I will discuss the reference locator sources that are traditionally used in criminal justice and criminological research as well as the currently available CD-ROM search of the literature and some of the other available sources.

Topic Selection

One of the most difficult tasks for many students is *research topic selection,* deciding what the topic of a research paper will be. Time and consideration before beginning the search of the literature will save you a great deal of effort in the long run. That is not to say that you should decide on a research topic and never change or develop that idea. Rather, it is important to get a sense for the focus of this study early in the process of searching the current knowledge base. Research ideas can come from newspapers, family conversations, friends, observations, reading textbooks, and any number of other sources. The basis of ideas is the imagination and creativity of the researcher and as such has virtually no limits. But how do you take these ideas and turn them into a viable research topic? One way is to engage in a definitional process wherein you define the topic through asking yourself a series of questions about what it is that you think you are interested in studying.[3] Figure 14.1 lists the types of considerations you could consider while deciding on the topic to be studied.

Figure 14.1

RESEARCHABLE TOPIC SELECTION CONSIDERATIONS

What am I most interested in studying?
Who are the subjects of study?
Where would I like to conduct the study?
During what time period would I like to conduct the study?
How will I study the subjects?

An example of applying these considerations could be taken from a newspaper. In the *Philadelphia Inquirer* one of the headline articles described a firebombing of a New York subway. I was struck by the potential for such violence in other cities such as Philadelphia and Washington, DC because of their large train-based mass transit systems. Since I cannot recall reading anything on the topic, I thought I would first attempt to flesh out this idea and make it a more researchable one.

Suppose that I am interested in studying commuter train lines because people live outside the city, in part, because of crime in the cities. This reduces the topic considerably as many train lines, and the one in New York, are only intercity lines. The subjects of my study would be people who use the train for commuting to and from work. That excludes those taking the train for other reasons, such as to go shopping or sight seeing. Since I regularly ride the PATCO train line into Philadelphia to the Amtrak station at 30th Street in Philadelphia, I would like to conduct my study on that train line. The PATCO line is very similar to many other commuter train lines that begin in suburbs and end in a large urban area (Long Island Rail Road, or BART in San Francisco) in terms of its distance and the types of people who use it. Since commuters take the train during rush hours, the study could be conducted during both the morning and evening rush hours. Last, probably the most logical and doable approach to studying such people is to conduct very short personal interviews based on a structured interview guideline. In this example, I have gone from an article in the newspaper to a researchable idea on commuter attitudes about crime on the trains they take into the city.

Preparation

Once you develop a researchable idea, the next step in conducting library research is *preparation for conducting research.* If you are fortunate enough to have a good university library that contains the major criminal justice/criminological sources, this process can be both fruitful and enjoyable. However, preparation before you go to the library will make your library time not only more productive but also more efficient. The researchable idea should be written down to fully describe the topic on a *researchable topic sheet* (see figure 14.2). Don't worry about being too organized on this topic description sheet. I generally hand write these sheets and continue to add words or phrases as I further develop the topic.

Once the researchable topic sheet is completed, you are almost set to begin the library search for literature on the topic of attitudes toward crime on commuter train lines. In order to locate sources on this topic you would typically consult with a "reference locator source." In this locator there is usually an alphabetic listing of concepts and topical areas with an accompanying full list of references. Hence, if helps a great deal to create a second list of your researchable topics in alphabetic order. The reference locator sources also

Figure 14.2
RESEARCHABLE TOPIC SHEET

Commuters
Commuter train
Attitudes about crime on the train
Attitudes about crime in the city
Male, female, white, black commuters
Suburb to city train lines
Rush hour study

Rush hours:
8:00–10:00 am
4:00–7:00 pm

Philly
New York
Washington

summarize the topics in the index to the sources. You then turn to the appropriate page number in the front of the reference locator to determine the specific reference that applies to the topic. For example, if you look up the concept "attitudes toward crime" in the back of the Criminal Justice Abstracts you might find a reference to page number 234, volume 12, edition number 2, where you would find the title, authors, source, and abstract of the article of interest. I usually look up all of my topics in the back of the reference locator and write down the page numbers, or abstract numbers. Then I look in the front of the reference locator for the sources and abstracts to ensure that I do not miss any sources.

Once you locate the sources of interest, you need to copy the page on a photocopier or write down the reference source listed in the reference locator.[4] At a minimum you should write down the author's name, the title, and the name of the book or journal, as well as the year, volume, number, and page numbers. I also record the locator I found the reference in just in case my library doesn't carry the journal or book and I have to use interlibrary loans to obtain a copy of the article or book.

Reference Locator Sources

There are basically three main reference locator sources available in criminal justice and criminology: the Criminal Justice Abstracts, the Criminology, Penology, and Police Science Abstracts, and the Criminal Justice Periodical Index.

Criminal Justice Abstracts

Perhaps the best reference locator available for criminal justice and criminological research sources is the set entitled the *Criminal Justice Abstracts*

(CJA). The Criminal Justice Abstracts contain references to all of the major criminal justice and criminology journals as well as the top journals in sociology that contain criminal justice research. In addition, many government documents, both state and federal, are referenced. The CJA has been in existence since the early 1960s and has been consistently improved and expanded to include additional sources and references. In fact, it is currently available on CD-ROM. It has been my experience, that the CJA is the best place to begin a library search for literature on criminal justice and criminological topics.

The Criminal Justice Abstracts are published in four editions per year (i.e., numbers 1, 2, 3, and 4) and are bound by libraries in year sets (volumes). In the index to edition number 4 is a "cumulative subject index" to the entire volume for a particular year. You would use this cumulative subject index to begin your search for references. In the older volumes of the CJA, the cumulative subject index provides a page number, which you use to locate the reference in the front parts of the volume. The abstracts are listed consecutively starting with edition number 1 and ending with edition number 4 for each particular year. In the newer CJA the numbers in the cumulative subject index reference the abstract numbers in the front of the book (see figure 14.3). Either way, it is quite simple to locate a set of references based on a few key works from your researchable topic sheet. In the front portion of editions 1, 2, 3, and 4, the CJA lists the author (or authors), the title of the reference, the source, including the journal name, year of publication, edition number, and the page numbers.[5] The CJA also provides an abstract or summary of the contents of the source so you can make a determination about whether the article, book, or document is appropriate as a basis for your current study.

Figure 14.3

EXAMPLE OF A CUMULATIVE SUBJECT INDEX IN CJA

Freudian approach to criminology 0852
Interrogations, confession and testimony 0247
Jurisprudence and 0684
Juror decision making 1469
Law and, international perspectives 1049
Law enforcement and 0565
Multiple sequential functional analysis 0765
Police interviewing 0984
Psychiatric study of arson suspects 0042
Psychological characteristics of male prostitutes 0452

Public Attitudes
New South Wales (AUS) anti-corruption commission and 1011
Police intervention in domestic disputes, Minnesota 0997
Public images of police officers and gender 0171
Public Intoxication
See Alcohol Abuse and Alcoholism
Public Opinion
Alternatives to death penalty, U.S. 1221

The following example demonstrates how one might use the CJA to look up "public attitudes" or "public opinion" toward the police. In figure 14.3, a rendition of the cumulative subject index from the 1993 volume of the CJA is shown. Suppose we are interested in the article on "public images of police officers" listed under the Public Attitudes heading. At this point we would turn to the front of the volume and find the source under the number 0171, provided in the cumulative subject index. We could read the source information and learn who wrote the article, its title, its source, and page numbers. In this case, the author and title are apparent. The article is a journal article that appeared in the 1992 edition of the journal of *Policing and Society.* The source numbers after the journal title (see figure 14.4) are translated as follows:

. . . *Policing and Society* 2(3): 219–232, 1992. [R 56755]

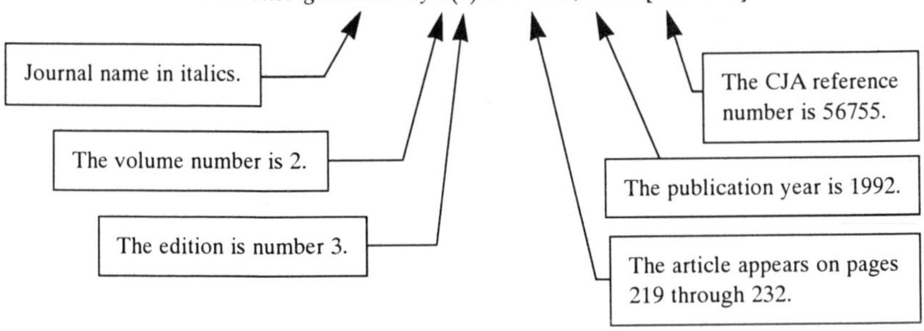

Because the abstracts for each year are listed in consecutive order beginning with 0001 for the first abstract of 1993 in edition 1 through whatever number of abstracts are included for the year, ending on the last page of the fourth edition for that year, it is easy to find a particular abstract in the CJA. At this point all we need to do is decide whether this article by Sandra Walklate is important to the study being contemplated. If it is, the call number for the *Policing and Society Journal* should be located in the card catalog. The University of Baltimore has a bound volume that is located in the library that lists the call numbers for all of the journals that the university and law school libraries subscribe to.

Criminology, Penology, and Police Science Abstracts

The *Criminology, Penology, and Police Science Abstracts (CPPA)* are very similar in set-up to the CJA in that they are produced quarterly and bound in yearly volume sets.[6] They also include a cumulative subject index as in the CJA. The difference between the CPPA and the CJA, at least insofar as I have found any difference, is that the CPPA tends to cover more non-United States sources than does the CJA. Hence, if you are interested in comparing policing in China and the United States, there is a better chance

Figure 14.4

LOCATED ARTICLE IN THE FRONT PART OF CJA 1993 (VOLUME 25)

0171-25 Walklate, Sandra. "Jack and Jill join up at Sun Hill: public images of police officers." *Policing and Society* 2(3):219–232, 1992. [R 56755]

A study considers public images of police officers in the context of gender. Data were obtained from 253 references submitted on behalf of 153 successful applicants to a police force in the southern U.D. from 1984–87. The individuals chosen as referees for the sample were predominantly male (male, 190; female, 56; unidentified sex, 7), and employed in middle-class occupations.

The referees' views of police officers were largely conservative. Challenging these views at an individual level appeared to be fraught with difficulties. Policewomen face resistance primarily because they potentially challenge the (private) structural location expected of them as women. Their moral worth must therefore be beyond doubt. This does not mean that some gains have not been made for policewomen, but these gains are marked and curtailed. A patriarchically structured concern was evinced to control women by controlling their sexuality, a process that is as effectively sustained by women for men as it is by men. The comments by both male and female referees support the argument that the wife/whore continuum operates and has impact in numerous ways.

of finding an article about policing in China in the CPPA rather than in the CJA. I have found that the abstracts in the CPPA tend to be a bit shorter than those in the CJA and hence sometimes are more difficult to use as a decision basis for getting the article or book.

Criminal Justice Periodical Index

The final major source of criminal justice and criminological references is the *Criminal Justice Periodical Index (CJPI).* The CJPI is produced three times a year by University Microfilms International. The CJPI is only a list of references—there are no abstracts. The references are grouped by topical heading, which makes it fairly easy to select articles. The only problem is that the reference tells you only who wrote the article, book, or document, its title, and source and nothing else. It takes a bit more time to use and collect references in the CJPI. The biggest advantage to the CJPI over both the CJA and the CPPA is that it contains more references to criminal justice trade journals such as *Corrections Today* (American Correctional Association) and *The Police Chief* (International Association of Chiefs of Police). If you are interested in practical level or applied problems, these trade journals are often excellent sources. In addition, the trade journals when they do report the results of research tend to present it in a very understandable and nontechnical manner. An example of a few lines in the CJPI (1994) is shown in figure 14.5. The microscopic print in the CJPI is difficult to read, but it is a quick reference source for criminal justice data.

Figure 14.5

EXAMPLE OF CJPI (1994)

If The Suit Fits . . . Overweight Troopers Say Standards Discriminate. *Law Enforcement News,* 20:402. (5/31/94). p1,6.+*.

Juries—Hearing-Impaired Jurors—Due Process. The *Criminal Law Reporter: Court Decisions.* 55:14 (7/6/94). p1321.

Klein, Sid, author. Americans With Disabilities Complaint Settled. *Law and Order.* 42:5 (5/94) p97.+*.

Obesity may be "Disability" Under ADA, But Case By Case Analysis Required. *Correctional Law Reporter.* 5:5. (2/94). p77.

Bulletin. 19:1 (7/28/94), p3.

You Be the Judge: U.S. v. Menon. *The Law Officer's Bulletin.* 18:25. (6/30/94). p148.

Pleas (Criminal Procedures)

Acquittal Of Co-Defendants Is No Reason To Dismiss Charge Against One Who Plead Guilty. *The Criminal Law Reporter: Court Decisions.* 55:14 (7/6/94). p1313.

Appeals—Failure To Raise Issue Below—State's Invocation of Fundamental Error Doctrine. *The Criminal Law Reporter: Court Decisions: 55:14.* (7/6/94). p1320.

Police

see also Arrest And Apprehension; Assaults On Police: Border Control: Campus Police; Civilians in Police Work; Criminal Investigation; Police—Ethics; Police Brutality; Police Dogs; Police Patrol; Police Questioning; State Police: Tactical Units: Traffic Police: Undercover Activity.

News Central America: Mini Police Directory. *Law and Order.* 42:5. (5/94). p6.

Figure 14.6

CRIMINAL JUSTICE ABSTRACTS ON CD-ROM (WinSPIRS®)

File Edit Utilities Records Options Help

Search For:

public images of police

Send | Index | Suggest | Thesaurus

Search History

No	Records	Search
#1	6670	Public
#2	135	Images
#3	9914	Police
#4	2	Public Images of Police

Show | Limit | Retype | Clear

Criminal | 1 of 2 in search #4

Retrieved Records

1 □	TI: Public images of the police in Northern Ireland AU: Brewer, John D. JN: Policing and Society 3 (3) pp 163–176 PY: 1992
2 □	TI: Jack and Jill join up at Sun Hill: public images of police officers AU: Walklate, Sandra JN: Policing and Society 2(3) pp 219–232 PY: 1992

Show Options | Show All Fields | Add to Search | Full Screen

Criminal Justice Abstracts on CD-ROM

A more contemporary way to conduct criminal justice library research is with a CD-ROM. Willow Tree Press, publisher of the CJA, has released a CD-ROM version of the CJA for DOS® and Windows 3.1®. The Criminal Justice Abstracts on CD-ROM are a phenomenal technological development. They allow you to quickly and easily search thousands of research articles in a matter of seconds. While both the DOS and Windows versions function equally well, I have found that the Windows version is a bit slicker than the DOS version. The search for "public images of police" produced the information on the WinSPIRS® version of the CJA shown in figure 14.6. The use of the CD-ROM version of the CJA is as simple as typing in words or phrases in the "Search For" box and letting the computer select references from the data base of all CJA abstracts from 1968 through 1995.

Summary

This chapter has discussed the techniques and sources that are used to conduct library research in criminal justice and criminology. There are essentially three main locator sources of criminal justice and criminology. The first, and arguably the best source, is the Criminal Justice Abstracts, generally considered to be the most comprehensive locator source for academic literature on criminal justice and criminology topics. The Criminology, Penology and Police Science Abstracts are also a good locator source. The particular advantage of the Criminology, Penology and Police Science Abstracts is that they tend to include more international journal and book references than do the Criminal Justice Abstracts. The Criminal Justice Abstracts are still more comprehensive than the Criminology, Penology and Police Science Abstracts for the major criminal justice, criminology, and sociology academic research journals in the United States and England. The Criminal Justice Abstracts also are available in a CD-ROM version, which makes it even easier to search for the authors or topics that one is interested in locating.

The third locator source is the Criminal Justice Periodical Index. The advantage of this source is that it tends to report more of the practitioner trade journal sources than do either the Criminal Justice Abstracts or the Criminology, Penology and Police Science Abstracts. The Criminal Justice Periodical Index is different than the other two sources in that it provides only references—not abstracts of topics.

Main Concepts

Criminal Justice Abstracts (CJA)
Criminology, Penology, and Police Science Abstracts (CPPA)

Criminal Justice Periodicals Index (CJPI)
Criminal Justice Abstracts on CD-ROM
research topic selection
preparation for conducting research
researchable topic sheet

Discussion Questions

1. What do the Criminal Justice Abstracts provide? Why are they generally considered the best criminal justice locator?
2. Which is the better way to get a researchable topic: reading newspapers or reading journal articles? Why?
3. What kinds of topics are the Criminology, Penology and Police Science Abstracts particularly well-suited for? Why?

Exercise

Conduct a library search on a topic for the past year in Criminal Justice Abstracts, Criminology, Penology and Police Science Abstracts, and Criminal Justice Periodical Index. Compare the results of this search. You may want to compare the types of sources that are obtained (i.e., popular press versus academic articles), the number of sources referenced, and other issues.

Notes

Chapter 1: Introduction to Research Methodology

1. Where the description of particular topics is less detailed, additional sources will be cited. While every effort has been made to provide as detailed a description of research methodology as possible, a complete knowledge of the technical intricacies of many of the current social science research methodologies is not necessary.

2. Basically, Dr. David B. Kalinich, my primary mentor, was referring to the fact that the field of criminal justice is often confronted with a situation it has not created but which it must address. For instance, legislatures across the United States are very interested in establishing intensive supervision probation programs. There is limited consideration, however, of whether ISP is either effective or appropriate based on objective assessment, nor are there general considerations of the appropriate program content. At this point criminal justice researchers may be asked to evaluate the program. Hence, the movie is half over—all that remains to be assessed is the ending.

3. The RAND Corporation funds many studies of criminal justice agencies and problems. Most of the outcomes of RAND's research, however, have been of an applied or prescriptive nature (i.e., there are specific practical recommendations). Cited from the American Society of Criminology's Presidential Address, 1991.

Chapter 2: Research Terminology

1. Both the American Jail Association and the American Correctional Association support this trend and several academic programs (e.g., Michigan State University, State University of New York at Albany, Sam Houston State University, to mention a few) have added more applied "administration" and "management" courses.

2. Babbie labels this type of mistake "ecological fallacy," which he defines as making assertions about individuals as the unit of analysis based on the examination of groups or other aggregations (Babbie, 1989, p. 86). While groups are collections of individuals, the data one collects can be generalized only to the unit of analysis that one collects. Babbie also defines the "individualistic fallacy" as reconciling general patterns on the basis of individual units of analysis.

3. Lemert's labeling theory suggests that offenders tend to take on the negative label "criminal" once the criminal justice system officially labels the person.

Chapter 3: Research Design

1. A discussion of the various formats for conducting survey research will be provided in chapter 6. These survey methods allow one to collect unbiased and

objective qualitative data from interviews or observations. This is an example of Sutherland's opportunity theory. See Hagan (1989) for further information.

2. Within the archives of the University of Baltimore library I was able to locate, in the process of determining what the archives contained, jail inspection reports dating from 1923 to 1980. I later contacted the Baltimore Grand Jury office and was able to get a complete 1980 to 1992 collection of Grand Jury jail reports. I am currently constructing a grant under which the research design for this data will be specified.

3. If you continue on to graduate school, you will be required to learn about other research designs. For further information about a range of research designs, see Ralph Taylor, *Research Methods in Criminal Justice* (New York: McGraw-Hill, 1994) or Frank E. Hagan, *Research Methods in Criminal Justice and Criminology* (New York: Macmillan, 1989).

Chapter 4: Data Measurement and Collection

1. I assume in this chapter that you have worked out the research design as specified in chapter 2. Hence, you already know which variables you are most interested in and which have the most impact on your research questions or hypotheses.

2. When there are other variables that explain the cause and effect outside the supposed variables, the alleged model is labeled "spurious." The outside variables are contradictory evidence that weakens the argument of cause and effect.

3. The UCR was begun in 1924 and has been administered by the Federal Bureau of Investigation since 1930.

4. Forty-two states require the law enforcement agencies that participate in the UCR program to report to the state UCR program. The state UCR program then reports to the FBI-UCR.

Chapter 5: Sample Selection Techniques

1. G.M. Camp and C.G. Camp, *The Corrections Yearbook* (South Salem, NY: Criminal Justice Institute, 1993).

2. Assuming that it takes one minute to fold the survey and stuff each envelope, an additional minute to open the returned completed survey, and one minute to code each survey into a computer-based data storage system, it would take 1,903 days (over five years) to complete only the data collection and coding stage of the project.

3. The formula for the standard error is $S.E. = s \div \sqrt{n}$.

4. I have not included a random numbers table in this text because I believe it is easier to use a calculator or computer to select simple random samples. However, if you find this method to be preferable you can locate a random numbers table in virtually any research methods text (see, for example, Babbie, 1989).

5. I use a Hewlett Packard 21S: Stat/Math © 1987 calculator for almost all of my calculator-based statistical calculations. While Hewlett Packard no longer makes this particular calculator there are many others on the market that are oriented toward statistical analyses (e.g. 28S).

6. Most spreadsheets and calculators will give you a decimal number for the generated random numbers. I simply move the decimal to the right the number of places required. For example, if I require two places, I would move the decimal point two places to the right.

7. A population consists of all possible subjects, such as all U.S. citizens. Conversely, a sampling frame is the population that is available for study. For example, we could have a sampling frame of inmates in Maryland prisons. This would not include the entire inmate population, but those available for our study. It would be better to have a list of all inmates, but a list of 19,000 inmates should suffice for most purposes.

8. See M.W. Klein, and C.L. Maxson, "Street Gang Violence," in Marvin E. Wolfgang and Neil A. Weiner (eds.), *Violent Crime, Violent Criminals* (Newbury Park, CA: Sage, 1989).

9. George Camp and Camille Camp report in their 1993 version of the *Correctional Yearbook* that there are 320,772 correctional staff.

10. For more information, see Michael Quinn Patton, *Qualitative Evaluation and Research Methods,* 2nd ed. (Newbury Park, CA: Sage, 1990).

11. The use of the three year difference in age is based on the fact that older burglars tend to be male and that most research shows that male burglars tend to be career criminals. Since there is no currently existing evidence that there is a similar pattern for female burglars, the effect size of three years difference seems conservative.

Chapter 6: Experimental Designs

1. The physical sciences (chemistry, biology, and physics) are considered "hard" sciences because they deal with clearly measurable phenomena or physical properties. That is, a chemist could collect a sample of three oxygen atoms from the atmosphere and these would behave the same as all other oxygen atoms.

2. A control group of narcotic-using inmates who recognize their problem and desire to be in a program such as Narcotics Anonymous is likely to be hard to come by. It may be considered unethical or may expose the administration to liability to assign individuals to N.A. and others to no treatment in a random manner.

3. See Cambell and Stanley, *Experimental and Quasi-Experimental Designs for Research* (1963) or Cook and Campbell, *Quasi-Experimentation: Design and Analysis Issues for Field Settings* (1979).

4. This is not to say that I do not endeavor to get all my students to understand my approach beforehand, just that the tendency is that those who have taken my classes in the past score 3% to 5% higher on my tests. I would also wager that this is very common for other faculty and that it is very difficult to change this effect in the typical college or university setting.

Chapter 7: Survey Research

1. I have conducted several studies of the national BJS jail survey data and have found it lacking in completeness. Many of the smaller jails report answers for half, or less, of the questions they were asked. This is not to say that the BJS study

is not valuable, just that there are problems with much of the survey research that is being conducted at the national level in the area of criminal justice.

2. The most popular windows programs are Microsoft Word 6.0®, Wordperfect®, and Ami Pro® by Lotus. Other programs, like Word Star, can be used for similar purposes. There are also several very good desk-top publishing systems that can be used to create professional looking surveys. Comparable hardware is also an important aspect of survey production and given the relative inexpensiveness of laser printers, questionnaires should be printed on nothing less.

3. In the actual administration of the questionnaire with the study sample, I would not ask for subjects' names. However, by getting the students' names I could match the responses for each person over the testing time period.

4. While there are certain abnormalities in the population (i.e., hermaphrodites) most individuals are clearly either male or female or are able to identify the category in which they believe they belong.

5. The cover letter should be printed on official stationery if possible. If that is not possible, it should be written on high quality bonded paper.

6. In a study I conducted a few years ago I contacted AT&T and inquired about the average number of unlisted numbers. I was told that they ranged from 5 percent to 40 percent, with the high-income communities in the higher percentage range.

Chapter 8: Observational Designs

1. In a search of the Criminal Justice Abstracts, 1968–1994 (Willow Tree Press, CD-ROM version) I was able to locate only forty field research studies. Therefore, there are hundreds of other articles and studies that are not observation based.

2. In some cases and studies one would use both quantitative and qualitative designs for different questions within an overall research project. In fact, the use of multiple measures, should they agree, can improve the validity and reliability of the results of studies.

Chapter 9: Secondary Analysis of Data

1. The ICPSR provides a complete listing of the publications that have resulted from the secondary analyses of the data sets that are housed at the archive. Some studies have resulted in several publications, whereas others have not been so prolific. Even though there have been many secondary analyses of the ICPSR data, there are virtually unlimited possibilities with these data.

2. The Survey of Inmates of Local Jails, for example, has several thousand cases and several hundred variables and has been conducted in 1978, 1983, and 1989. This represents a substantial cost and time investment that few academic or organizational researchers are either willing or able to assume.

3. Machine readable data sets are computer-ready data sets. The NACJD enters all of the data onto a computer disk or magnetic tape and mails that to the end users. In addition to the data set there is usually SPSS source codes that allow one to use the Statistical Package for the Social Sciences directly (i.e., the source code is the SPSS program to run the package). These features greatly facilitate the use

of these rather large data sets and remove the burdens and costs of data coding and program writing.

4. The Internet address for the ICSPR information is icpsr__netmail@um.cc.umich.edu. The address for the CDNet is icpsr.icpsr.umich.edu. And if your system still uses BITNET, the address is usersvcq@umichum.

Chapter 11: Basis Inferential Analyses

1. I have not included any of these probability tables in this book because I prefer that students focus on the methods rather than on the mechanical calculation of statistics. I have, however, included portions of statistical probability tables so you can at least get some sense of how I arrived at the values I use for the population estimates. In addition, computer-based software will give you an exact probability estimate, and the tables are unnecessary. Another source of probability values is through the use of many contemporary calculators (for example, my Hewlett Packard 21S STAT/MATH® calculator can give me probability estimates for the four most commonly used statistical probability tables).

2. In fact, Becker won the Pulitzer Prize in economics for his work on the rational choice model of employment and crime. His work in the late 1960s and early 1970s has resulted in several developments in criminological and human capital theory.

3. There are several statistical texts where these tests are fully illustrated and used (see Hinkle, Wiersma, and Jurs, 1994). You should consult these sources should you require one of the tests not listed in this text.

4. One particularly useful source for finding the appropriate tests that are available is Gopal K. Kanji's book *100 Statistical Tests* (1993). Any basic social science statistical text, however, should be sufficient for finding other tests for various situations. In addition, the most popular statistical computer programs provide descriptions of tests that they rely upon and usually provide relevant examples.

5. You should recognize, however, that this usually involves reducing the precision in the data. For example, if you have an interval measured variable such as age and a nominal level measured variable such as gender, the reduction in precision in the age variable would influence the inference you make from your inferential test at the nominal level.

6. The distinction of interval and ratio levels of measurement is less crucial than the distinctions between nominal, ordinal, or interval and greater. What this means is that tests that are appropriate for interval data are appropriate, at least in practice, for the ratio level of measurement.

7. The example I show here is for a large sample size. There is a small sample size version of the means tests in which the basic difference between the tests is the use of the z distribution in large samples and the Student's t distribution for small samples.

8. There are two requirements for the chi square test. One is that the sample size be at least twenty observations. Second, each expected frequency should be greater than 5. In terms of the second requirement, it is acceptable to still use the chi square test when 25% or less than the expected frequencies are less than 5, but once that threshold is crossed, the chi square is less reliable for making decisions about the null hypothesis.

9. Statisticians have developed tests, such as the "runs test for randomness" (see Kanji, 1993) that allow them to test whether the sample data are actually, not just theoretically, random.

10. For large samples (n>30) the only difference is in the calculation of a z value instead of a t-test value. The standard error formula is also altered because the samples are large (i.e., $\sigma_{\text{standard error}} = \sqrt{(s^2_{\text{one}} \div n_1) + (s^2_{\text{two}} \div n_2)}$) and the z population values should be used in the decision stage of the test.

11. To determine the sign of the population probability values when we have a directional test we refer to the research hypothesis. If the research hypothesis were written symbolically, it would be stated as follows:

$$\text{Research Hypothesis: Mean Weight}_{\text{before}} < \text{Mean Weight}_{\text{after}}$$

That is, the inmates will weigh on average more after the program than before. Since the implied direction of the test is that the second mean will outweigh the first, the population probability value should be negative. If the proposition was that the mean weights decreased over time, then the population probability value would be positive.

12. A calculated independent t-test value is 1.37 with a t critical population value of 2.228. Hence, the more powerful test (the t-test) would require that we retain the null hypothesis. This result may be due to the violation of the homogeneity assumption, however.

Chapter 12: Basic Qualitative Data Analyses

1. In one of the states where I recently conducted prison research, I collected a systematic sample of over 1,400 use of force reports, which detailed nearly eighty different variables about the use of force situations.

2. For example, in the study of the 1,400, use of force reports we also conducted using five hundred officer and inmate interviews, observational studies, and viewed video tapes of use of force incidents in real time. Since the data from all of these diverse qualitative and quantitative sources were in general agreement, we had more confidence in the validity of the use of force reports as well as the interviews.

3. In the 1,400 use of force reports mentioned in note 2, there were narratives of the substance of each use of force incident. These narratives, while hardly as descriptive as a case study, do provide one with insights into the organizational norms of correctional officers using force and the functional realities of such situations.

4. The six general types of qualitative research designs are: (1) human ethnology, where wherein the researcher attempts to understand through observation the range of behaviors that people naturally engage in; (2) ecological psychology, which emphasizes the interaction of the person and the environment through observational studies of persons in their environments; (3) holistic ethnography, an observational approach that attempts to uncover and document participants' perspectives; (4) cognitive anthropology, in which in-depth interviews are used to understand the cognitive meanings of people's perspectives; (5) ethnography of communication, the study of the results of communications (i.e., content analysis); and (6) symbolic interactionism, where the researcher is interested in understanding how individuals take and make meaning in interactions with others (Marshall and Rossman, 1989).

5. A literature review based on one article is hardly sufficient for most research projects, especially considering that there are several studies on newspapers and crime. However, for example purposes, and to focus your attention on one particular question, this is sufficient.

6. To select the sample of six sampling elements, I chose the following random numbers going through the random numbers table. I started with the random start and proceeded down each column of numbers until I reached the end of the table, and then I went to the top of the next column of two digits. Hence, I selected 98, 27 (in sampling frame), 59, 91, 83, next column, 61, 14 (in sampling frame), 75, 90, 55, 88, 36, 06 (in sampling frame), 64, 60, next column, 27 (already in sample), 37, 68, 15 (in sampling frame), 19 (in sampling frame), 46, 98, 67, 79, 59, next column, 84, 74, 04 (in sampling frame) . . . and that concludes the selection of a simple random sample of six days.

7. This program is funded by the U.S. Department of Education for three years.

8. The Ethnograph expects either text files or ASCII code to function. Most, if not all, computer-based word processors allow one to save data as plain text or text only, which is sufficient for the program to operate.

Chapter 13: Research Ethics

1. The initial mailing would cost $14,800 for copying 40,000 surveys, $7,400 for the follow-up surveys, $2,000 for the outgoing envelopes, $16,000 for the outgoing postage, and at least $15,200 for the return envelopes for a grand total of $55,400. There are very few grant sources that are readily available for that amount for just conducting an inmate survey considering there are several other research project costs (such as paying assistants, university overhead, and so on).

2. In 1995, the total federal and state prison population was 909,186; according to the Bureau of Justice Statistics.

3. This survey was based on our search and study of over three hundred past research articles on the fear of crime.

4. The Code of Federal Regulations, Article 45, Part 46, clearly states that research involving the use of survey procedures, as long as the subjects cannot be identified and will not be disclosed, is exempt from the federal human subject protection review policy (p. 117). As I read the Federal Code our research was exempt from review because it is nonintrusive and because subjects would not be identified by any means.

5. His concern was not off base given that the University of Baltimore is located in the midtown area of Baltimore, which is not necessarily a low crime area in a high crime urban area.

6. Muscle samples are generally taken from a person's thigh muscle (i.e., quadriceps) though the insertion of an ice-pick-like probe with a barb on the end, which tears out the muscle tissue sample upon removal. The sample is taken from a depth of one or two inches and is (in my experience) very painful.

7. On the other hand, maybe my students are very good to me and fill in my pretest surveys to help me out or perhaps they feel sorry for me and fill in the questionnaires on that basis. Either way, I have appreciated their cooperation throughout the past few years.

8. These are the two national organizations to which most criminal justice researchers belong.

Chapter 14: Library Research

1. I found that male populations appear to cycle from a peak (i.e., high population) to a valley (i.e., low population) every seven days. This generally corresponded to the court day when most bail decisions where made (Wednesdays), building to a peak on that day. Conversely, the female population took fifty-one days to go from peak to valley. This was due to the seriousness of their offenses and the lack of bail opportunities.

2. There has been very limited cross-overs between practitioners and academics in the current literature. However, many practitioners have published their ideas and research in their trade journals (e.g., *Corrections Today, Police Chief,* and so on).

3. This approach is merely one way to go about developing a researchable topic and is by no means the only way. One particular advantage of this approach, in my opinion, is that it can be applied to many situations and provides a very logical beginning point for formulating a researchable idea or topic.

4. A few companies make portable copiers that I have found are excellent for this purpose. They copy only a few lines at a time, and the copied references can be taped to an 8½-inch-by-11-inch sheet and then copied on a full-sized copier once all of the references are located.

5. In the case of a book, the CJA lists the title and publisher, and for documents, it lists the title and publishing agency.

6. The Criminology, Penology, and Police Science Abstracts have long been known as the Criminology and Penology Abstracts, and the Police Science Abstracts were housed as a separate collection. The publisher decided to incorporate the volumes of both the Police Science Abstracts and the Criminology and Penology Abstracts. So if you spot the former don't get confused. It's the same collection of abstracts. I believe the Criminology and Penology Abstracts are more general than the Police Science Abstracts and therefore may be more useful to you.

Glossary

acceptance error: Another term for beta error or TYPE II error.

accidental sample: A sample based on available subjects. For example, in studying the fear of crime you would be relying on an accidental sample if you talked to the first two hundred people who agreed to complete your survey. Accidental samples are notoriously inaccurate, and there is no way to estimate the true population values from such a poor sampling technique.

alpha error: Rejecting a true null hypothesis or TYPE I error. A way to decrease the chances of committing an alpha error is to increase the test precision through increasing the level of significance. However, this tends to lead to more beta errors.

alpha level: The chance that one is willing to take in committing a TYPE I error, or the probability that a TYPE I error (incorrectly rejecting a true null hypothesis) has been committed.

alternative hypothesis: The same as a research hypothesis. The hypothesis that is not directly tested in inferential analyses. The research can indirectly find support for the alternative hypothesis through rejecting the null hypothesis.

analysis of variance (ANOVA): A statistical test of the differences among the mean scores for three or more groups or variables. The ANOVA tests typically result in an F ratio.

applied research: A more policy-relevant form of research than basic research, which attempts to answer theoretical questions. Applied research attempts to contribute information that can lead to immediate decision making in criminal justice agencies.

association: A group of statistical measures that establishes the level of a relationship as well as its strength. In the context of this text association refers to the relationship statistics between nominal variables.

asymmetrical: A skewed or non-normal distribution is asymmetrical. If sliced in two halves, the distribution is asymmetrical if the two halves are not mirror images of one another.

averages: Point estimates of a distribution or variable. The three most typical averages are the mode (nominal level of measurement), the median (ordinal level of measurement), and the mean (interval or ratio level of measurement).

bar chart or graph: A simple pictorial representation of frequency distribution data for categorical or nominal variables.

Bar Chart of Gender

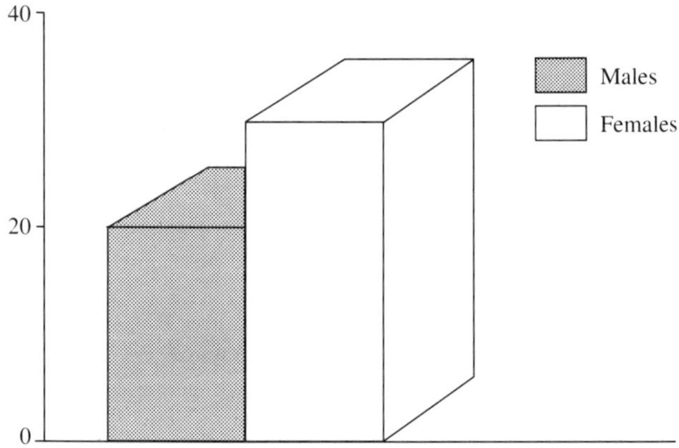

basic research: Research conducted to contribute to the criminological or criminal justice knowledge base. Basic research is most typically conducted on theoretical issues and usually has an indirect applicability to the operational criminal justice system.

bell-shaped curve: A symmetrical curve, also known as a "normal" curve.

beta error: The same as a TYPE II error. A beta error is committed when one retains a false null hypothesis in an inferential test. One way to reduce the chances of committing a beta error is to increase the size of the sample used in the research.

biased estimator: The sample standard deviation is a biased estimator because it tends to underestimate the population standard deviation.

bimodal distribution: A distribution with two modes.

case study: A typical qualitative study wherein the researcher gathers large amounts of qualitative data from individual cases. That is not to say that case studies cannot also collect quantitative data, only that it is more usual that the data collected tend to be interviews or observational.

categorical variable: The same as a nominal level of measurement. A categorical variable differentiates values only by kind. Examples are gender, yes/no opinions, or employed/not employed.

causal: One variable (the independent) causes changes in another variable (the dependent). Causality requires that the two variables (independent and dependent) be related, that the relationship be nonspurious (i.e., not caused by another variable), and that the independent variable precedes the dependent variable in time (e.g., alcohol consumption, the independent variable, can cause people to become drunk, the dependent variable; one cannot become drunk without having first consumed alcohol).

census: A study of the entire population. The Bureau of Justice Statistics regularly conducts a census of all adult correctional facilities in the United States.

Central Limit Theorem: A probability postulation that the larger the sample size, the more closely it will approximate a normal distribution. The larger the sample, the smaller the difference between the sample and the true population values.

central tendency: The measures of average and variation all measure the central tendency or the main descriptive characteristics of a distribution. For example, the average age of inmates is about 29.7 years, and the inmates vary by about 12 percent (CV) around that mean age.

chi square association: The measurement of a relationship between two nominally measured variables. The value can range from 0 (zero) or no relationship between the two variables to a maximum value of N (k − 1) where N = the number of study subjects, and k = the number of categories in the row or column variable, whichever is less.

chi square distribution: A probability distribution that can be used in concert with the chi square test to test hypotheses for nominally measured variables.

chi square test: The calculation of a chi square association value but used in concert with a chi square distribution to test a null hypothesis.

closed format questions: In surveys closed questions require the subjects of research to fill in specific information only within researcher determined and set categories. For example, the following question forces respondents to respond in one of two ways—male or female.

What is your gender ______ male ______ female

codebook: A list of variables in a study and how they have been written. For example, for the following question:

For what type of crime were you most recently convicted?
______ violent
______ property
______ other

the codebook would record 1=violent, 2=property, and 3=other and would also record the column location for the variable, such as the first column, as well as the column width. Basically, the codebook is a road map to a data set as in the following example

Codebook

NO.	NAME	COLUMNS
1	id code	1 to 3
2	variable 1	4
3	variable 2	5 and 6
4	variable 3	7
5	variable 4	8
6	variable 5	9
7	variable 6	10
8	variable 7	11
9	variable 8	12
10	variable 9	13

Data Set

1	2	3	4	5	6	7	8	9	10
001	1	12	1	2	3	2	1	2	1
002	1	23	3	2	3	2	1	3	1
003	2	24	2	3	2	2	1	3	1
004	2	25	1	2	3	2	1	3	1
005	1	27	2	3	4	2	1	4	1
......									
etc.									

coding: The process of turning raw data notes from interviews, data reports, or other sources of research data into a machine readable format.

cohort: A study that examines the same group of people over time. Cohort is another word for a panel study.

concept: An abstract idea. A group of concepts are typically collected into theories. Concepts are also used in the process of operationalization to determine the variables that should be included in the study.

concurrent validity: Determining validity of a variable by measuring its relationship with other variables that is believed to be valid. For example, in a study of prisoner intelligence based on a newly developed test, we would compare the results of the new test with those of tests that have been used in the past.

confidence interval: A range of values based on sample values that is predicted to contain the true population parameter.

constant: A measure that has the same value for all observations. In a study of rookie police officers, the subjects would all be twenty-one years of age.

construct validity: Determining validity by the extent to which variables measure the construct of research interest. One would measure several variables to see whether the variables all measure the same construct of interest. If so, they are considered valid.

content analysis: The analysis of the content of records of communications or administrative or operational activities.

content validity: Validity based on the researcher's judgment of the validity of the measures.

contingency coefficient: A normed chi square measure that can be used on nominal level variables. The contingency coefficient ranges from 0 to 1 in magnitude, and its formula is $C = \sqrt{X^2 \div (X^2 + n)}$

continuous variable: A variable that is measured at either the interval or ratio level of measurement, for example, crime rate or number of inmates.

control group: The group that receives no treatment in an experimental design. Control groups are used to compare the effects of an independent variable with a group where there is no such influence.

control variable: A variable that one does not want to examine. For example, in a study of recidivism rates one might want to control for the gender or race of the inmates.

convenience sample: A sample selected on the basis of availability rather than representativeness. If a researcher selected a sample of inmates from the jail in the county where she resided just because she knew the sheriff, that sample would be a convenience sample. There is no reason to believe the single jail population is representative of the over 3,000 jail populations in the United States.

convergent validity: Validity that is determined by using several measures of the same concept. The several measures should produce similar conclusions if there is convergent validity. For example, if IQ tests, grades, and scores on a standard test are valid people would score similarly on each of these three measures.

correlation: The amount of similarities in magnitudes of the variables. Correlation is another term for relationship. For instance, the correlation between the number of property crimes and the crime rate could be calculated.

correlation coefficients: Measures of the association between variables. There are several common correlation coefficients such as the Pearson's r and the Spearman's rho. Correlation coefficients measure whether both variables increase or decrease (i.e., positive relationship) or whether one increases and the other decreases (i.e., negative relationship). Correlation coefficients are summary measures of the amount of relationship.

covariance: The amount of similarities in the variation in variables. The covariance can be assessed through comparing the individual scores to their means and comparing such variation around the mean.

criterion variable: Another name for the dependent variable.

cross-sectional study: A study of an issue or research question at one point in time. That is, the Survey of Jail Inmates conducted by the Bureau of Justice Statistics in 1983 was a study of jail inmate attitudes on several hundred questions at one point in time.

cross-tabulation: A method of presenting variables (usually of a nominal level) so that their association or relationship is more apparent. For example, the following is a cross-tabulation of opinions of a sample of people toward the death penalty on the basis of their gender.

	For	Against	
Men	27	4	31
Women	7	22	29
	34	26	60

In this example the relationship from the raw data becomes more apparent in the cross-tabulation in the sense that there are more men that are in favor of the death penalty and more women that are against it in the sample of sixty people in this study.

data: The variables represent the data that are used in research. Data are bits of information collected from the study subjects. *Data* is plural and *datum* is singular. Hence, one would say the data *are* normally distributed, not the data *is* normally distributed. Data can be numerical, qualitative, or textual.

data entry: The process of creating machine readable data sets from the data collected from the study subjects.

data point: One datum, or the value of a variable for one individual in the sample (i.e., Alicia is thirty-five years old).

data set: A collection of variables for a group of subjects that have been studied. The U.S. Census is a data set for all of the population.

decision error: A mistake about the null hypothesis relative to making TYPE I or TYPE II errors.

deduction: Using logic that moves from general theories or principles to conclusions about particular instances. For example, one might study differential association theory and attempt to explain juvenile delinquency in Philadelphia.

degrees of freedom: The degrees of freedom to vary, given the reduction in a group of scores due to division or subtraction. From an applied perspective, one need only know the degrees of freedom calculation method, and therefore value, in order to use the population probability tables for inferential tests using chi squares, F's, and t's. In a two variable chi square the degrees of freedom = df = (number of rows − 1) × (number of columns − 1), for example.

dependent samples: Another phrase for samples that are taken of the same group over time. Typically, dependent samples are collected in a pretest and posttest experimental design where the researcher is interested in determining the difference on some dependent variable over time.

dependent variable: The "effect" in a study; the variable that is explained or influenced by the independent variable. For instance, suppose that the amount of crime a person commits depends on his or her age (in general, as age increases, criminality decreases).

descriptive statistics: A group of procedures that summarizes data through reducing its amount or better organizing it. Descriptive statistics generally include measures of average, variation, and relationship.

df: Shorthand for degrees of freedom.

dichotomous variable: A variable that can take on only two possible values for its attributes. For example, the variable gender is dichotomous because one's gender is either male or female. There are, for all intents and purposes, no other possible values.

direct relationship: Another way of stating there is a positive relationship.

discrete variable: A variable that has finite categories for its attributes. Each category is separate. For example, a discrete variable could be police officer rank (i.e., captain, lieutenant, sergeant, and officer). A study of police would have to measure their rank within one of these categories (or additional categories if they exist).

distribution: Another term for a variable that is plotted on a graph showing the lowest to highest values.

distribution-free tests: Also known as parametric tests. These tests (i.e., chi square, Mann-Whitney U, Wilcoxon T, etc.) do not require the data to meet the parametric assumptions of randomness, homogeneity, and normality.

ecological fallacy: A logical error that results when one attempts to make conclusions about individuals based on group data. For example, suppose you found that there is a correlation between the size of the state and the size of its crime problem and then attempted to generalize to cities. You would have committed an ecological fallacy in this case.

elaboration: A process of studying an association between two variables to further explain its meaning. Elaboration is typically done through the addition of control variables that help further explain the relationship between the original two variables.

empirical: Measurable. When one relies on the UCR as an empirical measure of crime rates, one is operating under the belief that the UCR is a measure of the amount of crime. Even qualitative textual data is presumed to be a measure of the topic under study.

empiricism: Belief that empirical data can lead to understanding problems and issues.

equation: A mathematical expression of the functional relationship between variables. Most statistical operations can be represented by equations. Equations provide statisticians with a means of providing a summary of the operations necessary to conduct a certain calculation or set of calculations.

Ethnography: A research method that relies on direct observation of social settings or systems, for example, an observational study of inmates in a podular cell block to study their interactional patterns. Ethnography is a basic form of qualitative research methods.

evaluation research: Research that attempts to answer practical-level and applied questions. Evaluation research often focuses on the evaluation of programs such as vocational education for inmates.

exhaustive: A reference to a nominal or categorical variable where all of the attributes cover every possible response that people could provide. For example, suppose we asked inmates about their marital status, whether they were single or married. This would not be exhaustive because it fails to include "separated" and "divorced." Hence, to include all attributes of the nominal variable marital status one would have to include the exhaustive categories of single, married, separated, and divorced.

expected frequency: The value that would occur in a chi square if there were no relationship between the observed variables. In the following example of opinions toward the death penalty by gender, the expected values are a function of the marginal summary frequencies.

expected value = (row total, 31) × (column total, 34) ÷ total sample size, 60

	For	Against	
Men	**27** (31 × 34) ÷ 60 = 17.57	**4** (31 × 26) ÷ 60 = 13.43	**31**
Women	**7** (29 × 34) ÷ 60 = 16.43	**22** (19 × 26) ÷ 60 = 8.23	**29**
	34	**26**	**60**

experiment: A study that attempts to approximate laboratory conditions. Experiments ideally include a group that is exposed to a treatment or independent variable (the experimental group) and a group that is not exposed to the treatment but which is used as a comparison to the experimental group (control group).

explained variance: The variance in the dependent variable that is explained by the independent variable. The amount of recidivism can be explained, for instance, on the basis of employment.

external validity: The amount of accuracy that the study has in terms of being able to generalize to groups that are not the same as the study subjects or context. External validity is very similar in meaning to "generalization."

F: A test value that corresponds to the Fisher's distribution. ANOVAs and homogeneity tests use the F population probability distribution. The F population probability values can be found in the F distribution, which is listed in most statistical texts.

face validity: Accuracy is established on the basis of the logical reasoning of the researcher. That is, the measures are presumed to be accurate because they appear to measure the concepts under study. The Uniform Crime Reports are a face validity measure of crime rates because they appear to accurately measure crime in the United States.

field experiment: The same meaning as a quasi-experiment in that the experimental design takes place in the "real" world. For example, instead of attempting to measure how people learn through the conduct of a laboratory-based experiment, the researcher would go into a school and conduct the experiment in the actual setting where education is supposed to take place.

field notes: The raw data from an observational or interview-based study. Researchers in qualitative research projects rely on the notes they take during their contact with the study subjects or situation.

fit: A statistical term that typically refers to the correspondence between the actual data and the population probability or statistical model.

formative evaluation: Formative evaluations focus on the overall assessment of the program utility and processes and whether anything can be done to improve these dimensions. In an evaluation of vocational education, the formative evaluation would focus on whether or not the program reduced recidivism and how the program was executed.

frequency: The number of times an observation occurs. In a categorical variable a frequency might be the number of men in the sample (i.e., the frequency of males). On the other hand, for a continuous variable a frequency might be the number of students that scored 80 percent or better on the midterm examination.

frequency distribution: The frequencies for all categories are typically presented in a tabular form that is known as a frequency distribution. For example, the frequency distributions for gender and midterm scores are shown below:

Frequency Distribution (Gender)

Category	Frequency
males	23
females	12
Total	33

Frequency Distribution (Midterm)

Category	Frequency
Above 80%	56
Below 80%	32
Total	88

F test: A statistical test that uses the F distribution. F tests typically are comparisons of the homogeneity of the variation in two or more variables.

generalizability: The extent to which the findings from a sample based study can be applied to a population. For example, it we studied the decision making of a random sample of judges, we would more than likely be interested in the extent to which the sample would allow us to imply that all judges make decisions consistent with the sample.

goodness-of-fit: The more lengthy phrase for "fit." Basically, the goodness-of-fit is the extent to which the sample fits the appropriate probability distribution. Typically social science researchers use the term goodness-of-fit in reference to chi square tests, F tests, and regression modeling although it is not limited to these applications.

graph: The same as "chart" or "figure." Any visual, and typically descriptive, depiction of data can be referred to as a graph.

H_0: The symbolic term for the "null hypothesis."

H_a: The symbolic term for the "research hypothesis." Many researchers also refer to the research hypothesis as the "alternative" hypothesis.

Halo Effect: Researchers may bias their results by giving higher scores to those who have scored high on previous tests or because they like or empathize with the subjects. For example, in a study of how criminal justice students perform on essay examinations vs. multiple choice tests, the researcher might include a Halo Effect for the students she "knows" are smart (i.e., she would give them the benefit of the doubt).

Hawthorne Effect: The tendency for subjects to change their behavior because they know they are being studied. For instance, in a study of inmates, the inmates would use noninstitutional language (i.e., they would not be profane) with the researcher. Hence, they would drop their "prison-speak" because they do not want the researcher to think ill of them.

histogram: A bar graph that represents the frequencies for interval or ratio level variables. The bars in a histogram are connected, whereas those in a bar chart (nominal or ordinal data) are not.

homogeneous: Similar in terms of variation or dispersion. One of the key assumptions of the data in parametric testing is that the background populations of the sample values are homogeneous (i.e., similar).

hypothesis: A speculation about the relationships, differences, or direction of theoretically or conceptually relevant variables. The null hypothesis is typically a statement of no relationship, no differences, or opposite direction, whereas the research hypothesis is one of relationship, difference, and greater or lesser magnitude (see chapter 11).

hypothesis testing: The process of applying inferential statistical tests to the null hypothesis speculation and making a decision (see chapter 11).

independent variable: The presumed explanatory variable or predictive variable. Some researchers also presume that the independent variable is causative, but causation is never an empirical concept, as it is a theoretical one.

index: A group of variables that together measure a general concept. For example, a fear of crime index might include questions on where people fear being a crime victim, the types of crimes they fear most, and so on. The idea behind the creation of indexes is to improve the validity and explanatory power of the variables.

inductive logic: Using specific cases or results to form generalizations or theories; the opposite of deductive logic. For example, if offenders were found to be young, uneducated, and urban residents, then the researcher might suppose that "urbanness" might be one of the causes of criminality.

inferential statistics: The implication that sample statistics are accurate indicators of population parameters. In inferential statistical analyses, one typically calculates a sample statistic and compares it to a population probability value (see chapter 11).

instrument: A method for collecting study data. For example, one might use a survey instrument to collect responses about the opinions of individuals toward the death penalty. In interview studies, the instrument is the interview guideline, and in observational studies, it is the paper on which the researcher takes field notes.

internal consistency: The extent to which the individual variables in an index or scale measure the same concept.

internal validity: The amount of the results of a study that can be imputed to actual differences rather than to problems with the research design. In a study that has methodological difficulties, it would be problematic to state that the study is internally valid.

interrater reliability: The degree of agreement in the data collected by several researchers contributing to the same data set. The more interrater reliability, the better the data. When data collectors disagree about the data, there is less reliability over the course of the data collection.

interval level of measurement: Data that allow one to distinguish observations by their kind, order, and exact magnitude. For example, an interval level variable would be age in years. We know that a twenty-year-old is different than a forty-year-old (i.e., they are different by kind). We also know that 40 is a higher number than 20 (i.e., they are different by their order), and we can determine their differences by exact magnitudes in the sense that the twenty-year-old is half as old as the forty-year-old (i.e., there are differences by exact magnitudes—years).

intervening variable: A third variable that helps to further clarify the relationship between two original variables. For example, suppose a researcher suggests that the quality of programs in prisons is related to the recidivism rates. A third variable that could help clarify this relationship might be the inmates' ages (the intervening variable).

interview schedule: A guideline used to conduct interviews so the researchers can collect more consistent data and so they do not forget to ask specific items of each study subject. Interview guidelines can be very structured (i.e., ask the same exact question in the same order for every subject) to very unstructured (i.e., general list of topics to be covered in the interview).

inverse relationship: Another term for a negative relationship. When there is an inverse relationship one variable increases as the other variable decreases. For instance, if employment and crime are inversely related, the percentage of the population employed would increase as the crime rate decreases.

joint occurrence: The chi square measures the amount of joint occurrence for two categorical variables such that the corresponding measurement of each of the subjects on both variables is simultaneously reported.

judgmental sample: A form of accidental or convenience sampling where the researcher attempts to include subjects that in his or her judgment are representative of the group to which generalization or study focus is directed.

Kolmogorv-Smirnov test: A test for normality wherein the researcher can determine if the sample data that have been collected conform to the normal distribution. If the data are not normal, nonparametric tests should be used with the data.

kurtosis: The symmetrical shape of the distribution of the data. The kurtosis can be flat (i.e., platykurtic), peaked (i.e., leptokurtic), or bell-shaped (i.e., mesokurtic). The characterization of the kurtosis of variables is not the same as assessing their normality but the type of symmetry in the distribution of data. However, if there is an extreme form of kurtosis (i.e., either platykurtic or leptokurtic), there is more likelihood that the distribution will be non-normal.

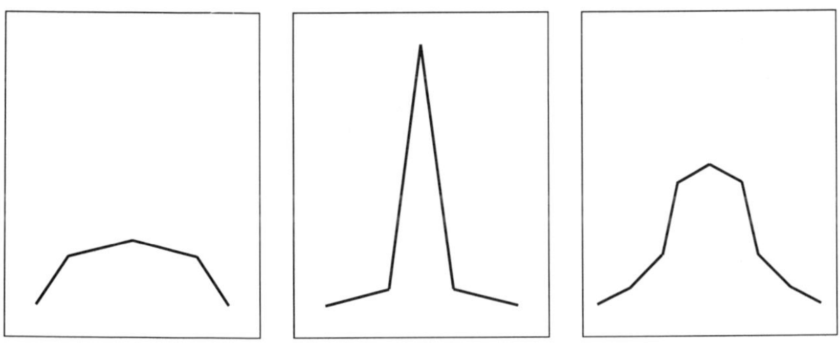

platykurtic leptokurtic mesokurtic

lambda: A measure of association (proportional reduction in error approach as opposed to a chi square approach) for nominal level data where one variable is dependent upon the other. Lambda ranges in value from 0 to 1.

leptokurtic: Very peaked distribution unlike the normal distribution (see *kurtosis*).

level of measurement: The amount of precision in the data that are collected from the sample. There are basically four levels of measurement that are commonly used (nominal, ordinal, interval, and ratio).

level of significance: The probability that would be produced by chance alone. The level of significance is selected in inferential tests (chapter 11). In general, the smaller the level of significance, the fewer decision errors about the null hypothesis. The most common level of significance in the social sciences is .05.

Likert scale: A scale created by Rensis Likert. Respondents are asked to fill in their responses to questions in specific preset categories of strongly agree, agree, disagree, and strongly disagree. Likert scales are very common in criminal justice and criminology studies.

longitudinal studies: Studies that are conducted over time.

Mann-Whitney U test: The nonparametric alternative to the independent t-test. Where the data are not homogeneous, random, or normal, the Mann-Whitney U test is appropriate.

mean: The mathematical average of a distribution of scores for a sample.

measurement error: Errors due to problems with the instrument or instruments created to collect the data. For example, if we were interested in measuring the attitudes of inmates toward officers and found out that they did not read the survey before they filled in a random series of responses, then the questionnaire technique suffers from a large amount of measurement error.

median: The middlemost value in a distribution of scores for a sample.

methodology: The study of research methods.

Milgram: A researcher who conducted unethically designed studies wherein study subjects were asked to shock others (who were working with the researcher) to study how much people obey authority.

mode: The most common value or score in a distribution of scores from a sample.

model: A logical collection of relevant concepts that attempts to explain some phenomenon. Models are precursors to the formulation and design of theories.

multiple correlation: A correlation with more than two variables from a sample.

mutually exclusive: When an observation cannot fall in more than one category of a nominal level variable. For example, if one is married and cannot also be divorced. Although a person that is married today could have been divorced in the past, they cannot be both married and divorced at the same time to the same person. Another example is gender. One cannot be both male and female at the same time.

N: The number of observations in the population (however, not all researchers conform to this convention).

n: The number of observations in the study sample.

negative skew: When a distribution is not normal, and there are more low values than high values. For example, in the following line chart, a negative skewness is shown in the number of witnesses to crimes committed in urban areas.

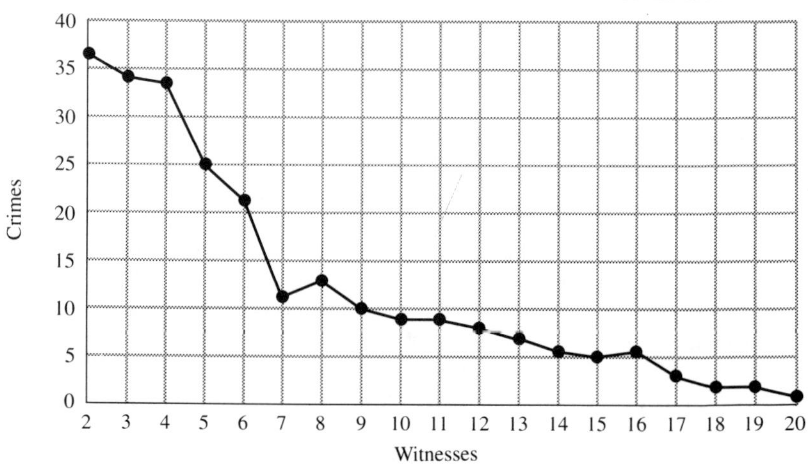

nominal level of measurement: The lowest level of measurement wherein observations can be differentiated only by kind. For example, we can tell the difference between men and women, but there is no other regularity to such data.

normal distribution: A theoretical distribution upon which statistical tests can be based, because it behaves in known ways. The deviations about the mean value are set are regular standard deviation units such that 68% of the scores fall between +1 standard deviation units and −1 standard deviation units. The basis of parametric tests is the normal probability distribution.

null hypothesis: A statement of no difference, no relationship, or opposite the directional research hypothesis (see *research hypothesis* or *alternative hypothesis*).

observational study: A research design wherein the researcher collects data on the basis of direct contact with the study subjects in the settings in which they are found. For example, a researcher might get permission to study the administrative process of the juvenile court through being permitted to observe their proceedings (he or she would take field notes on such an experiment as the instrument of data collection).

observed frequencies: In a chi square analysis, the observed frequencies are those values that are observed or collected from the sample subjects. For example, the observed values for the sample of sixty people toward the death penalty could be as follows:

	For	Against	
Men	27	4	31
Women	7	22	29
	34	26	60

open-ended questions: Questions on a data collection instrument (usually a survey) wherein the researcher does not restrict or categorize the responses before the study subjects respond to the study.

one-tailed tests: A test wherein the researcher has a directional hypothesis. One-tailed tests are generally more specific than nondirectional or relationship based hypotheses.

H_r: There are more male recidivists than female recidivists.

one-way ANOVA: A statistical test that allows one to compare the means of three or more groups. For example, we might compare the average recidivism rates for a sample of former prison inmates, offenders who served a sentence of probation, and a group of offenders who were sentenced to boot camp.

operationalize: The process of defining variables that represent specific concepts, or portions of concepts, that will be collected from the study subjects. When researchers operationalize they impose their ideas about how a concept should be measured on the study situation. For example, the concept of "criminality" can be operationalized as the number of arrests a subject has had in the past year.

ordinal level of measurement: A level of measurement that differentiates observations by both kind and order. For example, police officer rank differentiates officers (i.e., a patrol officer is different from a captain) and there is a specific order to the ranks (i.e., captain is a higher rank than lieutenant).

panel study: A longitudinal study wherein the same group is studied over time. A study of inmates from arrest through sentence completion to determine how the criminal justice system works in practice could be conducted by following the same group of people throughout the process.

parameter: A characteristic of a population (i.e., its mean, standard deviation, and so on) as opposed to characteristics of samples (e.g., statistics).

parametric statistics: A group of statistical tests that requires data that are normally distributed, have homogeneous background populations, and are randomly selected. Researchers typically test the normality, homogeneity, and randomness of data before using the parametric tests. In general the parametric statistics are considered to be superior to nonparametric statistics in terms of accuracy.

Pearson's correlation coefficient: A common correlation measure of the linear relationship between two interval or ratio measured variables (see chapter 10).

phi coefficient (ϕ): A measure of the association between two nominally measured variables when there are only two categories of each variable. Phi is appropriate then when one wants an association measure between gender (males or females) and opinion about the criminal justice system (good or bad).

pie chart: A chart that represents the proportions of categorical observations in each category. For example, the proportions of male and female inmates is shown in the following pie chart:

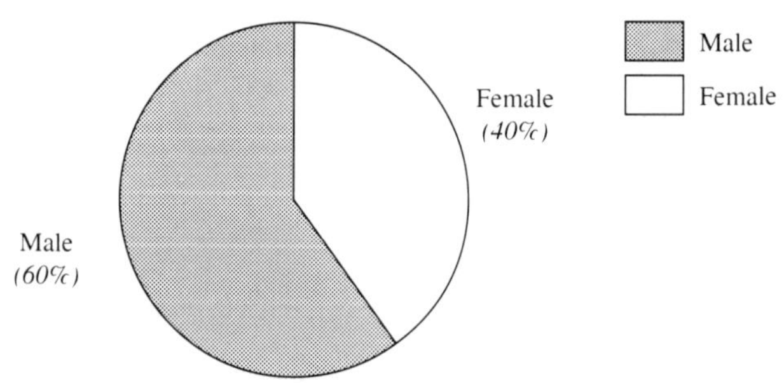

platykurtic: A flat distribution. See *kurtosis.*

point estimates: Averages (mode, median, and mean) are point estimates of the distribution of variables. Point estimates summarize the values in a variable in one number.

population: The total persons in a study. Most criminal justice research focuses on the study of samples in an attempt to generalize to the population.

positive skew: When a distribution is not normal and there are more high values than low values. For example, in the following line chart, a positive skewness is shown in the number of witnesses to crimes committed in urban areas.

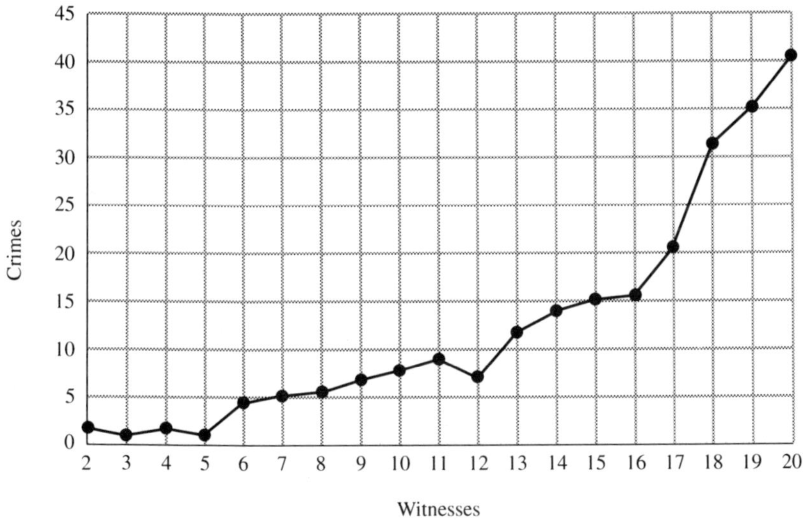

post hoc comparisons: After one conducts an ANOVA all that is known is that the means of the three or more groups are different. However, one has no idea which of the groups are significantly different from each other. Post hoc comparisons (e.g., Tukey, Shefle, and so on) allow the research to test such subgrouping differences.

posttest: A retesting of the study subjects once an experimental treatment has been given.

predictive validity: The ability of the variable to be consistent with past research; the ability of the variable to predict about performance in an experiment, for example.

pretest: Testing the study subjects prior to the experimental treatment.

probability: The likelihood that an event will occur. However, an inferential testing (as in chapter 11), probability is used to establish how populations should behave in the long run. That is, in inferential testing we generally compare a sample statistic with a population probability value in order to make a decision about our null hypothesis.

probability distributions: There are several distributions of population probability values upon which decisions about sample statistics can be based (e.g., t-distribution, F-distribution, normal distribution, chi square distribution, and so on).

proportional reduction in error: Measures the association between nominal or ordinal level variables through predicting the reduction in errors rather than on the basis of no association, as in the chi square approach. Common proportional reduction in error measures (PRE) are lambda and Gamma.

purposive sample: A sample selected either for a specific purpose or because the researchers believe, on the basis of their expertise, that the sample is fairly representative of the population. Purposive samples are nonparametric as they have limited basis in probability theory given the manner of their selection.

qualitatitive data: Variables that are non-numerical. Nominal variables can be assigned numerical labels, but such numbers have no mathematical meanings. Qualitative data can also refer to long interviews or field notes wherein the researcher has textual information.

quantitative data: Numerical data upon which most statistical analyses depend. That is, statistical analyses cannot be conducted on non-numerical data.

quasi-experiments: Experimental designs that take place in the "real" world wherein the independent variables may not be randomly assigned. Quasi-experiments are often necessary in criminal justice research because few prison wardens, for example, would allow a researcher to randomly assign inmates to programs.

questionnaire: A survey that the study subjects fill in themselves.

quota sample: A nonprobability sample by which the researcher can understand the general characteristics of the population (i.e., age, race, gender, and so on). For example, in a study of fear of crime on campus one might ask four women (on the basis of accidental selection) and six men to participate because the campus has 60 percent male students and 40 percent female students.

r: Symbol for Pearson's correlation coefficient.

r^2: Symbol for the coefficient of determination.

random error: Errors that are based on random variation in the data. This type of error cannot be controlled because it is actually in the data and not the result of the data collection as in measurement error.

random numbers: A table of numbers in which each and every number is not dependent upon the one that came before it or after it. Used to select random samples through attaching a numeric label to each subject in the population and moving through the table (i.e., down the columns) until the desired sample size is selected.

random sampling: Sampling where each and every element (i.e., possible subject in the population) has an equal and independent chance of being included in the study sample. Typically, random sampling is based on random numbers tables or computer generated random selection of subjects (see chapter 7).

range: A measurement of variation for ordinal level data that indicates the dispersion in the scores.

ratio level of measurement: Data for observations that differentiate the observations by kind, order, and magnitude and have a true zero point. Income is an example of a ratio level variable. For example, we know that a $10,000 per year salary is different than $30,000 per year (kind), that the second salary is three times higher than the first, and that there is a meaningful numeric difference between $1,000 and $1,001, and that there are some who have no income.

region of rejection: Area in the population probability distribution wherein it is unlikely that a sample value of the type found would be the case in, for example, 95 percent of the cases.

regression: A statistical technique used when one wants to predict the scores of a dependent variable based on the scores of one or more independent variables. A basic regression function is y = a + bx + e, where y is the predicted value, a is the intercept, b is the slope and x is the independent variable.

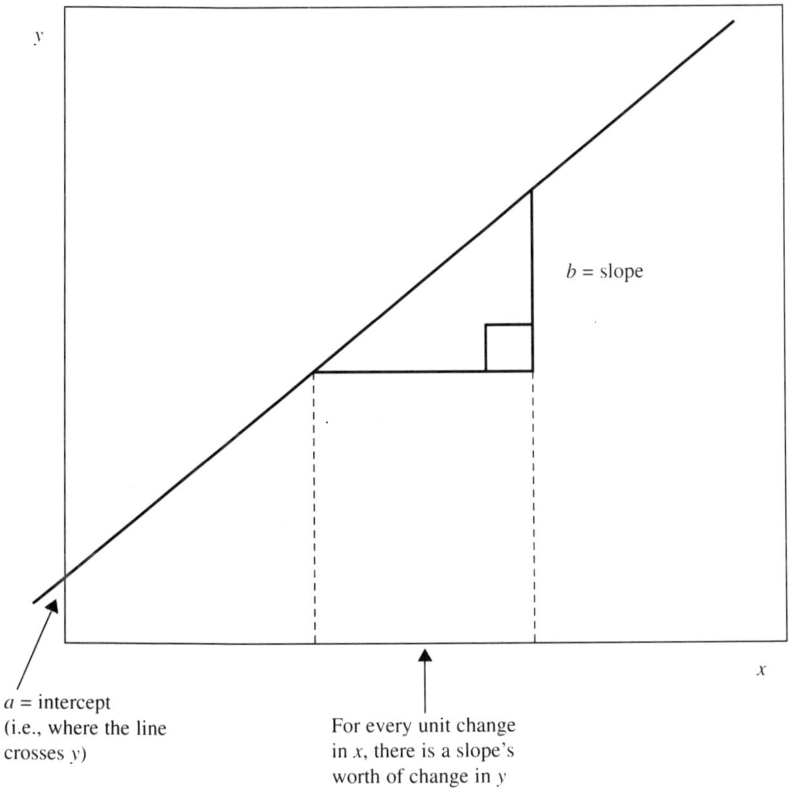

reliability: The amount of consistency in the measurements or observations that are used in a particular study. When there is a lot of consistency, the data are reliable.

replication: When a researcher repeats a prior study to attempt to get the same result to increase the believability and strength of research findings. The emphasis in criminal justice and criminological research has not been heavy on replication of past research.

research: A systematic investigation of phenomena, behavior, or processes that relies on empirical data and logical study and analysis.

research design: The road map or plan for conducting research. There are both quantitative and qualitative research designs, and many researchers will employ both in a given research situation.

research hypothesis: Another name for the alternative hypothesis.

sample: A group of subjects selected as a representation of the larger study population. Inferential statistics are calculated on the basis of sample data.

sampling error: The difference between the sample and the population from which it is drawn. The larger the sample, the more representative of the population it tends to be.

sampling frame: The actual list of subjects in the population from which the study sample is taken. Populations are rarely directly available for study, so researchers are forced to use the best possible list of the population. For example, in order to study probation officers I obtained a list from the American Correctional Association of the 4,700 probation officers that are members in the ACA. I then selected a sampling frame from that "population" upon which my study was based.

sampling with replacement: When a subject is selected from the sampling frame and then placed back into the sampling frame. Sampling with replacement is what probability theory assume happens when a study sample is selected: each subject has an equal and independent chance of being included in the study.

scale: A group of variables that are presumed to measure the same general dimension. The difference between a scale and an index is that the former has some order or intensity structure whereas the latter are merely like measures. For example, a scale on opinions toward the death penalty would measure whether the subjects agreed, strongly agreed, or disagreed, whereas an index would merely measure for or against.

scatter plot: A chart that shows the pattern of a relationship between two variables.

secondary analysis: A study wherein the researcher reuses the data that have been collected by other researchers. Typically, the second analysis uses the data for a different purpose than the first researcher had in mind.

selection bias: A threat to validity that relates to the selection of study subjects. If inmates in programs are evaluated, they might be different than inmates who would not choose to be in programs, and hence the data from such self-determined groups of inmates may not be generalizable to the population of all inmates.

significance level: The probability of rejecting a true null hypothesis (i.e., committing a TYPE I error). Also know as the alpha level.

skewness: The difference between a distribution of scores and a normal distribution. See *positive skew* and *negative skew*.

slope: The change in the dependent variable that is accompanied by a 1 unit change in the independent variable. For instance, suppose we found that years of education predicts the number of arrests based on the following regression equation: y = 12.34 − 2.75Xi + e. The slope (−2.75) shows that for every year of education, there is a 2.75 decrease in the number of arrests.

Spearman's rho: A measure of the relationship between two ordinally measured variables.

split half reliability: A test of the consistency of data measures based on a comparison of half the questions with the other half of the questions. High correlations between the two halves of a survey or questionnaire indicates high reliability.

SPSS: The statistical package for the social sciences; a comprehensive software system that conducts statistical analyses most commonly used in the social sciences. SPSS comes in DOS, Windows, and Mainframe computing versions as well as in a student version.

spurious relationship: When the relationship between two variables is explained by a third variable, the relationship between the original variables is spurious.

standard deviation: A measure of variation for interval and ratio measured variables wherein scores are measured in terms of their standard units from the mean score.

standard score: A transformation computed on individual scores in a distribution that makes them comparable to the standard scores for another distribution. A common standard score used in criminal justice and criminology is the z score.

statistic: A numerical characteristic of sample data.

statistically significant: When the sample statistic is significantly larger than the population probability value.

subject: An individual that is included in a study.

systematic sample: A sample wherein every nth element from the sampling frame is taken for the study sample. For example, in a study of 1,000 police officers, a systematic sample could take every tenth officer consecutively shown on a list as the basis for study. Systematic samples are pseudo-random in that if there is no bias in the list they tend to approximate a random sample.

test-retest reliability: Establishing reliability through the use of several applications of the same questionnaire and comparing the results of each application to the previous application. The more consistency there is in the results across applications (i.e., the more they are the same), the more reliable is the questionnaire instrument.

theory: A speculation about how phenomena, behaviors, or processes are caused or take place.

transformation: The adjustment of values through the use of creating percentages or turning them into logarithms. Transformation makes the data easier to handle at the analysis stage.

triangulation: Using more than one method to study the same thing (i.e., interviews, surveys, observation, and so on). The idea behind triangulation is that one can learn more about different aspects of the topic as well as collect measure that, if they agree, will contribute to the power of the results.

two-tailed or nondirectional test of significance: Used when one is interested in conducting a research study wherein only the differences between the groups are of concern. See *one-tailed test.*

TYPE I error: The chance of rejecting a true null hypothesis. This can be reduced through increasing the precision of the significance level.

TYPE II error: The chance of retaining a false null hypothesis. This can be reduced through increasing the sample size.

units of analysis: That which one collects data about. For example, a researcher can collect data from inmates (individuals as the units of analysis), cell blocks (groups as the units of analysis), prisons (organizations as the units of analysis), or officer logs (artifacts of communications as the units of analysis).

validity: The accuracy of one's measures; the degree to which the measured variables accurately measure the requisite theoretical concepts in one's study.

variables: The measured qualities or quantities of theoretical concepts. Variables consist of attributes. For example, the attributes of the variable "gender" are male and female, whereas the attributes of the variable "age" are the individual years.

variation: The amount of dispersion in the scores across the range of all scores in a distribution; how much the scores as a group differ from one another. Variation is the second key characteristic of the *Central Limit Theorem*; the first is the *average.*

weighted mean: Controls for the differences in sample sizes to produce a more accurate average of the measure across two groups. For example, suppose in our sample of twelve men the average age is 34.23 and for a sample of five women the average age is 23.61. Without controlling for the differences in the male and female samples, we might calculate the mean as follows: $(34.23 + 23.16) \div 2 = 28.9$. Yet this does not take into account that there are twice as many males in the sample than females. A weighted mean takes the sample sizes into account as follows: $[(34.23 \times 12) + (23.16 \times 5)] \div 17 = 30.97$. Hence, the weighted mean is a more accurate average measure.

Wilcoxon T test: A nonparametric alternative to the dependent t-test. This test is used when the data do not meet the parametric assumptions of normally distributed data, homogeneity of the background populations, and randomness.

z score: Common standard score that transforms data into a unit of normal distribution where the mean is 0 and the standard deviation is 1. Standard scores allow researchers to compare different distributions for different variables.

References

Alexander, S.L. (1991). Cameras in the courtroom: A case study. *Judicature, 74*(6): 307–313.

Allen, H., Carlson, E., and Parks, E. (1979). *Critical Issues in Adult Probation: Issues in Probation Management.* Washington, DC: U.S. Government Printing Office.

Archambeault, W.G. (1982). Management Theory Z: Implications for correctional survival management. *Federal Probation, 46*(3): 7–11.

Archambeault, W.G., and Archambeault, B.J. (1989). *Computers in Criminal Justice Administration and Management: Introduction to Emerging Issues and Applications.* 2d ed. Cincinnati, OH: Anderson.

Babbie, E. (1989). *The Practice of Social Research.* 5th ed. Belmont, CA: Wadsworth.

Bailey, K.D. (1978). *Methods of Social Research.* New York: Free Press.

Baker, T.L. (1988). *Doing Social Research.* New York: McGraw-Hill.

Balch, R. (1972). The police personality: Fact or fiction? *Journal of Criminal Law, Criminology, and Police Science, 63:* 117–124.

Becker, G.S. (1968). Crime and punishment: An economic approach. *Journal of Political Economy,* 76(2): 169–217.

Belkin, J., Blumstein, A., and Glass, W. (1971). JUSSIM: An Interactive Computer Program for Analysis of Criminal Justice Systems. Unpublished user's manual.

Binder, A., and Geis, G. (1983). *Methods of Research in Criminology and Criminal Justice.* New York: McGraw-Hill.

Boland, B., and Forst, B. (1984). *The Prevalence of Guilty Pleas.* Bureau of Justice Statistics. Washington, DC: U.S. Government Printing Office.

Boyle, G.J., and Langley, P.D. (1989). *Elementary Statistical Methods for Students of Psychology, Education and the Social Sciences.* Elmsford, NY: Pergamon Press.

Braswell, M.C., McCarthy, B.R., and McCarthy, B.J. (Eds.). (1991). *Justice, Crime, and Ethics.* Cincinnati, OH: Anderson.

Breci, M.G., and Murphy, J.E. (1992). What do citizens want police to do at domestics: Enforce the law or provide services? *American Journal of Police, 11*(3): 53–68.

Brent, E. (1984). Qualitative computing: Approaches and issues. *Qualitative Sociology, 7,* 34–60.

Bridgman, P.W. (1945). *The Logic of Modern Physics.* New York: Macmillan.

Bureau of Justice Statistics. (1983). *Report to the Nation on Crime and Justice.* Washington, DC: U.S. Government Printing Office.

Bureau of Justice Statistics. (1993a). *Correctional Populations in the United States, 1991.* U.S. Dept. of Justice. Washington, DC: U.S. Government Printing Office.

Bureau of Justice Statistics. (1993b). Highlights from 20 Years of Surveying Crime Victims: The National Crime Victimization Survey, 1973–92. Office of Justice

Programs, Bureau of Justice Statistics, U.S. Dept. of Justice. Washington, DC: U.S. Government Printing Office.

Burgess, E.W. (1923). The growth of the city. *Proceedings of the American Sociological Society, 18*: 85–89.

Burgess, E.W. (1929). Urban Areas. In *Chicago: An Experiment in Social Science,* T.V. Smith and L.D. White (Eds.). Chicago, IL: University of Chicago Press.

Camp, G., and Camp, C. (1991). *The Corrections Yearbook.* Salem, NY: Criminal Justice Institute.

Campbell, D.T., and Stanley, J.C. (1963). *Experimental and Quasi-Experimental Designs for Research.* Chicago, IL: Rand McNally.

Canter, S. (1993). Statistical analysis: State of the art. *PC Magazine, 12*(9): 227–287.

Carey, J.T. (1984). The professionalization of probation: An analysis of the diffusion of ideas. In *Probation and Justice: Reconsideration of Mission,* McAnany, P.D., Thompson, D., Fogel, D. (Eds.) Cambridge, MA: Oelgeschlager, Gunn and Hain.

Cavender, G., and Bond, M.L. (1993). Fear and loathing on reality television: An analysis of America's Most Wanted and Unsolved Mysteries. *Sociological Inquiry, 63*(3): 305–317.

Chapin, S.F. (1955). *Experimental Design in Sociological Research.* New York: Harper.

Chelimsky, E. (1991). On the social science contribution to governmental decision-making. *Science, 254*(11): 226–231.

Chiricos, T.G. (1987). Roles of crime and employment: An analysis of aggregate research evidence. *Social Problems, 34*(2): 187–212.

Clear, T.R., and Hardyman, P.L. (1990). The new intensive supervision movement. *Crime and Delinquency, 36*(1): 42–60.

Clear, T.R., and O'Leary, V. (1983). *Controlling the Offender in the Community.* Lexington, MA: Lexington Books.

Cloward, R.A. (1975). Social control in prison. In *Theoretical Studies in Social Organization of the Prison,* Cloward, R.A., Cressey, D.R., Grosser, G.H., McCleery, R., Ohlin, L.E., Sykes, G.M., and Messinger, S.L. (Eds.). Millwood, NY: Kraus Reprint Co.

Code of Federal Regulations. (1993). Protection of Human Subjects. Article 45, Part 46, Sections 101 to 409. Washington, DC: Office of the Federal Register, National Archives and Records Administration.

Conrad, P., and Reinharz, S. (1984). Computers and qualitative data: Editor's introductory essay. *Qualitative Sociology, 7*(3): 15.

Cook, T.D., and Campbell, D.T. (1979). *Quasi-Experimentation: Design and Analysis Issues for Field Settings.* Chicago, IL: Rand McNally.

Cressey, K.D. (1993). *Other People's Money: A Study of the Social Psychology of Embezzlement.* New York: Free Press.

Crew, B.K. (1991). Sex differences in criminal sentencing: Chivalry or patriarchy? *Justice Quarterly, 8*(1): 59–83.

Crime and Justice Data. (1992). CD-ROM issued by the ICPSR from the Bureau of Justice Statistics, U.S. Dept. of Justice.

Crime Victimization Data, 1973–1991. (1993). CD-ROM issued by the ICPSR from the Bureau of Justice Statistics, U.S. Dept. of Justice.

Crouch, B.M., and Damphousse, K.R. (1992). Newspapers and the anti-satanism movement: A content analysis. *Sociological Spectrum, 12*(1): 1–20.

Crowley, J.E. (1984). Delinquency and employment: Substitutions or spurious associations? In *Youth and the Labor Market*, M.E. Borus (Ed.). Kalamazoo, MI: Upjohn Institute for Employment Research.

Cullen, F., Link, B., Wolfe, N., and Frank, J. (1985). The social dimensions of correctional officer stress. *Justice Quarterly, 2*(4): 505–533.

Denzin, N.K. (1978). *Sociological Methods: A Sourcebook.* 2d ed. New York: McGraw-Hill.

Department of Justice. (1978). *The Nation's Toughest Drug Law: Evaluating the New York Experience.* Washington, DC: U.S. Government Printing Office.

Di Leonardi, J.W., and Curtis, P.A. (1988). *What to Do When the Numbers Are In: A User's Guide to Statistical Data Analysis in the Human Services.* Chicago, IL: Nelson-Hall.

Dillman, D.A., Christensen, J.A., Carpenter, E.H., and Brooks, R.M. (1974). Increasing mail questionnaire response: A four state comparision. *American Sociological Review, 39*: 755–781.

Elifson, K.W., Runyon, R.P., and Haber, A. (1990). *Fundamentals of Social Statistics.* 2d ed. New York: McGraw-Hill.

Erwin, B.S., and Bennett, L.A. (1987). *New Dimensions in Probation: Georgia's Experience with Intensive Probation Supervision.* U.S. Dept. of Justice, National Institute of Justice, Research in Brief. Washington, DC: U.S. Government Printing Office.

Evans, B.J., Coman, G.J., and Stanley, R.O. (1992). The police personality: Type A behavior and trait anxiety. *Journal of Criminal Justice, 20*(5): 429–441.

Felkenes, G.T., and Schroedel, J.R. (1993). A case study of minority women in policing. *Women and Criminal Justice, 4*(2): 65–89.

Fisher, R.A. (1971). *The Design Experiments.* New York: Hafner.

Fitzgerald, J.D., and Cox, S.M. (1994). *Research Methods in Criminal Justice: An Introduction.* 2d ed. Chicago, IL: Nelson-Hall.

Flanagan, T.J. (1980). Time served and institutional misconduct: Patterns of involvement in disciplinary infractions among long-term and short-term inmates. *Journal of Criminal Justice, 8*: 357–367.

Flanagan, T.J. (1982). Discretion in the prison justice system: A study of sentencing in institutional disciplinary proceedings. *Journal of Research in Crime and Delinquency, 19*(2): 216–237.

Gardner, R. (1981). Guard stress. *Corrections Magazine, 7*: 6–14.

Geertz, C. (1983). Thick description: Toward an interpretative theory of culture. In *Contemporary Field Research,* Robert M. Emerson (Ed.). Prospect Heights, IL: Waveland Press.

Glaser, B., and Strauss, A. (1967). *The Discovery of Grounded Theory.* Chicago, IL: Aldine.

Gleason, S. (1978). Hustling: The inside economy of a prison. *Federal Probation, 42*: 32–39.

Goetting, A., and Howser, R.M. (1986). Correlates of prison misconduct. *Journal of Quantitative Criminology, 2*(1): 49–67.

Greenberg, D.F. (1991). Modeling criminal careers. *Criminology, 29*(1): 17–46.

Greene, J.R., and Bynum, T.S. (1982). T.V. crooks: Implications of the latent role models for theories of delinquency. *Journal of Criminal Justice, 10*(3): 177–190.

Greenfield, L. (1986). *Probation and Parole, 1984.* Bureau of Justice Statistics. Washington, DC: U.S. Government Printing Office.

Groeneveld, T., and Brian, G.A. (1985). Short-term human relations training for corrections personnel. *Canadian Journal of Criminology, 27*(1): 97–101.

Groves, R.M., and Kahn, R.L. (1979). *Surveys by Telephone: A National Comparison with Personal Interviews.* New York: Academic Press.

Guide to Resources and Services. (1993–1994). Ann Arbor, MI: Inter-University Consortium for Political and Social Research (ICPSR).

Hagan, F.E. (1986). *Introduction to Criminology: Theories, Methods, and Criminal Behavior.* Chicago, IL: Nelson-Hall.

Hagan, F.E. (1989). *Research Methods in Criminal Justice and Criminology.* 2d ed. New York: Macmillan.

Hagan, F.E. (1993). *Research Methods in Criminal Justice and Criminology.* 3d ed. New York: Macmillan.

Hagan, F.E. (1994). *Introduction to Criminology: Theories, Methods, and Criminal Behavior.* 3d ed. Chicago, IL: Nelson-Hall.

Hagedorn, J. (1988). *People and Folks: Gangs, Crime, and the Underclass in a Rust Belt City.* Chicago, IL: Lake View Press.

Heal, K., and Ekblum, P. (1981). Coping with public demand: A challenge for police management. *Police Studies, 4*(3): 3–8.

Hepburn, J.R. (1985). The exercise of power in coercive organizations: A study of prison guards. *Criminology, 23*(1): 145–164.

Hepburn, J.R., and Albonetti, C. (1980). Role conflict in correctional institutions. *Criminology, 17*: 445–459.

Hessler, R. (1983). Using computers to organize qualitative field notes in a methods class. Paper presented at the 47th Annual Meeting of the Midwest Sociological Society, Kansas City, MO.

Hinkle, D.E., Wiersma, W., and Jurs, S.G. (1994). *Applied Statistics for the Behavioral Sciences.* 3d ed. Boston, MA: Houghton Mifflin.

Holmes, M.D., and Taggart, W.A. (1989). A comparative analysis of research methods in criminology and criminal justice journals. *Justice Quarterly, 7*(2): 421–437.

Homant, R.J., and Kennedy, D.B. (1984). A content analysis of statements about policewomen's handling of domestic violence. *American Journal of Police, 3*(2): 265–283.

Johnson, R. (1987). *Hard Time: Understanding and Reforming the Prison.* Monterey, CA: Brooks/Cole.

Johnson, R. (1990). *Death Work: A Study of the Modern Execution Process.* Pacific Grove, CA: Brooks/Cole.

Jones, A. (1986). Self-mutilation in prison: A comparison of mutilators and nonmutilators. *Criminal Justice and Behavior, 13*: 286–296.

Kalinich, D.B. (1980). *The Inmate Economy.* Lexington, MA: Lexington Books.

Kalinich, D.B. (1986). *Power, Stability, and Contraband: The Inmate Economy.* Prospect Heights, IL: Waveland Press.

Kalinich, D.B., and Senese, J.D. (1988). Police discretion and the mentally disordered in Chicago: A reconsideration. *Police Studies, 10*(4): 185–191.

Kanji, G. (1993). *100 Statistical Tests.* Newbury Park, CA: Sage.

Katz, J. (1983). A theory of qualitative methodology: The social system of analytic fieldwork. In *Contemporary Field Research,* R.M. Emerson (Ed.). Boston, MA: Little, Brown.

Katz, J., Capron, A.M., and Glass, E.S. (1972). *Experimentation with Human Beings.* New York: Russell Sage Foundation.

Kelling, G., et al. (1974). *The Kansas City Preventive Patrol Experiment: A Summary Report.* Washington, DC: Police Foundation.

Kerle, K. (1992). Editor's letter. *American Jails, 5*: 9.

King, G., Keohane, R.O., and Verba, S. (1994). *Designing Social Inquiry: Scientific Inference in Qualitative Research.* Princeton, NJ: Princeton University Press.

Klockers, C. (1980). The Dirty Harry problem. *Annuals of the American Political Science Association, 452*: 33–47.

Klofas, J.M., Stojkovic, S., and Kalinich, D.B. (1992). The meaning of correctional crowding: Steps toward an index of severity. *Crime and Delinquency, 38*(2): 171–188.

Klofas, J.M., and Toch, H. (1982). The guard subculture myth. *Journal of Research in Crime and Delinquency, 19*: 238–254.

Kraemer, H.C., and Thiemann, S. (1987). *How Many Subjects? Statistical Power Analysis in Research.* Newbury Park, CA: Sage.

Kratcoski, P. (1985). The functions of classification models in probation and parole: Control or treatment-rehabilitation? *Federal Probation, 49*: 49–56.

Kuhn, T.S. (1962). *The Structure of Scientific Revolutions.* 2d ed., enlarged. Chicago, IL: University of Chicago Press.

Lindblom, C.E., and Cohen, D.K. (1979). *Usable Knowledge: Social Science and Social Problem Solving.* New Haven, CT: Yale University Press.

Linguanti, F., and McIntyre, J. (1992). Public attitudes toward the police: Methodology and questionnaire. *Canadian Police College Journal, 16*(4): 251–262.

Lipton, D., Martinson, R., and Wilks, J. (1975). *The Effectiveness of Correctional Treatment.* New York: Praeger.

Liska, A.E., and Baccaglini, W. (1990). Feeling safe by comparison: Crime in the newspapers. *Social Problems, 37*(3): 360–374.

Longmire, D.R. (1991). Ethical dilemmas in the research setting: A survey of experiences and responses in the criminological community. In *Justice, Crime and Ethics,* Braswell, M.C., McCarthy, B.R., and McCarthy, B.J. (Eds.). Cincinnati, OH: Anderson.

Lorr, M., and Strack, S. (1994). Personality profiles of police candidates. *Journal of Clinical Psychology, 50*(2): 200–207.

Lundman, R.J. (1980). Police Behavior: A Sociological Perspective. New York: Oxford University Press.

Lutz, G.M. (1983). *Understanding Social Statistics.* New York: Macmillan.

Marquart, J.W. (1986). Prison guards and the use of physical coercion as a mechanism of prisoner control. *Criminology, 24*(2): 347–366.

Marshal, C., and Rossman, G.B. (1989). *Designing Qualitative Research.* Newbury Park, CA: Sage.

Martin, D.W. (1985). *Doing Psychology Experiments.* Monterey, CA: Brooks/Cole.

McCarthy, B.R. (1991). Ethics and criminal justice research. In *Justice, Crime and Ethics.* Braswell, M.C., McCarthy, B.R., and McCarthy, B.J. (Eds.). Cincinnati, OH: Anderson.

McDonald, W. (1985). *Plea Bargaining: Critical Issues and Common Practices.* Washington, DC: U.S. Government Printing Office.

McGahan, P. (1992). Public awareness of policing initiatives. *Canadian Police College Journal, 16*(1): 24–46.

Miles, M.B., and Huberman, A.M. (1984). *Qualitative Data Analysis: A Sourcebook of New Methods.* Beverly Hills, CA: Sage.

Milgram, S. (1963). Behavioral study of obedience. *Journal of Abnormal Social Psychology, 67*: 371–378.

Moos, R.H. (1968). The assessment of the social climates of correctional institutions. *Journal of Research in Crime and Delinquency, 5*(2): 174–188.

Nachmias, D., and Nachmias, C. (1981). *Research Methods in the Social Sciences.* 2d ed. New York: St. Martin's Press.

National Advisory Commission. (1973). *National Advisory Commission on Criminal Justice Standards and Goals, Courts.* Washington, DC: U.S. Government Printing Office.

National Crime Survey Codebook. (1992). *National Crime Victims Survey, 1986–1991.* 4th ed. U.S. Dept. of Justice, Bureau of Justice Statistics. Ann Arbor, MI: Inter-University Consortium for Political and Science Research.

Niederhoffer, A. (1967). *Behind the Shield: The Police in Urban Society.* Garden City, NY: Doubleday.

Northrop, F.S.C. (1965). *The Logic of the Sciences and the Humanities.* Cleveland, OH: World.

Patton, M.Q. (1990). *Qualitative Evaluation and Research Methods.* 2d ed. Newbury Park, CA: Sage.

Pearson, F.S., and Bibel, D.B. (1986). New Jersey's intensive supervision program: What is it like? How is it working? *Federal Probation, 50*(2): 25–31.

Petersilia, J. .(1991). Policy relevance and the future of criminology. *Criminology, 29*(1): 1–15.

Poole, E.D., and Regoli, R. M. (1980). Role stress, custody orientation, and disciplinary actions. *Criminology, 18*(2): 215–226.

Poole, E.D., and Regoli, R.M. (1983). Self-reported and observed rule-breaking: A look at disciplinary response. Paper presented at the American Academy of Criminal Justice Sciences Meeting, San Antonio, TX.

Powell, D. (1981). Race, rank, and police discretion. *Journal of Police Science and Administration, 9*: 383–389.

Pratt, C.E. (1992). The great police search. *Law and Order, 40*(1): 190–193.

Priestly, J. (1772). *The History and Present State of Discoveries Relating to Vision, Light, and Colours.* Report from the London Statistical Society.

Rapaport, E. (1991). The death penalty and gender discrimination. *Law and Society Review, 25*(2), 367–383.

Reeves, I.S.K. (1992). Smart shading: Judicious use of color benefits inmates and staff. *Corrections Today, 54*(2): 128–130.

Reiss, A.J. (1971). *The Police and the Public.* New Haven, CT: Yale University Press.

Reynolds, P.D. (1979). *Ethical Dilemmas and Social Science Research.* San Francisco, CA: Jossey-Bass.

Rosett, A., and Cressey, D.R. (1976). *Justice by Consent: Plea Bargains in the American Courthouse.* New York: Lippincott.

Rubenstein, M., Clarke, S., and White, T. (1980). *Alaska Bans Plea Bargaining* Washington, DC: U.S. Government Printing Office.

Rummel, R.J. (1970). *Applied Factor Analysis.* Evanston, IL: Northwestern University Press.

Schafer, S. (1969). *Theories in Criminology.* New York: Random House.

Seidel, J. (1983). The Ethnograph. Computer programs demonstrated at the 47th Annual Meeting of the Midwest Sociological Society, Kansas City, MO.

Senese, J.D. (1991a). Communications and Inmate Management: Interactions among Jail Employees. *Journal of Criminal Justice, 19*(2): 151–163.

Senese, J.D. (1991b). Jail utilization over time: An assessment of the patterns of male and female populations. *Criminal Justice Police Review, 5*(3): 241–255.

Senese, J.D. (1992). Control in prisons: An assessment of the use of force in American Prisons. Paper presented at the International Conference on the Present State and Future of the Prison System, Centre for the Study of Public Order, University of Leicester, Leicester, U.K.

Shadish, W.R., Cook, T.D., and Leviton, L.C. (1991). *Foundations of Program Evaluations.* Newbury Park, CA: Sage.

Sherman, L., Milton, C., and Kelly, T. (1973). *Team Policing: Seven Case Studies.* Washington, DC: U.S. Government Printing Office.

Skolnick, J. (1966). *Justice Without Trial.* New York: Wiley.

Smith, S.J. (1984). Crime in the news. *British Journal of Criminology, 24*(3): 289–295.

Sykes, G.M. (1958). *The Society of Captives.* Princeton, NJ: Princeton University Press.

Sykes G.M. (1967). *Crime and Society.* 2d ed. New York: Random House.

Taylor, S.J., and Bogdan, R. *Introduction to Qualitative Research Methods: The Search for Meanings.* 2d ed. New York: Wiley.

Teplin, L.A. (1986). *Keeping the Peace: The Parameters of Police Discretion in Relations to the Mentally Disordered.* U.S. Department of Justice, National Institute of Justice. Washington, DC: U.S. Government Printing Office.

Tifft, L. (1974). The cop personality reconsidered. *Journal of Police Science and Administration, 2:* 268–273.

Toborg, M. (1982). *Pretrial Release: A National Evaluation of Practices and Outcomes.* Washington, DC: National Institute of Justice.

Toch, H. (1977). *Living in Prison.* New York: Free Press.

Toch, H. (1981). Cast the First Stone? Ethics as a Weapon. *Criminology, 19:* 185–194.

Trojanowicz R., and Harden, H. (1985). *The Status of Contemporary Community Policing Programs.* East Lansing, MI: National Neighborhood Foot Patrol Center.

Tunnell, K.D. (1993). Political crime and pedagogy: A content analysis of criminology and criminal justice texts. *Journal of Criminal Justice Education, 4*(1): 101–114.

Uniform Crime Reports. (1991). *Crime in the United States.* U.S. Dept. of Justice, Federal Bureau of Investigation. Washington, DC: U.S. Government Printing Office.

Uniform Crime Reports. (1993). Crime in the United States. U.S. Dept. of Justice, Federal Bureau of Investigation. Washington, DC: U.S. Government Printing Office.

Van Voorhis, P., Cullen, F.T., Link, B.G., and Wolfe, N.T. (1991). The impact of race and gender on correctional officers' orientation to the integrated environment. *Journal of Research in Crime and Delinquency, 28*(4): 572–600.

Vera Institute of Justice. (1972). *1961–1971: Programs in Criminal Justice.* New York: Vera Institute of Justice.

Vigil, J.D. (1988). *Barrio Gangs: Street Life and Identity in Southern California.* Austin: University of Texas Press.

Vito, G.F., and Latessa, E.J. (1989). *Statistical Applications in Criminal Justice.* Newbury Park, CA: Sage.

Walters, S. (1992). Attitudinal and demographic differences between male and female corrections officers: a study in three midwestern prisons. *Journal of Offender Rehabilitation, 18*(1/2): 173–189.

Whitehead, J.T., and Lindquist, C.A. (1989). Determinants of correctional officers' professional orientation. *Justice Quarterly, 6*(1): 69–87.

Wilson, J.Q. (1968). *Varieties of Police Behavior: The Management of Law and Order in Eight Communities.* Cambridge, MA: Harvard University Press.

Wooldredge, J.D. (1991). Correlates of deviant behavior among inmates of U.S. correctional facilities. *Journal of Criminal Justice, 14*(1): 1–25.

Workman, J.P. (1992). Use of electronic media in a participant observation study. *Qualitative Sociology, 15*(4):419–425.

Zimbardo, P. (1963). On the ethics of intervention in human psychological researcher: with special reference to the Stanford prison study. *Cognition, 22:* 243–246.

Zupan, L.L. (1986). Gender-related differences in correctional officers' perceptions and attitudes. *Journal of Criminal Justice, 14:* 349–361.

Index

Abstract terms, 37
Academy of Criminal Justice Scientists, 335
Accidental sampling, 117–118
Administrative constraints, 326
AIDS research, 28, 330
American Association for Public Opinion Research, 335
American Civil Liberties Union (ACLU), 269–270
American Correctional Association, 159, 160
American Jail Association, 56
American Jails, 56–57
American Journal of Police, 350
American Probation and Parole Association, 160
American Society of Criminology, Academy of Criminal Justice Scientists, 335
Analysis of variance, 135, 282–284
Analysis of variance test, 285–287
Analytic induction, 302–303
Anonymity, 331, 340–341
Applied research, 25–26
Argot roles, 52
Artificial intelligence systems, 318–319
Association, 233–237
  chi square statistic, 235–236
  Cramer's V statistic, 236–237
  Spearman's Rho, 237–238
Attitude measurement, 68
Availability samples, 117–118
Averages, central tendency, 224–229

Babbie, Earl, 6, 144, 154, 326, 335
Background/demographic questions, 169
Bail, 18
Baker, T. L., 157
Baltimore City Pretrial Service Division, 25–26, 107
Bar charts, 222
Basic ethical agreements, 328–334
  fair reporting of results, 333–334
  harm-free research, 329–330
  honest researchers, 332–333
  on research subject protection
    anonymity, 331
    confidentiality, 331
    informed consent, 331–332
  voluntary participation of subjects, 330–332
Becker, Gary S., 246
Behavioral outcome, 12
Behavioral research, 11–12
Biased questions, 149–150
Biased sample, 111–112
Bivariate tables, 222
Blinder, A., 7
Body language, 185–186
Boland, B., 19
Bookmaker Corporation, 153
Bureau of Justice Statistics, 19, 100, 144–145, 148, 165, 180. *See also* National Crime Victimization Survey
  comparative studies, 201
  Law Enforcement Management and Administrative Statistics, 203
  National Archive of Criminal Justice Data, 209–210
  National Jail Census, 202
  National Jail Survey, 213–214
  Survey of Youth in Custody, 200–201
Bureau of the Census, 100, 148, 165. *See also* National Crime Victimization Survey
Burgess, E. Q., 38

Campbell, D. T., 127, 133
Canadian Police College Journal, 350
Capital punishment, student attitudes, 51
Case analysis, 299
Case loads, 19
Case studies
  data analysis example, 316–318
  definition, 315–316
  reasons for, 314–315
  uses of, 314
Categorical variables, 225
Cause and effect
  in data collection, 83–84
  no interference, 84–85
  relationship, 84
  time order, 84
Census questionnaires, 148

Central tendency
  averages
    mean, 228–229
    median, 226–228
    mode, 224–226
  definition, 224
  variation
    index of dispersion, 229–230
    range, 231
    shape of distribution, 229
    standard deviation and coefficient variation, 232–233
Charts
  bar charts, 222
  line charts, 223
  pie charts, 223
Chi square probability tables, 289
Chi square statistic, 235–236
Chi square test, 262–265, 280–282
Chronology strategy, 299–300
Clarification purpose for research, 53–54
Classical experimental model
  criterion for, 130–131
  matching, 132
  nature of, 129–131
  randomization, 132
  variations
    factorial design, 133–135
    Solomon four-group design, 133
Cleared offenses, 205
Clickbook software, 153
Closed-ended questions, 156
Codebook, 92–93
Code of Federal Regulations, 327, 330, 336, 337–344
  and Institutional Review Board, 341–343
Code of Professional Ethics and Practices of the American Association for Public Opinion Research, 335
Coding cases, 306
Coefficient variation, 233
Communication, content analysis, 308–310
Complete researcher, 178
Composite data measures, 78–81
Computer-assisted interviewing, 208
Computer-Assisted Telephone Interviewing, 165
Computer-assisted telephone surveys, 165
Computer-based qualitative analysis
  approaches to, 318–319
  artificial intelligence systems, 318–319
  DYNAKWIK, 321–322
  Ethnograph, 318–320
Concentric Zone Theory of Cities, 38
Concepts, 36–38
  as abstractions, 37
  determination of, 59–60
  as operational definitions, 37–38
  operationalization of, 61–62
Conceptualization process, 58–60
Confidentiality, 331, 340–341
Consortium Data Network, 212
Construct validity, 87
Containment theory, 39
Content analysis
  data investigation, 313
  definition, 308–310
  example of qualitative analysis, 308
  process, 310–314
Content validity, 86–87
Contingency questions, 156–157
Continuous data, 29–30
Contrasted design, 136
Control analysis, 69
Control group
  in experimental research design, 67–68
  matching technique, 132
  randomization, 132
Control variables, 36
Cook, T. D., 127
Correctional institutions
  AIDS research in, 28
  officers, 20–21
Correctional research, 19–21
Corrections Today, 56, 356
Correlates, 116
Courts
  case loads, 19
  importance of research for, 18–19
Cramér's V statistic, 236–237
Creating a data subset, 203–204
Crime story reporting, 310–314
Criminal justice
  studies of phenomena, 12
  study of processes, 12
  units of analysis, 30–32
  use of probability theory, 244–245
  use of survey research, 144–145
Criminal Justice Abstracts, 352–355
  on CD-ROM, 338
Criminal justice data
  National Crime Victims Surveys, 99–100
  self-report, 100
  Uniform Crime Reports, 98–99
Criminal Justice Periodical Index, 356–357
Criminology, 49, 56
Criminology, Penology, and Police Science Abstracts, 355–356
Criterion sampling, 110–120
Criterion selection
  example, 257, 260, 264, 270, 273, 276–277, 279, 281, 284, 289
  level of significance, 251–252
Cross-case analysis, 299
Cross-index telephone directories, 165

Cross-sectional studies, 40
Crowley, J. E., 41
Cyclical process of research, 9-11

Data
  accuracy in observational studies, 182-184
  creating subset of, 203-204
  on criminal justice, 98-101
  discrete versus continuous, 28-30
  federal sources, 204-210
  kinds of variables, 34-36
  from national data archives, 210-212
  non-criminal justice data sets, 201-202
  normally distributed, 268
  qualitative versus quantitative, 26-27
Data aggregation, 305-306
Data analysis, 11, 64-65
Data base management, 12
Data categorization, 304-305
Data coding, 213
Data collection, 63-64
  cause and effect, 83-85
  composite measures, 78-81
  field notes, 192
  fieldwork guidelines, 195-196
  for observational studies, 180-181, 190-196
  qualitative, 94-98
  quantitative, 91-94
  reconstructed notes, 193
  records study, 195
  redundant measures, 81-82
  tape recording, 193-194
  Uniform Crime Reports, 205
  value of, 77-78
  video tape recording, 194-195
Data grouping, 221
Data investigation, 303-305, 313-314
Data labeling, 305-306
Data meanings, 306-307
Data measurement
  instrumentation problems, 141
  levels of, 32-34
  qualitative and quantitative, 82-83
  reliability, 87-91
  validity
    construct validity, 87
    content validity, 86-87
    face validity, 85-86
    predictive validity, 86
Data set
  Ethnograph, 320, 322
  federal sources, 204-209
  national data archives, 210-212
Data set collection, 202-203
Degrees of freedom, 263
Delinquency
  and IQ, 33
  opportunity theory, 48
Department of Health and Human Services, 336, 337
Department of Justice, National Archive of Criminal Justice Data, 209-210
Dependent t-test, 272-274
Dependent variables, 35
  in experimental designs, 67
Descriptive analysis, 27-28, 218-219
  central tendency
    averages, 224-229
    variation, 229-230
  graphical displays, 219-223
  relationships
    association, 233-237
    Pearson's product moment correlation coefficient, 239
    Spearman's Rho, 237-238
Descriptive designs, 65-66
Developmental approach to interviewing, 162
Difference hypothesis, 247-248
Dillman, D. A., 160
Directional questions, 150
Directional research hypothesis, 248
Dirty Harry style, 17
Discrete data, 28-29
Distribution of scores, mean, 228-229
Distribution of values
  index of dispersion, 229-230
  median, 226-228
  mode, 224-226
  range, 231
  standard deviation and coefficient variation, 232-233
Double-barreled questions, 150
DYNAKWIK program, 321-322

Economic harm, 330
Empirical data, 8-9
Ethical agreements. *See* Basic ethical agreements
Ethical constraints, 328
Ethnograph, 318-320
Evaluation designation, 71
Evaluation designs
  needs assessment, 70-72
  outcome evaluation, 72-73
  process evaluation, 72
Evaluation purpose, 54-56
Exempted research, 338-339
Experience/behavior questions, 168
Experimental designs, 126
  classical model, 129-132
  quasi-experimental, 136-138

Experimental designs *(continued)*
single group, 127–128
validity problems
external validity, 138–139
internal validity, 139–141
variations on classical model, 133–135
Experimental mortality, 140–141
Experimental research designs, 66–68
External validity problems, 138–139
Extralinguistic observations, 187
Extreme case sampling, 119

Face validity, 85–86, 91
Factor Analysis, 79–80
Factorial design, 133–135
and effects of testing, 141
Federal Bail Reform acts, 18
Federal Bureau of Investigation, 9, 98–99
Uniform Crime Reports, 200, 203–207
Federal data sources
National Archive of Criminal Justice Data, 209–210
National Crime Victimization Survey, 206–209
Uniform Crime Reports, 204–207
Feeling questions, 168
Felkenes, G. T., 315
Field notes, 97–98, 192
Fieldwork guidelines, 195–196
File Transfer Protocol, 212
Focus groups, 148
as group interviews, 169–170
sampling, 119
Follow-up mailing, 159
Force narratives, 304
Forst, B., 19
Frequency tables, 219–222
F test statistic, 286
Full participant researcher, 175–176
Full participation data collection, 95
Functional adaptive theory of institutional adjustment, 52

Gallup poll, 116, 117
Geis, G., 7
Gender variable, 26
Glaser, B., 302
Goetting, A., 305
Goodness-of-fit test, 263
Government regulation, 335–336
Graphical displays
charts, 222–224
frequency tables, 219–222
nature of, 219
probability paper, 268
Greenberg, David, 25
Grounded theory, 302
Grouped data, 221
Group longitudinal studies, 41
Group questionnaires, 147

Hagan, F. E., 6–7
Hagedorn, J., 120, 167
Harmless research, 329–330
Harris poll, 116, 117
History, and validity of findings, 139–140
Home delivery questionnaires, 148
Honest researchers, 332–333
Household respondent, 165
Households, panel design, 207
Howser, R. M., 305
H test, 288–291
Hypothesis setting, 246–251
example, 257, 260, 262–263, 270, 273, 276, 279, 281, 284, 288–289
Hypothesis testing, 106, 245
logical trick, 250

ICPSR. *See* Inter-University Consortium for Political and Social Research
Idea formulation, 56–58
Independent t-test, 269–272
Independent variables, 35
Index Crimes, 205
Index of dispersion, 228–229
Inferential analysis, 27–28
Inferential statistical analysis, 244–245
Inferential statistics, 245
Inferential testing, 106
criterion selection, 251–252
decision/interpretation, 253–255
hypothesis setting, 246–251
multiple sample tests, 282–291
null hypothesis, 247–251
process, 245–246
research hypothesis, 246–251
single sample tests, 255–265
statistical tests, 253
test statistic, 252–253
two-sample tests, 265–282
Type I and Type II errors, 250–251
Informational data bases, 212
Informed consent, 331–332, 342
Informed consent explanation, 343
Institutional Review Board, 339–343
Instrumentation problems, 141
Interfering variables, 84–85
Internal validity, sources of problems
experimental mortality, 140–141
history, 139–140
instrumentation, 141

maturation problem, 140
testing, 141
International Association of Chiefs of Police, 204
Inter-University Consortium for Political and Social Research, 100
description of, 210–212
Interval level of measurement, 33
Interview
developmental approach, 162
limited structure, 167–168
semantic differential, 162–163
semi-structured, 167
structured, 166–167
Interview analysis
case analysis, 299
cross-case analysis, 299
Interview design, 207
Interview schedules
limited structure interviews, 167–168
semi-structured interview, 167
structured interviews, 166–167
Interview surveys
administration of, 169–170
nature of, 165–166
schedules, 166–168
types of questions, 168–169
Investigation, 54
IQ testing, 29–30
and delinquency, 33
Irrelevant questions, 152–153

Jail overcrowding, 82
Jails, research on, 56–57
Johnson, Robert, 168
Journal of Criminal Justice, 49, 56
Justice Quarterly, 49, 56

Kalinich, D. B., 350
Kansas City study, 17
Kelling, G., 17
Kerle, Ken, 56
Key events focus, 300
Klein, Malcolm, 115
Klofas, J. M., 350
Knowledge questions, 168–169
Known offenses, 205
Kolmogorov-Smirnov normality test, 268
Kruskal Wallis H test, 288–291

Language usage, 186–187
Law Enforcement Assistance Administration, 16
Law Enforcement Management and Administrative Statistics, 203
Law School Admissions Test, 86, 91
Legal constraints, 327–328
Legal intervention, 336
Level of significance, 251–252
Levels of measurement. *See also* Data measurement
in data collection, 63–64
interval, 33
nominal, 32
ordinal, 32–33
ratio, 33–34
Library research
preparation for, 352–353
reasons for conducting, 349–351
reference locator sources, 353–358
topic selection, 351–352
Life skills training program, 316–317
Limited structure interview, 167–168
Line charts, 223
Linguanti, F., 350
Linguistic behaviors, 187
Lipton, D., 6
Logical inquiry, 50–52
Logical structure, 8
of coding scheme, 93–94
Longitudinal studies, 40
Longmire, D. R., 335
Los Angeles gangs, 115
Lotus 1-2-3, 219, 222

Mailed questionnaires, 147
Manhattan Bail Project, 18
Mann-Whitney U test, 274–278
Martinson, R., 6
Maryland Department of Corrections, 257, 259
Maryland Occupational Training Skills Center, 316–317
Matching technique, 132
Matrix questions, 157
Maturation problem, 140
Maxson, Cheryl, 115
McCarthy, B. R., 331
McDonald's, 117–118
McIntyre, J., 350
Mean, 228–229
Mean squares, 286
table, 287
Means test, 259–262
Measurement. *See* Data measurement
Median, 226–228
Michigan Department of Corrections, 111
Microsoft Excel, 219, 222
Microsoft Works, 109, 222
Milwaukee gangs, 120
Minitab, 245
Missing values, 214

Mode, 224–226
Models, 37–38
Moos Correctional Institution Environment Scale, 91
Multiple data sets, 201
Multiple sample test
  analysis of variance, 282–284
  analysis of variance test, 284–287
  description of, 282–284
  Kruskal Wallis H test, 288–291
Multiple sample tests, 267
Multivariate tables, 222
Mutual exclusivity, 62

Nachmias, C., 171
Nachmias, D., 171
National Advisory Commission on Criminal Justice Standards and Goals, 18–29
National Archive of Criminal Justice Data, 100, 209–210
National Crime Victimization Survey, 99–100, 180
  appropriate uses of, 209
  description of, 206–208
  limitations of, 208–209
National data archives, 210–212
National Incident Based Reporting System, 98, 205
National Institute of Justice, 28, 200, 337
National Jail Census, 202
National Jail Survey, 213, 214
National Sheriffs' Association, 204
Needs assessment, 70–72
Negative skewness, 268
Niederhoffer, A., 17
Nominal level of measurement, 32
Non-criminal justice data sets, 201–202
Nonoccurrences, 190
Nonparametric tests
  chi square test, 262–265, 280–282
  Kruskal Wallis H test, 288–291
  Mann-Whitney U test, 274–278
  Wilcoxon t-test, 278–280
Nonparametric test statistic, 254–255
Nonprobability sampling
  accidental sampling, 117–118
  nature of, 114
  versus probability sampling, 105–106
  purposive sampling, 114–116
  quota sampling, 116–117
Normal curve, 269
Normality, 268
Normally distributed data, 268
Null hypothesis, 245
  criterion selection, 251–252
  example, 257, 260, 263, 270, 273, 276, 279, 281, 284, 289
  Type I and Type II errors, 250–251

Null hypothesis *(continued)*
  in inferential testing, 248–251
  making a decision/interpretation, 253–255

Obedience-to-authority experiments, 328, 329
Objectivity, 7–8
Observational studies, 69–70, 174–180
  advantages
    direct data collection, 180–181
    high feasibility, 181–182
    natural settings, 181
  approaches, 175
  case studies, 315–316
  complete researcher, 178
  data collection, 190–196
    fieldwork guidelines, 195–196
    recording observations, 192–195
    timing of, 191–192
  disadvantages
    lack of consistency, 184
    reduced accuracy, 182–184
  focus of, 179–180
  full participant researcher, 175–176
  general issues, 178–179
  participant researcher, 176–177
  problems with, 174–175
  researcher who participates, 177–178
  subjects of observation, 184–190
    body language, 185–186
    language use, 186–187
    nonoccurrences, 190
    physical setting, 187–188
    social setting, 188
    spatial behavior, 186
    unobtrusive indicators, 189–190
Observational study data analysis approach, 299–301
Offensive questions, 150
Office for the Protection of Research Subjects, 336
Office of Justice Programs, 200
Office of Management and Budget, 336
One-shot case study, 127
Open-ended questions, 156
Operational definitions, 37–38
Operationalization, 61–62
Operational settings, 180
Opinion/values questions, 168
Opportunity theory, 48
Ordinal level of measurement, 32–33
Outcome evaluation, 72–73

Panel design, 207
Parametric tests
  proportions test, 256–259
  two-sample tests, 267–268

Parametric test statistic, 254–255
Parens patriae attitude, 183
Participant researcher, 176–177
Part I crimes, 205
Particular longitudinal studies, 41
Part II crimes, 205
Patrol duty, 17
Patton, Michael A., 100, 166, 296, 299
Patton qualitative framework, 95
Patton's evaluation designation, 71
Pearson's product moment correlation coefficient, 239
Petersilia, J., 14
Philadelphia Inquirer, 352
Physical harms, 329
Physical records, 195
Physical setting, 187–188
Pie charts, 223
Pilot studies, 46
Place, sites, settings, and locations focus, 300–304
Planning, 49–50
Plea bargaining, 18–19
Police
  Dirty Harry style, 17
  importance of research for, 17–18
  minority women, 315
Police Chief, 56, 356
Police discretion, 17–18
Police patrol, 17
Police personality, 17
Policing and Society Journal, 355
Political constraints, 14–15, 327
Polling, 116–117
Population
  in data set collection, 203
  in observational research, 69
  in probability sampling, 106–113
  and probability theory, 245
  for sample selection, 62–63
  in sample selection, 104–105
  sample size, 120–122
Population values
  chi square test, 262–265
  criterion selection, 251–252
  hypothesis setting, 240–251
  means test, 259–262
  null hypothesis, 248–251
  proportions test, 256–259
  test statistic, 252–253
Population variances, 267
Positive skewness, 268
Positivistic School, 11
Posttest-only design, 129
Powell, D., 18
Practical research, 49
Pratt, C. E., 15
Predictive validity, 86
Pre-experimental designs, single-group, 127–129
Preparation for conducting research, 352–353
Preplanning, 170
Pretest, 67
  self-report questionnaires, 154–155
Pretest/posttest
  and history, 140
  of questionnaires, 149
Pretest/posttest design, 127–129
Priestley, Joseph, 11
Prisoners
  argot roles, 52
  life skills training program, 316–317
  research subjects, 343–344
Probability paper, 268
Probability sampling, 267
  and inferential tests, 106
  nature of, 106–107
  versus nonprobability sampling, 105–106
  simple random sampling, 107–109
  stratified random sampling, 112–113
  systematic random sampling, 109–112
Probability theory, 229
  basis of inferential analysis, 244–245
  statistical uses, 244–245
Probation and parole programs, 20
Probation classification, 19–20
Probation officer effectiveness, 78–79
Process evaluation, 72
Professional code of ethics, 335
Proportions test, 256–259
Psychological harm, 329–330
Pure research, 25
Purposive sampling, 114–116

Qualitative data, 8–9, 26–27
Qualitative data analysis
  analytic induction, 302–303
  case studies, 314–318
  computer-based, 318–322
  content analysis, 308–314
  grounded theory approach, 302
  influences on data, 307
  interview analysis approach, 299
  need for guidelines, 297
  observational study data analysis approach, 299–301
  process
    categorizing data, 304–305
    data aggregation, 305–306
    data investigation, 303–305
    data meanings, 306–307
  theoretical approaches, 301–303
  thick description, 301–302

Qualitative data analysis *(continued)*
unclear analysis problems, 296–297
Qualitative data collection
forms of recording, 97–98
framework, 95–97
Qualitative data sources, 298
Qualitative measures, 82–83
Qualitative research
focus of, 298
versus quantitative research, 297–298
Qualitative research designs, 68–69
content analysis, 69
observational, 69–70
Qualitative research sampling, 118
criterion sampling, 119–120
extreme, 119
focus group, 119
snowball sampling, 120
Quantitative data, 8–9, 26–27
Quantitative data collection, 91–92
codebook, 92–93
logical structure, 93–94
nature of, 94–95
Quantitative descriptive analysis, 219
Quantitative estimation techniques, 121–122
Quantitative measures, 82–83
Quantitative research designs
description of, 65–66
experimental, 66–68
problems with, 174–175
versus qualitative research, 297–298
relation between variables, 66
Quasi-experimental designs
contrasted design, 136
time-series, 136–138
Quasi-random sample, 114
Questionnaire, 89
Questions
biased, 149–150
closed-ended, 156
contingency, 156–157
directional, 130
double-barreled, 150
format guidelines, 151–154
for interview surveys, 168–169
irrelevant, 152–153
matrix, 157
offensive, 150
open-ended, 156
pattern-avoidance, 151–152
screening, 162
for self-report, 149–151
for self-report survey, 155–157
unanswerable, 150–151
vague, 151
Quota sampling, 116–117
Quota sampling frame, 116–117
Racial discrimination, 18
Random-digit dialing, 165
Random sampling
simple, 107
stratified, 112–113
systematic, 109–112
from telephone directories, 164
Range, 231
Ratio level of measurement, 33–34
Recidivism, 120
Reconstructed notes, 193
Recording observations, 192–195
Records, content analysis, 308–310
Records study, 195
Redundant measures, 81–82
Reeves, I. S. K., 10
Reference locator sources
CD-ROM *Criminal Justice Abstracts*, 358
Criminal Justice Abstracts, 352–355
Criminal Justice Periodical Index, 356–357
Criminology, Penology, and Police Science Abstracts, 355–356
uses of, 352–353
Rehabilitation orientation, 6
Relationships
association, 233–237
Pearson's product moment correlation coefficient, 239
Spearman's Rho statistic, 237–238
between variables, 66, 84
Reliability, 87–88
improving, 90–91
split-half technique, 89–90
test-retest, 88–89
Research
administrative constraints, 326
based on current literature, 348–351
basic ethical agreements, 328–334
constraints on, 14–16
in educational institutions, 337
ethical constraints, 328
exempted from regulations, 338–339
fair reporting of results, 333–334
harm-free, 329–330
impact on policy and practice, 14
importance for corrections, 19–21
importance for courts, 18–19
importance for policing, 16–18
importance of, 13–14
involving unobtrusive techniques, 338–339
legal constraints, 327–328
political constraints, 327
practical purpose, 49
in preexisting data, 339
pure versus applied, 24–26
quantitative versus qualitative, 297–298
reliance on sample selection, 104–106

review of, 339–343
theoretical purpose, 48
time factor, 40–41
voluntary participation of subjects, 330–332
Research designs
construction of
conceptualization, 58–60
data analysis, 64–65
data collection, 63–64
idea formulation, 56–58
operationalization, 61–62
sample selection, 62–63
as deliberate activity, 46–48
evaluation designs, 70–73
logical inquiry, 50–52
planning, 49–50
process specification, 50
purposes
clarification, 53–54
evaluation, 54–56
investigation, 54
simple reporting, 52–53
as purposive activity, 48–49
qualitative, 68–70
quantitative, 65–68
reasons for, 45–46
Researchers
honest, 332–333
self-imposed morality, 336–337
Researcher's identity, 332–333, 341
Researcher who participates, 177–178
Research hypothesis, 246–259
contrasted with null hypothesis, 248–251
example, 257, 260, 263, 270, 273, 276, 279, 281, 284, 289
test selection, 252–253
Research journals, 56
Research methods
basic dichotomies
descriptive versus inferential analysis, 27–28
discrete versus continuous data, 28–30
pure versus applied research, 24–26
qualitative versus quantitative data, 26–27
basic rules, 4–5
importance of studying, 2
individual concepts
concept analysis, 36–38
levels of measurement, 32–34
theories and models, 38–40
units of analysis, 30–32
variables, 34–36
and practitioners in criminal justice, 4
relevance, 3–4
traditional, 5–12
Research processes, 50
Research question, 310–311
Research subjects
anonymity, 340–341
approaches to protecting, 334–337
benefits from research, 343
confidentiality, 340–341
ethical protection
anonymity, 331
confidentiality, 331
informed consent, 331–332
informed consent, 342
informed consent explanation, 343
informed decisions by, 342–343
legal protections
and *Code of Federal Regulations*, 337–344
exempted research, 338–339
prisoner research, 343–344
review of research, 339–343
making informed decisions, 332
prisoner research, 343–344
voluntary participation, 330–332
Research topic selection, 351–352
Research topic sheet, 352–353
Resource constraints, 15
Response rates, 159–160
Review of research, 339–343
Roper poll, 116, 117

Sample selection, 62–63
Sample size, 120–122
Sampling
basics of, 105
population, 104–105
theoretical, 302
Sampling interval, 110–111
Saviano, Fortunato, 301
Scattergram, 223
Schroedel, J. R., 315
Scientific method, 5–6
Screening question, 162
Secondary data analysis
creating a data subset, 203–204
data set collection, 202–203
of existing data, 212–214
multiple data sets, 201
nature of, 200–202
trend assessments, 202
Self-imposed morality, 336–337
Self-report data, 100
Self-report questionnaires
administration of, 157–159
advantages and disadvantages, 160–161
format guidelines, 151–154
guidelines, 149–151
instructions for returning, 154
less common types, 148
main types of, 147
nature of, 146–149

Self-report questionnaires *(continued)*
  pretesting, 154–155
  response rates, 159–160
  types of questions, 155–157
Self-report survey, 144
Semantic differential, 162–163
Semi-structured interview, 167
Sensory questions, 169
Sentencing, sexual differences in, 28
Series longitudinal studies, 40–41
Simple random sampling, 107–109
  for content analysis, 312
Simple reporting, 52–53
Single group design, 127
Single group experimental designs
  posttest-only design, 129
  pretest and posttest design, 127–129
  single group design, 127
Single sample tests
  chi square test, 262–265
  description of, 255–256
  means test, 259–262
  proportions test, 256–259
Skewness, 268
Skolnick, J., 17
Snowball sampling, 120
Social Disorganization Theory, 36
Social setting, 188
Solomon four group design, 133
  and effects of testing, 141
Spatial behavior, 186
Spearman's Rho statistic, 237–238
Split-half technique, 89–90
Spreadsheet programs, 109
SPSS software, 245, 268
Stability of punishment hypothesis, 8
Standard deviation, 232–233
Standard error of the mean, 261
Stanley, J. C, 133
Statistical testing, 268–269
Statistical tests, 64–65
Statistical tests of inference, 253
Stojkovic, S., 350
Stratified random sampling, 112–113
Strauss, A., 302
Structured interview, 166–167
Study population, 62–63
Sums of squares, 285–286
  table, 287
Survey of Youth in Custody, 200–201
Survey Research Center, 211
Surveys
  in criminal justice research, 144–145
  interview, 165–170
  self-report, 144
  self-report questionnaires, 146–161
  telephone, 161–165
Sutherland, Edwin H., 48
Sykes, G. M., 52–53
Systat, 245
Systematic random sampling, 109–112

Tables
  definition, 219
  frequency tables, 219–222
Tape recording, 193–194
Telephone directories, 163–164
Telephone interview schedule, 162–163
Telephone surveys
  computer-assisted, 165
  interview schedules, 162–163
  nature of, 161–162
  selection of subjects, 163–165
Testing problems, 141
Test-retest, 88–89
Test statistic, 246, 252–253
  example, 259, 260–261, 264, 271–272, 273–274, 277–278, 279–280, 281–282, 284–285, 289
  parametric or nonparametric, 254–255
Text-analysis programs, 318–322
Theoretical approaches to qualitative analysis, 301–303
Theoretical purpose of research, 48
Theoretical sampling, 302
Theoretical systems, 38–39
Theories, 6–7, 38–40
Thick description, 301–302
Time factor, 40–41
  in data collection, 191–192
Time order, 84
Time-series design, 136–138
Time-series display, 223
Toborg, M., 18
Traditional research methods, 5–6
  aims of
    empirical data, 8–9
    logical structure, 8
    objectivity, 7–8
    theory, 6–7
  concerns of, 11–12
  cyclical process, 9–11
T-test
  critical values for, 271
  dependent, 272–274
  independent, 269–272
  Wilcoxon, 278–280
T-test of homogeneity, 267
Twain, Mark, 64
Two-sample tests
  chi square test, 280–282
  dependent t-test, 272–274
  description of, 265–269
  independent t-test, 269–272

Mann-Whitney U test, 274–278
parametric assumptions, 267–268
Wilcoxon t-test, 278–280
Type I error, 250–251, 252, 254–255, 310
Type II error, 250–251, 252, 254–255, 310

Unanswerable questions, 150–151
Uniform Crime Reports, 9, 77, 91, 203
appropriate uses of, 206–207
compilation of, 204–205
as data source, 98–99
problems with, 205–206
purpose of, 200–202
Units of analysis, 30–32
University of Baltimore, Office for Institutional Research, 115
University of Michigan, Inter-University Consortium for Political and Social Research, 100, 210–212
Unobtrusive indicators, 189–190

Vague questions, 151
Validity of data measurement, 85–87
Validity of findings
external, 138–139
internal, 139–140
Variables
association of, 233–237
in calculating range, 231
central tendency, 224
chi square statistic, 235–236
in composite measures, 80
correlates, 116
Cramer's V statistic, 236–237
for experimental designs, 66–70
in factorial design, 135
in frequency tables, 222
interfering, 84–85
kinds of, 34–36
noninterfering, 84–85
in observational studies, 184
in operationalization, 61–62
redundant measures, 81–82
relationship between, 84
relationships between, 66, 233–239
Spearman's Rho statistic, 237–238
in statistical tests of inference, 253
in stratified random sampling, 112
Variation
index of dispersion, 228–229
standard deviation and coefficient variation, 232–233
Vera Institute of Justice, 18
Victim surveys, 207–209
Video tape recording, 194–195
Voluntary participation, 330–332

Weberian Bureaucratic Theory, 87
Wilcoxon t-test, 278–280
Wilks, J., 6
Wilson, James Q., 16
WinSPIRS version of *Criminal Justice Abstracts*, 358